Taking Sides

BOOKS BY THE SAME AUTHOR

International Disaster Relief

Acts of Nature, Acts of Man

Disaster Assistance
(co-edited with Lynn H. Stephens)

Taking

America's Secret Relations
with a Militant Israel

Sides

STEPHEN GREEN

WILLIAM MORROW AND COMPANY, INC.

New York   1984

Library of Congress Catalog Card Number: 83-61736

ISBN: 0-688-02643-5

Printed in the United States of America

First Edition

1 2 3 4 5 6 7 8 9 10

BOOK DESIGN BY BERNARD SCHLEIFER

For my father, who would have understood

Contents

—1—

Peering into Dark Corners

THERE IS A CERTAIN excitement involved in doing research with original documents, and I remember the feeling I experienced in the fall of 1981 at the National Records Center in Suitland, Maryland. Physically, the reading room there is not much to look at—interior decorating has been done by the General Services Administration. But what goes on there is fascinating. At the back of the room a team of Japanese researchers pored over records from World War II. A woman from the Bolivian National Archives copied diplomatic documents to replace those destroyed in her country by fire, earthquake, and revolution. Others were there in a private capacity—tracing lost family records back to Civil War times and beyond.

Some, like myself, were writing books. I had requested access to the 1948 Jerusalem Consular File of the U.S. State Department, and was being assisted by Bill Lewis, a soft-spoken, competent archivist. But what he told me was puzzling indeed: there would be a delay in giving me the boxes containing the Jerusalem Consular File because they had first to be screened for "privacy" violations.

That did not make any sense. Surely the file had been checked before.

"Bill, do you mean to tell me that no one has seen that file since it was turned over to you by the State Department?"

"Well, the slip says no one has requested it."

Before they are released to researchers, records in the National Archives are, under the Federal Freedom of Information Act, supposed to be scanned for names of persons who may

9

appear in the documents in compromising situations. When these names are removed or blotted out, the file, assuming it is "open," i.e., either unclassified or properly declassified, may be released to researchers who are registered with the archives.

Actually, the process of gaining access to the records is quite simple and takes little more time than getting books from a public library—unless, that is, the file requested has to be screened the first time.

But I just could not believe what I was hearing. Nineteen forty-eight—Jerusalem. The birth of the State of Israel. Over the past years, the drama of the events that took place there and then has been described in dozens of books and hundreds of articles, depicted in movies, television dramas, and documentaries. How, I wondered, could no private researcher have previously asked to see the official reports of U.S. representatives on the scene? The American government and people had played, I knew, an important role in the birth of Israel. The people who participated in these events—some of them—became legends in their own time. And the events themselves have not diminished in importance with the years, for the war that began in Palestine in 1948 is still, unfortunately, with us.

It just did not make any sense. Until I got the files, that is. Knowing my work was stymied until I had them, Bill Lewis kindly speeded the screening process, and within a very few days a cart was wheeled up to me at the Suitland records center reading room. The file boxes smelled musty and were covered with dust, and the telegrams, letters, and reports in the folders from the U.S. Consulate in Jerusalem were yellowed and brittle.

I opened the folders and began to leaf through their contents. What was spread before me was not myth and legend, but the stories of real men and women who were struggling to make the best of a time of enormous tension and bitterness. There was drama enough—such as the story of the American Consul General in Jerusalem who was assassinated in the streets outside the legation only days after he had drafted a memo about measures needed to ensure the safety of the consular staff.

In poring through the files, seeing the communications about the ambushes and bombings, the battles, the diplomatic charges and countercharges that made up daily life in Jerusalem, I could see that what I was reading was not the heroic stuff of a very fictional *Exodus*, nor even that of some of the more recent "nonfiction" on the birth of Israel. The reality was so different from the myth as to be unrecognizable.

Moreover, there is a pattern easily discernible in what we popularly know and do not know about America's relationship with Israel. We are generally aware of the immediate recognition and warm support that President Truman accorded the State of Israel at its birth in 1948. We do not, however, know of the stolen advanced radar prototype that was presented to the Czechs (i.e., the Russians) that same year in exchange for the continuation of the flow of arms and trained soldiers out of Czechoslovakia and into Israel through the Zionist underground to fight the War of Independence there. We know of Moshe Dayan's exploits in the Suez War of 1956, but Americans are not generally aware of his efforts, two years earlier, to subvert the negotiations of his country's Prime Minister (Moshe Sharett) when the latter was endeavoring to conclude a peace with Egypt. We have read of and seen depicted the heroic thrusts of the Israeli Army in the Six-Day War, but we have no knowledge of the important assistance provided the Israelis by the U.S. Air Force in that war. Patterns.

In turn, this selective historical knowledge has led to fundamentally false impressions in America about Israel and about the Middle East dispute generally. For instance, there is and has been since 1948 a basic misperception in the United States about Israel's armed strength vis-à-vis the Arabs. Many of the chapters of this book will deal with that subject, citing some startling statistics from previously secret U.S. civilian and military intelligence files.

Another misunderstanding about U.S.-Israeli relations has to do with the informal alliance that many Americans believe has always existed between the two countries. While it is true that the relationship is unique in many respects, there have been times when we have been adversaries, or at least have acted as such. And then there is the question of the mutuality of our relations. Has it always been, to borrow President John Kennedy's phrase, "a two-way street"? It is doubtful.

This book is not a history of the Middle East, nor even a history of U.S.-Israeli relations. It is a collection of historical vignettes that have been—and I freely acknowledge this—carefully selected. Nevertheless, they have been meticulously documented, largely from a variety of official, heretofore unpublished U.S. government sources. To those who would criticize the book as selective history, I answer that much of what has been written on Israel in the West has been no less selective, including many if not most of the "classic" texts on U.S.-Israeli relations and histories of the many modern Middle Eastern wars.

The early chapters of this book are based almost entirely on documents available in the Modern Military, General, and Diplomatic branches of the National Archives in Washington. I have checked the footnotes herein with the archivists who assisted me in my research in these places, to ensure that the citations are sufficiently specific to permit the checking of my sources. The middle and later chapters are drawn largely from material available in several of the presidential libraries, most particularly the Dwight D. Eisenhower Library in Abilene, Kansas, and the Lyndon Baines Johnson Library in Austin, Texas. Here too, I have checked to ensure that the cited materials can be readily located by other researchers.

The one caveat I must make is that Executive Order 12356, promulgated by Ronald Reagan in mid-1982, permits reclassification of previously declassified documents. The Reagan Justice Department has encouraged a number of federal agencies to avail themselves of this new "opportunity" to return to an era when the processes of government were none of the American people's business.

My fear is that publication of this book, and that of others which have employed similar research techniques, will lead to a wholesale effort to close files, for the narrowest of short-term foreign policy and domestic political reasons. Nor do judicial appeals under the Freedom of Information Act provide a remedy. Federal district judges seem, at the present time, to be having great difficulty distinguishing between the concepts of political embarrassment and damage to national security. They are not one and the same.

In researching this book, I submitted more than 100 Freedom of Information Act (FOIA) requests to 22 different government agencies with rather limited success. Although the National Archives system (including the presidential libraries) and the FOIA offices in government agencies operate under the same regulations with respect to classification-declassification standards, the ways in which they relate to researchers could not be more different. The archivists are professionals dedicated to the most efficient use of the materials in their charge, within the constraints of Executive Order 12356, the Privacy Act, and, most of all, the sevére budget cuts they have suffered in the past few years. It did not take the current administration long to realize that reductions in funds for the National Archives and Records Service could kill two birds with one stone, by cutting expenditures while also effectively limiting the public's access to "public" documents. Nevertheless, though there are enormous backlogs and workloads at the National Archives, the spirit is willing.

By contrast, the FOIA process has in the past few years become an adversarial one with strong political overtones. Initial requests may simply be ignored for months until repeated follow-ups elicit *pro forma* responses. Once a researcher's request reaches an active pile, he or she may be threatened with exorbitant search and duplication fees.* When a request is denied— and it almost always is—the administrative appeals process is perfunctory and time-consuming. Two years after I submitted most of my requests, fully 30 percent of them remain unresolved.

To be sure, the FOIA offices have also received budget cuts and have large backlogs of work—for exactly the same insidious reasons as the archives. The difference is that FOIA case officers treat "backlog" as just one more weapon in the arsenal with which they defend their agency's business from the meddling inquiries of the American citizen. This from an administration that says it is defending the American citizen from the excesses of government!

A few disclaimers are perhaps in order. I am not a Middle East area studies expert, and have had to familiarize myself with the literature as I made my way along chronologically. Research and writing have required just under two-and-one-half years. I do not speak, read, or write Hebrew or Arabic. How much these skills would have contributed to the project is debatable, however, as neither Israel nor the Arab countries permit ordinary citizens, let alone foreigners, access to materials on the vast majority of the subjects addressed in the following chapters.

---

*At one point, I submitted an FOIA request for "after-action reports on the October, 1973, war in the Middle East" by the Defense Intelligence Agency. I was informed in writing that servicing my request would require 13,000 hours of search time at $16 per hour. If I would just send along the $208,000, they would get cracking on the matter.

My primary motivation for writing this book has been a nagging, nettling awareness over recent years that many if not most public statements by American politicians—particularly Congressmen—reflected an appalling ignorance of what has actually transpired between Israel and the United States over the 36-year history of our relationship. If you wish to test this proposition, approach your U.S. Senator, who last year doubtless read into *The Congresssional Record* some 20 to 100 speeches, statements, letters, and/or articles on the subject of Israel, and ask him or her to explain the Lavon Affair to you—an event that has had a greater impact on the political history of Israel than Watergate has had in the United States. It will be one of the few times you will see your Senator with furrowed brow, pursed lips, and no glib response.

My objective in writing this book is to bring into the public domain many hundreds of important documents and texts that, taken together, fill significant gaps in America's collective knowledge about our past relationship with Israel. Neither myths, disinformation, nor selective information constitute a healthy basis upon which to conduct our Middle East policy. As a great power, and possibly the one major country with residual influence on both sides in the Arab-Israeli dispute, the United States has a history of lost opportunities in that region. And this is due in no small part to our inability as a nation to learn from the past, because we have had access only to carefully selected portions of the past. Thus we are condemned to relive as spectators the sorry cycle of wars, terrorism, and instability that constitutes modern Middle Eastern history.

For the "Friends of Israel" who pointedly wear that self-designation on their sleeves, this book will present certain problems. Thoughtful friends of Israel, who are genuinely concerned about current trends in the Middle East, will I hope welcome the book. I have been heartened periodically, through the process of research and writing, by my discussions with the latter type of supporter of Israel—including several who carried passports from that country.

It is most ironic that as Israel's military might, and the aggressiveness and frequency with which that might is applied, have increased, Israel's security—internally and vis-à-vis her Arab neighbors—has declined. In many respects, as Martin Buber, Nahum Goldmann and Moshe Sharett, among others, have pointed out, militarism in modern Israel has produced a parody of the early dreams of a secure Jewish homeland. And the unusual relationship it has had with America has in no small way nudged Israel toward that belligerent militarism.

My sincere hope, then, is that this book may raise questions about these trends, and may lead to further research and writing that probe areas of U.S.-Israeli relations that deserve far greater scrutiny than they have received to date.

—2—

*An Uneasy Friendship
Is Born*

IT HAD BEEN A VERY, very long year—one of the longest, he thought, in his life. Colonel E. P. Archibald had been the senior American military attaché in Israel during the early months of that country's modern existence. Now it was almost Christmas, 1949, and Colonel Archibald sat down to report on his office's first year to his superiors in the Directorate of Intelligence at the Pentagon. He was frustrated, tired, and a little bitter.

His first recommendation, he said, was that consideration be given to downgrading his post in rank, when he came up for replacement one year hence. The Israelis were friendly enough socially, but they refused to play the game of diplomacy—the quid pro quo game—in terms of military intelligence:

> These people are anxious to obtain a great deal in the way of American training and equipment, but are willing to give nothing in return. To date they have told us nothing that was not obtainable from the newspapers. It may be that by assigning two full Colonels and a Navy Captain here at the beginning, we impressed these people with their importance to the United States and it might be a good idea if we let the pendulum swing in the opposite direction for a while. . . . the United States is not treated as a military friend or an ally.[1]

None of the three military attachés—Air Force, Army, and Navy—were allowed to have direct contact with their counterparts in the Israeli Defense Forces (IDF). Instead, they all had

16

to work through a "liaison office" of junior officers. The Air Attaché's plane was not allowed to fly over Israel at all. Every flight plan filed at Lydda Airfield near Tel Aviv, where the plane was kept, had to be accompanied by a signed statement: that the pilot was aware that should he fly outside the prescribed corridor between Lydda and the Mediterranean, he would be fired upon. Even in the corridor it was not safe. Archibald's plane had in fact been fired upon in March of 1949, a bullet passing harmlessly through the tail section as it landed at Tel Aviv.

Archibald had not always referred to the Israelis as "these people." In fact, he had been extremely positive about them when he arrived a year earlier. His first reports out of Tel Aviv had an almost breathless quality in describing the young country and his assignment in it. The problem, he thought then, was that the well-known close relationship between the U.S. and British intelligence services gave the Israelis good reason to fear that whatever was shared with U.S. military intelligence would find its way to the Arabs via the British.

> They are not too sure that America is 100% their friend yet. Should we back them with de jure recognition, United Nations membership and a loan they might be convinced. We have lost the friendship of the Arab nations and for that reason should do what we can to get the friendship of Israel. This little nation looks as though it has great possibilities. It will certainly be the outstanding country in the Middle East. . . . Israel is the horse to back in this area.[2]

The reason why Archibald, as Air Attaché, had a particularly hard job ferreting out information about Israel's Air Force, he thought, might have had to do with the large numbers of foreign volunteers (particularly Americans) who still, in 1949, flew for the Jewish state. Virtually all of Israel's pilots during the War of Independence had been foreigners. The Americans fighting for Israel had been violating the U.S. Nationality Act of 1940, which forbade U.S. citizens from serving in the armed forces of a foreign state "unless expressly authorized by the laws of the United States." Israel might have been trying to protect the Zionist volunteers.

During Archibald's first year in Israel, the United States did in fact accord Israel *de jure* recognition, and strongly backed the new nation for UN membership. And through the Export-Import Bank, the United States provided a critical loan to Israel of $135 million. But somehow, Archibald's hopes for close intelligence relations with Israel did not materialize.

True, the U.S. mission was the only legation in Israel during that year that was allowed to have military attachés at all. But increasingly, Archibald saw this as related to Israeli designs upon American military assistance, rather than as a manifestation of Israeli trust in the United States. While repeated requests for arms and training for the Israel Defense Forces were received, the U.S. Naval Attaché was being surreptitiously followed everywhere he was allowed to go in the country. The Army Attaché discovered that his phone was tapped. By August, 1949, the U.S. service attachés were frustrated and angry, one noting that

> [The] U.S. has been furnished with organizational schemes and OB [orders of battle] of practically every country in the world, the exception being Israel, U.S.S.R. and some of the satellites. . . . Even the simplest request such as . . . identifying insignias of units and formations, and general geographical locations of major commands is denied U.S. by Israel.[3]

Finally, in September, Archibald began to recommend against any assistance, any cooperation between the U.S. and Israeli militaries. Such assistance, he reasoned, should only be granted to an ally. Archibald's comments and complaints became so strong, in fact, that the Air Force Chief of Staff felt it necessary to reprimand him for bias against the country that, nine months earlier, Archibald had felt was the "horse to back" for the United States in the Middle East. By early 1950 Archibald was totally alienated, and wrote to Air Force Intelligence that relations between his office staff and their counterparts in the Israeli Defense Forces were so bad that there was no way, "except through actual spy operations," that military information could be obtained.

Archibald's colleagues were also undergoing similar transformations during this period. The U.S. Army Attaché in Tel Aviv, Colonel Andrus, wrote a memo in the last few months of 1949 to the Intelligence Division of the Army General Staff, citing "wanton killing of Arabs and . . . denying access to their own land."[4] In November a request for military training in the United States by the Israelis was turned down, and a very critical article by correspondent Kenneth Bilby appeared in the *New York Herald Tribune.* Colonel Andrus was outraged to learn that Bilby had submitted a draft of the article to Yigael Yadin of the Israeli Defense Forces, and had accepted his corrections. This was the second time, Andrus wrote to Army Intelligence, that the Israeli government had employed American journalists to "blackmail" the United States into providing training assistance. Curiously, it did not occur to Andrus to question in his report the professional conduct of the journalist in question.

Though Israeli methods were scorned by Andrus, their intelligence services had his respect. In November, 1949, he learned that his long-standing request for vacation in the States for himself and his wife had finally been approved. Israeli military intelligence told him—they had known for two weeks.

What was going on here? According to the public record of U.S. diplomatic and financial assistance at the time, according to the effusively warm statements of President Harry Truman and his Secretary of State, Israel was an ally. But Colonels Archibald and Andrus were military men, intelligence specialists, not politicians or diplomats. They were learning firsthand, in the field, what their superiors in the U.S. military and intelligence community already took for granted: that underneath their public, official relationship, Israel and the United States were acting as intelligence and security adversaries. In fact, when the State Department had first officially asked the Department of Defense to establish Army, Navy, and Air Force attaché offices in Tel Aviv, Acting Secretary of State Robert Lovett noted in a memo to Secretary of Defense James Forrestal that "the admixture of European races in Palestine offers a unique opportunity for Soviet penetration into a highly strategic area." The new attachés in Israel, he said, "should be qualified to observe Soviet activities, and should be thoroughly familiar with Soviet tactics." The State Department thought the matter so urgent that the normal procedures for selecting and briefing military attachés were bypassed, and Archibald, Andrus, et al. were rushed to Tel Aviv to begin tracking the presumed Soviet involvement there.

WASHINGTON'S INTERNAL
ASSESSMENT OF THE NEW JEWISH
STATE . . .

As early as 1946, the U.S. Army Intelligence had asked the Military Attaché at the American legation in Beirut, Lebanon, to report on the "Communist leanings" of the leaders of major Palestinian Jewish labor organizations, including *the* major one, the Histadrut. Certainly Palestine was not unique in receiving this kind of attention from the U.S. intelligence agencies—relations with the Soviet Union were deteriorating rapidly, and there was a general fear of Communist "penetration" in many parts of the globe. But in the Middle East there was oil. And by 1947, it was apparent to U.S. intelligence that the worldwide sympathy for Jewish immigration to the region, supported by an international Zionist underground, was destabilizing the area. In September of 1947 the Near East the CIA's "Review of the World Situation as It Relates to the Security of the United States" assessed these developments:

> Zionist leadership, exploiting widespread humanitarian sympathy with the surviving Jews of Europe, has pursued its objectives without regard for the consequences. The Arab reaction is bitter and potentially violent, endangering not only the Jews in Palestine but also the strategic interests of the Western powers in the Near and Middle East, since the Arabs now identify the United States and the United Kingdom with Zionism.

By early 1948, U.S. government intelligence estimates reflected a deep concern that international Zionism was dragging the United States into a dangerous program of territorial conquest in the Middle East. In March, 1948, a Joint Chiefs of Staff paper on "Force Requirements for Palestine," anticipating the termination of the British Mandate, predicted that the "Zionist strategy will seek to involve [the United States] in a continuously widening and deepening series of operations intended to secure maximum Jewish objectives." The JCS listed the objectives as (a) initial Jewish sovereignty over a portion of Palestine, (b) acceptance by the great powers of the right to unlimited immigration, (c) the extension of Jewish sovereignty over all of Palestine, (d) the expansion of "Eretz Israel" into Transjordan and into portions of Lebanon and Syria, and (e) the establishment of Jewish military and economic hegemony over the entire Middle East.

The JCS paper added ominously:

> All stages of this program are equally sacred to the fanatical concepts of Jewish leaders. The program is openly admitted by same leaders, and has been privately admitted to United States officials by responsible leaders of the presently dominant Jewish group—the Jewish Agency.[5]

U.S. intelligence officials were particularly interested in the Jewish terrorist gangs that were harassing the British mandatory government: the Stern group and the Irgun. In November, 1947, the American Consul General in Jerusalem had transmitted to the State Department in Washington documents obtained from the Jewish Agency (via the British) that linked Stern and Irgun leaders to the Soviet and East European legations in Beirut. An Irgun leader by the name of Menahem Begin was said in these reports to have regularly accepted funds from Eugenie Podvigin, the Second Secretary of the Soviet legation in Beirut.[6]

There are reasons to doubt the veracity of the Jewish Agency report. The Jewish Agency and its leader, David Ben Gurion, had for years been trying to discredit and/or destroy Menahem Begin and the Irgun, in a campaign known at the time as "the Season." In this effort, Ben Gurion and his colleagues had worked closely with British intelligence to seek out Irgun arms caches and kill Irgun leaders. On the morning of June 20, 1948, the dispute was carried to extreme lengths when Ben Gurion ordered his colleagues Yigal Allon and Yitzhak Rabin to use cannon and mortar fire on Begin and the *Altadena*, an Irgun gunrunning boat. The man who would one day become Prime Minister of Israel narrowly escaped with his life, at the hands of the country's first Prime Minister.[7]

Although the State Department probably discounted the Jewish Agency version of Begin's Soviet contacts, knowing as it did of Begin's extreme right-wing politics, it may have been less sanguine about the Stern group. Army Intelligence in Paris at the time reported on Soviet-sponsored training for the Stern group leaders, and alleged close working contacts between that organization and the Palestinian Communist party. Nor did the State Department believe reports in May of 1948 that there were 8,000 Soviet soldiers fighting with the Jewish Army. The U.S. Consul General in Jerusalem, Thomas Wasson, responded to department inquiries by characterizing the information as "rumors . . . yarns . . . pure poppycock."

Nevertheless, U.S. intelligence followed with great interest the immediate diplomatic recognition accorded Israel by the Soviet Union in the hours after the Tel Aviv declaration. Poland, Czechoslovakia, and the other East Bloc countries followed suit. Of even more interest was the flow of emigration out of Eastern Europe during 1948. As was the case in the American zone of occupied Germany, the Zionist "welfare" and recruiting organizations were not seeking the young, the old, and the infirm— they wanted soldiers. The senior representative of the American Joint Distribution Committee in Warsaw assured the U.S. Embassy that there would not be a flood of emigration out of Poland to the new State of Israel, as "Israel was only interested at the present time in the immigration of potential soldiers, and there are not in Poland today more than 2000 Jewish youths of military age who are not encumbered by families."[8] Nevertheless, American intelligence followed the flow of emigration carefully. Of the approximately 1.5 million Jews living in Europe after the war, fully half were behind the Iron Curtain.

Reports coming from the U.S. missions in Eastern Europe in mid-1948 emphasized the possibilities for infiltration of Soviet agents into the Jewish fighting units that flowed out of the region and south through Yugoslavia, Italy, and France. As the Israeli government was formed, Army Intelligence drew ominous attention to the birthplaces of the members of the Ben Gurion cabinet, many of whom came from Eastern Europe.

When the first Ambassador from the USSR to Israel arrived in Tel Aviv on the evening of August 8, 1948, the U.S. Embassy, which was lodged in the same hotel as the Soviets, reported on the event in great detail. The U.S. mission noted disappointedly that despite the late hour of the Russians' arrival, a large crowd of several hundred persons gathered to cheer the Ambassador. The report ended on a high note, though, gleefully recounting the resentment of the exhausted Israeli hotel staff when the Russian delegation insisted on being served a full five-course dinner at 3 A.M.

In a way, the suspicion and antipathy of the U.S. intelligence community may have worked to Israel's advantage. At the end of 1948, more than six months after the declaration of Israeli independence, the United States still had not granted *de jure* recognition, and the Truman administration was not yet committed to meeting the urgent financial needs of the new state. The U.S. Ambassador in Tel Aviv, James G. McDonald, saw an opportunity, and began to wave the Soviet flag in the face of the President and the State Department, arguing repeatedly and forcefully for *de jure* recognition and for U.S. support for the Export-Import Bank loan.

McDonald was an ardent Zionist, and his appointment had been strongly opposed for that reason by Secretary of Defense Forrestal and Undersecretary of State Lovett, among others. Israel was in the midst of its first national election campaign in December, 1948, and McDonald warned his superiors in Washington again and again that the Soviets might be planning "campaign tricks" to influence the election in favor of the small Israeli Communist party or the larger socialist Mapam party. What were urgently needed, McDonald wrote, were concrete manifestations of U.S. support to "strengthen those elements here who stand clearly for Western system political freedom and socio-economic justice," by which McDonald meant the "moderate" Mapai party and David Ben Gurion. It worked. The loan and the recognition were approved on January 25, 1949, just prior to the election.

During 1949, communism was a common theme of the reporting from both the military and political staffs of McDonald's embassy in Tel Aviv, though, as we shall see, those two staffs drew quite different conclusions regarding U.S. action in the face of the perceived threat. In March, yet another warning came about the possible political implications of Israel's absorption of all those poor immigrants from the East Bloc countries. And in April, a detailed analysis of "Certain Communist Tactics" was dispatched to Washington.

In September, a 14-page study on "Communism in Israel" was sent, along with a plea from the Chargé d'Affairs, Richard Ford, for additional staff for the embassy to work full time on tracking the Red threat, which was seen to have "increased materially in strength." The report was written in a rather journalistic style and was replete with the terminology that would become so tragically common in America over the next few years: "fellow travelers . . . parrots of the party line . . . 'agents provocateurs' . . . carefully camouflaged Communist machinations . . . vitriolic drippings from the Party-sponsored daily newspaper," and my favorite, "sorry creatures of chaos."

At one point Richard Ford's "study," as he called it, described a visit to a small Arab village near the Transjordanian border, during which he met three Israeli officials, recently arrived from Russia. "All three," he said, "were of the thick-necked, gorilla shouldered, crouched headed type of Russian peasant who might have left the steppes only yesterday."

It is no surprise that, in the face of such a palpable, physical Soviet threat, Ford concluded that the situation fairly cried out for U.S. involvement. In his words: "It goes without saying of course that heroic measures will be required in stopping the already well advanced Communist encroachment."[9]

. . . AND ITS PUBLIC POSITION

The creation of a Jewish homeland in the Middle East as a legal and diplomatic entity took place in a remarkably short space of time and with strong, warm support from the United States, the reservations of the U.S. intelligence community notwithstanding.

In 1942, the major world Zionist organizations met in New York at the Biltmore Hotel and called for the creation of a Jewish state in the entire area of the British Mandate in Palestine. The Biltmore Program, as this plan was called, was unofficial in a legal sense, and was not at the time even approved by the Zionist Organization in Palestine.

By 1946, with the extent of the devastation of European Jewry now known, several Zionist groups vied for support in America and Europe, each with different objectives and timetables for the establishment of a Jewish national home in the Middle East. Late in the year, both the Executive of the Jewish Agency and the World Zionist Congress backtracked from the "maximalist" position of the Biltmore Program, and endorsed a form of partition that was termed a "viable Jewish state in an adequate area of Palestine."

In November, 1947, the United Nations General Assembly

first gave a concrete legal form to Jewish national aspirations when it passed a partition plan that, had it ever been implemented, would have created both a Jewish and a Palestinian Arab state in what was then the UN-mandated British territory of Palestine.* What the General Assembly did not vote, however, was any detailed procedure for the creation of the two new states.

The member states of the UN were still arguing about the procedures and timing of partition when, in March of 1948, the Jewish Agency announced that a provisional government was being formed in the Jewish portion of Palestine. Within weeks, blue and white flags appeared, stamps were issued and taxes were levied. Israel began to acquire the appurtenances of a nation-state. In May of 1948, when David Ben Gurion proclaimed the creation of the new state and recognition was granted by both the U.S. government and the Soviet Union, the form and shape of the new state was still not determined. It was not until January of 1949 that a permanent government of Israel was elected, and an armistice was declared that froze the borders of the new state.

In less than a decade, "Israel" had been transformed from the shapeless aspiration of a portion of the world Jewish community into a modern nation-state that had achieved political acceptance around the world and, as we shall see, a position of total military predominance in the Middle East.

The critical role played by the United States government, and most particularly by President Truman, in the birthing of the new State of Israel is generally accepted by historians of these remarkable events. Three former Israel Prime Ministers who were deeply involved in the diplomatic, military, and financial aspects of the creation of the state, David Ben Gurion, Moshe Sharett, and Golda Meir, have paid elaborate homage in their writings to the U.S. assistance. Gideon Raphael, who has recently published a most detailed and authoritative diplomatic history of Israel, has said of Truman's early diplomatic recognition, transmitted minutes after the Ben Gurion declaration, that

---

*The voting of the General Assembly partition plan on November 29, 1947, is often cited as having provided a basis in law for the declaration of the State of Israel in May of 1948. If that is true, and it is certainly a plausible position, then the partition plan also lies dormant as a legal foundation for the creation of the Arab State of Palestine, if and when (and where) that is "declared."

it had "placed the new state firmly on the political map of the world."[10]

Repeatedly during these critical years, Truman intervened to assist the Zionist leaders who were working for the creation of Israel. He pressured Britain to accept more refugees in Palestine, supported the original UN partition plan, appointed an ambassador to Tel Aviv who was strongly predisposed to favor Israel against the Arabs, and arranged the Export-Import Bank loan and a temporary credit, in response to a Jewish Agency request for the same. As the end of the British Mandate approached, Truman appealed publicly to the Arab nations not to attack the new Jewish state. After the Ben Gurion declaration and the commencement of open hostilities, the U.S. delegation at the UN repeatedly took Israel's side in disputes over successive armistice lines that gave the Jewish state ever larger portions of Arab Palestinian land. Finally, in January of 1949, when a more or less permanent armistice had been achieved, the Truman State Department began to lobby hard for UN membership for Israel, which was granted in May of that year.

Perhaps less well known is the behind-the-scenes U.S. support in the days and weeks just prior to the declaration on May 14, 1948. As it became apparent that the Arab states were mobilizing to invade Palestine, and were already providing active support to armed Arab bands that were crossing into the mandate territory to help local Arabs against the Jewish settlers, the State Department in Washington called in Arab diplomats to accuse them of aggression, and to warn them of the consequences and the "serious U.S. concern" about a possible invasion of Jewish Palestine. Moshe Sharett, Foreign Minister of the provisional Israeli government, was even allowed to use U.S. State Department code-telegram facilities to communicate quickly from New York with David Ben Gurion at the Jewish Agency (i.e., provisional government) headquarters in Tel Aviv.

The fact that the Soviet Union immediately granted both *de facto* and *de jure* recognition to the new State of Israel doubtless muted somewhat the negative reaction of Arab governments to the multiple evidences of U.S. support for the Jewish nation. Nevertheless, virtually every U.S. Embassy in the region was busy reflecting to Washington the outrage felt by Arab governments, particularly in May and June, 1948. One particularly poignant example was an aerogram from the U.S. Ambassador in

Beirut, summarizing articles in the Lebanese press for the last week of May:

> Editorialists still differentiated between their dislike of American policy and their feelings toward individual Americans. *Beirut* took the occasion of the return of [American University of Beirut] President Bayard Dodge to say: "Noble Americans who have lived many years among the Arabs resent President Truman's recognition of the Israeli State." . . . And on the President: "Truman does not fully realize his responsibilities. . . . From the presidential chair have radiated the most beautifully humane principles in history—in the times of Washington, Lincoln and Roosevelt."[11]

The British were very unhappy, also. In November, 1948, as Israeli soldiers swept through areas designated for the Arabs in the UN partition plan, and cease-fire after cease-fire was broken by both sides, British Prime Minister Clement Attlee warned Truman that "Palestine" had supplanted Berlin as the major threat to world peace, and would be the test both of the viability of the UN and the future of Anglo-American cooperation.[12]

Through all of this, and in the face of mounting evidence that U.S. support for Israel was becoming increasingly costly, President Truman stuck by his guns. In September of 1949, Deputy Undersecretary of State Dean Rusk could write to Clark Clifford in the White House that each and every item of support for Israel pledged in the Democratic party platform of June, 1948, had been "literally and fully carried out."

There is no need to reexamine here the old issue of the motivations for Truman's Middle East policy, i.e., whether "naked pressure" from Jewish American groups, directly and via the Democratic National Committee, or altruistic concern for the plight of European Jewry was the root cause of that policy. (Truman in his *Memoirs* says it was both.) Much has been written on this subject, and none of it is relevant to the remainder of this chapter. The point should be emphasized, however, that in terms of the official acts and diplomatic postures of the United States government, Israel's leaders had no reason to view America as other than a staunch friend and ally.

But something unusual had occurred during the bitter struggle to establish a Jewish homeland. It had to do with the Israeli leadership, and their unique outlook on the world. The political and military figures (they were often both) who worked to create Israel out of Jewish Palestine did so in the shadows. The immigration was illegal. The international arms trafficking was illegal. And the explosive acts of violence against the British Palestine government carried always the risk of imprisonment, or worse, from the dreaded British Criminal Investigation Division, known familiarly as the CID. But those who led the Zionist underground emerged in mid-1948 to become the politicians and diplomats of the new state, and they carried the ethics of the underground into the embassies, conference halls, and assemblies in which they now moved as official representatives of the new nation.

DIPLOMACY IN A WAR ZONE

In January, 1948, the U.S. consular staff began to note a slight change in "official" Zionist tactics. It had to do with the Semiramis Hotel in the middle-class Arab district of Katamon in Jerusalem. In the early morning of January 5, the Semiramis disappeared, blown up with 175 pounds of dynamite. Twenty-three persons were killed—all civilians—including the Spanish Consul. This in itself was not so unusual—both Arab and Jewish terrorists had committed similar acts of carnage for several years in Palestine, and the Irgun and Stern gangs had even evolved a complex rationale—almost a political philosophy—around such acts of violence.

But this, as U.S. Consul General Robert Macatee noted in his report, was different. For one thing, the Haganah, an arm of the Jewish Agency (which was about to become the provisional government of Israel), claimed responsibility for the explosion. The act achieved precisely nothing in terms of the Arab-Israeli struggle . . . except perhaps to send Jerusalem Arabs a message to leave Palestine. And that, of course, was the whole point. From Macatee's report to the State Department:

> First reaction in Jerusalem regarded this act so completely motiveless as to place in category of nihilism . . . it cannot be excluded that opinion in [the local Jewish community]

may have forced hand of Jewish Agency plus further justification in Jewish Agency mind that "this is war." [13]

It was to be a special kind of war—one waged against civilians, in which a major objective of both sides was to be the forced movement of populations. It occurred to the U.S. Consul General that in such a war, the diplomatic community would be at risk, so he led a delegation from the consular corps to visit a Jewish Agency official, Golda Meir, to plead the cause of diplomatic immunity. Mrs. Meir, whose organization had blown up the hotel, agreed to make an appeal to the "Jewish community" to take special care for the safety of consular personnel.

By early 1948, the Jewish Agency was calling upon the U.S. Jewish community for arms, money, and volunteers. And in late January, Moshe Shertok, who headed the agency's delegation to the UN, sought more formal, "official" assistance. Shertok visited the U.S. mission to the UN to ask that the U.S. government sponsor the Jewish Agency's admission as an interested party to the Security Council's debates on Palestine. It was a reasonable request, and the State Department did in fact support Jewish Agency participation in the UN discussions. Shertok also asked that the U.S. government support a UN policy that would permit the Jews to import arms into Palestine, but would prohibit the Arabs from doing so. The Jews, he said somewhat disingenuously, wanted to organize a militia. The U.S. government knew a great deal more about Zionist underground preparations for war than Shertok realized, however, and this proposal met with little success.*

Back in Jerusalem, the U.S. Consulate was battening down the hatches for the war that everyone knew would come, irrespective of what was said or resolved in the UN. The consulate installed a radio to permit direct contact with Washington, along with an electric generator, a reserve gasoline tank, and a water cistern. In March, Arab gunmen entered the car of one of the U.S. consular officers and ordered him to drive on. An Arab interpreter employed by the consulate was in the car as well, however, and he managed to convince the gunmen to desist. The incident brought home to the consulate just how difficult it was going to be to stay *hors de combat*.

*Moshe Shertok would later change his name to Moshe Sharett and become Foreign Minister, then Prime Minister of Israel.

It was with the Jewish community in Jerusalem that the U.S. Consulate's relations began to deteriorate, however. On the 11th of March, an Arab driver of the Consul General's car loaded it with dynamite and drove into the compound of the Jewish Agency headquarters, flags flying. Using a timed detonator that allowed him to escape, the driver exploded the car, killing several people and doing considerable damage. Although there was never the slightest intimation that anyone other than the driver at the consulate was involved, the Consul General was mortally embarrassed, and the threatening calls in "grammatical Hebrew" began coming into the consulate's phone operator the next day.[14]

About one week later, a speech made in New York created even more suspicion in the Yishuv (the Jewish community in Palestine.) Warren Austin, the U.S. Ambassador to the UN, announced in the Security Council that the United States no longer thought the UN partition plan could be carried out. He called for an immediate truce in Palestine, to be followed by a temporary UN trusteeship when the British Mandate terminated. The proposal, if it had been implemented, would have knocked the legal underpinnings out from under the Jewish Agency's plans to announce a new Jewish state on May 14, 1948.

In Jerusalem, the speech caused what the Consul General Robert Macatee described as "consternation, disillusion, despair and determination" in the Jewish community. In Washington, Presidential Assistants Clark Clifford and David Niles prevailed upon Truman to issue a written statement that undercut Austin's speech. Partition was still the basic U.S. policy, he said, and the trusteeship proposal was only a temporary measure intended to keep the peace in Palestine until such time as partition could be implemented. The damage, however, had been done.

As the end of the British Mandate drew closer, the scale of violence between Arab and Jew in Palestine escalated. On the early morning of April 9, a combined force of 100 Irgun and Stern gang members entered a small Arab village outside Jerusalem and killed 250 men, women, and children, most of whom were blown up with dynamite inside their own stone houses. The next day, David Shaltiel, the Haganah commander in Jerusalem, described the village that had been attacked as "one of the quiet villages in the area that had not been connected with any of the gang attacks since the start of the present campaign; one of the few villages that has not let foreign gangs in."[15] In response to Shaltiel's statement, the Irgun released a letter in which Shaltiel had given the Stern and Irgun gangs permission to attack the village. Twenty Haganah soldiers, it was later learned, had participated in the attack.

A new American consul general, Thomas C. Wasson, had just taken up his post in Jerusalem. His reaction to the attack upon Deir Yassin, as the village was called, was one of outrage and despair. In addition to his duties as Consul General, Wasson was also the American representative on the UN Security Council's Truce Commission, and Wasson now reported to Washington that after Deir Yassin, he saw little chance for a cease-fire and truce.

As if to prove him right, the Arabs retaliated. On April 13, Arab units attacked a ten-vehicle convoy that was resupplying Hadassah Hospital on Mount Scopus in Jerusalem and was traveling under the protection of the symbol of the Red Cross. Thirty-four were killed and 21 wounded. Among the dead was Dr. Haim Yassky, the hospital's director. In reporting this attack, *The New York Times* indicated that the majority of victims were doctors, nurses, and patients. No mention was made by the *Times* of arms having been found in the convoy trucks and ambulances after the attack.[16] The Arabs, however, maintained that the primary purpose of the convoy was to resupply a secret armed garrison, including artillery units, on Mount Scopus.

Thomas Wasson's reports on the attack to the State Department were specific on the disputed matter of the arms. On April 15:

> American correspondent eyewitnessed removal from trucks large quantities arms and ammunition and speculated whether for escort or other purpose.

And on April 17:

> . . . queried as to whether convoy included armored cars, Haganah guards, arms and ammunition in addition to doctors, nurses and patients, Kohn [of the Jewish Agency] replied in affirmative saying that it was necessary to protect convoy.[17]

In the days just before the termination of the mandate on May 14, 1948, Wasson was in daily contact with British officials. On May 13, he reported the British view that Deir Yassin might be repeated by the Jews to deliberately provoke a premature attack by the Arab armies poised on Palestine's borders. And on May 20, 1948, about one week after the British had left and the new State of Israel had been declared, Wasson reported to Washington that the Arab Legion had begun to shell the Hadassah Hospital after Jewish forces there fired on the Arabs from the hospital. The Jewish Agency, he said, had refused to remove its soldiers from the hospital area in spite of pleas from the International Red Cross delegate, Jacques de Reynier, that it do so, and in spite of repeated offers from the Arab Legion to afford the soldiers protection if they were disarmed.

And then Wasson himself was assassinated, by a sniper. It happened around midday on May 22, as he was returning from a UN Truce Commission meeting at the French Consulate, walking in an alley just behind the U.S. Consulate. He was wearing a bulletproof vest, as a U.S. consular guard and a naval radioman had been shot by snipers in previous days. The bullet entered Wasson's shoulder near the armpit, at a downward angle, and ricocheted off the inside of the vest, doing enormous internal damage. Wasson was taken to the Hadassah Hospital, where he died the next day.

Ten minutes before Wasson was shot, an American consul and vice-consul had been fired upon by a sniper in exactly the same place. The alley was surrounded by derelict buildings, and neither had any idea who had shot at them, as they saw no one and the area had been infiltrated by both Arab and Jewish irregulars, who shot at each other fairly regularly.

The New York Times, however, left no doubt as to who had killed Wasson. The front-page story announcing his assassination quoted Haganah sources saying the Consul General "had been shot by an Arab sniper."[18] Subsequent articles quoted an anonymous UPI correspondent and then an anonymous "Jewish nurse" as having heard Wasson on his deathbed say that "the Arabs had done it." The Consul and Vice-Consul who were shot at on the same day (one of whom was with Wasson in the hospital) do not recall any such accusation, and doubt that one was made.[19]

On June 5, 1948, two weeks after the killing, *The New York*

Times carried a small article in which the Acting Consul General in Jerusalem was quoted to the effect that no deathbed statement was made, and that it was unlikely Wasson knew the identity of his assailants.

But the State Department conducted no formal investigation into the circumstances that might have pinpointed the responsibility for Wasson's assassination. Nor does the Jerusalem Consular File for 1948 in the National Archives contain any reference to Wasson's killing, nor any communications about notice to kin, burial arrangements, and so on. When the Consul and Vice-Consul who had served with Wasson completed their tours in Jerusalem and returned to Washington, however, they were questioned closely by the State Department about whether Wasson had in fact been working at the time he was killed. The department, it seems, had doubts about whether Wasson's name should be added to the list of Foreign Service officers who have died "in the line of duty," inscribed on the tablet at the C street entrance of the State Department Building.

In mid-June of 1948, an uneasy truce was imposed on Arabs and Jews in Palestine under the auspices of the United Nations. And in the weeks that followed, the War of Independence was won. As UN and U.S. officials watched helplessly, arms and volunteers poured in to the Haganah, and to the Irgun and Stern gangs. The Jewish forces did not violate the truce agreement; in Mark Twain's words they "flung it down and danced upon it." Virtually every United States government agency represented in the Middle East documented the Jewish truce violations and predicted their adverse effects on the prospects for peace between Arab and Jew in the region.

The U.S. Military Attaché in Baghdad reported that King Abdullah of Transjordan had had to cease his Army's practice of returning Jewish female prisoners of war under flags of truce, because of repeated instances in which the Haganah had fired upon the Arabs on their way back to their own lines.[20]

Much more disturbing, however, in terms of any hope for an eventual settlement of the basic issues, were the violations that were to permanently alter the rough balance of power that existed in Palestine when the truce was first declared. During late June and early July, the U.S. Consuls in Jerusalem and Haifa reported massive amounts of new arms and thousands of trained soldiers being flown in from Eastern Europe, the use of Arab prisoner-of-war labor to build new fortifications, and forced movements of Arab civilian populations to allow repositioning of Haganah troops, all violations of the UN truce agreement and/or the Geneva Conventions.

The U.S. Director of Central Intelligence, Admiral R. H. Hillenkoetter, noted this change in the strategic balance in a memorandum to President Truman. "The Truce," he said, "has favored the Jews." But Hillenkoetter also perceived the long-term significance of this change in the strategic balance:

> The success of the Arab campaign is doubtful in view of acute ammunition shortages. Unless the Arabs can force political concessions from Israel within the next two months, they will probably be compelled by logistical difficulties to withdraw most of their army units from Palestine. However, they can be expected to support guerrilla activities indefinitely. Arab guerrilla incursions, political nonrecognition and economic sanctions will completely isolate Israel from the rest of the Near East. Under such circumstances, its security will be continuously threatened, its economy stifled, and its future existence consequently will be entirely dependent on the continuing good will of some outside power or powers.[21]

Hillenkoetter wrote this on July 8, 1948, as the first UN truce was disintegrating. Over the next ten days, Jewish forces advanced on three major fronts. And on July 19, Count Folke Bernadotte was able to achieve a second truce.

At this time, the Central Intelligence Agency estimated that Jewish forces outnumbered Arab forces "in or near Palestine" by just over two to one. The Jews had heavy artillery and a large, modern air force. "The truce," the CIA said, "resulted in so great an improvement in the Jewish capabilities that the Jews may now be strong enough to launch a full scale offensive and drive the Arab forces out of Palestine."[22] In sum, in a very real sense the Israeli War of Independence was not won during the fighting, but during the first UN truce. The new Jewish state would not have to be negotiated on the basis of partition, nor would it even have to be negotiated. The international Zionist underground had taken care of that.

As Israel grew stronger militarily, its approach to the question of secure borders altered accordingly. On August 3, Irgun leader Menahem Begin addressed a crowd of 4,000 persons in Zion Square in Jerusalem. All of Jerusalem including the Arab Old City, he said, should be included in the new Jewish state, and eventually all of Transjordan should be annexed as well. Force should be used against any international troops that interfered.

Begin did not at this time, of course, speak for the government of Israel. But Golda Meir did, as a senior official in the Foreign Ministry and Minister-designate to the USSR. In mid-August, Mrs. Meir spoke with the new U.S. Consul General in Jerusalem, John MacDonald, and told him among other things that Israel could no longer accept the internationalization of Jerusalem (as stipulated in the UN partition resolution of November, 1947) and would have to have all of Negev in any future negotiated settlement. MacDonald passed this news on to the State Department, together with reports that Jewish forces in Jerusalem were firing repeatedly on Arab troops, and that the latter were in most instances not returning the fire, i.e., were abiding by the truce agreement.*

In Washington, Secretary of State George Marshall noted the new Israeli belligerence and reacted angrily. In May and June, the United States had repeatedly, publicly branded the Arab states as aggressors, in the United Nations. Now, Marshall said in a memorandum for the President, Israel was engaged in "systematic violations of the UN Truce" including forward movement of Israeli troops from agreed truce positions, continued firing against Arab positions, and organized violations of the UN arms embargo.

Israel had become the aggressor. Marshall proposed to President Truman that the Israeli Ambassador to Washington, Eliahu Epstein, be called in and informed that the U.S. government "shall be not less zealous in the Security Council to oppose aggression from the Israeli side as we were when the attack was launched by the Arab side." Further, Marshall proposed that the prospect of U.S. *de jure* recognition of Israel, U.S. support

---

*The State Department even knew why the Arabs were not firing back. The U.S. Military Attaché in Cairo had recently reported that the Arab Legion was almost completely out of ammunition.

for Israeli UN membership, and the Export-Import Bank loan
should all be used to pressure Israel to abide by the UN truce
agreement rather than recommence hostilities.

Marshall then reminded President Truman (as had the CIA
the previous month) that renewed fighting between Israel and
Transjordan could conceivably force the United Kingdom to
honor its treaty commitments to the latter . . . "with the result
that the two great Anglo-Saxon partners would be supplying and
aiding two little states on the opposite sides of a serious war,
from which only the Soviet Union could profit." [23]

Standing between Arab and Jew during both truces were
United Nations observers and International Red Cross personnel. The instances of Jewish forces firing upon UN peacekeeping
troops increased perceptibly in August until, as Consul General
MacDonald reported, they were occurring many times daily.
Several in the UN observer force were wounded. There was a
certain logic to the deterioration of relations between Israel and
the UN peacekeeping force, MacDonald concluded. At the beginning of the truce, UN forces had protected the Jews from
stronger Arab forces, at least in Jerusalem. By August, however, the positions had reversed. Now UN Mediator Bernadotte
and his forces were considered by the Jews, said MacDonald, to
be an "obstacle to their military conquest of Jerusalem and perhaps the remainder of Palestine."

From Tel Aviv, Ambassador James McDonald suggested to
Washington at about this time that the UN peacekeeping forces
be strengthened. But when the State and Defense departments
responded, in late August, with an offer to the UN to augment
U.S. participation in the peacekeeping forces by 125 additional
military observers, an extraordinary thing happened.

On August 24, Ambassador McDonald wrote both President
Truman and Presidential Assistant Clark Clifford, outside State
Department channels, to warn that U.S. support of UN policies
in Palestine might well lead the United States into open, armed
hostilities with Israel. To the President he added:

> Striving to see the whole problem objectively, I have
> reached the conclusion that the Jewish emphasis on peace
> negotiations now is sounder than the present U.S. and UN

emphasis on truce and demilitarization [of Jerusalem] and refugees.[24]

The Ambassador's observations were not well received in Washington, at least not by the Secretary of State. A week later, in a long telegram approved by President Truman, Marshall responded that maintaining the truce, agreement on demilitarization of Jerusalem, and settlement of the refugee question were not alternatives to a lasting peace agreement, as the Israelis had suggested; rather they were "essential preliminary steps" toward peace. As for the UN, Marshall was hopeful that "wise counsels" in Israel would come to realize that "the new state cannot exist except by acceptance of [the] international community." While the governments of Israel and the United States were not in a state of open, armed hostilities, some Israelis were apparently unaware of that.

On August 22, George Paro, the Chief Code Clerk at the U.S. Consulate in Jerusalem, was kidnapped. Paro was kept for less than 24 hours, and although he was roughed up a bit and interrogated more or less constantly, he was returned without serious harm having been done. Consul General MacDonald's reporting on the affair emphasized that it was a maverick Stern gang operation, and that Paro had been mistaken for a British CID (counterintelligence) operative.

There is reason to doubt both conclusions. The moment Paro was kidnapped, his official diplomatic passport was taken. No effort was made by his captors to verify his identity by contacting the U.S. Consulate, as Paro repeatedly pleaded they do. During his interrogation, Paro was taunted with the accusation that the U.S. Consulate was responsible for the wounding of Vivian Herzog, a Jewish Agency official injured in the Jewish Agency headquarters bombing the previous March, which had involved the Consul General's automobile. Finally, when Paro was "released," he was taken to a Haganah police post where he was kept a further eight hours without explanation.

In September, relations between the U.S. and Israeli governments deteriorated still further. The State Department announced that full *de jure* diplomatic recognition of Israel would only be granted after Knesset elections were held the following year. The Truman administration was following CIA recommendations on this matter, concerned that a pro-Soviet government might be formed to supplant Ben Gurion. In Tel Aviv, Ambassador McDonald was furious at the delay in recognition, and warned that this would "only encourage the Jews in their aggressive attitude."

Then there was the matter of the "emigration" of Jewish displaced persons (DP's) from the American zone of occupation in Germany. As previously indicated, the efforts of Haganah and Irgun were concentrated on the recruitment, by various means, of persons of military age and training to go to Israel and fight. It was precisely this flow of recruits that UN Middle East Mediator Bernadotte wished to stop. He requested that U.S. officials temporarily prohibit the exit of men of military age from the American zone of Germany, and the United States agreed.* The provisional government of Israel delivered a strong note of protest to the State Department.

On September 16, the Israeli Foreign Minister, Moshe Shertok, publicly accused UN Mediator Bernadotte of bias against the State of Israel and in favor of the Arab states. That same day, Bernadotte had signed his Second Mediation Plan, which stipulated, among other things, creation of a Palestinian Arab state that would include the Negev, the demilitarization of Jerusalem, and provision for the repatriation and/or compensation of Palestinian Arab refugees.

The next day, Bernadotte was dead. The Mediator was shot at a roadblock set up in a Jewish-occupied area of Jerusalem. On September 18, the day after the assassination, Consul General MacDonald assured Secretary of State Marshall that the maverick Stern gang was responsible, and that the Israeli government was taking every step possible to apprehend the killers, including mass arrests of Stern gang members. There is no doubt that the Stern group was involved, nor that the government did in fact round up many Sternists after the murder. But there is strong evidence that the Israeli government was itself directly involved in the killing, and that the U.S. government secretly investigated this involvement.

In the days immediately preceding Bernadotte's assassina-

---

*The UN Security Council had, the previous June, adopted a motion calling upon all members to assist the UN Mediator in carrying out his proposals to, *inter alia*, determine whether immigration was being used by one side or the other to achieve military purposes, and in such an event, to refuse such "immigrants" entry into Palestine.

tion, the Israeli press carried out a campaign of vilification of the UN Mediator and the Truce Commission, in particular the American, French, and Belgian members of the commission. The General Zionist paper of Tel Aviv, *Haboker,* questioned whether the American member of the Truce Commission, Consul William C. Burdett, might not be anti-Semitic.* *Hayam,* the paper thought by the U.S. Consulate to be the "spokesman of the Jewish Agency," attacked both the Mediator and the Truce Commission.

On the night of September 17, the date of Bernadotte's death, the Czech Consulates in both Jerusalem and Haifa worked until midnight. Some 30 visas were processed for the Stern gang members who had been involved in the planning and excecution of his assassination. The passports on which the visas were stamped had been delivered late in the day with the "recommendation" of the Israeli government that the visas be approved. All of the passports had valid Israeli exit permits, granted in the hours just after the killing.[25]

Between September 18 and September 29, most if not all of the 30 left Israel on flights for Prague, Czechoslovakia. Three of the 30 left directly from Jerusalem, on September 18, the day after the shooting. Those who left had in fact been rounded up and interned in Jerusalem, in the hours after the killing, during the Israeli government "purge" of the Stern gang. But beginning on September 18, those involved in the murder were permitted to slip out of jail, and were flown secretly to Prague.[26] About a week after the murder, the Belgian Consul General in Jerusalem stated that he had "reliable information" that some or all of the 30 Stern gang operatives flying to Europe intended to kill "members" of the United Nations Security Council, which was then in session in Paris.[27]

By mid-October, the U.S. government believed that the Israeli government, or some part of it, had directly participated in Bernadotte's assassination. Robert Lovett, Acting Secretary of State, assigned a special unit in the department (within the Intelligence and Research Section) to investigate the matter, calling this unit the Acquisition and Distribution Division. As inquiries were sent out to the field (primarily to Israel and Czechoslovakia) in the course of the investigation, respondents were asked to address replies to this unit using the reference IAD-137.

*By which, it is assumed, *Haboker* meant anti-Jewish.

It was primarily the scale, precision, and speed of the evacuation-escape that made the department suspicious that the Stern gang was not involved alone, and the details of the escape were a major focus of the department's investigation. But the Czech connection was also worrying, and in the two to three months after the killing, the U.S. Air Attaché in Prague investigated aircraft manifests for flights between Israel and Prague both before and after the murder. This led to the suggestion that the operation might have been planned and prepared in Czechoslovakia, and that a specially trained squad had been flown into Israel from Prague for that purpose.[28]

On October 19, 1948, the Security Council "noted with concern" that Israel had submitted no report to that body regarding its investigations into the assassination.

But it was not until eight months later, on May 3, 1949, that Israel finally submitted its accounting. It revealed that the majority of the Stern gang members rounded up in the "purge" had been released within two weeks. Those not released were held until a general amnesty was granted on February 14, 1949. In granting the amnesty, the Israeli special military court stated that it was ". . . unable to establish with any degree of certainty that the murder of Count Bernadotte was carried out by order of LEHI [the Stern gang]."

The assassins of Folke Bernadotte were never put on trial in Israel. And in Washington, the State Department never revealed the results of the investigation of the Acquisition and Distribution Division.*

Two days after Count Bernadotte died in his jeep, the U.S. Army Attaché in Jerusalem, Major Nicholas Andronovitch, was having a drink at the Sports Club. A group of uniformed Israelis at the next table were discussing the assassination, and one of them said that "the American Consul's turn is next." When asked whom they meant, one of them responded, ". . . the present Consul, he will get his soon."[29] Consul General MacDonald took the threat seriously enough to relay the overheard conversation back to the State Department. MacDonald had, two days previously, telegrammed the department that a minimum of six guards should be on duty at all times at the consulate. And within

---

*A detailed, balanced account of Count Bernadotte's murder is contained in Sune O. Persson's *Mediation and Assassination: Count Bernadotte's Mission to Palestine 1948* (London: Ithaca Press, 1979).

a week, the Acting Secretary of State had recommended to the Defense Department an augmentation of the marine guard at the Jerusalem consulate, from 13 to 27 men.

Press coverage of Bernadotte's murder in America was relatively sparse and mild as compared to that in Europe. Nevertheless on September 20, the Military Governor of (the Jewish section of) Jerusalem, Dov Joseph, requested that the U.S. Consulate cease transmitting the daily pooled report for American correspondents. The reasons given were that such a transmission was contrary to the Post Office Ordinance, and prevented the military censor from doing his duty. The ordinance in question was several months old, and the military censor in Jerusalem had already told the AP correspondent that he had no objection to the latter's using consular radio facilities. The State Department concluded that Joseph's real concern was political, not military censorship, but agreed to abide by whatever arrangement the Military Governor worked out directly with the correspondents. The department pointed out, via Consul Burdett, that it did not wish thereby to "convey acceptance of his right to impose censorship on grounds of military security."

In October there were other pressures brought to bear on the consulate by Dov Joseph and his government. First, he implied that Army Attaché Andronovitch was spying, and forbade him to cross into Arab-controlled areas around Jerusalem, for which the consulate had official, consular responsibilities, including protection of American citizens caught in the fighting. Then, the Israeli Foreign Ministry objected to U.S. Marines bearing arms "in the streets," i.e., when escorting attachés or consular officers on official business. In Haifa late in the month, Israeli naval vessels fired across the bow of a ship's boat from the U.S.S. *MacKenzie,* which was one of three U.S. Navy destroyers then on duty with the UN Mediator for Palestine. The boat that was fired upon carried both U.S. and UN flags. An apology was delivered by the Israelis, but the point had been made. The Mediator's presence was not appreciated. And just in case the point had been missed, the Israelis fired on the U.S.S. *Gainard* a few weeks later, on December 13, 1948.

Meanwhile, Israeli troops recommenced the fighting. The truce was ended. When UN observers approached the Jewish forces to ask that the shelling cease, they were told, ". . . We

have orders to shoot. If you want us to stop, see Ben Gurion."
Colonel Moshe Dayan, the Israeli commanding officer in Jerusalem, then barred the UN observers from the area south of the
city, where the Israelis were launching a major offensive against
the Egyptians.[30]

The fighting was particularly bitter around Jerusalem, and
the consulate reported another Deir-Yassin–like massacre of civilians at Dawaymeh, an Arab village in the Galilee area. UN
observers were able to get through the lines and verify this incident. The Jewish soldiers invaded and looted a Christian con-
vent at Tiberias. Again the UN confirmed the event and made a
report, and the U.S. Consulate was obliged to write the State
Department a bitter dispatch summarizing "the Jewish attitude
in Jerusalem towards Christian institutions."

By November, the arms shipments and troop arrivals from
Czechoslovakia were so frequent that complaints began to be
voiced in the United Nations that the Czech-Zionist connection
constituted an "intervention by a foreign power" in the Middle
East war, in violation of both the partition plan and the various
UN truce agreements. The Israeli response to that produced one
of the more bizarre events in the War of Independence—the
Foreign Ministry of Israel announced that the country was being
invaded from all sides by a huge British army. The British were
flooding Transjordan and Iraq with heavy arms, tanks, and aircraft from Libya. Roads were being built for the attack north
from Akaba on the Red Sea. Troop concentrations were reported in the Negev and in Hebron.

It was a dramatic turn in the war . . . except that it never
happened. When asked by the State Department for details of
the invasion, the Jerusalem consulate responded: "Reports UK
troop movements this area considered entirely unfounded. PGI
[Provisional Government of Israel] apparently hoping divert attention from Czech airlift."

By this time the Israelis, in fact, did not even need the Czech
arms. The only Arab army still able to fight was that of the
Egyptians, and it was virtually encircled on the southern front at
Al Faluja. The UN Truce Commission wanted to stop the fighting, but could not convince the Israelis to allow shipments of
food and water to the surrounded Egyptian troops.

And there were other problems. Ralph Bunche, the new UN
Mediator for Palestine, described for the Security Council

"three outstanding problems" to be overcome if the council truce resolution voted on November 4 and the armistice plan voted on November 13 were to be given effect:

1. Israeli refusal to allow UN-escorted supply convoys through to the Egyptian force which has been encircled at Al Faluja for more than six weeks, or to permit their evacuation;
2. Israeli insistence that its deployment of "regular mobile forces" permit it to occupy many positions in the Negev occupied by Egyptian forces prior to the fighting which began on October 14; and
3. Israeli refusal to withdraw its military forces from Beersheba.[31]

From the perspective of the UN Mediator, whose objectives were an end to the fighting, formal armistices between Israel and other warring governments, and, eventually, an agreed resolution of the fundamental issues dividing Arab and Jew in the Middle East, it was perfectly logical to view Israeli military intransigence as a barrier, a "problem" in the path toward peace in the region. Ralphe Bunch was serving the principles of the United Nations Charter.

But the Israeli position was no less logical. Israel wanted the Negev. The Bernadotte Plan (to which the United States, in November, 1948, was fully committed) would, if implemented, deny them this area. But just as the Galilee region had been won on the battlefield during the first two rounds of fighting, the Negev could be won in the next round. And if it was to be won, the Egyptian Army would have to be destroyed, Beersheba would have to be held, and the international community would have to accept the principle that, irrespective of population settlement patterns, Israel had a right to keep that land which its mechanized, mobile forces had conquered.

Foreign Minister Shertok had explained this to Secretary of State Marshall the previous month. He had told Marshall in Paris that the principle objection of his government to the Bernadotte Plan lay in ". . . the assignment of the Negev to the Arabs." Marshall elaborated in a memorandum of the conversation:

Mr. Shertok pointed out that the Arabs frequently argued that a Jewish State which followed a policy of unrestricted immigration would soon press for additional territory. Mr. Shertok believed, on the other hand, that if the Negev were lost to them Galilee would not be adequate to absorb immigration into Israel.[32]

Israel had a "charter" also. But it was not like the UN Charter, a collection of timeless principles to govern the affairs of nations. Israel's charter was more land. David Ben Gurion and the provisional government of Israel hadn't the luxury of principles, timeless or otherwise. There were still hundreds of thousands of Jewish DP's in Europe who dreamed of a national homeland in Palestine. Space was needed for these people. It was almost done now, in October and November, 1948. Militarily, Israel stood astride Palestine and indeed all of the Middle East. Now the battlefield would be that of international diplomacy.

And Israel knew she had a powerful friend in the battle to come. The United States went to the polls in the first week of November, 1948, and elected a president pledged to a Democratic party platform that included the following statement:

> We approve the claims of the State of Israel to the boundaries set forth in the United Nations' resolution of November 29 [1947] and consider that modification thereof should be made only if fully acceptable to the State of Israel.

After the election, if any doubt remained in the international community as to whether the President-elect intended to honor this commitment, it was put to rest. In a speech before the UN General Assembly, on November 20, 1948, Dr. Philip Jessup, a member of the U.S. delegation, reiterated the pledge word for word. The fact that this approach to the "Palestine problem" was completely inconsistent with the Bernadotte Plan and was, in fact, inconsistent with *any* scheme of mediation of the territorial disputes between Arabs and Jews in the Middle East did not seem to bother President Truman. Israel had, in effect, a diplomatic blank check from the Truman administration.

THE DRAWING OF A CLEAR, STRAIGHT LINE

Predictably, one year later the United Nations Palestine Conciliation Commission in Lausanne, Switzerland, was still trying to draft a final plan for peace between Israel and her Arab neighbors, including agreed borders. The United States delegation seemed to be vacillating on the issue of the final inclusion, within the borders of Israel, of the Negev region. Hal Lehrman, an influential journalist from the American Jewish publication *Commentary,* was in Lausanne discussing the negotiations with the Israeli delegation:

> "If we have to choose between the Negev and America's friendship," one very high and usually very calm Israeli spokesman has sadly told me, "we will keep the Negev. It is the one area where large settlement of our people is possible."[33]

The Israeli diplomat understood the distinction between friend and ally. By contrast, the vacillation at Lausanne by the United States, and indeed the general inability of the Truman administration during the years just before and just after the War of Independence to evolve a coherent Palestine policy, derived in large part from Truman's failure to distinguish between U.S. and Israeli national security interests.

Colonel E. P. Archibald also understood. He was neither a diplomat nor a politician, and was in all likelihood not even aware of the pledges in the national platform of the Democratic party. He was, in late 1949 (at the time of the Lausanne negotiations), a military officer in the service of his country. He was U.S. Air Attaché in Tel Aviv. In August, he wrote to the Director of Intelligence of the U.S. Air Force to request permission to apportion part of his representation allowance to his enlisted men. "It so happens," he said, "that some interesting pieces of information have been obtained by the Crew Chief of the Air Attache airplane at various times through his association with members of the Israeli Air Force." Archibald suggested to the Air Intelligence Directorate that it might be profitable to arrange for the Crew Chief to periodically entertain some of his Israeli associates, "in order to create a spirit of friendly cooperation and to exploit this source of information."[34]

His eight months of service in Israel had made crystal clear to Colonel Archibald the line between U.S. and Israeli national security interests. He had taken a page from the Israeli book.

3

U.S. Intelligence and the Zionist Underground

IN ONE SENSE, the war for Palestine in 1948–1949 was World War III. While the scope of the fighting was limited to a small section of the Middle East, the input into the war was truly worldwide. On the Arab side, some 20,000 soldiers in units from the armies of Egypt, Transjordan, Iraq, Syria, and Lebanon participated, though only two of those armies—the Egyptians in the Negev and the Transjordanian Arab Legion in the Jersualem area—had any sustained involvement in the fighting.

On the Jewish side, thousands of tons of weapons, including planes, tanks, and artillery, were mobilized and tens of millions of dollars were generated by a network that covered Europe, North and South America, North and South Africa, and even China.* Many thousands of trained soldiers and pilots with experience in the armies and air forces of both Western and East Bloc countries were also rushed into the fighting on the Jewish side, some as immigrants to Palestine and some as volunteers. Others were mercenaries whose involvement was strictly a business proposition.

U.S. intelligence officers, both military and civilian, were fully aware of the scale and the methods of the Zionist underground. And finally it was this awareness, much more than any concern about "Soviet penetration" of the new Jewish state, that colored their view of the war in Palestine. Of particular interest to the FBI, the CIA, and the intelligence services of the

---

*The Irgun, today generally thought to be a minority "extremist" group within the Zionist underground, had units in 23 countries worldwide, engaged in fund-raising, recruiting, hiring, training, purchasing, and shipping operations.

47

Army, Navy, and Air Force were the illegal activities of American citizens involved in supporting the Jewish war effort. In
most cases, these activities involved violations of the U.S. Neutrality Act, the U.S. Nationality Act of 1940 (previously mentioned) and/or the Arms Export Control Act, but there were
also instances of theft and even espionage.

Unlike the White House staffers, many members of Congress, the Democratic National Committee, most American
journalists, and the "man in the street," the U.S. intelligence
community did not view the Zionists as amateurs or romantics,
and as we shall see in this chapter, they most certainly did not
view the Jewish forces as underdogs, even long before the outbreak of large-scale fighting in Palestine.

"SECURITY PROBLEMS" IN THE
GERMAN DP CAMPS

Peter Rodes, the Director of Intelligence for the Office of
Military Government for Germany—U.S. (OMGUS), was puzzled and frustrated by the activities of Zionists in the DP camps
in early 1948. On January 10, his weekly intelligence report to
the Pentagon detailed thefts of weapons and ammunition from
the U.S. arms depot in Landshut, Bavaria. He guessed at the
time that the stolen items—.45 ammunition and hand grenades—might have been destined for Palestine. It was a logical
conclusion, as many of the DP's were leaving to fight for Eretz
Israel, and Rodes no doubt also was aware that there had been
Zionist raids on arms depots in the United States.

Then there was the problem of the emigration itself. In the
American zone of occupation, tens of thousands of Jewish displaced persons waited through 1946, 1947, and 1948 for an opportunity to resettle permanently in North America, Europe, or
the Middle East. When the State of Israel was declared and war
broke out between Arabs and Jews in Palestine, many of the
DP's turned to the Jewish Agency for assistance in traveling to
the new homeland. Immigration into Palestine was controlled by
the British Palestine government prior to May, 1948, and by the
United Nations Security Council after that time. From Germany, DP's were frequently able to leave with arms pilfered or

illegally purchased from U.S. surplus stocks with the aid of the Jewish Agency. But these were viewed by OMGUS as relatively minor security problems.

Until, that is, the "recruitment" began. The Jewish Agency was not the only organization helping DP's to emigrate. The Irgun Zevai Leumi was also active in the camps, and it provided "assistance" of a different sort.

American military and intelligence officials in Germany, many of whom had personally witnessed the liberation of the death camps at the end of the war, were generally sympathetic to the plight of the DP's, and many were even (privately) supportive of emigration to Israel. But the Irgun was something else. From the OMGUS weekly intelligence report for January 10, 1948:

> Tensions and clashes in the Jewish DP camps are now on the increase. They are spreading to various parts of the U.S. zone and are gaining momentum. In the back of it all is an attempt and determination of the "Irgun Zevai Leumi" to gain control of the camp administrations and institutions.
>
> They find it hard however to take over committees that are democratically elected and are working under an Army charter and subject to public control and scrutiny. Irgun, therefore, seems to concentrate on the DP police force. This is an old technique in Eastern Europe and in all police states. By controlling the police, a small, unscrupulous group of determined people can impose its will on a peaceful and inarticulate majority; it is done by threats, intimidation, by violence and if need be by bloodshed. . . . they have embarked upon a course of violence within the camps.
>
> Irgun is the military arm of the Revisionists, an organization of Zionist extremists who are advocating that the solution of Palestine tolerates no compromises and that the Arabic side should not be considered at all. The Revisionists are a small minority within the Zionist organization. The overwhelming majority of Zionists are moderates and rational human beings who are animated with an idealism and with a spirit of self-sacrifice, who aim and dream to establish in Palestine a Jewish Community founded on the principles of social justice and mutual aid according to the dictates of the ancient prophets of Israel.

Peter Rodes, commenting on the above report, which had been extracted from the weekly intelligence summary of the U.S. Constabulary, found it to be "over-simplified" but "interesting" and "valuable."[1]

Subsequent OMGUS intelligence reports, however, returned again and again to the brutal tactics employed by the Irgun to raise funds and recruit soldiers for Palestine among DP's. In July, 1948, DP's in Berlin who claimed to have just arrived from Poland were found instead to have fled the American zone to avoid the Irgun "recruitment" drives. In Duppel Center DP Camp, Irgun recruiters beat some of those who refused to "volunteer" to fight the Arabs in Palestine, and others were threatened with death if they refused to go. While prospective recruits were being persuaded, the main gates to the camp were closed to prevent escape.[2]

Some of the camps began to report around this time that the Haganah was adopting violent tactics similar to those of the Irgun. An elite, paramilitary group within the Haganah called Sochnut began to appear in report after report of threats, beatings, and intimidation. The targets of these efforts were not the old or the infirm of course, but able-bodied persons (especially males) between the ages of 17 and 35. Of particular interest were "tank and truck drivers, radio operators, all types of mechanics and pilots." Although the OMGUS authorities only began to notice this selection process in mid-1948, it had in fact been practiced for many months, especially by the Irgun.

Harried and frightened by the recruitment drives, DP's of military age began to marry in unusual numbers and to escape from the camps. . . . Jewish victims of Nazi terror again were forced to flee friends and family, to escape Zionist terror. Speaking of particular DP camps, Peter Rodes said:

> It is reported that over 300 persons have left Tikwah for Israel. Of this number, about 65 percent have been forced to go through the application of various degrees of pressure. . . . at the Wetzlar Jewish DP camp . . . the Chief of the DP police is allegedly in charge and is paid by Haganah. He is alleged to be making frequent night trips to other Jewish DP camps in an effort to locate Jewish DP's who left Wetzlar to escape Haganah recruitment.

Even with such tactics, Rodes did not feel that high percentages of the DP's would actually be emigrating to Palestine in the near future, because

> . . . it is extremely doubtful that that many DP's are in the right age group for military service and there are few indications that, at the present stage, people of non-military age or capabilities are being encouraged to go to Israel.[3]

By mid-year, what the OMGUS reports described as "terrorist tactics" had become standard operating procedure for the recruiters from both the Haganah and the Irgun. A typical incident occurred at the Kriegslazarett camp in Traunstein, Bavaria:

> At about 0130 hours, 14 June, a group of six to eight "Ghuis" from the recruitment organization Palestina Amt entered the room of Aaron Stanner and assaulted the six occupants of the room, allegedly because one of Stanner's sons refused to enter the Jewish Army. During this time, the camp police had put a cordon around the building to prevent anyone from entering or leaving. About this same time, Josef Fisch, another DP, entered the camp and was going to his room in the same building. The "Ghuis" were just leaving the building as he arrived. Thinking Fisch was going to the aid of the Stanners, they beat him into unconsciousness. At about 0200 Stanner tried to put through a call to Military Government Traunstein but was unable to get past the camp switchboard.

And later the same day:

> As 14 June was a Jewish holiday of mourning, camp inhabitants who were not willing to go to Israel were warned not to enter the synagogue because they would be forced to leave. Most people warned did remain at home.[4]

THE RECRUITMENT OF AMERICAN
MILITARY OFFICERS

A form of Zionist underground recruitment that concerned
U.S. military and intelligence officials even more was that of
direct approaches to American military personnel, including
those on active duty. And this was occurring closer to home.

In 1948, the U.S. Code provided that any American citizen
who accepted and exercised a commission to serve a foreign
country that was at war with any other foreign country with
which the United States was at peace should be fined not more
than $2,000, or imprisoned not more than three years, or both.
The legislation upon which this federal law was based is known
as the Neutrality Act. Retired officers of the Regular U.S. Army
were also prohibited, in this case by the U.S. Constitution, from
accepting any emolument, office, or title from a foreign government. Reserve officers not on active duty could have accepted
such a position, but Army regulations at the time provided that
such an act would be grounds for immediate discharge of the
officer concerned. On August 7, 1947, the State Department
had issued a circular (number 747) stating that American citizens, military or civilian, who entered foreign armed forces
"cease to be entitled recognition as citizens during the period of
such service" and should lose their passports.

As early as January, 1948, the State Department asked the
Jerusalem consulate to report "as soon as possible" on the mili-
tary and political activities of Americans in Palestine. Many
American citizens were already fighting for the Haganah.

In March of 1948, First Lieutenant Jack Hirshorn, himself an
active duty officer stationed at Gunter Air Force Base, Mont-
gomery, Alabama, tried to recruit an officer of Air Force Intelligence to fly for the Jewish forces fighting in Palestine. Hirshorn
explained that as a non-Jew, the officer could not of course pilot
for the Jewish Army, but it would be arranged for him to fly for
one or another of the Arab air forces, the purpose being to hi-
jack the fighter craft, or cargo plane with supplies and equipment, and to fly the aircraft to the nearest Jewish base.[5]

Not all the approaches were this exotic, but throughout 1948
and 1949, and particularly just before and after the declaration

of Israeli independence, the Zionist underground attempted to recruit (i.e., suborn) literally thousands of U.S. servicemen throughout the United States and Europe. U.S. intelligence officials followed the trend very carefully, and took steps to counter it. Particularly disturbing were reports from the Security Group of Army Intelligence that

> There presently exists among [the Haganah and Irgun] a plan to recruit former Army officers who are proficient in the use of all kinds of weapons to serve as instructors for recruits of the Jewish Armed Forces. It was reported that there is someone in the Pentagon who has access to officers' AGO [Adjutant General's Office] files and who is making available to these organizations the names of former officers thus qualified.[6]

The information contained in these files was classified. The Army officers whose names were referred to the Haganah and Irgun, and were subsequently approached, were being asked to violate the Neutrality Act as well as their oaths as commissioned officers. Finally, those who accepted to serve for Israel were often issued fake passports.

One retired Regular Army officer implicated in the recruitment scheme by Army Intelligence was Colonel David "Mickey" Marcus. Marcus had been New York Governor Thomas Dewey's predecessor as District Attorney in Manhattan, and had also been Adjutant General on the staff of General Lucius Clay in Berlin. An Army Intelligence report in April, 1948, concluded that "Marcus is thoroughly loyal and any apparent Jewish-Palestinian activity is for political purposes to help Dewey." He subsequently joined the Haganah and became the most prominent American military officer to fight for Israel. Less than a month after this report was written, Marcus was appointed commander of the Jerusalem front for the new Israeli Defense Forces. Moshe Dayan credits him with helping the Jewish forces in Palestine make the conversion from an underground force to a modern regular army. Marcus gave his life in the effort, though; he was accidentally shot by an Israeli sentry during the night. Marcus may indeed have been loyal to the United States, but his commitment to the Israeli cause was total.

In May of 1948, an investigation of the matter revealed to

Army Intelligence the possible identity of the "someone in the
Pentagon" who was making AGO files available to the Haganah
for purposes of recruitment. He was Lieutenant Colonel Elliot
A. Niles. According to the agent report on the investigation,
Niles was "an ardent Zionist, formerly a high official of the
B'nai B'rith, and lately in charge of veterans liaison for the Veterans Administration." Niles and one other person working in
AGO, the report concluded, had photostated the "66-I cards"
of likely candidates for the Haganah, and sent them to Palestine. These, together with confidential efficiency-report files,
were thought to be the basis for selection of prospects for
Haganah service. This particular report was adjudged by its author to be rated A-2, i.e., A for "source completely reliable,"
and 2 for "information probably true." Colonel Niles's brother
was David K. Niles, then an aide to President Truman, and one
of the two or three most influential persons in the White House
on Middle East policy matters.[7]

During May of 1948, Zionist recruiters seemed to be coming
through the windows and doors and hospital wards of the U.S.
Army. Captain William Young, still partially paralyzed on one
side from his war injuries, was approached in that month by a
Haganah representative. A gentleman by the name of Levine
wanted to have information about and access to officers in the
hospital who were awaiting discharge. Young was still an in-pa-
tient at Walter Reed hospital in Bethesda, Maryland, but had
frequent business dealings in downtown Washington, and was
able to meet his contact regularly during these trips. As with the
Air Force case in Alabama, the primary interest of Army Intelligence was not in Young, nor the Zionist recruiter, but in finding whether and how the Zionists had managed to penetrate the
hospital staff.[8]

The money being offered to experienced soldiers who would
go to Palestine was considerable. Pilots were offered $600 per
month plus expenses, a slightly better salary than pilots in the
U.S. military were receiving in 1948. And the contacts by
Haganah were not always subtle. Two Army Privates in uniform
were stopped at a traffic light in Norwalk, Connecticut, in May,
1948, and offered $25 per day to fight in Palestine. When the
enlisted men replied that they were members of the National
Guard, one of the recruiters answered, "Oh, that's all right. We
have connections who can get you out of that."[9] Indeed they
did.

ZIONIST ARMS FOR PALESTINE

For about five years, from 1945 to 1949, the flow of arms and men from the American Zionist underground into Palestine accelerated at a steady pace. Most of the arms were purchased; some were stolen. But all were illegal. In addition to the Neutrality Act and the Export Control Act, previously mentioned, two presidential proclamations, numbers 2549 (1942) and 2776 (1948), prohibited the export from this country of arms, ammunition, and other implements of warfare.

The U.S. Zionist groups, some connected with the Haganah and others with the Irgun, operated quite openly. Ads seeking volunteers were taken in major newspapers. Certain organizations maintained hotel suites in New York where volunteers were interviewed and briefed prior to departure for the Middle East. Although law enforcement agencies across the country vigorously prosecuted violators, and were especially tough on the export of arms, judges frequently treated the offenders lightly. In the New York area particularly, those convicted were often let off with suspended sentences or nominal fines.

This is not surprising when one considers that the gunrunning and other similar activities were occurring exactly at the time when the world was learning the full extent of the horrors of the Nazi death camps. To most of the American public at the time, American Zionists who were assisting the remnants of European Jewry to establish a home in Palestine were engaged in a humanitarian effort. And since the event, popular history has depicted those involved as flamboyant but principled romantics. If there was lawbreaking, it has been seen as moral lawbreaking. Typical of this approach is A. Joseph Heckleman's in *American Volunteers in Israel's War of Independence:*

> How is it that normally loyal, patriotic citizens deliberately break the laws of their country?
> . . .We suggest that it was ultimate faith in their government that led these men to defy it. Was not a firm, viable Jewish Homeland an extension of the humanitarian justification for World War II? Was this not a specific instance of the promotion of higher purposes which give governments a moral justification? Was the firm support of the

United States for a Jewish State not repeatedly on record
. . . including immediate de facto recognition of Israel by
the United States May 14, 1948?[10]

To the U.S. intelligence community at the time, however,
the Zionist underground looked a bit different.

There was the matter of the scale of the assistance, for one
thing. It is doubtful that U.S. intelligence had an estimate of
the total amounts of illegal arms pouring into Jewish Palestine–Israel, particularly in the period 1948–1949, when the flow
became a flood. But documents from numerous U.S. legations
and Embassies at the time show that they followed the traffic
carefully, and considered it to be a major destabilizing factor in
the struggle going on in the Middle East. Heckleman reckons
U.S. private assistance to the Jews in Palestine during the war at
1,300 volunteer fighters and $15 million to $20 million. Both figures are probably very conservative. And American volunteers
constituted but a fraction of the total. As previously noted, a
substantial portion of Israel's command structure and virtually
all of its Air Force were composed of foreign volunteers. In
1948–1949, the Arabs were not fighting the Jews of Palestine.
They were fighting the combined forces and resources of the international Jewish community.

A rough measure of the amounts involved is indicated by
State Department and Attaché reports of some of the individual
purchases, or attempted purchases. In February, 1948, the U.S.
Embassy in London reported an attempt by one Edward
Kreisler to purchase from surplus British stocks, export to the
U.S., and transship to Palestine some 100,000 military rifles,
along with 300 million rounds of ammunition. The "order" was
valued at $10 million.[11] In May of 1949, the U.S. Air Attaché in
Rome reported that an Israeli agent had asked for prices from
an Italian munitions manufacturer, for a list of anti-aircraft cannon and torpedoes. The cannon alone were valued at over $10
million.

Weapons imported on this scale gave the Palestinian Jews a
military predominance in the Middle East. Later in this chapter,
I will examine in more detail the Myth of the Miracle Victory. It
is sufficient here to say that before, during, and after the War of
Independence in 1948, the Palestinian Jews enjoyed a substantial advantage over the combined Arab forces in both equipment

and men at arms. In the latter half of 1948, as one UN cease-fire after another was broken and Israel expanded its borders repeatedly, the Jewish position on the UN arms embargo became harder and more strident. In July of 1948, the American Consul in Haifa reported to the Department of State:

> Jews becoming more and more defiant in breaking truce as they say UN observers have no enforcement power to back up decisions of [arms embargo] violations.[12]

Another matter of concern to U.S. intelligence was the type of weapons that the Israelis were bringing or attempting to bring into the Middle East, primarily from surplus stocks stored in Europe following the Second World War. Repeatedly during April, May, and June of 1948, the U.S. Military Attaché in Brussels reported to Army Intelligence that the Belgian Office of Mutual Aid was asking for a statement of policy on the sale of certain U.S. Army supplies in their possession to the Jewish forces in Palestine. The response, from the Plans and Operations Division of the Army, was that while the U.S. government had no control over surplus property once it was sold to a foreign government, resale to third countries was against the (then current) policies of the Department of State, and such sales could prejudice the receipt by the country involved of any future requested assistance.

In June of 1948, the U.S. Military Attaché reported preparations of a Belgian firm to export to Palestine 10 tanks, 26 U.S. armored cars, and 64 half-trucks. And in that same month, the Belgian Military Attaché in Washington requested samples of stocks of toxic ammunition from a captured German chemical ammunition dump in Bavaria.[13] A few days later, the U.S. military attaché in Cairo reported that there had been "reliable indications" in Tel Aviv and elsewhere in the area that the Jewish forces were preparing to use gas to attack Arab population centers.

Then there were reports that the Zionist arms underground was co-opting leaders in Latin America in the violation of U.S. laws. In June, 1948, the U.S. Air Attaché in Mexico City reported that Mexican President Miguel Alemán had received $1.5 million from the Haganah for his "cooperation" with one of the bogus airlines that shipped arms to Palestine, Lineas Unidas de

Panama.[14] Another form of cooperation was the issuance of
fake receipts for arms shipments to countries that then permitted transshipment to Palestine. Generalissimo Anastasio
Somoza, dictator of Nicaragua, was very helpful in this regard,
according to Heckleman, and received $200,000 in a New York
bank account from the Haganah for his troubles in 1948.

On occasion, Zionists involved in the arms trade interfered
directly in the conduct of U.S. foreign policy. In July, 1948, one
such person, who claimed to officially represent the government
of Israel, berated the U.S. Ambassador in Helsinki for having
told (as he had been instructed to do) the Finnish government of
U.S. support for the UN arms embargo. The Israeli informed
the Ambassador that his action was "in conflict with present
American policy toward Israel," and that he was going to make
a report on this transgression to the Israeli Embassy in Washington. Sadly, the Ambassador thought the contact sufficiently important to write the Secretary of State about the matter.[15]

THE CZECH CONNECTION

The gunrunning, the abuse of DP's in occupied Germany,
the systematic violation of the Neutrality and Nationality acts—
all of these were aggravations to the U.S. military and intelligence communities, but they were little more than that. The
documentation indicates, to be sure, that each of these became
the subject of extensive investigations. The FBI, for example,
collected literally tens of thousands of pages of field reports on
the exportation of illegal arms to Palestine. But none of these
matters directly threatened the national security interests of the
United States. Until, that is, the focus of the Zionist arms underground shifted to Eastern Europe.

During January–April, 1948, Major Stephen J. Meade, the
U.S. Military Attaché in Beirut, began to report on mysterious
night landings at a small rural airport in Ryak, Lebanon, in the
Bekaa Valley. The landings occurred frequently and several involved more than one plane at a time. Over a period of three
months, dozens of landings occurred and were reported by
Meade. In the several instances in which the landings were observed personally by the Military Attaché, heavy crates were

loaded by a Lebanese arms smuggler, Darouiche Beydoun. Meade subsequently learned from the Lebanese Army Chief of Staff that the crates contained arms bound for the Jewish forces in Palestine.[16]

Leaders who figured prominently in the Zionist movement at the time, and subsequently in Israel's political history, have tended to deny that imported weapons reached the Jewish settlements in Palestine prior to the declaration of Israeli independence on May 14, 1948. In writing of the "miracle victory" of 1948, former Prime Ministers David Ben Gurion and Golda Meir have taken such positions in their autobiographies. Mrs. Meir dates the commencement of the foreign shipments at "the start of the war," i.e., mid-May, 1948.[17] Moshe Dayan does not even acknowledge the existence of foreign arms shipments in his autobiography. The reports of Major Meade, among others, bring into question the candor of these individuals, who were all in a position to know better.

Meade was not certain about the origin of these air shipments, and it was not until March 31, 1948, that U.S. intelligence officials learned of the new source of arms supply (and, to a certain extent, training) for the Zionist underground: Czechoslovakia.

In the last week of March, the Military Attaché in Prague had reported that the Stern gang was recruiting in the Czech Army with, he thought, the approval of the Soviet government.[18]

And on the last day of March, an American Skymaster DC-4 owned by Ralph Cox, Jr., of New York City landed unsignaled at Prague airport with a cargo of seven tons listed as "surgical instruments and small tools." What attracted the attention of U.S. intelligence agents was the fact that Czech secret police guarded the loading carefully. The plane then took off, overflying both U.S. and British occupation zones in Germany without the proper clearances, thence to an old Royal Air Force airfield at Beit Darras in Palestine, landing by night with the assistance of flares. A British infantry division encamped 15 miles away noticed nothing. The arms and ammunition were off-loaded and taken to the nearby Jewish community of Beir Turya.[19]

At the Palestinian end of the flight, Major E. H. Whitaker reported on the landing and the disposition of the arms. The last paragraph of his report contained the following statement:

Arab residents in the village of Beit Darras and Sawafir Ash Shamaliya which are adjacent to the drome report that Jewish planes of the Auster variety land there quite regularly and that they were in no way surprised by the arrival of the Skymaster.[20]

When the plane returned to Prague, the U.S. Consulate summoned the American crew for questioning, and the story of the "Czech connection" of the Zionist underground began to unfold.

The reports of the incident out of Prague and Palestine were treated by U.S. intelligence with the utmost seriousness. On April 12, 1948, Rear Admiral Hillenkoetter, the new Director of Central Intelligence, sent a memorandum to the President, the Secretary of State, and the Secretary of Defense entitled "Clandestine Air Transport Operations in Europe." Hillenkoetter described several instances of clandestine arms transport by air, of which the Beit Darras flight was only one. Such flights, he said, "into areas of extreme political sensitivity . . . are increasing. U.S.-owned aircraft and U.S. crews are directly participating in these activities." Further such "irresponsible activities," he told the President, could have "unfavorable effects on the U.S. national security," among which he listed "embarrassment to the U.S. through smuggling of arms to either side in the current Palestine hostilities . . . objections by friendly governments and . . . furtherance of the objectives of unfriendly nations in activities over which the U.S. has no control."[21] Hillenkoetter could not foresee just how true his warning about "furtherance of the objectives of unfriendly nations" would turn out to be.

One aspect of the Zionist arms traffic out of Prague that particularly disturbed the State Department was the evidence of the direct involvement of the Czech government. Security police guarded the loading of every plane bound for Palestine, and in April, the CIA discovered that some of the Zionist arms had actually been transported as far as southern France by Czechoslovak Airlines (CSA). In June, Secretary of State Marshall sounded out Ambassador Laurence Steinhardt in Prague about the likely effect of an official protest. The latter felt that such a protest would fall on deaf ears, in view of the acute shortage of hard foreign currency reserves in Czechoslovakia, and the general deterioration of U.S.-Czech relations. The embassy did not know yet how many dollars were involved in the traffic, but thought them to be "substantial."

By mid-July a permanent crew of American pilots and mechanics was ferrying Czech-made arms to and from Israel. U.S. officials tried physically to stop the flights, and threatened to lift the passports of those involved. In each case, Czech authorities protected the American Zionists. Finally, the U.S. Military Attaché recommended, to the Chief of Staff of the Army Intelligence Division at the Pentagon, that the crew of one of the Zionist planes be notified that "unless aircraft and crew proceed Wiesbaden prior July 25 noon it will be shot down on sight by intercepting fighters."[22] In consultation between the Army and the State Department, it was decided, however, to try to exhaust all other measures before resorting to force.

The State Department was, nevertheless, furious at the spectacle of Americans breaking American laws behind the protective shield of the Czech government. If there was any doubt about the direct involvement of the Soviet government in all of this, that was dispelled in late July when the Soviets intervened with the Czechs to release an Israeli agent who had been jailed in Prague for blackmail.

In early August, Admiral Hillenkoetter sent a second memorandum to President Truman, noting the greatly increased scale of the operation in Czechoslovakia and the direct involvement of the government, particularly the Czech security police. Czechoslovakia, he said, had become "the main operational base for the extensive underground organization engaged in clandestine air transport of war material to Palestine."[23] One aspect of the operation noted by Hillenkoetter had been previously reported by Army Intelligence and by the State Department: some of the Americans involved were apparently being made to work involuntarily. Passports had been lifted and no visas issued; security police had told these American "volunteers" that they could not leave the perimeter of the airport. Whether such restrictions originated with the Czech government or with the bogus Zionist airline was not known.

In mid-August the U.S. government decided to turn up the heat. The State Department informed the Americans that if they stayed in Czechoslovakia to work for the Zionists, they "must look to that Government for protection and deposit their American passports with the Embassy." A formal note of protest was

filed with the Czech Foreign Ministry, and the UN Mediator in
Palestine, Count Bernadotte, was informed by the United States
of the details of the operation, and the belief of the government
that a violation of the UN truce terms might be occurring in
Czechoslovakia. The Czech Foreign Ministry was given a copy
of the note to Bernadotte.

Within less than a month, the Czech government informed
the State Department that all of the Americans had left Czechoslovakia. The embassy knew better, though, as a former Czech
Air Force officer had already told the U.S. Military Attaché that
the Zionist air operation had been dismantled and moved out of
Prague to a small airfield at Malacky, north of Bratislava, far
from the prying eyes of the U.S. Embassy.

The new base was not just an air transport depot. Russian
and Czech Air Force officers trained Israeli Defense Force pilots. Fighters and bombers purchased by Israel were recondi-
tioned there and used for training. Soon, the U.S. Air Attaché
learned of other airfields, like Kunovice, near Brno, at which
fighters (British Spitfires and German ME-109's) were being
sold, dismantled, and loaded into the Lineas Unidas de Panama
cargo planes for shipment to Israel.

In some cases, the Panamanian flag on the tail assembly of
the cargo planes was painted over with an American flag, to
facilitate passage over the U.S. zone of occupied Germany, en
route to Israel. The Air Attaché noted in an intelligence report:
"Positive proof of this illegal use of the American flag should
provide ample grounds for legal international action against this
brigand carrier corporation."[24] In the bowels of the Pentagon,
some analyst may have seen this and thought back wistfully to
the recommendation made a few months earlier by the Military
Attaché in Prague, to shoot such planes down on sight.

By now, tens of millions of dollars were involved in the
Zionist Czech operation. The Army Intelligence estimate that
the purchases, training, and illicit shipments to Israel now constituted a $300-million business annually was probably a bit
high, but in November, one single airplane purchase (for 75
fighters and 13 spare engines) amounted to over $4 million. Pay-
ments were made in either gold or dollars, both desperately
needed by the Czech Communist regime.

The Israeli Air Force was not the only beneficiary of the
Czech connection. In mid-November, the U.S. Air Attaché in

Prague reported that between 4,000 and 5,000 Israeli military personnel were being trained in Czechoslovakia: 1,500 infantry troops at Olomouc, 500 nurses and auxiliaries at Velka Strebna, radio and telegraph operators at Liberec, electromechanics at Pardubice, and tank and airborne troops at České Budejovice. The trainees were of many nationalities, though they were primarily East European, English, and American. The commanders of the training centers were Israeli nationals. For the Americans, recruitment and personnel administration matters were handled out of Prague by two American Jewish "welfare" organizations, the Hebrew Immigrants' Aid Society and the American Joint Distribution Committee.[25] At several of the training centers, Soviet and Czech Army officers provided "political education" sessions along with the training.*

Suddenly, in October, 1948, the future of the entire Zionist operation in Czechoslovakia was at risk. Army Intelligence and State Department sources in Europe and the Middle East began reporting that Moscow's attitude toward Israel generally, and the Zionist-Czech connection specifically, had changed. The State Department surmised that pressure was being brought to bear from Moscow on the Czech government to terminate all training and air transport operations, in spite of the obvious financial benefits involved. Alternatively, it was felt that the Czech Ministry of the Interior might have been getting unpleasant feedback on the political indoctrination sessions that accompanied the training—resistance from the trainees may have begun to convince the Soviets and Czechs that "far from creating [a] fifth column they may actually be training an army of potential enemies." At about the same time the press in Israel began to report on changes in the attitudes of the Polish and Romanian capitals toward Zionist organizations there—attacks on headquarters, arrests of the leaders, and so on.

But it was in Czechoslovakia that the training and resupply efforts essential to the Jewish war effort in Palestine were located. Air freight companies in Strakonice and Brno that had been flying to Israel two planeloads per day of light machine guns and other arms were suddenly closed down. U.S. Army Intelligence received word that the Israeli Air Force trainees

*Subsequent intelligence placed the infantry training at Mikulov and increased the estimated number of soldiers to 2,000. In late December, this contingent, named the Gottwald Brigade, was trucked to northern Italy and departed for Israel from the port of Rimini aboard a former Dutch ship, the S.S. *Kedwa*.

had been told that all training would cease, and they would soon depart for Israel. In December, a high-level Czech delegation including the Czech Foreign Minister traveled to Moscow, and Zionist leaders in Prague were quietly told to wind down their operations before the return of the delegation.

But mysteriously, the cloud passed. When the delegation returned from Moscow, the U.S. Embassy reported that the Israeli legation showed "general relief." And at the end of December, as previously noted, the Gottwald Brigade was allowed to depart with its arms. Sales and shipments of Czech tanks, aircraft cannon, antitank guns, and ammunition continued into January and February of 1949. Relations between Israel and Czechoslovakia, at least for the time being, had returned to normal.

What brought about this reprieve? The documents suggest a couple of possibilities. In December, one of the DC-4 Skymasters returning to Prague from Tel Aviv brought one and one-half tons of fresh oranges, which, it was announced in the Czech press, were a gift from "children of Israeli Trade Unionists to their small Czechoslovak friends." A more likely explanation for the sudden resumption of the "Czech connection," however, is contained in two reports in Army Intelligence files that originated within a day of each other, on December 27 and 28, 1948, from Prague and New York City.

On December 17, a four-motored Skymaster circled in over Ruzyne airport outside Prague, landed, taxied immediately to the far end of the field, and parked behind a hangar. Extraordinary precautions were taken to keep the aircraft's presence secret. Later in the day, when it attempted to take off from Ruzyne, the aircraft developed engine trouble and was immediately wheeled into a hangar. A heavy guard of Czech secret police was posted at all entrances.

One of the Czech police, however, was an informant of the U.S. Embassy, and he managed to view the cargo of the plane, which he later described to the U.S. Air Attaché as "small machine guns and rifle ammunition." The aircraft took off from Ruzyne on the day after Christmas, December 26, 1948.

But before it departed, a small but important Christmas present was left with the security police. From the Air Attaché's report:

Of interest is the arrival on this aircraft of a gift from Palestine to the Czech Government which the source described as being a small framed motor vehicle having a cup-shaped apparatus on the back and believed by the source to be a small mobile early approach radar.[26]

In his report on the event, the U.S. Air Attaché noted that a member of his staff had positively identified the two pilots of the plane as being Americans previously involved in clandestine Zionist arms operations. Both of the pilots (Elieser Rav and David Herzel), and in fact all of the crew, carried Israeli passports. Herzel's passport had been issued in Israel five days previous to the arrival of the plane at Ruzyne, on December 12, 1948. Herzel later in the week met in a downtown Prague hotel with a member of the Air Attaché's staff, and gave his name as Raab.

The Air Attaché filed his report with Army Intelligence on December 27, 1948. The next day, an Army Counterintelligence Corps detachment filed a report from First Army Headquarters in New York City. It cited an informant, a member of the Czech General Staff, to the effect that he had, two years previously, dispatched an assistant military attaché to the Czech Embassy in Washington with a high-priority mission: to submit reports on American radar development and on new American inventions in this field. The informant thought that the Assistant Attaché was still assigned in Washington, and might be compromised and used as a double agent.[27] What he did not know was that the intelligence requirement carried by the Assistant Attaché to Washington had already been fulfilled.

THE MAKING OF A MIRACLE VICTORY

> The Jews have four or five thousand Palmach troops and a paper army of fifty thousand in the Haganah, but they have only ten thousand rifles. The Macabees can put a thousand men out, no more, with light arms. They have no artillery, their air force is three Piper Cubs, and their navy is those illegal-immigrant runners tied up at Haifa. The Jews are outnumbered in soldiers forty to one, in population a hundred to one, in equipment a thousand to one, and in area five thousand to one.
>
> —LEON URIS in *Exodus*

I have the honor to report, after hearing innumerable mysterious references to the "Secret Weapons of Israel," that I am
convinced they consist of three, i.e. (1) Determination, (2)
Courage, and (3) Necessity. . . . In retrospect, the achievements of the Israel civilian army against better armed and
numerically superior Arab forces is an achievement that cannot always be explained on technical or logical grounds. . . .*
                    —CHARLES F. KNOX, JR., Coun-
                    selor of Mission, U.S. Embassy,
                    Tel Aviv, in a letter to the Secre-
                    tary of State, November 30, 1948

The idea that the victory of the Jews in the battle for Palestine was a miracle victory against overwhelming odds is arrant
nonsense. More precisely, that idea is unsupported by the documentation. U.S. military and intelligence professionals followed
quite closely the preparations for war in the Middle East, as the
British Mandate drew to a close. The United States fully expected to be asked—and finally was asked—to help fill the
peacemaking vacuum left when the British withdrew, as part
of a United Nations presence in Palestine. Contingency planning naturally included assessments of the size of the force required to keep Arabs and Jews apart. U.S. policymakers at
the time realized that "peacekeeping" might well involve dis-
arming of and/or full-scale fighting with one or both sides in the
dispute, as indeed it had for the British during the mandate
period.

Fortunately, the vast majority of persons engaged in strategic
planning for the United States at the time were thorough professionals who had little use for legends and myths. They were
more concerned with numbers of soldiers, arms and equipment,
training, sources of resupply, financial resources, and the like.
And in these hard terms, the prospects for the new Jewish state
looked bright indeed, before, during, and after the declaration
of Israeli independence in May of 1948.

In the months following the end of the Second World War,
pressure from the international Zionist movement on Britain to
allow more and more of Europe's displaced Jews to resettle in
Palestine mounted steadily. The Truman administration, which
was itself being criticized for dragging its feet on Jewish resettle-

*Knox must have been writing for posterity. Foreign Service officers usually feel that
their opinions on virtually any subject, particularly one so sensitive as this, are "Top
Secret," "Secret," or, at the very least, "Confidential." Knox chose to designate this
particular letter "Unclassified."

ment to North America, began to see the merits of a Jewish homeland in the Middle East. In August, 1945, Truman wrote to British Prime Minister Clement Attlee, asking that 100,000 additional Jewish immigrants (the British were already admitting 1,500 per month) be allowed entry to Palestine as soon as possible. Attlee was not enthusiastic about the idea. At the time the British were maintaining an army of approximately 80,000 men in Palestine, partly to deal with the violence generated by a rising tide of Arab resentment of the *existing* levels of Jewish immigration. Attlee proposed that an Anglo-American Committee of Inquiry be established to formulate a common policy on the intertwined problems of the destitute Jews of Europe and the Palestine question. Truman agreed, and in January of 1946, a committee of distinguished public figures from the two countries began taking testimony and collecting evidence.

One subject that soon became an important focus of the testimony was the extent of Jewish military and paramilitary preparations in Palestine, about which most of the American committee members seemed to know little and be very curious. The testimony and evidence put before the committee on these subjects were extensive, and were subsequently sent separately by the British Chiefs of Staff to the U.S. Joint Chiefs of Staff (JCS). After review of the material, JCS issued it as a memorandum for information on May 9, 1946.[28]

The Chiefs of the British Middle East and Palestine commands estimated the Haganah had "a reasonably well-trained and equipped force of about 65,000 persons with a reserve of perhaps up to 40,000." All of the reserve had received some kind of military training. Within the Haganah, the British Chiefs said, was a mobile field army of 16,000 persons and an elite strike force, the Palmach, of 2,000 to 6,000 men, all of whom were trained on and carried automatic weapons.* When pressed as to whether the Haganah was an "army" or a guerrilla force, the British Chiefs noted that it had a complete chain of command, from a general headquarters through zone commands, down to battalions, companies, and platoons. The Haganah had

---

*Many in the Palmach had in fact been trained by the British, as part of the Jewish Settlement Police. The Jews took maxium advantage of this training program, by joining and then quitting, ensuring a steady flow of trainees into and out of the force. This continued even as Irgun and finally Haganah forces were ambushing and blowing up British military and police detachments during the final years of the mandate.

"transport and all the machine guns, rifles, mortars together with ammunition that it needs."

Every combat member had a personal arm, rifle, submachine gun, or pistol. Rifle grenades and other types of grenades were extensively used. The Haganah had large numbers of light machine guns, sufficient to provide one for each section, and "fair numbers of medium and heavy machine guns." They had large numbers of two- and three-inch mortars, antitank mines, homemade flamethrowers, and "a number of heavier weapons such as pompoms, piats, bazookas and field pieces [artillery], but the ammunition supply for these is somewhat problematic."

Already in 1945, the composition of the Jewish immigrants into Palestine—legal and illegal—was changing: people of military age, many of whom had already had military training and/or experience in Europe, predominated. So the Haganah was growing monthly. And alongside the Haganah, the Jewish settlements had the extremist Irgun ("3000—5000") and Stern group ("several hundred"), which were also very well armed. The British Chiefs thought that the Jews would win a war with the Arabs in the short run, could in fact occupy most if not all of Palestine, but in the longer run, economic and supply factors would favor the Arabs unless the Jews were resupplied from outside the Middle East.

A year and a half later, in November, 1947, the U.S. Army Intelligence Division was asked by the CIA to do the military section for an estimate that the agency was preparing on the "Consequences of the Partition of Palestine." The total strength of the Arab forces in Palestine, the Army said, was 33,000, most of whom were members of poorly equipped "quasi-military organizations." The largest number of Arabs that would ever be mobilized against the Zionists was between 100,000 and 200,000, including soldiers from all the surrounding Arab states. In an all-out war, however, Army Intelligence estimated that the Jews could mobilize *and arm with modern weapons* some 200,000 men and women "who have had some combat and supply experience at one time or another."[29]

How could this be, in view of the fact that the Arab population of Palestine alone outnumbered the Jews by over two to one? (In late 1947, the official UN estimates for Palestine were: Arabs, around 1.3 million; Jews, just over 600,000.) Another Army ID document, prepared in December, 1947, for the Assistant Secretary of State for Occupied Areas, provides part of the answer. An age breakdown of the males in Palestine showed Arabs again outnumbering Jews by about two to one (626,000 to 321,000), but showed Arab males only outnumbered Jewish males in the 20–39 "military" age group by 149,000 to 121,000. By late 1947, the Jewish Agency's and Irgun's selective immigration policies were already having the intended effect.

In early 1948, the Secretary of State received word that the British War Disposals Board had, against the UN embargo policy of Her Majesty's government, sold 21 reconnaissance aircraft to a Jewish company in Palestine. The British Foreign Office was furious, as a few weeks after the transaction, it already had evidence that the planes were being armed. And in February, 1948, the FBI learned of the shipment of 2,200 modern machine guns from New York City to the Haganah, via South America. The guns had been manufactured in the United States by a Jewish-owned zipper company.

In that same month, the American Consul General in Jerusalem wrote to the State Department noting a change in Jewish tactics in the skirmishes with Palestinian Arabs: now, he said, the Jews were taking the offensive, demolishing Arab strong points, raiding Arab villages in strength, and blowing up selected Arab civilian quarters. Such tactics were relatively new, he noted, and were designed, according to his Jewish sources, "to force the Arabs into a passive state."

Army Intelligence received a field report in February, after a visiting U.S. Military Attaché was able to inspect Jewish arms-manufacturing facilities in Tel Aviv and the Galilee. British officers, he said, thought the Sten guns and mortars made by the Jews were superior to those made in England. The Army knew from other sources that the explosives and armor used in this new industry were supplied from the United States and Europe.

In March, 1948, U.S. intelligence learned of another accidental loophole in the British arms embargo: 13 overpainted, armored half-track troop carriers were delivered to Jewish forces in Haifa "for agricultural use." British customs officials finally realized that a mistake was being made, and prevented delivery of the remaining 37 half-tracks on the ship. These, together with the flights in the Bekaa Valley of Lebanon and the first arrival of an arms flight from Czechoslovakia, meant that the arms of the Jewish forces in the northern sector of Palestine had been considerably strengthened some six weeks before the termination of the mandate, in, around, over, and under the noses of the British. The British Foreign Office's Palestine Desk now estimated that Jewish forces would overwhelm Jerusalem, Arab Legion and all, once the expected fighting began.

In April, Army Intelligence was told by the Jewish Agency that 150,000 were then under arms. Mortars had been obtained or built that would fire shells weighing 38 kilograms. And for the first time, via Major George Fielding Elliott, a British military author who had the confidence of the Haganah, Army Intelligence learned something of that organization's permanent training facility at Natanya, near Tel Aviv. Sufficient equipment for the training of all Haganah artillery personnel was reported, including 25-pound and 6-pound pieces. Fifteen armored cars were seen, along with the usual assortment of machine guns and mortars. The training, which Elliott judged to be excellent, was run by senior officers who had served with the Jewish Brigade of the British Army, in the Mediterranean during the Second World War. Training in intelligence (including aerial reconnaissance) and communications was witnessed as well. Major Elliott concluded that as of April 1, 1948, the Haganah was well prepared for large-scale, set-piece battles if it came to that, and Palestine was invaded by regular armies from nearby Arab states.

In early May, in the days just prior to the outbreak of the full-scale war involving the other Arab countries, the U.S. Secretary of Defense had estimates from both Admiral Louis Denfeld, Chief of Naval Operations, and Undersecretary of State Lovett to the effect that Jewish forces in Palestine were superior in manpower, equipment, and training vis-à-vis the combined Arab forces. The Jerusalem consulate reported to the State Department that the Arabs were confused and resigned, and were already leaving Palestine in large numbers.

On May 13, the day before the end of the mandate, Secretary of State Marshall predicted in his "Daily Report Palestine" that the combined Arab armies would be no match for the Haganah, noting that

> This does not mean, however, that over long period Jewish State can survive as self-sufficient entity in face of hostility of Arab world. If Jews follow counsel of their extremists

who favor contemptuous policy toward Arabs, any Jewish
State to be set up will be able to survive only with continuous assistance from Abroad.[30]

From Jerusalem, the U.S. Consul General reported: "Considerable doubt exists that Arab armies other than Arab Legion
will do more than cross Palestine Frontiers and await developments." And later: "Jewish Agency spokesman when asked by
American correspondent whether Jewish Agency would regard
invasion of Palestine by Arab armies as releasing Agency from
obligations of 29 November resolution, replied that Ben Gurion
had always said that main aim of Jews was to get all of Palestine."

What had happened? How had it all become so clear, so
quickly? On May 18, four days after the invasion, the Army
Intelligence Division held a special briefing for the Chief of
Staff. The fighting in Palestine was summarized:

> Upon the termination of the British Mandate, the procla-
> mation of the Jewish State was countered by the entry into
> Palestine of the regular armed forces of the Arab League
> States of Egypt, Transjordan, Iraq, Syria and Lebanon.
> These forces, now either inside Palestine or on its borders,
> total some 20,000 men. The organized Arab guerrillas al-
> ready operating within Palestine number some 13,000. Op-
> posing these forces are over 40,000 full-time Jewish troops,
> supported by some 50,000 militia.[31]

The Jews had outnumbered the Arab forces, regular and irregular, by nearly three to one, in terms of forces actually participating. The Army Intelligence Division added that the Jews
enjoyed the advantage in strength, training, discipline, leadership, combat experience, and reserves of arms and ammunition.
The Arabs had the advantage in artillery, in aircraft, and "possibly" in armor. With the lifting of the British naval blockade,
however, these latter advantages were quickly being overcome
as trained volunteers, arms, and aircraft were flooding in from
Eastern Europe.

At the end of the first month of fighting, in mid-June, 1948,
as the scope of the Jewish victory became apparent, the Joint
Chiefs of Staff updated their intelligence estimate of the pre-

vious March. JCS tried to gauge the manpower reserves of the two sides, and concluded that the Jews had a maximum mobilization potential of 185,000, and the Arabs approximately 140,000, in terms of the number of soldiers who could actually be committed to fighting in Palestine.

In July, the most effective fighting force that the Arabs had, the Arab Legion in the Jerusalem area, was virtually out of ammunition and without any immediate source of resupply. In August, the Israeli Defense Forces received a shipload of armored cars and tanks. By November, the British estimated that the Israeli Air Force had amassed some 150 to 160 planes, virtually all of which (U.S. intelligence knew) were being flown by foreign volunteers. What was happening in the latter half of 1948 was that the caveat seen in virtually all previous military and intelligence estimates of Arab and Jewish strength was being activated. It had been said, time and again, that the Arabs would lose but would eventually gain the upper hand *unless the Jews were resupplied from Europe and America.* After March, 1948, U.S. intelligence knew that the floodgates were open on illegal shipments. And after January, 1949, the flood was legal, as the UN arms embargo was lifted.

In addition to being generally better equipped than and numerically superior to the Arab forces, the Jewish Army was more mechanized and mobile. The result was that in the vast majority of individual engagements, Jewish solidiers simply outnumbered Arab soldiers. In most instances—the exceptions being several engagements against the Arab Legion in the Jerusalem area—it was superior Jewish numbers and firepower that carried the day.

In early 1949, after it was all over, the U.S. Ambassador to Israel, James McDonald, wrote to the Secretary of State on the subject of the "Possible Reason for Strictest Military Secrecy in Israel." It was his opinion as a layman, McDonald said, that Israel's absolute secrecy about its order of battle was in fact an effort to conceal weakness.

In a four-page message to the Secretary of State, McDonald said he recalled that at the beginning of the War of Independence, Washington and London estimates of the strength of the Haganah had been at "12,000, while other information (possibly for propaganda purposes) placed the numer as high as 55,000."

It was well known that Israel "has little effective artillery," he said, "no fire power other than light weapons," and "a limited number of fighter-bomber aircraft." (British estimates of an Israeli Air Force of 104 planes were exaggerations, said Mc-Donald.) The Israelis might seem to have more soldiers than they actually had, he said, because they were "shifted rapidly from front to front, wherever the Arab pressure is greatest, in order to give the illusion of a much greater force than exists." McDonald then estimated the current Israeli strength at

> . . . 30,000 at present, with an additional 30,000 over-age auxiliaries (including women) who are called up intermittently. . . . The rumored figure of an "Israeli Defense Army" of 80,000 fighting men is, in the opinion of the Counselor [himself] an exaggeration.

McDonald then embellished his message to the Secretary of state with a story of "217 picked Palmach boys" who had recently taken the village of Safed in a dramatic midnight attack, routing some 6,000 Iraqi and Syrian troops. It was obvious, McDonald said, that no military commander would send 217 boys against 6,000 men if he had an alternative—the 217 were all that could be spared for the operation.[32]

It will be recalled that at the time of McDonald's message, the United States government was beginning to receive repeated requests for military aid from the government of Israel. The U.S. Embassy was the only one permitted by the Israelis to have a military attaché's office, and Colonel Archibald suspected that this had something to do with all these requests.

In an effort to clarify the question of legitimate Israeli defense needs, the U.S. Army requested, in April of 1949, that the Military Attaché (Colonel Andrus) in McDonald's own embassy convey his best estimate of total Israeli strength. On May 10, 1949, the Military Attaché informed Army Intelligence that even after 10 percent had been demobilized, following the armistice in January, the Israelis maintained a standing army of 95,000 to 100,000, with some 20,000 to 30,000 reserves.[33]

In September of 1949, *Haboker,* the right-wing General Zionist daily newspaper in Tel Aviv, noted:

Our Jerusalem correspondent understands that USA Ambassador to Israel, Professor James McDonald, will return to Israel for a short time only, and will continue with his present functions. Adversaries of Israel in the State Department oppose the return to Israel of this friend of the Jews, and they want the appointment of a neutral envoy.

Indeed.

U.S. estimates of the size and capabilities of the armies of the Middle East states after the war was over continued to rate the Jews superior to the combined Arab forces. The CIA monthly review of the world situation for April, 1949, referred to the "indisputably superior strength of Israel" as against the combined Arab states. And in March and April of 1950, the U.S. Air and Naval Attachés in Tel Aviv revised upward their estimates of the strength of the Israeli Air Force and Navy, based upon acquisitions that were being made at a furious pace at the time in the United States and in Europe. The new estimates: 163 aircraft and 19 naval vessels.*

In March of 1952, JCS Chairman General Omar Bradley met in Washington with Ambassador Eban of Israel. Eban urged that Israel be included in any Western-Oriental Middle East defense organization that might be in the planning stages and, further, requested U.S. arms assistance for Israel. When Bradley's memorandum on the meetings was disseminated to the other Chiefs, a background note was added that contained the following comment:

Israel has consistently been unwilling to furnish the information necessary to evaluate her military capabilities, and, furthermore, has taken elaborate steps to prevent U.S. attaches from obtaining pertinent information. Any assessment of legitimate Israeli military needs is therefore highly speculative. Nevertheless, available intelligence on Arab and Israeli forces and attitudes leads G-2 to believe that the

---

*The issue of the strength of the Israeli Defense Forces just after the War of Independence apparently remains an important one to the U.S. State Department. In February, 1982, I was asked by the National Archives to return certain documents so that they could be "tabulated" for record-keeping purposes. The State Department then asked the Air Force, as the originator of certain of the documents, to reclassify certain of them that dealt with estimates of Israeli Defense Forces strength in 1949 and 1950—some 32

present Israeli military establishment exceeds that needed for defense against the Arab States. Israel is, in fact, restrained from aggression against the Arab states primarily by Israeli fears of Western power disapproval and restraint.[34]

Estimates of the small size of Jewish forces similar to those fabricated by Ambassador McDonald have survived to be repeated again and again in popular histories of the War of Independence. Larry Collins and Dominique Lapierre in their book *O Jerusalem* (1972) recall that the Haganah had only 18,900 men "fully armed and in position" on May 14, 1948. The reason, they say, was a lack of weapons—the Haganah had only about 15,000 rifles and 7,000 Sten guns. In *Israel, the Embattled Ally* (1978) Nadav Safran states that at the time of the Arab invasion, Israel had "over 30,000 troops, three quarters of which were organized in combat formations."

In this way, not in the fighting in 1948–1949, was Israel's "miracle victory" achieved. In books, movies, and TV shows in the 50's and 60's, the Jewish state was depicted as having defeated the Arabs against overwhelming odds, contrary to virtually every professional strength estimate of the opposing forces that was made at the time of the war itself.

to 33 years ago. This was done, even though reclassification of the documents was a clear violation of the executive order then in force governing the handling of classified material, E.O. 12065. With the aid of attorneys from the American Civil Liberties Union, I convinced the National Archives and Air Force to re-declassify the documents that are the basis of parts of this last section. But the latter-day McDonalds are still hard at it.

4

The 1953 Aid Cutoff:
A Parable for Our Times

THE SEPARATE ARMISTICE AGREEMENTS concluded in 1949 between Israel and the Arab states did little more than end the large-scale fighting. Jewish refugees from Europe and Jewish money from around the world poured into Israel in those first few years after the War of Independence. The scale of both frightened the Arabs, who watched, frustrated, as Israel became a diplomatic and military (though not an economic) reality. In the early 1950's some 800,000 Palestinian refugees huddled just outside the borders of the new state, a constant reminder of the scale and totality of the Arab defeat.

Member states of the United Nations created bureaucracies to deal with the annoyances of truce supervision and refugee aid. In May of 1950, Britain, France, and the United States issued the Tripartite Declaration regulating arms shipments to the region and opposing any attempt to modify the armistice lines by force. It was all essentially negative diplomacy, and merely served to freeze and formalize the state of war that still existed between Arab and Jew in the Middle East. The Cold War loomed in policy circles in 1949 and the early 1950's; other trouble spots—Greece, Berlin, Korea, and Iran among them—drew attention away from the region.

It was an unhealthy, unnatural situation. It more or less assured another outbreak of war, and in the meantime prevented any form of regional economic, social, or political collaboration. In Asia, Africa, and Latin America, regional organizations and development schemes bloomed in this period, but in the Middle East, the only growths were malignant plans for rearmament, guerrilla warfare, unified commands, and territorial expansion.

76

CREATING FACTS ON THE JORDAN RIVER

To Dwight David Eisenhower, the idea of a Jordan River Development Authority made sense. Southern Lebanon, northern Israel, and western Syria and Jordan—all with desperately undeveloped agricultural economies—lay within the catchment basin of the Jordan River. More than half of all the Palestinian refugees lived in this area as well, virtually all of them dependent upon the United Nations Relief and Works Agency for Palestine (UNRWA) for the international charity that kept them alive. If only some of these refugees could be permanently resettled on lands made productive by the irrigation water and power, which the waters of the Jordan could provide . . . It was a tempting prospect, and a constructive policy goal.

Aware that the Arabs and Israelis had different comprehensive schemes for development of the Jordan Plain, Eisenhower and his Secretary of State, John Foster Dulles, urged the United Nations to take the lead in developing a unified plan that could be acceptable to all of the countries with riparian rights in the Jordan River system.* The Hashemite Kingdom of Jordan had already finalized its version of a regional scheme—the Bunger Plan—and had, in 1952–1953, convinced both the U.S. government and UNRWA to earmark funds for the commencement of work on one of the Jordan tributary rivers, the Yarmuk. Israel objected that, as a lower riparian state on the Yarmuk River, it should be consulted on any scheme involving the river. Accordingly, work on the project was delayed. Allocation of the earmarked U.S. and UN funds was postponed. The Jordanian government was bitterly disappointed, but the new Eisenhower administration insisted that development of the Jordan River valley should be a cooperative venture involving all of the affected states.

In the previous year, 1952, UNRWA had asked the Tennessee Valley Authority in the United States to prepare a desk study that would synthesize the essential features of both the Arab and the Israeli unilateral schemes. Now, with work on the

---

*A concise review of the various unilateral and multilateral plans for Jordan River valley development is presented by Samir N. Saliba in *The Jordan River Dispute* (The Hague: Martinus Nijhoff, 1968), Chapters 5 and 6.

Jordanian Bunger Plan aborted, both U.S. and UNRWA officials pressed the TVA to complete a unified plan. With the help of a firm of engineering consultants in Boston, the TVA was in the final stages of preparation of the plan in September, 1953, when the U.S. government learned that Israel had begun, on a crash basis, to construct a canal that would divert much of the water of the Jordan into Israel at a point near B'not Yaakov Bridge, about midway on the river between Lake Huleh and Lake Tiberias. *

Several aspects of the Israeli project were disturbing to U.S. and UN representatives in the field. For one thing, in the first week of September, when Major General Vagn Bennike, the Chief of Staff of the UN Truce Supervision Organization (UNTSO), had first learned of the project, the Israelis had explained to his subordinate that it was only a small diversion to provide waterpower for an electricity-generating station on the shore of Lake Tiberias. A few days later, however, when Bennike went to see the work for himself, he discovered bulldozers and other pieces of heavy equipment at work constructing a canal large enough to divert a substantial portion of the Jordan's waters into Israeli territory, far more than that which would be necessary for a hydroelectricity project. Bennike was well aware that the main difference between the unilateral Arab and Israeli plans was that Israel had proposed to divert a large amount of water out of the Jordan Valley altogether, to be transported by viaduct and canal to the Sharon Plain and eventually to the coastal areas of the northern Negev Desert.

There were other elements of the project that were suspicious. Two months previously, the Israeli government had loudly endorsed regional cooperation and the U.S. and UN efforts to complete a unified plan. The U.S. Foreign Operations

*It was not the first diversion of Jordan River water by Israel. In March, 1951, Israel had moved bulldozers and military units into the demilitarized zone on the Syrian border, and over the protests of the UN observers in the area and the U.S. State Department in Washington, began draining Lake Hula, which is part of the Jordan River system. Syrian villages were fired upon by the Israelis, and though Syrian troops moved closer to the border, they did not return the Israeli fire. U.S. Major General A. R. Bolling, Assistant Army Chief of Staff for Intelligence, noted at the time that "apparently, Israel is prepared to risk military operations against any of the Arab States, and several recent Israeli actions appear to have been designed, at least in part, to provoke Arab initiation of hostilities." (See memorandum for the Chief of Staff from Major General A. R. Bolling, dated April 4, 1951, in Army Chief of Staff Decimal File, 1951–1952, File 092 Israel, Record Group 319, Records of the Army Staff, National Archives.)

Administration, which had funded several internal Israeli water projects and had recently assisted the Ministry of Agriculture in Israel in developing a national plan for the country's water requirements, had no knowledge of the diversion project at B'not Yaakov. The work on the canal had actually begun on September 2, but no non-Israeli had been informed of the project until several days later. Finally, there had been no line item for the project in the Israeli national budget.[1]

The canal construction was actually not in Israel, but in a demilitarized zone (DMZ) established according to the 1949 armistice that terminated hostilities between Israel and Syria. The agreement, which had been negotiated by UN Mediator Ralph Bunche, required Syrian forces to withdraw from an area of Palestine they had occupied during the war. The DMZ was to be controlled by UN troops responsible to the Israeli-Syrian Mixed Armistice Commission. Both parties had formally agreed to refrain from actions that would (a) affect the military balance in the DMZ or (b) disturb the normal activities of the civilian inhabitants of the zone. Disputes about military or civilian matters were to be resolved by the three-member mixed armistice commission, which in turn was responsible to the UNTSO Chief of Staff, Major General Bennike.

After investigating the construction site at the end of the first week of September, Bennike dispatched a letter to the government of Israel asking that the work on the canal be halted, citing violations of the armistice agreement between Syria and Israel, and adding that the reduction in the water level of the Jordan caused by the diversion would adversely affect both Syrian and Jordanian farmland, and thus likely lead to disturbances of the peace. Israel's response was to reject Bennike's request, and to speed up work on the canal, increasing the crews to three shifts, some working under floodlights at night. Syria, with Bennike's support, then brought the matter before the UN Security Council.

IKE CREATES SOME FACTS OF HIS OWN

In Washington, Eisenhower and Dulles watched these events with growing frustration. The administration had just prevailed

upon Jordan to stop its project on the Yarmuk River, pending
finalization of the unified plan, and following complaints from
Israel about Jordan's "preemptive" unilateral scheme. In July,
Israel had endorsed the principle of regional cooperation. Now,
the bulldozers growled through the night under klieg lights while
Syrians and Jordanians—and Major General Bennike—looked
on helplessly.

It was not just the B'not Yaakov diversion project that disturbed the administration. Two weeks previously, Israeli troops
had moved into Egyptian territory and killed 22 persons. When
the United States government sent a note of protest to Tel Aviv,
the Israeli government did not even reply. Israeli troops had occupied the DMZ's created by the various armistice agreements,
and had obstructed the movement of United Nations observers
when they had tried to verify these violations. *

On September 18, 1953, Secretary of State Dulles informed
the Israeli Ambassador in Washington that U.S. economic aid to
Israel was suspended as of that day, until Israel agreed to cease
work on the B'not Yaakov diversion canal. Specifically, an allocation of $26 million from Mutual Security Act funds, due to
be sent to Israel in a matter of weeks by the Foreign Operations
Administration, would be "deferred" until Israel saw fit to cooperate with the United Nations in the Middle East. There would
be no public statement at that time. The check just would not be
issued.[2] Furthermore, the President had instructed the Treasury
Department to draft an order removing the tax-deductible status
of contributions made to the United Jewish Appeal (UJA) and
to other Zionist organizations raising private funds for Israel in
America.

A COUNTRY WITHOUT AN
ECONOMY

These were not symbolic gestures. At the time Israel was not
only not self-supporting, it had virtually no national economy in

---

*These and other charges were made by the State Department in a formal note issued
on October 18, 1953. The government of Israel responded that Washington did not fully
appreciate the fact that Israel was a small country surrounded by hostile and more powerful neighbors. (*The New York Times,* October 19, 1953, 1:5.)

the traditional sense. The country's two main products were citrus fruits and chemicals dredged from the Dead Sea. Revenues generated from these exports provided between 18 and 25 percent of the national budget. The remainder was made up of foreign loans, charitable contributions from American and European Jewry, and direct grants-in-aid advanced by the U.S. government.

In late 1953, contributions from American Jews were falling off at a steady rate, and numerous large short-term foreign loans would fall due in the coming winter. Israel had a cash-flow problem. But more important, the country seemed to be without the resources to break out of the cycle of borrowing to meet current expenditures. In October, 1953, a memorandum from a staff member of Eisenhower's Science Advisory Committee described the basic problem:

> The fundamental cause of Israel's economic and financial plight is that too many people have been admitted too rapidly into a country which possesses almost no natural resources.

Referring to a speech by Israeli Prime Minister David Ben Gurion calling for preparations for the entrance of 2 million more Jewish refugees from the Middle East and Eastern Europe within the next ten years, the committee opined:

> This unrealistic approach can only lead to further economic and financial difficulties, and will probably result in additional pressure to expand Israel's frontiers into the rich lands of the Tigris and Euphrates Valleys, and northward into the settled lands of Syria.[3]

During the period 1949–1953, official U.S. "development" assistance to Israel averaged just over $70 million per year.* In addition, approximately $20 million in foodstuffs was sent annually. Private contributions from the American Jewish commu-

---

*In fiscal year 1952, Israel received 93 percent of all official U.S. assistance sent to the countries of the Middle East. IN FY 1953, the figure dropped to 87 percent. (NSC paper 5428, entitled "United States Objectives and Policies with Respect to the Near East," dated July 23, 1954.)

nity in this period were even more important, running around
$150 million annually. But it was not enough. The "develop-
ment" assistance voted each year by the U.S. Congress could
not be used for development. In fiscal year 1952, 87 percent of
that aid was used to buy food and fuel and to pay off short-term
foreign debts. In FY 1953, the figure rose to 90 percent.[4] Congress fully appreciated Israel's cash-flow problems, and looked
the other way at these violations of the public laws governing
U.S. foreign assistance.

But Congress could and did insist that the government of
Israel undertake remedial measures to put its financial house in
order. Formal, written assurances were asked and received from
the Israelis for the establishment of a bureau of the budget and a
general accounting office on the American model; creation of a
balanced foreign-exchange budget; biweekly reports to the U.S.
Congress showing debts paid, new obligations incurred, and
debts outstanding; and finally a commitment by Israel to make
an intensive effort, supervised by a group of American financial
experts, to convert some $50 million in short-term debts to
long-term ones.[5] Humiliating it may have been, but necessary
it was.

It was not the United States or the international Zionist community that saved Israel financially in the early 1950's, however;
it was the Federal Republic of Germany. In March of 1953, the
West German government agreed to pay Israel $840 million in
war reparations. The first $100 million was to be paid in FY
1954—an amount equal to 30 percent of all of Israel's imports in
the same period. Menahem Begin's Herut party condemned the
agreement as an "act of disgrace and bankruptcy" and threatened to sabotage the first shipments of German goods. But in
New York, the *Times* summarized the significance of the arrangement:

> Many an Israeli repeated today, not without seriousness,
> an old saying that a miracle always came to Israel's
> rescue in the hour of need. They recalled the time when
> Soviet support at the last minute insured the adoption
> by the United Nations General Assembly in 1947 of a reso-
> lution for the partition of Palestine, and the time when the

arrival of Czechoslovak and other arms at the last minute enabled Israelis to withstand the Arab assault in 1948.[6]

Even with the German assistance, though, Israel's cash-flow problems were serious in the fall of 1953 with all those short-term notes coming due, and Dwight David Eisenhower and John Foster Dulles were not unaware of this fact. Congress, after all, was receiving biweekly reports of Israel's bookkeeping.

On September 23, Major General Bennike finished his report on the implications of the diversion canal for UN peacekeeping in the region, and formally asked Israel to cease work on the project. On September 25, and again on October 8, the State Department pressed the Israeli Ambassador in Washington to transmit to his government the expression of strong U.S. support for cooperation with Bennike, and both times reiterated that no further allocations of Mutual Security Act (economic development aid) funds would be made until that cooperation was forthcoming. Each time Secretary Dulles emphasized that the work could be stopped "subject to possible reversal or appeal by Israel to the United Nations Security Council." And each time the Israeli Ambassador was asked to understand that the United States could not support the role of the UN in the region on the one hand, while providing aid that assisted Israel in doing precisely what UNTSO had asked it not to do, on the other.

If there was a pleading quality about these representations, they nevertheless fell on deaf ears. The response of the Israeli government was negative. Construction on the nine-mile diversion would be completed as quickly as possible. For the time being, however, the dispute was a private one. No public announcement was made regarding the U.S. aid sanctions. Until, that is, the raid at Kibya rendered a public aid cutoff morally as well as diplomatically imperative.

THE KIBYA MASSACRE

The raid on a small West Bank Jordanian village by Israeli commandos on October 14–15, 1953, was a "reprisal" action similar in many ways to numerous such operations conducted before and since. Indeed, from a perspective in time after the war in Lebanon in 1982, in which tens of thousands of Lebanese and Palestinian civilians were slaughtered, it is difficult to see the importance of Kibya, in which 53 civilians were killed. But at the time, the raid had enormous significance, including an immediate impact on U.S.-Israeli relations.

After the fact, it became necessary for Israeli public figures to explain Kibya in the broad context of Arab population figures and designs on Israel's destruction, and, if possible, oblique references to the holocaust in Germany. Abba Eban in his autobiography says of the operation:

> The United States opposed our retaliations without suggesting an alternative method of defending our lives. The idea that Arabs could kill Israelis without any subsequent Israeli reaction was close to becoming an international doctrine.*

Eban depicted a small country facing a "torrent of violence" in 1953 from its Arab neighbors—"with military units and marauders . . . bringing mutilation and death to our civilians in frontier areas. . . ."[7]

The facts of the raid itself were verified by a United Nations observer team, and have never been in dispute. An Israeli military unit of between 250 and 300 soldiers entered the Jordanian village of Kibya from three sides on the night of October 14, 1953, blasting its way through defenses (it was a border village in a demilitarized zone) with heavy mortars and "bangalore torpedoes." Automatic weapons and grenades were used to force fleeing residents back into their homes, whereupon dynamite was used to blow up 41 residences and 1 school building with people in them. Fifty-three civilians were killed, most at the

---

*The official records of the Israel-Jordan Mixed Armistice Commission suggest that something close to the opposite was true. From June, 1949, to October, 1954, armed border crossings occurred roughly an equal number of times from the Israeli and Jordanian sides, but Israeli soldiers were involved more than twice as many times as Jordanian soldiers. Two hundred fifty-eight Israelis were killed or wounded in incidents for which Jordan was officially condemned for truce violations 60 times by the commission. During the same period, 474 Jordanians were killed or wounded in incidents for which Israel was condemned 95 times. See *Violent Truce* by Commander E. H. Hutchinson, VSNR (New York: Devin-Adai Company, 1956), pp. 90–92.

doorways of their houses. The fighting and demolition operation took seven hours, and lasted well into the next morning.*

An act of desperation carried out in reprisal for "mutilation and death" rained upon Israel by Arab "marauders"? Yes, it was that. Three civilians had been murdered two days previously by Jordanians on the Israeli side of the border. But Kibya was also a training exercise for a new, special unit of the Israeli Defense Forces, planned and executed respectively by two men, both of whom would later become Minister of Defense of Israel: Moshe Dayan and Ariel Sharon.

In the years since Kibya, Israeli government officials who were much closer to the affair than Abba Eban, who was a diplomat in New York at the time, have provided a somewhat less rhetorical, more candid explanation for the raid:

The leaders of the IDF—Chief of Staff General Mordechai Makleff and the head of the Operations Branch, General Moshe Dayan—had become genuinely concerned about what they considered to be the "lowered fighting standards" of the IDF, in the months just prior to Kibya. In several small-scale "reprisal raids" into Arab border villages in early 1953, the IDF detachments involved returned with men killed and wounded without having fulfilled their missions. Makleff and Dayan, newly promoted at the time, were determined to change that. One of the steps taken was to form Force 101, a commando unit with special training in night warfare and demolitions. The commander of this new unit was to be the "daring and combat-wise" Major Ariel Sharon. For many months after its formation, Force 101 would be the only IDF unit to carry out reprisal raids. Dayan would later say that it "operated with such brilliance that its achievements set an example to all the other formations in the army."[8]

One of Force 101's early achievements was to blow up the village (and villagers) of Kibya. Dayan's memoirs, however, contain no mention of the raid, and for very good reason: it was an illegal operation, and those involved were not acting in an official capacity for the IDF or for any other branch of the Israeli government, as the raid had not been approved by the Prime Minister's Defense Committee.

---

*This description of what happened at Kibya is taken from the report to the United Nations Security Council by Major General Bennike on October 27, 1953. The text of the report was printed in full in *The New York Times* the following day.

On October 14, newly appointed Acting Prime Minister
Moshe Sharett convened a meeting with Defense Ministry officials to discuss the diversion canal on the Jordan River, which
had been ordered by then Acting IDF Chief of Staff General
Dayan the month before. Present at the meeting was Acting
Minister of Defense Pinchas Lavon. The primary reason that
virtually everyone was "acting" was that Prime Minister Ben
Gurion had recently departed for an extended vacation to a kibbutz in the Negev, during which time Ben Gurion wished it to
appear that he was no longer running the government.

During the meeting Gideon Raphael, who was then Coun-
selor in charge of Middle East and United Nations affairs for the
Foreign Ministry, was called to the telephone and informed by a
colleague that a major retaliatory raid had been planned by
Dayan, Sharon, and others, for later on that evening. Raphael
passed a note to the Acting Prime Minister who, startled, suspended the meeting and took Defense Minister Lavon aside.

Sharett demanded that Lavon stop the raid, but Lavon insisted that the operation had the authorization of Ben Gurion,
and refused. Ashen-faced, Sharett quickly terminated the meeting, and began to try by phone to contact Ben Gurion to argue
the wisdom of the raid. All of those involved were aware that
the national economy was *in extremis,* and that Eisenhower and
Dulles had just invoked an aid suspension, citing Israel's lack of
cooperation with the United Nations. Surely Ben Gurion would
see that the raid was poorly timed and could have grave international consequences for Israel. But Sharett was unable to contact Ben Gurion at his small kibbutz in the desert. He was
"unavailable" and no one knew where to find him. *

And the next morning, the extent of the disaster was apparent. Force 101 had slaughtered and dynamited more than 50 civilians, most of them women and children. A UN observer team
had departed Jerusalem for Kibya at 6:30 A.M. In terms of diplomatic impact, the worst could be expected. Before the morning was out, Ben Gurion stated that he had never given his
consent for the raid. Defense Minister Lavon must have been
mistaken.

*The details of the meeting and Sharett's efforts to head off the Kibya raid are taken
from Gideon Raphael's *Destination Peace,* pp. 32 and 33. Sharett's *Personal Diary,*
recently published in Hebrew in Israel, also confirms the meeting and relates Sharett's
surprise, then horror, at the Kibya operation. Excerpts of the *Diary* dealing with Kibya
appear in Livia Rokach's *Israel's Sacred Terrorism* (Belmont, Mass.: Association of
Arab-American University Graduates, 1980), pp. 14–18.

Lie begat lie. At a meeting of IDF and Foreign Ministry officials the following day, October 16, it was suggested that the
Israeli government officially deny that the IDF had anything to
do with the raid, and say that it was the spontaneous act of inhabitants of Israeli border villages seeking revenge. Sharett opposed this, saying that no one in the world would believe such a
story. It had been a huge operation with heavy weapons, and
the mixed armistice commission had already visited Kibya and
made a preliminary report. Ben Gurion supported the idea of
"stonewalling it," however, and three days later made a radio
speech denying all IDF involvement. *

As expected, after inspecting the site of the carnage, the Israeli-Jordanian Mixed Armistice Commission of the United Nations condemned the raids as violations of the Israel-Jordan
Armistice Agreement. Three villages had in fact been attacked—all of them in a demilitarized zone. In London on
October 16, the Foreign Ministers of Britain and France and the
U.S. Secretary of State met and agreed to jointly place the incident before the United Nations Security Council, invoking the
Tripartite Declaration of May, 1950. And in Washington that
same day, a State Department press officer termed Kibya "the
most serious of a long line of incidents along the borders between Israel and the Arab States." On October 18, the department issued a formal statement that described that attack as
"shocking" and used the occasion to confirm publicly that aid to
Israel had been (previously) suspended.[9]

Viewed from either side of the Israel-Jordan border, Force
101 had been a very expensive training exercise.

"AN ACT OF UNWARRANTED DURESS"

It was the first and only time that an American president has
cut off all aid to Israel. Later, in other similar crises, there
would be short delays in shipment of certain weapons systems,
but never a cutoff of the main economic-aid pipeline. In Israel,
the Ministry of Finance scrambled to raise the funds to meet
short-term notes coming due, notes that the $26-million aid al-

---

*To this day, that is the official Israeli government position on the affair. One can't help
but wonder, as Rokach does in *Israel's Sacred Terrorism,* whether those who developed
this fabrication considered the danger in which it immediately placed those Israeli border
villages, at a time when cries for revenge were being heard throughout the Arab world.

location would have paid. Israeli businessmen told *The New York Times* that the aid sanctions could in the medium term mean higher unemployment and a substantial slowdown in development programs.

In America, the Jewish community was stunned. In the days after the cutoff was made known, Eisenhower and Dulles repeatedly assured questioners that the action was not related to Kibya, but was a response to a general pattern of Israeli noncooperation with the United Nations. But that seemed to be putting a bit too fine a point on the matter. The moral condemnation was there—official moral condemnation from Israel's closest and most valued friend. And the situation promised to get worse. The result of the tripower statement to the UN Security Council was that the council requested Major General Bennike to return to New York the following week to report on conditions in the troubled Middle East. The State of Israel for the first time in its short history faced diplomatic isolation and condemnation.

The American Zionist organizations, which raised over $150 million annually for Israel, were not without their political resources, to be sure. But Dwight David Eisenhower would be a tough nut to crack. Near the beginning of his first term and enormously popular, Ike had a public image of fairness and strong moral character. He would not be vulnerable to oblique allusions to anti-Semitism. Nor, for that matter, would John Foster Dulles, whose strong, traditional religious convictions were well known. And there was no party platform pledging Eisenhower to unreserved support for Israel, as there had been in 1948. Eisenhower was not even a politician, strictly speaking (he had flirted with the idea of running as a Democrat), and generally seemed to care little for party politics.

But the aid cutoff simply could not be ignored. What U.S. Zionists needed first was a sign. And on the evening of October 18, the day that the State Department publicly revealed the cutoff, they got it. An attaché of the Israeli Embassy, Eliashev Ben Horin, in Atlantic City addressing 1,000 members of Mizrachi, the women's religious Zionist organization, complained bitterly that Israel was "being hauled before an international tribunal." Ben Horin, who was a last-minute replacement for Ambassador Abba Eban, then detailed what he said was "intolerable" Arab agression on the Israel-Jordan border: 421 Israeli civilians killed or wounded in 866 armed attacks in the previous three years alone, and 160 instances of UN condemnation of Jordan for "proven violations" of Israeli borders.* Ambassador Eban had used the same figures earlier that day in a statement issued to the Security Council.[10]

In the days that followed, the battle lines were drawn up. On October 19, the State Department made known the outlines of the unified plan for Jordan River development, which Israel was in effect scuttling by its unilateral action in commencing a major river diversion at B'not Yaakov. The plan would cost $121 million, the lion's share of which would presumably be funded by the United States. Israel's share of the total flow of the Jordan River watershed would be 33 percent.† More important, a large portion of Jordan's share would be devoted to a resettlement scheme for 200,000 Palestinian refugees *in Jordan,* thus reducing considerably the pressure for repatriation to the refugees' previous homes and lands in the State of Israel.

But U.S. Zionists were little interested in details or percentages. The aid cutoff carried implications of blame with which they were very uncomfortable. More than anything else, it was unwarranted duress."[11] The choice of words was perhaps coincidental.

On October 21, Congressmen began to weigh in on the issue. Representative Emanuel Celler of Brooklyn termed the aid cused "the State Department" of "obvious bias." And the next day, a huge celebration of Jerusalem's 3,000th birthday at Madison Square Garden in New York City provided an ideal forum to extend the criticism. A capacity audience of 20,000 persons heard Dr. Israel Goldstein, the chairman of the affair, say that "Peace will not be helped by withholding aid as an instrument of unwarranted duress."[11] The choice of words was perhaps coincidental.

On October 21, Congressmen began to weigh in on the issue. Representative Emanuel Celler of Brooklyn termed the aid

*Ben Horin was a bit disingenuous. The figures he gave for numbers of armed attacks and for Israeli casualties do not match official UN figures for the period (see page 84n.). The number of condemnations is accurate, but the Attaché neglected to mention that the vast majority of these "border violations" involved unarmed refugees trying to return to their homes in Palestine.

†The significance of this figure is that only 23 percent of the flow of the Jordan watershed originates in Israel. The unified plan would have given Israel nearly a 50 percent greater share of the Jordan flow than that which it would have received had the waters been apportioned strictly according to watershed sizes. See Saliba, op. cit., p. 98.

cutoff a "snap judgment" by the State Department. Celler was perhaps uninformed of the repeated meetings with the Israeli Ambassador in which Secretary Dulles had beseeched Israel to reserve judgment on the unified plan, or at least to cooperate with Bennike until all of the riparian states had had a chance to review the plan. The next day, Senator Herbert Lehman also criticized the State Department, though he added that he did not condone "the recent tragic raid by armed Israeli villagers." The word was filtering down.

President Eisenhower saw the wave of criticism that was forming, and did not flinch. On October 21, at a press conference, he was asked by Milton Friedman of the Jewish Telegraphic Agency whether Secretary of State Dulles had consulted him before announcing that aid to Israel was being cut off. The President looked at Friedman and said, "Yes." The next question was taken.

Inevitably, an attempt was made to use the aid cutoff as a partisan political issue. New York City was in the midst of a mayoral campaign, and one of the candidates, Democrat Robert Wagner, accused Dulles of "intemperate and cruel action" against the "greatest bulwark for democracy and freedom in the Middle East." Wagner said that "Arab propagandists" were trying to "veer the Eisenhower Administration into an anti-Israel course." Mixing his facts up a bit, Wagner attributed the cutoff to the Kibya raid. Two days previously, both Dulles *and* the Israeli government had acknowledged that the suspension had been in effect several weeks before the attack.* Numerous other politicians, including many from New York, hastened to register themselves in the lists of State Department critics. Senator Irving Ives and Representative Jacob Javits were careful in doing so, however, to specify Dulles and the department in their criticism, and not Dwight David Eisenhower.[12]

On October 23, the aid cutoff was publicly condemned by the American Jewish Congress, the American Jewish Palestine

---

*The next day, Arthur Krock in a *New York Times* editorial surmised that Wagner's remarks may have "reflected no New York electoral considerations, but only his heartfelt championship of a 'valued ally.'" Or, he said, Wagner's statement may have been a naked appeal "to what became known in the First World War as 'hyphenated Americanism.'" Krock ended by reminding Wagner that more than a New York City election was at stake here—U.S. national security interests were involved as well. The Eisenhower administration, from the latter perspective, intended to "restore a balance [in U.S. policy] which its predecessors upset in the Middle East." (*The New York Times*, October 23, 1953, 22:5.)

Committee, the National Council of Jewish Women, the Labor Zionist Organization of America, the Zionist Organization of America, and the Zionists-Revisionists of America, and also by James G. McDonald, now home from his assignment in Tel Aviv. On October 24, Hadassah, the largest of all the Zionist organizations in the country with more than 300,000 members, joined the chorus of critics. Hadassah termed the cutoff "an attempt to coerce a friendly government to surrender what it believes to be its legitimate rights in peaceful development of its own resources." Hadassah did not think it important to note that those resources were in a DMZ that Israel had solemnly agreed not to develop, in the 1949 Israel-Syria Armistice Agreement.

On October 25, the volume of criticism was turned up, and its character declined. The American Jewish Committee, in conference in Chicago, blamed the UN for the rising tide of violence in the Middle East. In New York, a member of the Jewish Agency Executive referred darkly to "powerful anti-Israel forces" abroad in the land, poisoning relations between the United States and Israel. And in Jerusalem, David Ben Gurion echoed this, condemning "world forces which cannot be reconciled with Jewish independence" before a group of 150 visiting Jewish businessmen. "There are many, and they are powerful," he said, "who believe religiously that we ought to be the eternal wanderer because of something that happened 2000 years ago in this very country." It was a barely masked allusion to John Foster Dulles.

On October 26, Senator Ives and Representative Javits, along with many heads of American Jewish organizations, bearded the lion in his den at the State Department in Washington. Dulles had prepared a statement for the event that he intended to release to the press, explaining, as he later wrote in a memorandum of conversation on the meeting, "the reasons behind the temporary suspension of funds, and restating the fact that there had been no change in our basic friendship for Israel."[13] The group unanimously urged, according to Dulles, that no such statement be made. They opposed any explanation of U.S. actions, however delicately phrased, if it implied any criticism of the State of Israel.

The next day, on October 27, Major General Bennike issued a detailed report to the Security Council that was, as expected, strongly condemnatory of Israel. Bennike distinguished, in his report, between the seriousness of punitive raids by civilians, which increased tensions, and formal military actions, which reflected the conscious flouting by governments of the armistice agreements and carried the risk of full-scale engagement with the military forces of the other side.

And then it was over. On October 29, President Eisenhower announced that Israel had agreed to stop work on the diversion project, and that it would cooperate with the Security Council's efforts to reach a solution to Jordan River development that would take into account the legitimate rights of all riparian states. And a few hours later, Dulles announced that the $26 million allocation was ready to be transmitted immediately. Aid to Israel had been restored.

Zionist organizations across the country generally hailed the President's decision, though some added the caveat that they thought the aid cutoff had been ill advised in the first place. An Israeli official addressing Hadassah summed up the feeling of most when he expressed "general satisfaction that the incident was closed."

ON STATESMANSHIP AND PANDERING

In the years since 1953, there have been many crises in U.S.-Israeli relations in which the kind of pressure just described has been brought to bear on a U.S. president. But in not one instance (including Eisenhower's second, better-known battle with American Zionism during the 1956 Suez Crisis) has an American president stood his ground as firmly or achieved the desired results so completely as did Dwight David Eisenhower in 1953. To be sure, the dispute over development of the Jordan River raged for years after 1953. In that respect, the aid cutoff resolved little. But the B'not Yaakov–Kibya affair was a high-water mark in one significant way. A strong case can (and will) be made that Eisenhower was the last American President to actually make U.S. Middle East policy. Since 1953 Israel, and friends of Israel in America, have determined the broad outlines of U.S. policy in the region. It has been left to American Presidents to implement that policy, with varying degrees of enthusiasm, and to deal with tactical issues.

A student of the affair cannot help but observe that there was a disconcerting uniformity to the press releases, resolutions, and speeches of Zionist organizations and officials, as this "mini-crisis" moved from phase to phase. And there was a marked similarity between the positions taken by American Zionists and those taken by the government of Israel at each stage, day by day. Not once in any of the statements of Zionist organizations—as reported at the time—nor in any of the records of meetings of administration officials with Zionist Congressmen, was there any suggestion that Israel reconsider *its* decision to unilaterally divert the river in violation of the armistice agreement, while the administration was being asked to reconsider the aid cutoff.

It was Moshe Dayan's decision to dig the diversion canal, and it was David Ben Gurion's decision to attack Kibya, using Force 101. Those actions were not debated or approved beforehand in the proper Israeli policy fora, and were in fact vehemently opposed by the Israeli Foreign Minister and Acting Prime Minister, Moshe Sharett. There can be little doubt that both decisions had catastrophic consequences for Israel diplomatically, in terms of relations with the Eisenhower administration and the Jewish state's public image in the United Nations.

Whose interests were represented then, by the frenetic campaign in New York and Washington against the aid cutoff? Put another way, would it have really served the interests of the people and government of Israel (not to say the United States) if the Eisenhower administration had succumbed to the pressure and validated the approach to Arab-Israeli problems symbolized by Force 101? The lies about Kibya and the interplay involved in those lies, between Prime Minister Ben Gurion and Defense Minister Lavon, led in a matter of a few months to the Lavon Affair, the longest and most destructive political scandal in Israel's history. Consciously or unconsciously, through their unquestioning support of the Israeli hard line, American Zionists paved the way to that scandal.

5

A Conspiracy Against Peace

AT THE END OF 1953 David Ben Gurion was exhausted and frustrated. After having headed the Jewish Agency and the provisional government in the struggle to create a new State of Israel, he had served for the first five years of its existence as both Prime Minister and Minister of Defense concurrently. His use of the IDF for repeated thrusts into nearby Arab states was, in the early 1950's, becoming controversial within his own country, as well as in the UN. The small parties composing the Israeli left, together with a large and growing faction within the ruling Mapai party itself, increasingly disagreed with the policy of "reprisal." Then, the diplomatic debacles of Kibya and B'not Yaakov heightened the volume and frequency of these criticisms and Ben Gurion, 67 years old and tired of haggling about tactics, decided to retire from public life for a year or two. Or at least, that was what he said.

The move was not entirely voluntary. Several times during the last months of 1953, Ben Gurion was unable to convince a majority of his own cabinet to approve large retaliatory raids into nearby Arab countries. The person around whom such opposition coalesced was Ben Gurion's number two, Foreign Minister Sharett, whose distinguished career had closely paralleled his own. Through the years of Zionist struggle for a homeland, Moshe Sharett had raised funds and negotiated the necessary assistance and recognition in America and in Europe. In the United Nations, he had represented Jewish Palestine and then the provisional government, and with the declaration of the new state in May of 1948, he had been the logical choice to become Israel's first Foreign Minister.

Despite their years of collaboration, deep philosophical differences existed between Sharett and Ben Gurion. It was more than a disagreement about tactics. Sharett had spent part of his childhood in an Arab village and spoke Arabic well. He had studied Islamic history, culture, and politics. He saw Israel's enemies as a proud, sensitive people with whom an accommodation had to be made if Jews were to live and prosper in peace in the Middle East. To Moshe Sharett, in sum, the Jewish homeland was and would remain a Middle Eastern state, its future inextricably bound up with the future of the Christians and most especially the Muslims of the region. Finally, the Foreign Minister's years of close contact with other governments and with the United Nations had also imparted to him a deep respect for international law and for the uses of allies and the goodwill of the international community.

David Ben Gurion, on the other hand, did not accept the existing armistice lines as more than just that. Several million new Jewish refugees would soon come to Israel, he hoped, and new lands would be needed to house and feed these people. The Negev Desert, if irrigated and developed, could help to meet this need (hence the B'not Yaakov canal diversion), but Ben Gurion was not prepared to renounce what he felt were legitimate historical Jewish claims to additional territory, notably in Judea and Samaria on the West Bank of the Jordan. The Arabs were unlikely to negotiate peace on these terms, of course, unless obliged to do so under extreme duress, and arranging that duress was exactly what Ben Gurion had in mind. His tactics were large, set-piece "retaliation" raids against both civilian and military targets. His strategy was military superiority based upon maximum self-reliance. His goal was an expanded Israel.

On certain fundamentals, these two protagonists could agree. Certainly neither man was prepared to diminish Israel as the price of peace with the Arabs. Neither was willing to take back Palestinian Arab refugees displaced during the War of Independence, or would accept a retreat from land taken by Israel during the 1948 conflict. But within this context, Sharett felt that there was still room for negotiation toward peace with the Arab states, after five years of boycotts and of mutually costly warfare along troubled armistice lines. Sharett thought that peace was possible and diplomacy therefore desirable. A lasting peace, he hoped, could be negotiated on the basis of the 1949 armistice lines.

Ben Gurion was not pleased when the Mapai party congress chose Sharett to replace him. His last official act as Prime Minister in December of 1953, therefore, was to appoint as Chief of Staff of the Army a kindred spirit with whom he had a close personal relationship: Moshe Dayan. Another hard-liner, Pinchas Lavon, was made Minister of Defense. Ben Gurion then "retired" to a small kibbutz in the Negev Desert. Frequent, sometimes weekly, meetings with his appointees permitted Ben Gurion to continue to influence if not direct defense policy, in spite of the fact that nominally and legally such policies were subject to the concurrence of the Prime Minister of Israel, Moshe Sharett. *

Thus did one of the strangest years in Israeli history develop. While the IDF continued to mount Kibya-like operations across the borders in three countries, and offensive espionage and sabotage operations on Arab capitals, frequently without the knowledge of the Knesset or Sharett, the Prime Minister himself was making secret direct and indrect contacts with the most important Arab head of state, Gamal Abdel Nasser of Egypt, to try to negotiate a final peace between Arab and Jew in the Middle East. In 1954 and early 1955, then, Israel had two foreign policies, contesting one with the other. One important distinction between the two, however, was that Moshe Sharett's policy of negotiation (he called it a "diplomatist" approach) was the legal foreign policy of Israel, as he spoke with the authority of the Prime Minister of the state. But these negotiations had to be conducted in the strictest secrecy, as neither Sharett nor Nasser could be seen, in his own country, to be bargaining on essential issues until substantial progress toward a peace agreement could be assured.

THE PARTY OF THE SECOND PART

To say that peace with Israel was a major concern of Gamal Abdel Nasser in 1954 would be stretching the point. Nevertheless, an opening for peace developed in that year, as Nasser and his Revolutionary Command Council (RCC) consolidated their

---

*An excellent account of the Sharett–Ben Gurion rift, derived largely from Hebrew-language sources, is contained in Professor Avi Shlaim's *Conflicting Approaches to Israel's Relations with the Arabs: Ben Gurion and Sharett, 1953–1956* (Washington, D.C.: International Security Studies Program, Woodrow Wilson International Center for Scholars, Smithsonian Institution, 1981).

power in Egypt; for Cairo, unlike other Arab capitals, was not preoccupied with bitterness about issues such as the 1948 war, the Jewish homeland in the Arab midst, or the Palestinian refugees. There were too many pressing problems at home.

The Egyptian revolution of July 23, 1952, which brought Nasser into public life, was in a sense inevitable. The last few years of the reign of King Farouk had been almost purely, perfectly corrupt, and had brought Egypt to the brink of bankruptcy. Nepotism, embezzlement of government funds, importation of luxury goods, and generally profligate lifestyles had preoccupied the ruling elite, while rapid population growth, widespread communicable disease, and illiteracy had immobilized the masses. In the last two years of the King's rule, Egypt's total gold and foreign exchange holdings had been depleted by 25 percent.

For almost 15 years, Gamal Abdel Nasser and other young Army officers had watched colonial England, the ruling Wafd party, and the Egyptian royal family mismanage the country and squander its resources. A secret Free Officers Society had formed just after World War II, with cells in all elements of the Egyptian military. Initially, the primary objective of the society had been to rid Egypt of British rule. During the war against Jewish Palestine in 1948–1949, however, the government and senior officers had purchased faulty surplus arms in Europe, had sent the Army into battle without adequate supplies of ammunition, and then had lied to the Egyptian public about the progress of the war. It was too much for the young Free Officers Society. When, in 1952, Farouk announced that his incompetent brother-in-law would become Minister of Defense, Nasser's group moved quickly and effectively. There was little resistance and there were few casualties. Farouk was exiled and power vested in the Revolutionary Command Council (RCC).

Neither the Free Officers nor the new ruling junta, however, had a plan for reform of the government. Both groups contained right-wing Muslim Brotherhood members, Communist sympathizers, monarchists, and constitutionalists, among others. Most of the revolutionaries were not ideologists at all, but simply nationalists who could not stand any longer to watch the British and the royalists play polo while Egyptian peasants were mired in a filthy, dusty existence that had changed little since the Middle Ages.

In the two years after the revolution, the RCC moved

quickly to bring the Egyptian economy under control. Cost-of-living allowances for government employees were reduced, as were subsidies for food staples. Higher duties were placed on imports, particularly luxury goods, and total imports were cut by 17 percent in the first year alone. The net trade deficit in the first year of the new regime was reduced by 39 percent. New programs were instituted for electrification, irrigation, improved communications, and housing construction.[1]

In all of this, however, the RCC was reacting to conditions more than it was following any preset development plan. First, the Army knew, discipline and common sense had to be imposed upon the chaotic economic and social conditions that had induced the take-over to begin with. When Colonel Nasser, who had for years been the most influential of the Free Officers, replaced Major General Mohammed Naguib as the Premier in early 1954, one foreign observer described the new leader as "a dictator by default of a revolution without a doctrine."

Nasser's tasks were formidable. In addition to the raft of new development projects, the new Premier was, by mid-1954, locked in negotiations with Britian to end the then 72-year British occupation of the Suez Canal Zone. The Muslim Brotherhood, in the name of Islamic fundamentalism, vehemently opposed many of the RCC reforms, and took its opposition into the streets. * Simultaneously, Nasser was trying to regularize relations with the United States, find the enormous funds required for the Aswan Dam project, modernize the pitifully outdated Egyptian Army, and deal with a burgeoning Communist party.

It was in the context of Egypt's overwhelming, immediate problems, then, that Nasser viewed the simmering dispute with Israel. The latter was simply not a priority. Moreover, Egypt in early 1954 did not have the financial resources for both economic development and mobilization for a war with Israel. Not that a war against Israel could have been waged effectively. In early 1954, Egypt had the same outdated equipment with which it had fought the 1948 war, and had approximately 50,000 to 60,000 men under arms. Israel had an army that, in its peacetime configuration, had only about 30,000 regulars, but it could mobilize, equip, and field an army of 200,000 reservists within two to three days. Moshe Dayan summed up the military situa-

---

*In October, 1954, this opposition would culminate in an attempt on Nasser's life as he addressed a crowd in Alexandria.

tion one year later when, meeting with the Israeli Ambassadors to Washington, London, and Paris, he said:

> . . . we face no danger at all of an Arab advantage of force for the next 8–10 years. Even if they receive massive military aid from the West, we shall maintain our military superiority thanks to our infinitely greater capacity to assimilate new armaments.[2]

Gamal Abdel Nasser was a military man and little else but that in 1954, and he well understood the realities of Egypt's military position vis-à-vis Israel. He had faced the Israelis in battle himself, as one of the senior officers in the Al Faluja campaign, in the latter stages of the 1948 war. Later, Nasser admitted to CIA official Kim Roosevelt that the Egyptians had been humiliated in battle, but maintained that he and his fellow officers were resentful of "our own superior officers, other Arabs, the British and the Israelis—in that order."[3] Shortly after the 1949 armistice agreement with Israel, the Free Officers Society had undertaken a reexamination of the Palestine question, and had even contacted leftist political groups in Egypt that had previously supported the partition plan, to discuss possible new directions for Egyptian policy on Palestine.[4] In other words Nasser, unlike some of his Arab colleagues, had always been flexible on the subject of Israel.

Kim Roosevelt was not the only foreigner to whom Nasser, in 1954–1955, expressed a tolerance and respect for Israel. British Labour Members of Parliament Richard Crossman, Maurice Orbach, and George Brown have all since written of conversations with the Egyptian Premier in this period, in which he spoke of his desire for peace with Israel. The U.S. Ambassadors in Egypt at this time, Jefferson Caffery and Henry Byroade, reported exactly the same thing to Washington.

Moreover, Nasser's actions fitted his words. Senior UN officials in the Middle East in the period from late 1953 to February, 1955, repeatedly noted in their official reports the relative restraint in the use of force exercised by Egypt, compared both to Israel and to the other Arab states.* Nasser also seemed am-

---

*The field reports of UNTSO Chiefs of Staff Vagn Bennike and Burns and Israeli-Jordanian Mixed Armistice Commission Chairman Hutchinson contain frequent references to this effect. The latter two officials have elaborated on this point in subsequent published writings as well, respectively in *Between Arab and Israeli* and *Violent Truce.*

bivalent about arming Egypt. In October, 1954, he became one of the few heads of state ever to refuse military aid from the United States. Two months earlier, a top-secret declaration of Egypt's eligibility for such aid had been signed by President Eisenhower. The idea was to include Egypt (and possibly Israel as well) in a Middle East security pact against the presumed threat of attack from the Soviet Bloc nations. Iraq had already accepted an offer of U.S. arms. Israel had wanted the arms badly, but had refused to accept a U.S. military advisory unit required by Congress (of all the states concerned) to ensure that the arms were used for defensive purposes only. Nasser's reservations were different, however: Egyptian Foreign Minister Fawzi informed U.S. Ambassador Caffery in Cairo that his country would prefer economic to military aid.[5]

The next year, 1955, Ben Gurion and Dayan would convince Nasser to change his priorities by mounting a series of devastating retaliatory raids that would again humiliate the Egyptian Army. Nasser would finally seek his arms from the United States—and get them from the Russians—but not before he and Israeli Prime Minister Sharett came very close to resolving the Arab-Israeli dispute once and for all.

A UNIQUE OPPORTUNITY FOR PEACE

In a sense, the idea of negotiations with the Arab states had existed since the founding of the State of Israel. As the arms poured into Jewish Palestine and the IDF advanced in late 1948, hundreds of thousands of Palestinian Arabs fled to nearby countries. The end result was the creation of a Jewish state in what had been largely a non-Jewish area, in terms of land ownership. * Naturally then, the establishment of the legal entity of Israel by force of arms was coterminous with the creation of a state of war with nearby Arab countries. Moshe Sharett, as Israel's first Foreign Minister, secretly began conversations on the basic issues of the Arab-Israeli dispute with King Abdullah of

*There is no dispute about this. Official UN estimates of the percentage of land owned by Jews in mandated Palestine at the time the State of Israel was declared in May, 1948, vary from 6 to 15 percent. David Ben Gurion and Moshe Sharett (then Moshe Shertok) both made estimates in this range in testimony before the United Nations Special Committee on Palestine (UNSCOP) in 1947, as representatives of the Jewish Agency.

Transjordan in 1948, even before the end of the War of Independence. For obvious reasons the two men could not meet personally, so an intermediary was required—Jean Niewenhuys, the Belgian Consul General in Jerusalem at the time.[6]

Following the signing of the armistice agreements terminating hostilities in 1949, Israel's announced policy was to seek a permanent peace accord with each of the Arab nations that had participated in the war. For their part, Arab leaders refused— publicly at least—to negotiate with a government whose legitimacy they did not recognize. In December of 1952, the Political Committee of the United Nations General Assembly approved the Israeli position on negotiations over strong objections by member Arab states, by calling for direct Arab-Israeli talks on the major outstanding issues—Arab refugee resettlement, compensation claims, and boundary adjustments. "Neutral" countries, led by Norway and Canada, drafted the proposal. The Soviet Bloc countries abstained. Iraq and Syria led the opposition.[7]

In March of 1953, the U.S. State Department outlined proposals for Arab-Israeli peace for discussion at an Arab League meeting, as part of a plan for the establishment of a Middle East defense organization involving (it was hoped) all of the countries of the region. Again, the Israeli government was receptive and the Arabs were not. But that same month, *The New York Times* reported that a "distinguished individual" was in fact already conducting secret negotiations at the "highest level" in shuttle diplomacy between Cairo and Tel Aviv, and that the two sides did not appear to be very far apart on such basic issues as refugee resettlement and the future status of Jerusalem.[8] The *Times* did not reveal the identity of that mysterious intermediary, but British Labour MP Orbach (who would himself act as a go-between in 1954) later wrote that he believed the "distinguished individual" to be UN Mediator in the Middle East Ralph Bunche, who at the time was director of the Department of Trusteeship at the United Nations.*

In his book *The Jewish Paradox,* Nahum Goldmann describes having tried to contact Nasser through another UN inter-

---

*Nasser later acknowledged that mediation had occurred, but denied Bunche's role as mediator. He hedged his denial, however, by saying that Bunche had had no talks *with him.* In March of 1953 the nominal head of state in Egypt had been Major General Naguib. Nasser's role as the real power in the Revolutionary Command Council was little known at the time.

mediary at about this time. Goldmann, the first President of the
World Jewish Congress, was one of the founders of the modern
State of Israel in that he played a major role in obtaining support for the state from the Truman administration just after the
Second World War. Goldmann asked Dag Hammarskjöld to
propose to Nasser that in exchange for a peace treaty and formal
recognition, Israel would become a member of a confederation
of Middle Eastern states along the lines of the European Common Market, which was formed later. Nasser, Hammarskjöld
reported, was very interested in the proposal, but was doubtful
that a capitalist Israel could fit into a nonaligned Middle East.

Goldmann pressed on, asking President Nehru of India to
bring the matter up a second time with Nasser. Again, the Egyptian Premier expressed interest in a confederation as a basis for
serious negotiations. This time however, he told Nehru that he
doubted Ben Gurion could be convinced to participate officially
in negotiations on such a basis. He was probably justified in his
skepticism. At another point in his book, Goldmann notes that
neither the Jewish people nor their representatives had yet
learned the difficult art of negotiation, which, he said "presup-
poses a certain equality between partners." One party might be
objectively stronger, but there had to be a psychological common ground, or the matter becomes one of diktat and submission, not negotiation.[9] Indeed, the significance of Ben Gurion's
resignation and Sharett's assumption of the prime ministership
in early 1954 was that for the first time, Israel had a leader who
viewed Arabs as people, as equals and possible future neighbors
and friends.

Through 1954, others recognized this "opening for peace,"
and offered to help continue the discrete contacts between
Nasser and Sharett. Jean and Simonne Lacouture have described these efforts:

> . . . indirect but generally encouraging contacts were made
> between Nasser and Sharett through various intercessors,
> usually British, such as Labour M.P.'s Richard Crossman
> and Maurice Orbach. To the latter, Nasser spoke of his
> "hopes" and his "lively sympathy for Mr. Sharett."[10]

Over the period of several months, Maurice Orbach shuttled
back and forth between Cairo and Jerusalem or Tel Aviv, dis-

cussing a seven-point proposal put forward by Sharett.* Orbach discussed this process in some detail in two articles published in the October and the November-December, 1974, issues of *New Outlook Magazine*. How far did these talks go? In an interview in an earlier (January, 1965) issue of the same magazine, Orbach indicated that sometime in 1954, an Israel-Egypt peace treaty had actually reached the drafting stage.

Inevitably, these efforts at third-party mediation led to frequent, direct contacts between official representatives of the two leaders. Sharett even prepared the way legally for this diplomatist approach to the Arab-Israeli dispute by putting the matter before the Israeli Knesset. In a long, anguished speech to the Israeli legislature in May, 1954, Sharett complained bitterly about U.S. arms aid to Iraq† and Soviet diplomatic support of the Arabs, but he insisted that Israel

> . . . is ready at any time to enter into negotiations with any of the neighboring Arab states concerning either a final and comprehensive peace settlement or any partial or interim arrangement aimed at paving the way toward peace.[11]

And four months later, in September, Sharett went back to the Knesset to seek a formal endorsement of his efforts to reach a peace agreement with Egypt, specifically. By a vote of 54 to 9, with 7 abstentions, Sharett received his mandate to negotiate.[12]

In fact, the Israeli Prime Minister had already initiated formal—though ultrasecret—contacts with Nasser. Gideon Raphael, former Israeli Deputy Foreign Minister, has written that around the time of the Egyptian-British Suez Canal Agreement in July of 1954, Israeli officials met with Nasser to "reassure him of Israel's understanding of his aspirations and its keen interest in negotiating a peaceful settlement with him." Raphael

---

*The seven parts of the proposal were: (1) no "inflammatory" sentences at the trial of the Lavon group (Israeli spies arrested in Cairo in September and October, 1954), (2) release of the *Bat Galim* (an Israeli ship that had been captured endeavoring to pass through the Suez Canal), (3) free passage through the canal for cargoes destined for Israeli ports, (4) cessation of "hostile propaganda" and "political warfare," (5) cessation of border incidents, (6) establishment of secret contacts between official representatives to work out details of the above, and (7) secret high-level exchange of views on future Israel-Egypt relations.

†In fact, by mid-1954, the United States had also begun to provide military assistance to Israel in the form of "reimbursable procurement" of military equipment, and training of IDF officers.

describes these contacts as "intimate" and "intense," but, writing in 1981, judged that they "did not yield significant political results." The meetings between Arab and Israeli representatives occurred more or less continually during the last half of 1954. At one point, Raphael himself headed a team of negotiators that discussed with Nasser's "special envoys" means of resolving the specific issues dividing their two countries, such as "practical arrangements for free passage of Israeli shipping through the Suez Canal."[13]

Professor Avi Shlaim, Israeli Fellow during 1980–1981 in the International Security Studies Program at the Woodrow Wilson Center in Washington, D.C., has described in a published working paper the way in which these peace efforts were undercut:

> Whether these talks, fraught as they were with uncertainty and ambiguity, would have produced even a limited political agreement had they been permitted to run their course, there is, of course, no way of telling. For while Sharett was exploring every possible avenue for bringing about an accommodation between Israel and Egypt, his defense minister was being equally energetic in pursuit of his own goal of escalating the conflict and sowing confusion and chaos in the Arab world.

Why? Professor Shlaim:

> Lavon [the Israeli Defense Minister] and Dayan [the IDF Chief of Staff] regarded Sharett's activist diplomatic strategy as not simply naive but actually dangerous in as much as it invited interference and the application of pressure on Israel by the United States and the United Nations.

How? During 1954 and 1955, the IDF mounted a series of full-scale military operations into Egypt, Jordan, and occasionally Syria, directed against both military and civilian targets, designed to either humiliate the neighboring governments or to force them to respond in kind. Professor Shlaim has characterized these raids as

> . . . a series of operations, some of which were carried out without Sharett's knowledge and with the conscious aim of foiling his conciliatory diplomacy.[14]

THE OTHER AGENDA

David Ben Gurion had never wanted to negotiate with the Arabs, in the usual sense of that term, and long before Sharett had assumed office as Prime Minister, he had been made fully aware of Ben Gurion's antipathy toward these efforts. Through late 1953, before, during, and after the Kibya attack, Sharett had watched with growing alarm as the scope and intensity of the IDF's "retaliations" into neighboring states had increased. Gideon Raphael remembers this period as the point at which Sharett finally decided, after 25 years of uneasy collaboration, to break with Ben Gurion and his followers:

> It took Sharett a while to recognize that the growing thrust and volume of the counteraction was not merely accidental, resulting from local tactical considerations, but an integral part of the plan to break the backbone of Arab belligerence and end the unfinished war by decisive military action when international circumstances were propitious. When he realized that this was the basic aim of Dayan's policy, his opposition to particular actions hardened.[15]

It was the international reaction after the Kibya raid that finally gave Sharett the opportunity to confront the militarists within the Mapai party councils, and to obtain a (temporary) agreement on a hiatus in the IDF policy of large-scale reprisal attacks into neighboring states.

It was in this poisoned atmosphere that David Ben Gurion announced his retreat from government and from Mapai party affairs, and the appointments of Pinchas Lavon as the new Minister of Defense and Moshe Dayan as the new Chief of Staff of the IDF. Sharett's *Personal Diary* reveals that he was immediately put on guard, predicting to Ben Gurion that Dayan's "great talent for conspiracy . . . will yield many complications."

These were not long in coming, for as Sharett began in early 1954 to initiate contacts with Gamal Abdel Nasser, Dayan and Lavon set in motion their own agenda. In January, Dayan convoked a meeting of the Mapai Ministers to propose a series of military moves into Egypt designed to precipitate a war with that country. The next month, both Lavon and Ben Gurion (the

latter from his retirement retreat) proposed what Sharett referred to as a "blitz-plan" to invade and occupy territory in
Syria, at a time of political turmoil in that country. Aside from
the obvious benefit of giving Israel control of more of the head-
waters of the Jordan River, Lavon suggested, an invasion and
occupation of the Golan would demonstrate Israeli strength and
determination to U.S. policymakers, and would dissuade them
from looking to "northern tier" Arab states for defense of the
Middle East against Soviet intrusions. Again, Sharett convinced
the cabinet to veto the proposal. The militarists would have to
wait until 1967.

In late February, Ben Gurion, Lavon, and Dayan proposed
Israeli support for the establishment of a Christian state in
southern Lebanon as a buffer in the north between Israel and
Muslims in Lebanon and Syria. Ben Gurion said that a "historic
opportunity" existed to divide Christian and Muslim in Lebanon, and create confusion and civil war. Sharett doubted that
Maronite Christians in Lebanon would lend themselves to a plan
that would probably drive Lebanese Muslims (who were a majority in the provinces of Tyre, Bekaa, and Tripoli) into the
arms of Syria. Again, the cabinet supported Prime Minister
Sharett. The militarists would have to wait until 1982.[16]

In March, an Israeli bus was attacked at a point in the Negev
between Eilat and Beersheba. Ten passengers were killed. It
was the worst attack on Israeli citizens since the 1949 armistice.
A national uproar ensued, in which Israeli news media called for
revenge. While the Israeli-Jordanian Mixed Armistice Commission of the United Nations was trying to establish responsibility
for the attack, Sharett relented under pressure and agreed to a
retaliatory raid into Jordan, the only one he was to approve during his tenure as Prime Minister. The IDF struck into Jordan on
March 28, killing nine civilians at Nahalin.[17]

And after Nahalin, Arik Sharon's Force 101 began to mount
frequent, destructive night raids into the border areas of nearby
states, particularly Jordan, without seeking the approval of the
Prime Minister's Defense Committee, as required by Israeli law
at the time. The obvious reason for such deviousness was to cir-
cumvent Sharett's opposition to such tactics. For Sharon, it was
no doubt a matter of tactics, but for his superiors, turmoil on the
borders and military operations against the Arabs generally soon
assumed a new dimension, a new rationale, for it was at about
this time that Ben Gurion and Dayan learned of the secret feel-

ers that the Prime Minister was putting out to Nasser to commence peace negotiations. The stage was set for the "operation" that would create the most disruptive political scandal in the history of the State of Israel.

THE LAVON AFFAIR

At the end of June, 1954, Modiin, the Israeli military intelligence organization, activated a ring of spies ("moles") in Cairo, ordering it to begin sabotage operations against selected Egyptian, British, and American targets. The Alexandria post office was fire-bombed on July 2. On July 14, the United States Information Agency offices in Cairo and Alexandria were damaged by fires started by phosphorus incendiary devices, as was a British-owned theater. On July 23, the group bombed the Cairo central post office and tried to set fire to the Rio Cinema in Alexandria. This last operation failed, as a stateless Israeli named Philip Nathanson was arrested when a small phosphorus bomb he was carrying, in his trouser pocket in an eyeglass case, detonated.

Nathanson was hospitalized and interrogated by the Cairo police. His house was searched. Incendiary bombs were discovered that same day in two other Cairo theaters, but the following morning, July 24, one of the devices exploded in a valise stored at the Cairo railroad station.

Within a few hours of Nathanson's arrest, two accomplices were arrested—Victor Levi and Robert Dasa—and others in the ring were being sought. On August 2, the U.S. Embassy security officer, W. Angie Smith III, was called to the Cairo police headquarters and given a full briefing on progress in the investigation. And within a few weeks of the first arrests, the entire ring had been rolled up—11 arrests had been made. The two leaders of the ring, Abraham Dar (alias John Darling) and Auraham Seidenwerg (alias Avri El-Ad, alias Paul Frank), fled Egypt and were not arrested.

Zacharia Mohyeddin, Egyptian Minister of the Interior, announced the arrests on October 5, 1954, and indictments were filed a week later accusing the 13 of espionage and sabotage. On December 11, trials commenced before a military tribunal in Cairo. These were open, and were well attended by members of the diplomatic community in Egypt and by other foreign observers, including several from Western human rights and civil liberties organizations. During the trials, one of the accused committed suicide in his jail cell. In early January, 1955, the trials terminated, and on January 27, two of the accused were convicted as charged and were sentenced to hang. The two leaders were sentenced to death in absentia. Six received prison terms and two were acquitted. Four days later, on January 31, Dr. Moussa Marzouk and Schmuel Azar were executed by hanging at Bab El Halek Prison, Cairo. *

In December, 1954, even while the trials in Cairo were under way, Prime Minister Sharett appointed a commission of inquiry to determine responsibility for authorization of what was at the time widely considered to be a failed intelligence operation. The common perception in Israel, then and now, was that the operation had targeted American and British institutions in an effort to damage relations between Egypt and these countries at a time when (a) the British and Egyptians were negotiating a British withdrawal from the canal zone and a turnover of British bases and facilities to Egypt, and (b) the Americans were seriously considering arms aid to Egypt as part of a U.S.-supported Middle East defense organization.

If the primary objective of the operation was sabotage of Egypt's relations with the United States and Britain, then the overwhelming evidence presented and made public at the trials, that the spy ring was recruited, trained, equipped, and funded by Israeli military intelligence, did indeed make the operation an IDF failure and an Israeli national shame. Certainly the operation was *perceived* as a failure in Israel, for there ensued a terrible outcry for investigation of the affair.

The appointment of a commission of inquiry (called the Olshan-Dori Commission) by Prime Minister Sharett was necessary because (a) Sharett himself had been unaware of the operation until after the arrests began in late July, (b) the operation had not been made known to the cabinet Defense Committee, which by Israeli law had to approve foreign intelligence opera-

*The facts of the sabotage operation, arrests, and trials that are presented here are drawn from a memorandum entitled "The Lavon Affair," prepared by Clyde R. Mark for the Congressional Reference Service on December 21, 1972; from "Limited" Foreign Service Dispatch 194 from U.S. Embassy, Cairo, to Department of State, Washington, dated August 3, 1954; and from newspaper accounts of the affair that appeared in *The New York Times* during the period from October, 1954, to January, 1955. See Appendix, Document 7.

tions, and (c) Modiin (military intelligence) Director Colonel Benjamin Gibli and Minister of Defense Pinchas Lavon were publicly accusing each other of having originally authorized the sabotage operations.* Moshe Sharett described in his diary the bitter public spectacle that was occurring at the time the commission was appointed:

> I would never have imagined that we could reach such a horrible state of poisoned relations, the unleasing of the barest instincts of hate and revenge and mutual deceit at the top of our most glorious Ministry [Defense].[18]

When the findings of the Olshan-Dori Commission were presented to the Prime Minister on January 12, 1955, they were inconclusive:

> In the final analysis, we regret that we have been unable to answer the questions put to us by the Prime Minister. We can only say that we were not convinced beyond any reasonable doubt that Col. Benjamin Gibli did not receive orders from (Lavon). We are equally uncertain that the Minister of Defense did in fact give the orders attributed to him by Gibli.[19]

Soon afterward Lavon submitted to the Prime Minister several "proposals for change" in the Ministry of Defense, among which were recommendations for the firing of Modiin Director Gibli, Director General Shimon Peres, and Chief of Staff Dayan. Sharett rejected the proposals and asked for Lavon's resignation instead, which the latter tendered on February 2, 1955. In an effort to restore order in the now demoralized Ministry of Defense, Sharett asked David Ben Gurion to again take up the Defense portfolio, which he did.

The matter did not rest there. Lavon became Secretary-General of the Histadrut, Israel's largest labor federation, later that year. His feud with Ben Gurion continued unabated for several years in speeches, leaks to the press, and attributed articles. Finally in 1960, Lavon, while on a trip to Europe, discovered evi-

---

*It will be recalled that Lavon and then Prime Minister Ben Gurion had engaged in a similar exercise in finger pointing in October, 1953, on the issue of who had authorized the Kibya massacre.

dence that Benjamin Gibli and Moshe Dayan, his accusers, had perjured themselves before the Olshan-Dori Commission by falsifying documents that made it appear that Lavon had in fact ordered the sabotage operation.[20] Lavon immediately returned to Israel and demanded a reopening of the investigation. The Knesset Committee of Defense and Foreign Affairs agreed, but under pressure from then Prime Minister Ben Gurion, turned the investigation over to a Committee of Seven Ministers from all the coalition parties. The committee, after reviewing the new evidence, exonerated Lavon, whereupon Ben Gurion resigned as Prime Minister. At Ben Gurion's insistence, however, the Mapai Central Committee ousted Lavon as Secretary-General of the Histadrut.

The issue surfaced again in 1964 when Ben Gurion, now retired, asked the Israeli Attorney General and the Minister of Justice to once again investigate the affair. When they agreed to this, then Prime Minister Levi Eshkol resigned. When a new government was formed under Eshkol, he wrote a letter to Lavon declaring that the latter's previous ouster as Histadrut leader "no longer had any significance," and inviting Lavon to resume his participation in Mapai party affairs.[21]

Was the Lavon operation a failure for Israeli military intelligence? As indicated above, that has been the conventional wisdom both in and outside Israel since 1954. And certainly if one accepts the idea that the primary objective of the July, 1954, sabotage operations was in fact to scotch the Anglo-Egyptian Suez Canal negotiations and damage U.S.-Egyptian relations, the operation would appear to have failed abjectly. The Suez Canal Agreement was announced in late July, 1954, and was formally signed three months later. American relations with Nasser did eventually sour, but it was the Czech arms deal, not the damaged USIA libraries, that brought this about.

In several important ways, however, the "Lavon group's" sabotage operations were an unqualified success. Consider for a moment: what if the target of the operation was not Gamal Abdel Nasser's relations with the British and the Americans, but rather Moshe Sharett's relations with Gamal Abdel Nasser? What if the object of the exercise was to discredit Sharett's diplomatist approach to Israeli foreign affairs, and bring Ben Gurion back to power? I am suggesting, of course, that the Lavon group may have been intentionally exposed by the Israeli government, or some part of the Israeli government, in order to achieve these objectives.

Preposterous? Perhaps not. The March, 1979, "Foreign Intelligence and Security Services" survey of Israeli intelligence services, prepared by the Directorate of Operations Counterintelligence Staff of the U.S. Central Intelligence Agency, assesses Israeli intelligence services as "among the best in the world," with "expert personnel" and "sophisticated techniques." Deserving of particular praise in the survey report was the "old guard" of intelligence officers in Israel who served in the Haganah during the War of Independence, and who constituted the core of Modiin (and Mossad) at the time of the Lavon operation.

And yet, in oh so many ways that operation was incredibly amatuerish. Avri El-Ad, who as Paul Frank was truly an Israeli master spy in Egypt during the early months of 1954, was asked by his superiors in Modiin to take charge of a group of young, inexperienced, barely trained operatives in Cairo. When Paul Frank was sent back to Egypt to assume charge of this group, some of the Egyptian money he was given had the stamp of the Israeli Central Bank on it. When the orders to actually commence sabotage operations were transmitted to the gang in Cairo (via radio), passports and additional money were supposed to have been sent to facilitate escape of the group members after completion of the mission. The passports and money never came. The incendiary devices that were used in the operation were totally undependable—one igniting prematurely in a theater ticket booth, and one in the pants pocket of the unfortunate Philip Nathanson.

When the arrests of Nathanson and the other "minor" group members began in late July, Avri El-Ad was still circulating in Cairo as Paul Frank, and still had the full confidence of the Egyptian intelligence services. The director of Egyptian counterintelligence, Colonel Osman Nourian, told Frank in confidence that his opposite number in Israel was giving him a hand in smashing the spy ring. Later, Frank escaped from Cairo to Europe before he could be arrested, but Modiin Director Gibli tried to convince him to return to help rescue one of the jailed group members at a time when Frank's identity was already known to the Egyptians! Finally, when, after both the 1956 Suez War and the 1967 Six-Day War, Israel had an opportunity to exchange captured Egyptian soldiers for the remaining Lavon group members in jail in Cairo, no effort was made to do so. And when the members of the group were finally released and returned to Israel, they were immediately inducted into the IDF and given rank. The telling of their story, should they ever choose to try it, was thus made a very serious offense.

Avri El-Ad personally confirmed to the author in 1982 that he now believes his cover and those of the rest of his group were intentionally blown by Israeli intelligence. Ezie Rahaf, a Modiin operative who was to have joined El-Ad in Cairo in early 1954 as the communications officer for the sabotage group, refused the assignment, later telling El-Ad that he had done so because he had suspicions that a double cross was in the works. Many years after the operation when El-Ad had emigrated to the United States, Lieutenant Colonel Mordechai "Motke" Ben Zur, who had been his immediate superior in Modiin, confirmed to El-Ad that the operation had been consciously, intentionally revealed to the Egyptians. El-Ad himself, still loyal to his former employers, does not believe it was Dayan and Modiin who did it, however, but rather the rival Israeli intelligence service Mossad, headed in 1954 by Isser Harrel.

Mossad had agents in Cairo at the time, El-Ad reasons, who could have given the assistance to Egyptian counterintelligence referred to by Colonel Nourian. There was little communication (at that time) between Mossad and Modiin, and therefore it is quite likely that Isser Harrel would not have realized that Paul Frank, who had previously produced valuable hard intelligence on the new Egyptian ground-to-ground rocket, and on Egyptian defense plans for the Sinai, was also a member of the sabotage ring. Mossad might not have known, in other words, that they were sacrificing Frank and his contacts when they passed the word to Egyptian CID about the sabotage ring. Finally, Mossad and Isser Harrel had much to gain from blowing the whistle on a Modiin operation, for after the Lavon trials in December, 1954, Modiin was disgraced and Mossad was placed in firm control of all foreign intelligence operations.

Certainly, none of this is conclusive evidence that the operation was intentionally revealed, and one might also question the objectivity of Avri El-Ad, who was subsequently brought to trial and convicted in Israel for having himself exposed the operation. But the proposition of a double cross by those in the IDF who authorized the operation, or by Mossad, does account for many aspects of the Lavon affair that are very, very difficult to explain otherwise.*

About the results of the exposure of the Lavon group there can be little doubt, whatever was the principal rationale for mounting the operation. David Shaltiel, commander of IDF forces in Jerusalem during part of the War of Independence, met Avri El-Ad in Tel Aviv not long after the latter returned to testify in the Olshan-Dori Commission hearings in late 1954. He said to El-Ad, "Because of you, Avri, there's no peace." That assessment of the impact of the Lavon Affair is also held by the CIA. In 1961, when Ben Gurion resigned as Prime Minister in protest against the decision of the Committee of Seven Ministers to exonerate Lavon, CIA Director Allen Dulles prepared for President Kennedy a retrospective report on the Lavon Affair. In it he assessed the effect of the operation on the secret peace negotiations:

> It was under Sharett's quiet and deft diplomacy that the first and only link Israel has ever had with Egypt was forged. [Here the CIA has excised a portion of the document.] He attached major importance to this channel through which he hoped to negotiate a lasting peace between the Arabs and Jews. . . . The disillusioned Nasser, believing [the Lavon Group] had been used to deceive him, ordered a discontinuation of all contacts with the Israelis, leaving bitterness in both camps. . . . As a result of the findings of the Olshan-Dori Commission which have never been made public, both Lavon and Gibli, though neither was accused of malfeasance, were asked to resign their positions by Mr. Sharett because they had destroyed his peace negotiations.[22]

Was it Ben Gurion who set the operation in motion? Was it, as El-Ad thinks, Isser Harrel and Mossad? Was it Dayan with Ben Gurion's approval, from his retreat in Sde Boker? Of

---

*Avri El-Ad's book *Decline of Honor* (Chicago: Henry Regnery Company, 1976), written with James Creech III, is a primary source for this section, though many of the facts cited, such as the accidental explosion of the phosphorus bomb, are verifiable in other, official documents. El-Ad's book itself, however, apparently has some credibility with the CIA, as it is listed as a "principle source" in the CIA's survey of "Foreign Intelligence and Security Services—Israel," cited above.

Dayan's involvement, there can be little doubt. He took, after all, enormous risks in himself falsifying, or allowing someone else to falsify, letters authored by him that were introduced (without his disavowal) as evidence before both the 1954 and the 1960–1961 official commissions of inquiry that investigated the affair. Moshe Sharett's diary certainly leaves little doubt that he felt Dayan was involved in both the operation itself and the sordid attempt to pin the blame on Lavon after the operation "failed."[23]

After the Lavon group trials, Nasser mounted a series of armed incursions into Israeli territory, which led to the IDF raid on Gaza on February 28, 1955, in which nearly 40 Egyptian soldiers were killed. And the humiliation of the Egyptian Army at Gaza, in turn, led Nasser to seek from the Russians the offensive weapons that his army now demanded and that the Eisenhower Administration was unwilling to provide. As one historian has observed, "With the Gaza raid, the countdown to war began."[24] It would be another eight months before Ben Gurion would formally replace Sharett as Prime Minister, but the Lavon operation effectively ended Israel's (and Egypt's) brief flirtation with a diplomatist foreign policy. The conspiracy against peace had succeeded.

There was to be no peace treaty in the Middle East in 1954, nor even any partial agreement between Israel and Egypt on specific issues such as the Arab economic boycott, free right of passage in the canal for Israeli shipping, and so on. No matter that so many people in the region and elsewhere seemed to want peace. No matter that so many instrumentalities for negotiations—organizations and willing individuals—existed, nor that the heads of state of the two major disputant countries were prepared to and did in fact take great political risks to initiate contacts with each other. Nineteen fifty-four and early 1955 became instead the period in which the next great Middle East war was made inevitable. A student of this period is left with the uncomfortable thought that it only requires a few powerful persons who want war, to bring that war about.

AMERICA ASLEEP AT THE WHEEL

It was as if Moshe Sharett had never existed, or at least had never assumed the mantle of power in Israel. In late 1953,

Sharett had faced down the Ben Gurion policy of massive re-taliation in both the cabinet and the Mapai Central Committee. Then he became Prime Minister and conducted a series of open Knesset debates, obtaining approval for his efforts at negotia-tion with the Arabs. Finally, through intermediaries and then in direct negotiations involving teams of representatives, Sharett and Nasser negotiated on both short- and long-term issues divid-ing Jew and Arab in the Middle East.

But in Washington, the State Department was apparently unaware of these developments, or at least failed to appreciate their importance—failed, in other words, to perceive any impor-tant difference between Ben Gurion's and Sharett's foreign pol-icies. Strangely, Eisenhower and Dulles had for several years been consciously positioning the United States to participate in, even play a leading role in, Middle East peacekeeping.

In July of 1953, for instance, President Eisenhower had ap-proved National Security Council policy paper 155/1, entitled "U.S. Objectives and Policies with Respect to the Near East." The paper's somber premises were the decline of Western influ-ence in the strategically important Middle East, due to Arab belief that the United States was following a pro-Israel policy. The continuing Arab frustration at the status quo was said to be exacerbated by the Palestinian Arab refugees and the border disputes that swirled around them. The Soviet Union was seen to be maneuvering to take advantage of these frustrations. In the classic Cold War terminology of the time, the report con-cluded gloomily: "Unless these trends are reversed, the Near East may well be lost to the West within the next few years."

At the heart of NSC 155/1 was a clear, unequivocal state-ment of United States impartiality in the region.

> The United States should . . . make clear that Israel will not, merely because of its Jewish population, receive pref-erential treatment over any Arab state; and thereby dem-onstrate that our policy toward Israel is limited to assisting Israel in becoming a viable state living in amity with the Arab states, and that our interest in the well-being of each of the Arab states corresponds substantially with our inter-est in Israel.

The specifics of this policy included a reaffirmation of the 1950 Tripartite Declaration regarding the use of sanctions against any state in the region that committed aggression against a neighboring state, preparedness of the United States to use force if necessary to deal with aggressors refusing to withdraw their forces behind the 1949–1950 armistice lines, and a pledge that the United States would seek a resolution of the Palestinian refugee problem involving all of the states of the Middle East, including Israel. The United States would also "use our influence to secure Arab-Israel boundary settlements, which may include some concessions by Israel," and would "discourage further large-scale Jewish immigration to Israel." The status of Jerusalem was to be resolved in a manner "acceptable to the states directly involved and to most of the nations of the free world." Finally the United States would "progressively reduce the amount of economic aid to Israel, so as to bring it into [an] impartial relationship to aid to others in the area."*

Preventing Soviet penetration of the Arab world was not the only reason for this new policy of strict impartiality. The United States would need influence with both sides in the Arab-Israeli dispute if it was to play an active role in mediation. And activism for peace was also at the heart of NSC 155/1—it pledged the United States to "assume an increased share of responsibility toward the area," and to "increase its efforts to achieve a settlement of the political differences among the states of the area."[25]

Why were these good intentions not translated into action in 1954, when the twin opportunities of Nasser and Sharett appeared on the scene? One clue is provided by the record of the reports that the State Department was receiving from the U.S. Embassies in the region at the time. In April of 1954, the department dispatched a "Top Secret" circular telegram to American legations in virtually all of the Middle East capitals, asking suggestions for the best procedures to start the negotiating process among the disputants.

From Beirut, Ambassador Raymond Hare (who would later become Assistant Secretary of State for Near Eastern Affairs) noted a sinister, irresponsible motive for Israel's policy of massive retaliation:

Israelis deliberately engaging series of military, quasi-military and political actions aimed at keeping frontiers in tur-

---

*An appendix to NSC 155/1 indicated that in fiscal years 1951–1953, the U.S. government provided official development aid to Israel totalling $159 million. The Arab states together received $20 million in the same period.

moil and so depreciating value of UNTSO machinery that UN and great powers will feel impelled seek some new arrangement more to Israel's advantage.

The United States needed to address this Israeli policy before direct negotiations would be a realistic objective in the region:

> Our declared policy of impartiality is sound but in existing circumstances it would be inconsistent with sound political judgment to interpret impartiality in terms of holding both sides equally responsible. The fact is that Israel has gotten out of line and real impartiality requires getting her renew play according to rules. After all, a referee does not cease being impartial when he penalizes an offending team.

In the short term, said Ambassador Hare, what was needed was a *modus vivendi* in the form of a "genuinely respected armed truce." And the international community owed it to the peoples of the Middle East to see that this modest amount of peace and order was enforced:

> Israel came into being as result action by the international community and it will take further action by the international community to settle her as peaceful Near Eastern state. . . . UN supervisory machinery should be strengthened and its authority imposed with rigid impartiality.[26]

The U.S. Ambassador in Tel Aviv, Francis Russell, tried to analyze the root causes for the lack of progress in moving toward peace in the region:

> Israel-Arab border problem . . . stems in part from presence of several hundred thousand Arab refugees along border with juxtaposition Arab poverty and Israel's comparative wealth; in part from feelings of Arab elements that infiltration is effective adjunct to Arab economic boycott; in part from Israeli Government's excessive harshness in attempting deal with infiltrators, which increases dimensions of problem, and policy of refusing participate in partial measures in its attempt secure full peace agreements. To extent first is cause, it can be dealt with only by resettlement of refugees. Second can be effectively dealt with only

by convincing Arab leaders that prolongation of infiltration is against their interests. Third by insistence to Israeli Government of folly of its policies.[27]

U.S. Consul General S. Roger Tyler, Jr., in Jerusalem, like Ambassador Hare in Beirut, thought that Israel's harsh tactics reflected conscious, long-term policy:

Israel actions belligerent to an incredible extent. She obviously spoiling for fight, *not* realizing any complications beyond her own ambitions. Syrian refusal to fire on Israeli boats . . . denied Israel chance to start shooting there. Since Jordan did not reply in kind to Nahalin raid Israel probably awaiting for next "infiltration killing" to make another raid which will force public opinion in Jordan to make "warlike" (Israel terminology) gesture for which Israel has set stage.[28]

When asked by the State Department what he thought the U.S. response to such actions should be, Tyler was unequivocal:

I feel strongly that we should confront Israel with known facts of her statements calling for easing of border tension as contrasted with her hostile acts of reprisal raids and sabotaging local commanders' agreements and rules of MAC procedure. . . .

Tyler anticipated the criticisms his observations might generate, as any American must who speaks objectively about Israel:

Above reflections not anti-Israel but from belief Israelis not only key to peace in area but by patience and justice a possible leader of a democratic Middle East. If Israel [a section here was withheld from release by the State Department] cannot be made to realize the consequences of her acts, she may perish and not impossibly the world with her. She must be patient and know that we will support her if she does and that because we disapprove certain of her acts does not mean we are deserting her. But there is a limit.[29]

These assessments from U.S. diplomats in the field were remarkable for their uniformity and candor, but also for their failure to detect, in April of 1954, any change in Israel's warlike posture following Ben Gurion's resignation and Sharett's succession to power. It will be recalled that U.S. Zionists had created a firestorm of protest in October, 1953, when aid was cut off during the B'not Yaakov–Kibya crisis. Were U.S. policymakers in 1954 distracted by the hard-line militancy of Congress and the American Jewish community, and thereby missing the more complex, more pluralistic attitudes on peace and war in Israel itself? Possibly so. Certainly Ben Gurion had then (and has now) more admirers in the United States than did Sharett. In any event, the perceptual failure in the reports just cited was, quite understandably, soon reflected in policy circles in Washington.

On July 6, 1954, approximately one year after NSC 155/1 was approved by President Eisenhower, the NSC Planning Board proposed amendments to that paper. A supporting memorandum transmitted to the NSC by Executive Secretary James Lay echoed the negativist observations sent to Washington a few months earlier:

> On the Arab side, small scale infiltration persists on the part of individuals and small groups acting on their own responsibility. There is no evidence of organized military activity by the Arab states acting in concert or by any individual Arab state. On the other hand, the Israeli Government, concerned at the failure of its efforts to secure peace on the basis of the status quo, appears to be following a deliberate policy of reprisals based on the theory that matters will have to be made worse before they become better.

TO THE BRINK OF PEACE

These assessments by U.S. diplomats and policymakers were not inaccurate. In fact, they were true in ways and for reasons that their authors at the time did not even fathom.* But these

---

*The files of the State Department and the CIA, according to those agencies' official responses to FOIA requests in 1982, contain no reports or analyses that reflect an appreciation for or even an interest, in 1954–1955, in the rationale for or implications of the Lavon Affair. The fires in the U.S. cultural centers, and even the trials of the spies, were treated as minor events at the time. Because Israelis—presumed allies—had covertly attacked U.S. facilities, the matter was simply an embarrassment to be ignored. It was not until many years later, when the affair had led to the domestic crises in Israel of 1960 and 1964, that State or the CIA made any attempt to understand what all the fuss was about.

assessments *were* misplaced, for they were true descriptions, not of Israel's foreign policy, but of schemes and machinations of the Ben Gurion–Dayan faction within the ruling Mapai party (with Menahem Begin's Herut party shouting encouragement from the wings). Israel, however, was legally ruled in 1954 by a Prime Minister whose striving for peace was genuine, and whose actions suited his words. Ironically, the failure of U.S. policymakers to draw this distinction lulled the Eisenhower administration into inaction at the very time when U.S. pressure, properly applied, might have tipped the balance in favor of Sharett and peace in Israel, and might have led directly to the successful completion of the negotiations with the Arabs that NSC 155/1 so devoutly desired.

Even without U.S. help, Moshe Sharett did not succumb easily. Contrary to what some historians have argued, the collapse of the secret peace talks, the return to the Defense Ministry of David Ben Gurion, and the Gaza raid did not signal an abrupt change in Israel's foreign policy. For in the 15 months that followed Gaza, Moshe Sharett battled Ben Gurion and Dayan at every turn, and with a great deal of success. In March of 1955, Ben Gurion proposed to the cabinet that all of Gaza be occupied by the IDF, and populated by soldier-farmers who would establish a buffer zone between Israel and Egyptian coastal areas. The cabinet voted with Sharett. Within days of that vote, Ben Gurion proposed that Israel unilaterally abrogate the Egypt-Israel Armistice Agreement. Again the cabinet accepted Sharett's warning that the world would view this as Israeli preparation for war. This time, however, the vote was very, very close.

When the Mapai party lost seats in the Knesset in the election of July, 1955, Ben Gurion's return to power as Prime Minister became more or less inevitable. Still Sharett did not give up. In August, he opposed plans for another major IDF raid on Egypt at Khan Yunis, relenting only after both Ben Gurion and Dayan threatened to resign their posts. Finally in November, the tension between "Sharettism" and "Ben Gurionism" within the government became unbearable, and Moshe Sharett resigned as Prime Minister. In an effort to avoid a complete split in Mapai, however, he reluctantly agreed to resume his former duties as Foreign Minister.

Even in this subordinate role, Sharett managed to forestall

the war that Ben Gurion and Dayan so fervently wanted. In December, the cabinet was asked to approve a full-scale invasion of the Sinai, the object of which was to be the capture of the Strait of Tiran. Once again, Sharett convinced a majority of the cabinet to oppose the plan. In March, 1956, Ben Gurion proposed that the IDF move in to occupy the El Auja region of the demilitarized zone, and that "civilian" settlements be built there, in violation of the armistice agreement. One last time, Sharett prevailed. Ben Gurion informed the cabinet that only his devotion to duty in perilous times kept him from again offering his resignation.[30]

The Eisenhower administration, which had been entirely passive on the subject of Middle East peacekeeping in 1954, finally and rather pathetically decided in 1955, during the "transitional" period in Israeli foreign policy described above, to try to head off the inevitable war. Senior CIA officials (Kim Roosevelt, Miles Copeland, et al.) were dispatched to Cairo to facilitate "secret" negotiations between Nasser, who no longer believed in a negotiated settlement of the Arab-Israeli dispute, and Ben Gurion, who had never believed in such a thing. Concurrently, Eisenhower sent his personal emissary, Robert Anderson, to try in a more formal way to bring the two sides together. It was a futile effort—too little, too late. The reception that Roosevelt and Anderson received from Nasser was a rejection so peremptory that John Foster Dulles and Dwight Eisenhower reacted as if they had been personally slighted.

Years later Henry Byroade, the Assistant Secretary of State for Near Eastern Affairs for most of this biennium and U.S. Ambassador in Cairo for the remainder, remembered the year 1954 as a missed opportunity for the United States:

> I wake up at night wondering what we might have achieved then if only we had tried, if only we had known. We didn't realize that it would be our last chance.[31]

In the succeeding 20 years, the Middle East would experience four devastating wars and a bitter hardening of both the Israeli and the Arab positions. The United States would, in effect, have to choose sides in the dispute, thus forfeiting any real possibility for American mediation of the core issues. The inability of the Eisenhower administration to recognize the significance of Ben Gurion's retirement and Moshe Sharett's peace initiatives stands as one of the major U.S. policy failures in the history of the Middle East conflict to date.

6

The Suez War:
Tripartite Deceit

GOVERNMENTS DO NOT PROCEED as boldly and directly toward warfare as did Britain, France, and Israel in 1956 without the assurance of total military superiority, without the assurance, in fact, that the other side can provide no effective resistance to the planned attack. This was precisely the case in the Suez War. Indeed, the bizarre diplomatic behavior of Britain, France, and Israel, in the months just prior to the outbreak of hostilities, can only be understood in the context of overwhelming military force poised to strike at Egypt at a time when looming presidential elections in the United States and uprisings in Poland and Hungary ensured that the superpowers would be too preoccupied to intervene.

Each of the three invading countries had its own reasons for action. Britain—most particularly Prime Minister Anthony Eden—bitterly resented Nasser's nationalization of the Suez Canal in July of 1956. The take-over was legal, as compensation had been promised. It was effective, as Nasser and his new national Suez Canal authority soon proved that they could manage and operate the canal as well as or better than the old colonial company. Increased traffic volume in the weeks after the take-over assured that Europe's oil lifeline would not be disturbed. But it was all very, very humiliating to an England whose empire was crumbling in the mid-1950's.

France too had owned part of the old canal company, and was affronted by Nasser's action. But it was what Nasser as a leader represented in the Arab world that most disturbed France and Prime Minister Guy Mollet: in particular, the moral and

tangible support that Nasser was providing to the Algerian revolution. One primary objective of the British and French in the
war was to depose Nasser as Egyptian head of state, and thereby
diminish his position in the Arab Middle East, and in the third
world generally.

Israel in 1956 despaired of any international action that
would force Nasser to allow her right of passage through the
Strait of Tiran—Israel's commercial window to the Indian
Ocean. More importantly Nasser, humiliated by the Gaza raid
in early 1955 and by subsequent IDF incursions into Egyptian
territory, had asked for and was now receiving large new supplies of arms from a familiar actor in the Arab-Israeli dispute—
the Soviet Union. The absorptive capacity of the Egyptian
Army was limited in the short term, but over several years,
given the opportunity, Egypt could, with the help of Soviet
trainers, advisers, and mechanics, pose a potential threat to Israeli military hegemony in the Middle East.

U.S. Secretary of State John Foster Dulles discussed this
new "Soviet factor," and its possible impact in the long term
upon the strategic balance in the Middle East, with President
Eisenhower and Robert Anderson just prior to the latter's peace
mission in the region in January of 1956. After coldly reviewing
the levers that the United States had with Nasser to prevent an
outbreak of fighting—withholding aid to the Aswan Dam project and the manipulation of cotton prices to "destroy or help
Egypt's market"—Dulles turned to Israel:

> I said I felt that the Israelis should realize that their posi-
> tion had been completely altered by the entry of the Soviets
> into the picture. Up until now, Israel had been strong and
> somewhat arrogant, relying upon the fact that the western
> powers were the only purveyors of arms to the area and
> that this fact, coupled with their natural sense of discipline
> and organization, enabled them to maintain a military su-
> periority over their Arab neighbors. But with Soviet sur-
> plus available to the Arabs they, with their population of
> about 40,000,000, had an absorbent capacity which could
> not possibly be matched by the 1,500,000 Israelis.

Dulles added, hopefully, that Israel would henceforth "have
to play the part of the good neighbor to the Arabs and not seek

to maintain itself by its own force and foreign backing."[1]

About six weeks later the State Department asked the Joint Chiefs of Staff to review the strengths and capabilities of all of the major Middle Eastern countries, and in particular to detail the equipment Egypt was receiving from the Soviet Bloc. The JCS response was delivered on February 27, and indicated a relative parity in manpower and naval strength between Israel and the combined Arab governments. The Arab states, due largely to recent shipments of planes to Egypt from the Soviet Union, were even thought to have a numerical edge in air power. Many of the Arab planes were, however, thought to be "non-operational." More importantly, the report noted that

> . . . with the exception of Lebanon and Jordan, the Arab States have very weak systems of supply, transport and evacuation, and are incapable of sustaining troops in combat for any significant length of time. . . . [Israel's] logistics system can provide excellent support for combat troops.[2]

The report concluded that Israel could sustain combat operations for 90 days—about three times as long as the Arabs could.

In March, Israel began to augment her supplies of modern arms, receiving her first shipments from France of advanced Mystère Mark II fighters. Agreements were also concluded for rapid delivery from France of AMX and Sherman tanks. Britain agreed to sell Israel Meteor night-fighter jets. Israel's purchases in Europe—with funds provided in large part by private contributions from the U.S. and European Jewish communities *— suited the Eisenhower administration perfectly, because they satisfied Israel's security concerns without jeopardizing U.S. relations with the Arab world, as official U.S. arms assistance would have done.

In April, the Chairman of the Joint Chiefs of Staff, Admiral Arthur Radford, informed the Secretary of Defense that if Israel initiated hostilities before midsummer, she could, in less than a month, defeat the Egyptian Army in the Sinai and contain the ground forces of the other Arab states. And at the end of April, the JCS did a more detailed study of the military capacities of

---

*The donations were not entirely private insofar as the United States was concerned. The U.S. government was subsidizing these contributions to Israel's armory by declaring the gifts to Israel to be tax exempt.

the countries of the Middle East. Most of the equipment that
Egypt had received, this report said, could not be effectively
utilized by them for at least a year. Furthermore, when one
compared the combat-ready forces that could be mobilized in
the region, Israel's troops outnumbered those of all Arab countries by 200,000 to 190,000. In terms of quality of training, numbers of technically trained specialists, and domestic production
of weapons in relation to armed forces requirements, Israel had
a decided edge over the Arab states taken together. More important, the Arabs possessed "no joint command organization
which could effectively direct combined operations" and had
"woefully weak systems of supply, evacuation and transport."
Finally, the report concluded, "Arab stockpiles of munition and
other supplies are hardly sufficient for operations lasting 30
days."[3]

Through the summer, both Israel and Egypt continued to
receive arms at an alarming rate. And in August, Admiral Radford was again asked to estimate the military capabilities of Israel and the Arab states. He responded:

> The Joint Chiefs of Staff now consider that Israel has a
> degree of military superiority which it will retain for the
> next three months. At the end of this period and until
> about April 1957, the military power of the two sides will
> be roughly in balance. After the spring of 1957, a margin of
> Arab military superiority will become manifest and, if pres-
> ent trends continue, will gradually increase.[4]

From August through October, 1956, as France and Israel
planned a coordinated attack on Egypt and Britain somewhat
hesitantly participated in the plot, the French stepped up the
pace of the arms shipments. Weapons more sophisticated than
any ever before seen in the Middle East poured into Israel, limited only by the ability of the IDF to absorb and "train up," and
by the number of French trainer-advisers available to do the
job. Both countries faced a self-imposed deadline—the attack
had to come during the U.S. presidential election campaign that
would end on November 6.

On October 29, the day upon which the attack commenced,
the JCS issued a "Special Watch Report" from its Intelligence
Advisory Committee:

1. The Watch Committee has examined new evidence of heavy Israeli mobilization on a scale which would permit Israel to:

a) occupy Jordan west of the Jordan River;
b) penetrate Syria as far as Damascus and occupy portions of this territory;
c) penetrate Egypt to the Suez Canal and hold parts of Sinai for a considerable time, depending on logistical limitations;
d) break the Egyptian blockade of the Gulf of Aqaba and keep the waterway open to Eilat;
e) gain air superiority over the Egyptian Air Force alone, or in combination with air forces of the other Arab States. . .

And then a remarkable statement:

f) probably carry out any or all of the above, even in the face of the combined resistance of contiguous Arab States.

Israel had amassed the most powerful military force in the history of the Middle East. Not since the apex of the Ottoman Empire in the 16th century had one of the countries of the region so dominated the Middle East militarily.

The Intelligence Advisory Committee noted:

The scale of the Israeli mobilization and its damaging effects on the economy, together with Egyptian preoccupation in Europe, French material support to Israel and the complicated inter-Arab rivalries in and over Jordan, particularly the growth in Egyptian influence in Jordan, all provide a favorable opportunity for a major attack.[5]

The "JCS Special Watch Report" in this last section reflects a certain naïveté. Israel had never in its short eight-year history provided more than 25 percent of its national budget from export earnings, and could not pay for normal government outlays, let alone a major expansion of its armed forces. The size of the Israeli mobilization, therefore, was limited by the size of fund-raising campaigns then ongoing in Europe and (primarily) in America. The impressive paraphernalia of the IDF was not purchased; it was donated.

The report was also somewhat outdated in its speculation regarding the immediate use to which the Israelis might put this Army, for as the report was being dispatched to U.S. military bases in Alaska, Colorado, France, Japan, London, and elsewhere, the IDF was already on the march. Forty-five thousand Israeli troops had, in the late afternoon of October 29, begun to cross the Egyptian border. Thirty thousand Egyptian troops faced them in the Sinai, and that included a ragtag "Palestinian Division" armed with pre–World War II weapons. Israel's Air Force of some 155 warplanes faced an Egyptian Air Force with 70 operational combat planes.[6]

The Israelis were not operating alone. French ships already patrolled the Israeli coastline. Seventy-two French jets—36 Mystères and 36 F-84 Thunderstreaks—had been stationed about ten days prior to the attack at airports in remote areas of Israel to protect nearby cities. As the fighting spread into the Sinai, French Nordatlas transport planes, flying out of Tymbou Airfield in Nicosia, Cyprus, dropped supplies to Israeli units. French fighters may even have directly participated in the Sinai battles, providing air cover for Israeli troops.*

Even more help was on the way. Executing a plan developed secretly some two-and-one-half months previously, British and French forces were, on October 29, preparing to follow within hours of the Israeli attack with a full-scale invasion of their own, involving more than 70,000 troops, including crack units of British commandos and French paratroops. Support would be provided by 240 combat planes, 130 warships including 7 aircraft carriers, 80 transport ships, and hundreds of landing craft, and some 20,000 vehicles. The expeditionary force that the British and French were sending to assist in the attack on Egypt was equivalent in size to that which the Allies had put ashore in the Anzio invasion in World War II.[7]

As the Israeli Army moved into the Sinai it was then, charac-

---

*The French Defense Ministry denied providing direct air support to Israeli troops during the campaign, and in fact denied for many years that any form of collusion with Israel had occurred before or during the Suez War. The *Manchester Guardian,* however, verified the French air support, including use of napalm against the Egyptian forces in the Sinai, in interviews with French pilots in Israel. (*The New York Times,* November 21, 1956, 6:3.)

teristically, taking very few risks. But it would not be as easy as planned.

A PREVENTIVE INVASION

The signing of the Soviet arms deal and the projected time frame for receipt, absorption, and deployment of the new weapons by the Egyptian Army set the timetable for war in the Middle East, at least from the standpoint of Israel. Diplomats would continue to meet and confer on the "issues" that composed the Arab-Israeli dispute, but all of that became, in late 1955, a kind of shadow play. In November, David Ben Gurion replaced Moshe Sharett as Prime Minister, and Israel was once again a country ruled by an army. To the IDF, Nasser's new Soviet-assisted Army was the only important issue. The gaining of rights of access through the Strait of Tiran via negotiations would be of little use to Israel if the Egyptian Army was reaching parity with the IDF. Indeed, Ben Gurion's strategy vis-à-vis the Arabs on all issues was firmly based upon an assumption of total military superiority.

There were in the United States senior government officials who recognized all of this. Not surprisingly, they tended to be military men. In October, 1955, the Deputy Director for Intelligence of the Joint Chiefs of Staff, Admiral Edwin Layton, addressed a memorandum to the JCS Chairman in which he warned that Soviet arms had just become the single most important factor in Arab-Israeli relations—more important than border disputes, water rights, or the settlement of Palestinian refugees. Admiral Layton explained:

> While the Israelis probably recognize that the military effects of this arms deal will not be felt immediately (it is estimated that a minimum of one year will be required after delivery before effective use by Egypt of most of the equipment could be made), they probably believe there is only limited time to deal with the situation. One solution which is probably receiving serious consideration in Israeli government circles is that of "preventative war" while Israel still retains military superiority.[8]

Subsequent writings by Israeli leaders of that period indicate that Layton's assumptions here were quite accurate.*

Egypt had agreed to purchase fighters, bombers, tanks, PT boats, submarines, and other items of equipment from the Soviets for $90 million in Egyptian cotton, but at concessionary prices. The JCS estimated that the cost to the United States of equivalent American arms would be $200 million. For a few months in late 1955 and early 1956, Israel turned to the Eisenhower administration to ensure her continued military preeminence in the region. On the advice of Secretary of State John Foster Dulles, the President refused Ben Gurion's repeated pleas for arms, however, citing the Tripartite Agreement of 1950 as the reason. White House memorandums from this period indicate there were other reasons, though, notably concern over Arab reaction and a belief that more arms would simply further solidify Ben Gurion's intransigence on all those "issues" that divided Arab and Jew.

So Israel turned to France, and by the end of May, 1956, copious shipments of French arms were arriving in Haifa and Tel Aviv. Abba Eban informed Secretary Dulles that his government was reconciled to the fact that the United States would not be a major supplier of arms.† Israel was, he said, getting "from one source or another" the arms that the IDF needed.[9]

Sometime in June, David Ben Gurion's (and Moshe Dayan's) plans for the preventive attack against Egypt were finalized. All that remained was for the right occasion to arise that would provide the justification for a full-scale attack without incurring the extreme wrath of the United States, Britain, and France—the Tripartite Agreement signatories. There was, as well, one more bit of domestic housekeeping necessary—getting rid of Moshe Sharett. Gideon Raphael, Israeli Deputy Foreign Minister at the time, describes how this matter was handled:

When [Ben Gurion's] plans for preventative action against Egypt matured in June he convinced himself that Sharett might eventually frustrate them. Without any substantive

---

*See for example Dayan, op. cit., Chapter 12.

†Although the United States was not supplying arms to Egypt—any arms—even when the Soviet arms purchase was rumored, the United States was secretly licensing private suppliers to ship "minor items of munitions, spare parts, etc.," to Israel in early and mid-1956.

discussion or an explanation of his true reasons he asked for Sharett's resignation from the post of Foreign Minister. Sharett, who had often contemplated handing in his resignation, was flabbergasted by the suddenness of the Prime Minister's blow. His relationship with him over the previous few years was far from harmonious, but Sharett had never suspected that Ben Gurion would terminate their close association of nearly twenty-five years with such painful abruptness.[10]

The decks were now cleared for action. And as if on cue, Gamal Abdel Nasser provided the needed occasion the following month, on July 26, 1956.

In late 1955 and early 1956, Nasser had pushed hard to obtain financing for a development project that had become almost an obsession for him—the Aswan High Dam. At a cost of over $1.3 billion, it would be the largest development project yet attempted in any third-world nation. As planned, Aswan would increase the total arable land in Egypt by 30 percent, and would provide that country with 50 percent of all the electrical power produced on the continent of Africa. The two primary sources to which Nasser looked for help on the project were the World Bank and the United States government. Negotiations with bank President Eugene Black were hard but, from Nasser's perspective, successful. Egypt agreed to allow the bank to supervise its foreign debt schedules, and accepted a bank loan for about half of the foreign currency needed for the project, at the then-current market rate of 5.5 percent interest.

The United States also had conditions, however, and these were even harder to meet. Egypt would make no more arms purchases from the Soviets, would accept U.S. and British monetary conditions for the loans as they were presented, and would conclude a peace agreement with the Israelis. The U.S. conditions were finally and firmly detailed to Ahmed Hussein, the Egyptian Ambassador to the United States, by Acting Secretary of State Herbert Hoover, Jr., in Washington in May of 1956.[11]

Taken together, the various World Bank and U.S. conditions for Aswan Dam financing amounted to a surrender of a considerable amount of national sovereignty, of control over Egyptian economic and foreign policy. Nevertheless Nasser decided to accede to Hoover's conditions as well, though he was not optimistic about the results because of the countervailing pressures on the U.S. government. The British and French were not likely to encourage the Eisenhower administration to support the project. The Baghdad Pact countries of Iraq, Iran, and Turkey were not enthusiastic about a project that would further enhance Nasser's preeminence in the Arab world. Finally, the cotton, Israel, and China lobbies in Congress each had its own reasons for opposing U.S. assistance.*

Nasser was not surprised, then, when Secretary of State Dulles formally withdrew the pledge of U.S. support for the Aswan project on July 19, leaving Egypt two options if it wished to proceed with construction: accept Soviet aid and the inevitable Soviet conditions, or find a way to finance the dam with Egyptian funds. At the time, Egypt had two major sources of foreign currency earnings: cotton exports, and the small stipend provided by the largely British- and French-owned Suez Canal company as a tip of the hat to Egyptian national sovereignty. Cotton earnings alone would not finance the project, and were in any event partially mortgaged to pay for Soviet arms. Nasser's choice was nationalization of the Suez Canal—the Aswan High Dam would be built with revenues from the passageway through which was carried the majority of Europe's fuel supplies.†

On July 26, on a hot, dusty evening in Cairo, standing on a podium in Liberation Square before a quarter of a million of his countrymen, President Nasser read his proclamation:

> The Universal Suez Maritime Canal Company S.A.E. is hereby nationalized. All funds and rights and obligations connected therewith are transferred to the State. All bodies and committees at present existing for its administration are dissolved. . . .

In Britain and France, the reaction was violent. Prime Minister Anthony Eden learned of the proclamation at a dinner party he was hosting at 10 Downing Street. Immediately, the dinner broke up and a cabinet meeting was held to discuss the situa-

*Egypt had recently enraged the China (or, more properly, Taiwan) lobby in Congress by granting diplomatic recognition to the People's Republic of China.

†The JCS estimated at the time of the take-over that Western Europe oil consumption stood at 2 million barrels per day, of which 1.2 million–1.3 million was carried by tanker through the Suez Canal.

tion. "The Egyptian has his thumb on our windpipe," said Eden, and then took the position with his Ministers that he would hold until the invasion some three months later: military action would be the British response. The British Chiefs of Staff were ordered to begin planning the campaign to retake the canal that very morning—it was already past midnight.[12]

In retrospect, Prime Minister Eden would have done well to carefully study Nasser's proclamation, and the speech made with it that evening, before committing himself to a course of action. For while Egypt could not hope to defeat or even seriously delay the forces that the British (with or without allies) could send against her, the seeds of an eventual diplomatic victory for Egypt lay concealed in Nasser's statement. First, Nasser indicated in the proclamation itself that share- and bondholders in the canal company would be compensated for the precise value of their holdings, as estimated at the closing rate on the Paris Bourse on the day before the action was taken. In spite of the subsequent invasion by Britain and France, which cost more than 3,000 Egyptian lives, the promise of compensation was fulfilled, and the last payment to shareholders was eventually made on schedule in January of 1963.

Second, in his proclamation Nasser revealed that as he was speaking, the government of Egypt had already physically taken control of and was managing the canal company and the canal itself. It was a hint. In the days and weeks to come, the traffic through the canal would continue to flow smoothly. On the day after nationalization, forty-nine ships—four more than the average—moved through the canal.[13] The U.S. government watched the flow carefully, as of course did the countries of Western Europe. From the time of nationalization until the day of the invasion, no unusual backlog of traffic waiting to transit the canal ever occurred. Nasser was also careful not to violate the terms of the Treaty of 1888, guaranteeing free rights of passage through the canal—in the weeks after nationalization, two ships under charter to Israel were even allowed to pass.[14]

In sum, Nasser's expropriation of the Suez Canal was, in terms of applicable laws and treaties, entirely legal. It was in no sense a casus belli for Britain or France. It did not even involve Israel. Within a week of the proclamation, however, the British Army took steps to reinforce the British troops stationed in Cyprus. The French Foreign Minister, Christian Pineau, con-

sulted with Anthony Eden in London concerning possible joint
military action against Egypt. The French Defense Ministry contacted the Israeli Embassy in Paris to obtain "up-to-the-minute
information on the strength and locations of the Egyptian formations—land, sea and air" to commence the planning for a
joint attack.[15] This the Israelis gladly provided. It was the first
small step toward war.

In Washington the Pentagon was unaware of these initial secret contacts regarding a possible coordinated attack, but it did
read the overall signs remarkably well. On August 17, 1956,
three weeks after the nationalization of the canal, the Office of
the Secretary of Defense asked the Pentagon's Joint Intelligence
Group (JIG) to analyze "the feasibility of a preventative war
aimed at stalling the rate of Arab cohesion" in order to "support
policy decisions of the Secretary of Defense." The JIG responded that there was a likelihood "in the short term" of a
"short, blitzkrieg type of war" by Israel against Egypt in order
to bring down Nasser's government, to destroy his Army, to
"gain territorial objectives," and finally to "effect a forced relocation of nearby refugee camps." The report implied that Israel might decide to move before November, 1956, when Egypt
would have absorbed sufficient Soviet arms to pose a threat to
Israel.[16] It was a remarkable bit of forecasting. And rather per-
ceptive analysis, as well.

A DIPLOMATIC DANCE,
SIGNIFYING NOTHING

For a decade after the Suez War, histories of the event took
at face value the diplomatic dance that occurred in August and
October, 1956. Various conferences and meetings were convened, plans were developed, and organizations were formed,
largely at the behest of Eisenhower and Dulles, in an effort to
prevent the war. Not until the mid-1960's, however, was the extent of the deception by Britain, France, and Israel during these
months fully revealed.

Within a few days of Nasser's proclamation, President
Eisenhower wrote Prime Minister Eden advising against a resort
to force unless and until "every peaceful means" of ensuring
international interests in the canal's operation had been re-

solved. At about the same time, Secretary of State John Foster Dulles was sent to London to consult with British and French officials, to propose an international conference of some twenty-four involved nations, including Egypt, and to produce a plan for operation of the canal by an "international authority."*

In fact, two reports emanated from the conference. The majority, composed of the United States, Britain, France, and some 15 other Western-oriented canal users, proposed to return control of the canal to the countries that had signed the Convention of 1888. A minority report, signed by India, the Soviet Union, Indonesia, and Ceylon, provided for retention of Egyptian control, with an advisory body to oversee "user interests."

Australian Prime Minister R. G. Menzies was designated to deliver the majority report to Nasser a few days later, which he did, presenting it as an ultimatum, whether it was intended as such or not. When, as expected, Nasser rejected the idea of a return to international control, U.S. Secretary of State Dulles floated the idea of a Suez Canal Users' Association (SCUA). A second conference in London on September 19–21, involving practically the same cast of characters, embraced the idea. On October 5, Britain and France agreed to take the SCUA proposal to the United Nations Security Council. When this was finally done, however, on October 13, the British and French UN delegations insisted that Egypt accept the majority report of the first London conference as part of the Security Council resolution. Egypt denounced the idea as presented, and when the resolution was finally put to a vote on October 13, the council passed a watered-down proposal based upon "six broad principles" that left effective control in the hands of Egypt. It was at this point, as legend would have it, that Britain and France decided to resort to force.

Only it did not happen that way. In the last week of July, shortly after Nasser's proclamation on the canal, the French Defense Ministry contacted the Israeli Military Attaché in Paris to determine whether Israel would be willing to participate in a joint British-French "military action" in Egypt, at least to the extent of supplying intelligence on the strength and locations of Egyptian military formations. By mid-August, as the first London conference was convened, the British and French De-

---

*Nasser at the last moment decided not to attend the conference because of vitriolic public attacks upon him by Eden just prior to the event.

fense ministries had put the finishing touches on Operation Musketeer, a joint military operation to seize and hold the Suez
Canal Zone. And on September 1, several days before Australian Prime Minister Menzies had given Nasser a chance to
react to the majority proposal of the first London conference,
the French Defense Ministry contacted the IDF to see whether
Israel would wish to participate in Musketeer.

On September 29 through October 1, over a week before
Britain and France took their case to the Security Council (without consulting the United States), the French General Staff
hosted a delegation from the IDF at Sèvres, near Paris, to discuss details of Israeli participation in Musketeer. Moshe Dayan
headed the Israeli delegation. Upon his return from Sèvres on
the first day of October and almost two weeks prior to the Security Council votes on the "six broad principles" and the
London conference majority proposal, IDF Chief of Staff Dayan
called a meeting of the IDF General Staff to give them an
"Early Warning Order" of an imminent campaign against the
Arabs "with France, and perhaps with Britain." And by October 8, still prior to the farcical discussion in the UN of the "six
broad principles" and so forth, Dayan had already convened his
IDF Staff Group for approval of Operation Kadesh, code-
named after the site of the "last sojourn in the Sinai wilderness
by the children of Israel before continuing to the Promised
Land."[17]

There was going to be a Suez war whether Eisenhower
approved or not, and whatever the outcome of the diplomatic
maneuvering within and outside the UN. The delay after September 1, when Britain, France, and Israel first began in a general way to discuss a coordinated "military action," was due to
the complexities and the size of the invasion, not to any genuine
desire to "exhaust every peaceful means" of resolving the canal
problem, as President Eisenhower wished.*

On October 19, the U.S. State Department noted an "increasingly reasonable attitude" on the part of President Nasser,
and a few days later, on October 24, urged the Egyptian Foreign
Minister in New York to submit concrete written proposals to

*The preceding account of concurrent public and secret diplomacy just prior to the Suez
War is drawn from three primary sources: Chapter 10 (entitled "The Suez Canal Crisis")
of the "Top Secret" JCS history 1955–1956, Records of the United States Joint Chiefs of
Staff, Record Group 218, National Archives; Moshe Dayan's *Story of My Life;* and
Donald Neff's *Warrior at Suez.*

the British and French prior to the opening of talks on SCUA at the UN, scheduled to begin on October 29. The day after the State Department approached the Egyptian Foreign Minister, Israel secretly declared a full mobilization of its reserves—150,000 men. There would be no more talks, and as Dayan would write years later, these late-hour diplomatic efforts reflected nothing more than the naïveté of the Eisenhower administration.

On October 25, the very day that Israel mobilized, Israel's Ambassador to the United States, Abba Eban, addressed the Security Council and solemnly pledged:

> The Government of Israel will faithfully observe the cease-fire so long as the cease-fire is observed by the other side. It will start no war. It will initiate no violence.[18]

On Sunday, October 28, Ambassador Eban paid an official visit to Secretary of State Dulles. Eban confided that Israeli intelligence had recent information that Eygpt was planning to attack Israel soon.[19] It was a scene reminiscent of the visit to a previous U.S. Secretary of State, Cordell Hull, paid by Japanese Ambassador Kichisaburo Nomura on December 7, 1941. As Hull had in the previous instance, Dulles received Eban politely. He did not inform Eban that the United States had aerial reconnaissance that clearly showed who was preparing to attack whom. Dulles received Eban as if he were an honorable man, and the accredited diplomatic representative of a friendly country.

Even after the attack the effort at deception continued. On October 30, the IDF Senior Foreign Liaison Officer informed the U.S. Military Attaché in Tel Aviv that the IDF had merely "penetrated and attacked Fedayeen bases in Kuntilla and Ras El Naqueb area."[20] That same day Ben Gurion telegrammed President Eisenhower that Nasser had surrounded Israel with a "ring of steel." And in late November, weeks after a cease-fire had been declared, the Eisenhower administration was still trying to figure out whether and how France and Britain had coordinated the attack with Israel. The *Jerusalem Post* first revealed that Ben Gurion had secretly visited France to plot the attack, in an article published on November 24, 1956. U.S. Ambassador Edward Lawson immediately raised the matter with the Israeli Foreign Ministry, which "denied categorically" that any such visit had taken place.[21] The State Department pursued the matter in Paris just to make sure, however. On November 29, U.S. Ambassador Clarence Douglas Dillon reported back:

> [Foreign Ministry] Director General Afrique-Levant Roux yesterday categorically denied reports of Ben Gurion's visit Paris late October or early November. Roux said despite secrecy top-level plans that juncture, he would certainly have known of Ben Gurion's presence Paris.[22]

It was not only a coordinated attack, but a coordinated deception, with two of America's "allies" using the same terminology to lie to the Eisenhower administration, even after the invasion was carried out.

"WE SHOULD TRY TO BE MORE PRECISE"

It would be inaccurate to portray the Eisenhower administration as a hapless victim in all of this. None of the four countries directly involved in the war—Britain, France, Israel, and Egypt—could understand exactly what U.S. government policy was on the looming conflict, because none of them was receiving clear signals from Washington about that policy. Even senior administration officials themselves realized and regretted the policy muddle. In March of 1956 the Joint Middle East Planning Committee had sent a strong policy memorandum to the JCS Chairman, Admiral Arthur Radford. The Arabs, said the committee, had taken the "blind" attitude that Israel did not exist. The Israelis had been "arrogant" in dealing with their Arab neighbors. But blame was also allocated to the West, and by implication, to the United States:

> . . . the western powers have been vacillating, unsure of themselves. The worst mistake the western powers have made has been to try to be friends with both sides—an utter impossibility.[23]

Others, higher in the administration, voiced similar criticisms. At the end of March, Henry Cabot Lodge, Jr., U.S. Ambassador to the UN, wrote a strong "personal and private" letter to John Foster Dulles ("Dear Foster"). UN Secretary-General Hammarskjöld, he said, could only deal with disputants on the basis of voluntary arrangements dealing solely with the carrying out of the existing armistice agreements. What was needed, wrote Ambassador Lodge, was a "realistic, comprehensive program for dealing with the issues basic to the Palestine question." Lodge continued:

> The problems of refugees, territorial adjustments and economic development can be dealt with effectively only by bringing to bear the full resources of this government. They will not settle themselves, nor does it appear that they can be settled piece-meal. Unless these problems are dealt with more realistically than they have been in the past eight years, we will . . . increasingly run the risk of actually having a war this year.[24]

It was just about as strong a letter as one can safely write to one's boss. And it was of course prophetic.

Even Dulles seems to have realized that the United States was sending "mixed signals," at least to Egypt's Nasser. In late April, the Secretary wrote to his subordinate, William Rountree, Assistant Secretary of State for Near Eastern Affairs, saying that Nasser could hardly be expected to conform to U.S. policies (viz., Soviet arms, peace with Israel) if he did not know what those were. "We should try to be more precise," Dulles concluded.[25]

The predicament faced by the administration was perhaps exemplified by the story of Operation Stockpile. By mid-September, it was apparent to U.S. military and civilian intelligence officials that the British and French and/or the Israelis were preparing to make war on one or more of the Arab countries—Egypt in the case of the British and French, and Jordan or Egypt in the case of the Israelis. This created certain problems for the administration. It all had to do with the Tripartite Agreement of May 25, 1950, the cornerstone of U.S. military and political policy in the region. Point 3 of the Tripartite Agreement was the following:

> The three governments take this opportunity of declaring their deep interest and desire to promote the establishment and maintenance of peace and stability in the area and their

unalterable opposition to the use of force between any of
the states in that area. The three governments, should they
find that any of these states was preparing to violate frontiers or armistice lines, would, consistently with their obligations as members of the United Nations, immediately
take action, both within and outside the United Nations, to
prevent such violations.

In April of 1956, the Joint Strategic Plans Group of the JCS
had produced a memorandum on "Combined Planning Pursuant
to the Tripartite Declaration of 1950," in which was contained
the "intelligence view of the most likely way in which hostilities
may start." The JCS predicted, based upon their consultation
with the British Chiefs of Staff, that aggression by Egypt was the
most likely way for war to start, and the attack would probably
first occur against Israel.[26]

Accordingly, in May of 1956, the Defense Department, on
instructions from the White House, mounted Operation Stockpile, a top-secret plan to make certain advanced military equipment available to "the victim of aggression in the event hostilities appeared imminent" in the Middle East. The Department
of the Air Force was directed to initiate preliminary planning for
the delivery, on short notice, of twenty-four F-86 aircraft from
U.S. operational units in Europe to air bases in Israel. Along
with the planes, Israel was to be provided with howitzers,
mounted recoilless rifles, rocket launchers, mortars, antitank
and antipersonnel mines, and 30 days' supply (90,000 cubic feet)
of ammunition for these weapons.

The memorandum creating the stockpile indicated that base
and transit rights for the weapons would be handled by the State
Department and would be "ostensibly" considered as "normal
reserves for U.S. forces in Europe and the Mediterranean." The
directive to the Secretary of the Air Force further noted:

Attention is directed to the sensitive nature of this operation and to the need for unusual security precautions to
prevent possible leaks. Premature disclosure of any details
of this operation would jeopardize the whole operation and
could cause serious international complications. Therefore,
this matter will be handled on a strictly "need to know"
basis.[27]

With all the precautions, there was still the possibility that news of the operation would somehow leak out, so Secretary of State Dulles directed a subordinate to prepare a statement to be used in such an event. Other materials were prepared for use by the Arab states, and for this purpose were stockpiled on board Sixth Fleet ships in the Mediterranean.

The problem was that by September, with national elections approaching, with the Suez Canal nationalized, and with Britain and France (the other two signers of the Tripartite Agreement) plotting with Israel to attack Egypt, any thought of making weapons available to the Arabs was preposterous. On September 28, 1956, Secretary of State Dulles sent the President a memorandum noting that

> I am inclined to agree with the Defense Department that it is now unlikely that we should be giving military assistance to the Arabs and am disposed to agree that the Defense Department may discontinue this part of the operation. Do you agree?[28]

The President agreed. Operation Stockpile was canceled.

The plain fact was that by September–October, 1956, the administration had, as a practical matter, very little leverage to apply to the disputant parties. All of the screws that the administration could turn on Egypt, for example, had already been turned. The offer of assistance on the Aswan High Dam had been withdrawn in July. Arms assistance had been denied Nasser all along. Even the food assistance provided under the PL 480 and CARE programs in Egypt had long since been suspended.

Britain and France could of course have been influenced by the President, but neither he nor John Foster Dulles thought that this would be necessary. Until the last ten days or so before the invasion, traditional diplomatic means were being used to achieve a compromise on the canal nationalization issue, and Washington's more or less open channels to London and Paris led Eisenhower and Dulles to hope that eventually a settlement would be reached and the need for the use of military force by Britain and France obviated.

Israel, of course, was in a fundamentally different situation vis-à-vis the United States as compared with the other three countries. As had been the case in 1953 during the B'not Yaakov canal dispute, Israel in late 1956 was virtually living from hand to mouth, and was almost totally dependent upon private and official government aid from the United States. In early October, when the administration had discussed U.S. guarantees for a $75 million Export-Import Bank loan, Secretary of the Treasury George Humphrey had informed Eisenhower that the bank was balking because Israel was over-extended in loans, and had virtually no foreign-currency earning power. Israel, said Humphrey, was simply a bad credit risk.[29] So as in 1953, Eisenhower did have a powerful hold on Israel. The problem was that more was at stake now for Israel than the irri-gation of the Negev—Egypt's Sovietized Army did pose a po-tential threat to the Jewish state, if only in the long term.

Then there was the presidential election campaign that was winding to a close as Israel planned its attack upon the Sinai. Eisenhower had repeatedly informed Israeli officials and repre-sentatives of American Jewish organizations that he would not be swayed by "domestic political considerations," even in an election year.* Nevertheless, he chose not to threaten to with-draw aid until October 27, when Israel's general mobilization was well underway. The horse, at that point, was out of the barn.

It was not until the invasion of Egypt had already begun that steps were actually taken to cut the flow of aid to Israel. On October 31, development assistance, technical assistance, and shipments of agricultural products under PL 480 had been stopped, though cargoes then in transit and projects underway had been allowed to proceed. The Export-Import Bank loan of $75 million had been delayed. All forms of military assistance, including those in the pipeline, had been terminated. All export licenses had been canceled for shipment of munitions or other military goods.[30] Finally, the Eisenhower Administration was being precise.

---

*In April, 1956, Eisenhower had told Rabbi Hillel Silver, of the Zionist Organization of America, at the White House that the election campaign would not be a consideration for him in determining whether or not to provide arms aid to Israel. Silver had re-sponded: "You can be re-elected without a single Jewish vote."

AFTERTHOUGHTS ON THE SUEZ WAR

Sometimes, in affairs of state as in sports, it is better to be lucky than to be proficient. The Eisenhower administration, which for months had failed to act to head off the Suez War, emerged from that war with its reputation in foreign affairs actually enhanced. Working through the UN and through direct, tough, bilateral diplomacy, the United States government was seen to be responsible for the prompt withdrawal of British and French forces from Eygpt soon after the fighting stopped. Although Israel lingered in the Sinai for four months, she too finally, reluctantly withdrew; and again the international community credited the Eisenhower administration for applying the pressure to achieve this result. In the Arab world and in the halls of the United Nations, Dwight Eisenhower was seen as a wise and fair peacekeeper.

But the fighting itself entailed grave risks, for the United States, of tragedies that were, one by one, narrowly averted. For example, the U.S. Navy successfully evacuated thousands of American citizens from Egypt, Jordan, Syria, and Israel. In the case of Egypt, men, women, and children were literally plucked from the midst of the fighting, and there were some close calls. A White House decision to evacuate all Americans from Cairo was finally made on October 28, and the operation itself commenced on the morning of October 30. Some 15 U.S. transport planes were waiting on the tarmac at Cairo West Airport to begin the airlift just as British bombers were arriving to bomb the airport. It was only at the last moment that Prime Minister Eden ordered his planes to delay the dropping of their bomb loads.[31]

The vast majority of the Americans in Cairo—some 1,528—were finally evacuated from Alexandria on November 4 on U.S. navy ships. For several days, those ships had been trapped in Alexandria harbor, fearful of departing because of information—which ultimately proved to be false—that the entrance to the harbor was mined. During the wait, British and French planes carried out bombing runs in the harbor, and there were several near misses on the American ships. To make matters worse, on the day before the final evacuation, an Egyptian destroyer anchored near the U.S. ships and began firing on the attacking aircraft.[32]

Then, U.S. military forces nearly had to fight in the war. Soon after Britain and France joined the invasion of Egypt, Premier Nikolai Bulganin of the Soviet Union warned that unless the Western powers withdrew, World War III could be started. For weeks thereafter, Bulganin publicly threatened to send "volunteers" to the Middle East. It was never done, but U.S. forces in the region and in Europe as well were placed on alert status just in case the Soviets did intervene in the conflict directly. Two reinforced marine battalions, armed with tactical nuclear weapons, were sent to the area prepared to "fight their way into Cairo" to evacuate U.S. citizens, if that became necessary. One unit of marines with tanks and artillery actually moved into Alexandria harbor while the evacuation of civilians was under way. A U.S. naval base in Morocco and the Dhahran oil fields in Saudi Arabia were also thought to be threatened by "Arab extremists," and the marine contingents had sealed orders to protect these facilities if it became necessary.[33] Fortunately, it did not.

Less than a week after the fighting stopped, the Foreign Liaison Officer of the IDF notified the foreign Military Attachés in Tel Aviv that a two-day tour of the Sinai would be conducted during which the Attachés would be allowed to examine and photograph captured weapons and supplies of Soviet origin. It was a harbinger of an aspect of U.S.-Israeli relations that would grow through future years and future wars. By 1973, weapons systems evaluation and testing would be one of the central elements of the U.S.-Israeli "friendship."

Despite superior numbers, weapons, air cover, training, preparation, mobility, and logistical support, the Israeli-British-French invasion of Egypt in 1956 was not a walk in the park. The British and French had the capability, of course, of sending specialized forces for special jobs. Well-equipped amphibious forces pushed ashore at either end of the canal. Paratroops were used extensively for specific military objectives. Air cover was total—the British and French air forces between them destroyed 95 percent of the Egyptian Air Force on the ground.

There was an interesting difference in the "design" of the

Egyptian and Israeli armies, however, and the Sinai fighting pitted strength against strength. Egypt, which called incessantly for an Arab effort to drive Israel into the sea in the early 1950's, had built an army that, as Edgar O'Ballance observed in his classic *The Sinai Campaign of 1956*, was uniquely defense-minded. "It would appear that the 'attack' had not been seriously studied or practiced," O'Ballance noted of the Egyptians.[34] And the Egyptians, who were defending their own territory in the Sinai, had defensive positions that were "always well sited, well concealed, had mutually interlocking fields of fire, good communication, were sited in depth and had protective wire and minefields."[35]

By contrast the Israelis, who always spoke in the early 1950's of the need to conclude peace agreements with their neighbors, had built an army with one and only one purpose—as a mobile strike force able to move quickly and deeply into a neighbor's territory. In his autobiography, Moshe Dayan describes at some length his efforts to use Ariel Sharon's Force 101 as a model for paratroop and other units of the IDF, trained and equipped to undertake "special operations across the border."[36]

Air cover was a decisive factor in the Sinai campaign. After some initial staffing runs on the morning of October 30, the Egyptian Air Force generally left the skies to the Israelis. Israeli pilots on that first full day of fighting flew twice as many sorties as the Egyptians, who were simply not well trained on their new equipment. By the end of the day on October 31, the Israelis were flying "many times" as many sorties as the Egyptians.[37] On the evening of October 31, the British and French air forces came into play, concentrating their attacks on Egyptian airfields. Now, the Egyptian soldiers in the Sinai were reduced to fighting planes with tanks in open territory. Accordingly, Nasser made the decision on the evening of October 31 to withdraw his troops to the canal zone, as they had no chance without air cover. Not that the Israeli pilots had an easy time of it. Egyptian anti-aircraft fire was extremely accurate, and overall in the Sinai campaign, the Israelis lost twice as many aircraft as did the Egyptians.*

*Homer Bigart, reporting from Jerusalem for *The New York Times* on November 15 (page 3, column 5), quoted official Israeli figures of 11 losses for Israel and 9 for Egypt. Edgar O'Ballance, writing in 1959 (op. cit., p. 180), said the Israelis had admitted 14 lost aircraft, and gave his estimate as 20.

The most dramatic aspect of the fighting on the first and second days was perhaps the Israeli paratroop drop, under the command of Ariel Sharon, at the Mitla Pass some 150 miles into Egyptian territory. Sharon thought the position was undefended. It was not. Then the drop was made in the wrong place, and poor defensive positions were taken by the Israelis.* Finally Sharon, against the strict orders of his commander, advanced from his positions up into a narrow defile, suffering extremely heavy casualties at the hands of the Egyptians. The pass was taken by the Israelis, and then abandoned. Dayan, writing in his autobiography, later termed these "tactical mistakes."[38] The pass was finally secured by the Israelis after two days of hard fighting when the Egyptian defenders, on Nasser's orders, withdrew to the canal zone.

Another key battle in the Sinai was Abu Ageila in the northern Sinai. Again, the Israeli attackers were caught in the open by well-entrenched Egyptian defenders, and took heavy losses in three days of fierce fighting. Again, the Egyptian soldiers abandoned their position when ordered to do so by their Commander in Chief, moving off under cover of darkness toward the port city of El Arish.[39]

Edgar O'Ballance summarized the fighting in these two "decisive" battles in this way:

> Neither in the Hittan Defile [Mitla Pass] nor in the area around Abu Ageila did the Israelis have it all their own way; slowly they got the upper hand, although not without some hard fighting on their part. The Egyptians made a stand and for a short while fought back hard, and especially when their line of retreat was cut off, as in the Hittan Defile, did they stay and fight to the bitter end.[40]

O'Ballance was severely critical of the qualities of leadership of most of the Egyptian officer corps, however, and thought the Egyptian soldiers to be generally less well trained and less motivated than were the Israelis.

On the Suez Canal front, the going was also very rough. In the battle for Port Said, crack British Red Devil paratroop units were met by the Egyptians with what one British correspondent

---

*These points are made by O'Ballance, op. cit., pp. 86–89.

described as "a screeching, crackling hell of lead."[41] Lieutenant General Sir Hugh Stockwell, British Army task force commander at Port Said, later said the Egyptians had fought "jolly well. . . . They fought very toughly, a good deal tougher than we anticipated."[42]

General Sir Charles Keightley, British-French Commander in Chief, summed up the Egyptian performance at Port Said, which was the main battle in the Suez Canal Zone, in terms very similar to those O'Ballance used in describing the Sinai campaign. Egyptian soldiers, he said, had fought well, but were poorly led. Hanson Baldwin, military analyst of *The New York Times,* summarized the Egyptian performance at Port Said this way:

> Most British fighting men with whom this correspondent talked—especially the Royal Marine commandos and British parachute troops—praised the Egyptians' courage and said they had been surprised at the tenacity of the defense.[43]

In another article on the battle, Baldwin noted that victory for the greatly superior British-French force was never in question. "But if the Egyptians had learned to use effectively the weapons they had," he added, "the story would have been very different."[44]

On November 14, IDF Chief of Staff Dayan spoke to the international press about the war. Israel could have won it in five to seven days without British and French help, he said. Dayan did not want to answer questions about alleged synchronization of the Israeli and the British-French attacks, "But we knew something was going on in Cyprus," he said. The Egyptians, he said, "showed little stubbornness, and were particularly inept at Sharm al-Sheikh."[45]

—7—

Making an Israeli Bomb, 1948–1967

EARLY DECISIONS (1948–1957)

AMONG THE REFUGEES WHO streamed into Palestine just before, during, and after the Second World War were many eminent physical scientists. For centuries, Europe had received from the Middle East innovations in mathematics and the sciences. Now in the space of a few short years, Fascist terror and the Zionist underground were combining to bring advanced scientific knowledge back to the region in a rush. From universities and laboratories in Berlin and Prague, Warsaw and Bucharest, came people familiar with advanced scientific procedures and very aware of the role that modern science could play in the tasks of nation building that faced the Jewish homeland.

Not surprisingly, then, within a year of the establishment of the State of Israel, the groundwork was being laid for a nuclear program. A survey of the mineral resources of the Negev Desert revealed phosphate deposits containing uranium. A group of young nuclear scientists was sent abroad for specialized training and research, sponsored by the Israeli Defense Ministry. And in 1949, the Weizmann Institute in Tel Aviv established a Department of Isotope Research.[1]

European-educated minds and funds from the Diaspora in the United States and Europe provided the basis for a program, but assistance would be needed from a country with a large industrial base, to provide the paraphernalia of reactors, cooling plants, and related installations required to process and manage fissionable material. In 1949, Prime Minister (and Defense Minister) Ben Gurion decided to ask France for the required collaboration. It was a wise choice, and the beginning of a relationship that would mutually benefit the economic systems and defense programs of France and Israel for over 20 years. The capacities and resources of the two countries nicely complemented each other, but there were more specific reasons for the "marriage":

> Since a large number of French atomic scientists in the postwar period were Jewish, numerous unofficial contacts were easily established over the years. Many Leftist-leaning French scientists had close associations with leading members of the Socialist party and with Leon Blum who, in turn, had close ties with Israel. Others, like Frederic Joliot-Curie, the High Commissioner [of the French Commissariat of Atomic Energy], had played an important role in the Resistance, where many of the French connections with Israel were forged.[2]

It would not in any sense be a one-way relationship. Even in the very early 1950's, Professor Israel Dostrovsky was completing work at the Weizmann Institute that he had begun at London University, to develop a new process for the production of heavy water.* Other Israelis were working on new methods for the extraction of uranium from phosphates and other low-grade ores. Both processes greatly interested the French.

In 1952, the Ben Gurion government established the Israel Atomic Energy Commission (IAEC), with Professor Ernest Bergman as Chairman. From the beginning, the IAEC worked closely with its French equivalent, the Commissariat of Atomic Energy (CEA). Technical exchanges were begun in 1953, and a formal agreement on cooperation between France and Israel in nuclear research was drafted that same year, but the fact of this accord was unknown to the Israeli public until late in 1954. In fact, the entire Israeli nuclear program was so secret that even the existence of the IAEC was kept from the Israeli public for two years.

French sales of conventional arms to the Israelis began in 1955 and continued for over a decade. Here too, the arrangement was mutually beneficial. In the years 1955–1967, Israel

---

*A costly material used in the cooling and controlling of nuclear fission processes.

spent over $600 million for arms from France, which included a nuclear reactor ($75 million) and some 300 military aircraft. One senior French military official estimated that the Israeli aircraft orders during these years may, by increasing production volume, have cut assembly-line prices by one third, resulting in enormous savings for the French Air Force.[3]

Israel's decision (i.e., Ben Gurion's decision) to build a nuclear reactor at Dimona in the Negev Desert, and to accept French assistance in doing so, was an important turning point in Israel's nuclear program, though it was not Israel's first reactor. Following the establishment of IAEC in 1952, the United States had agreed to help Israel construct a small 5,000-kilowatt reactor at Nahal Soreq near the Mediterranean coast. Part of the Eisenhower administration's Atoms for Peace program, the Nahal Soreq project was carried out under strict safeguards and included specific provisions for regular U.S. inspection of the entire site.* The small size of the reactor precluded production of militarily significant quantities of plutonium, in any event.

But Dimona was a different story. In early 1957, Israel and France signed a secret agreement for construction of a 24,000-kilowatt (thermal) reactor to be fueled with natural uranium and cooled with heavy water. Although the plans apparently did not include provisions for a separation plant, which would permit reprocessing of the reactor's spent fuel rods into weapons-grade plutonium, the size and design of the plant were a clear sign that Israel, with French assistance, had opted to take the first steps toward an atomic weapons program.

This decision was of course not made public, but the significance of it was clearly understood within Israel's tiny nuclear establishment. Six of the seven members of the IAEC promptly resigned, including Israel Dostrovsky, the scientist whose remarkable work in heavy-water production had been so important in inducing the French-Israeli arrangement in the first place. Even more interesting was what followed:

> Professor Bergman continued to hold the title of chairman of the Israeli Atomic Energy Commission, although he had no commission over which to preside. Incredibly enough no inquiry was held into the reasons for the resignations, and

---

*In 1964, responsibilities for inspection at Nahal Soreq were shifted to the International Atomic Energy Agency (IAEA) by agreement between Israel and the United States.

no one bothered to appoint a new commission. The Knesset did not demand an explanation. The chairman continued as before to act solely within the framework of the Defense Ministry, which controlled all nuclear development in Israel for both peaceful purposes and security needs.[4]

Although the United States was officially unaware of the Dimona reactor until 1960, and remains to this day officially unaware of its military purposes, the Eisenhower administration in 1957–1960 knew of the curious organization table of the Israeli nuclear program, which subsumed all nuclear enterprises within the Defense Ministry "for reasons of administrative efficiency." In addition to the financial and technical assistance to the small Nahal Soreq reactor under Atoms for Peace, the U.S. government was directly involved in nuclear research at the Weizmann Institute. A substantial part of the institute's operating budget was provided by the U.S. National Institutes of Health and by the U.S. Air Force, which, together with the U.S. Navy, funded classified nuclear physics research at Weizmann during this period.[5] From the beginning, then, the Eisenhower administration was involved.

Nevertheless, the joint French-Israeli plan for the Dimona reactor was kept a secret from the United States. When the Eisenhower administration inquired about the 1957 IAEC controversy or about the establishment of a strict security zone and the heavy construction going on at Dimona in the desert, David Ben Gurion responded with solemn assurances that what was being built was a "textile plant." Later, that was changed to a "pumping station."[6]

One might wonder why, in 1957, Israel would assume the costs and risks of a nuclear weapons program. The previous year, Israel had consolidated her unquestioned and unquestionable conventional military superiority in the Middle East. With British and French assistance, she had crushed the army of her only important rival in the region. Shimon Peres provided the likely explanation in 1962 when, as Permanent Secretary of the Israeli Defense Ministry, he spoke of the IDF concept of non-conventional "compellence" in an interview with the Israeli daily *Davar*. Later, a noted Israeli expert on his country's nuclear weapons program, Yair Evron, explained this concept:

. . . acquiring a superior weapons system would mean the possibility of using it for compellent purposes—that is, forcing the other side to accept Israeli political demands, which would presumably include a demand that the territorial status quo be accepted and a peace treaty with Israel be signed.[7]

THE DECISIONS REVEALED (1960)

By 1960 the "pumping station" story was beginning to wear a bit thin. In the three previous years, Israel had worked closely with France on preproduction design of the Mirage airplane, which was capable of delivering nuclear bombs.[8] And in February of 1960, the French began a series of nuclear tests in Raggan and Ekker in the Saharan reaches of Algeria.[9] It is reasonable to assume that the CIA knew that Israeli scientists observed and participated in these exercises. In March of 1960, during a visit by Prime Minister Ben Gurion to the White House, Eisenhower hinted broadly that "nuclear weapons" would not augment Israel's security situation vis-à-vis its Arab neighbors, and added that he "doubted that the USSR would give nuclear weapons to the UAR."[10]

Ben Gurion's primary purpose in the meeting had been to convince Eisenhower that the United States should agree to supplant France as Israel's major arms supplier. Eisenhower politely declined, suggesting that Israel should look to Britain, France, and West Germany. Citing U.S. intervention in the Suez War in 1956 and in Lebanon in 1958, the President assured Ben Gurion that the United States would not stand idle in the event of the threat of destruction of any Middle East country. To become a major arms supplier for any country in the region, however, would mean that the United States would forfeit its role as a potential mediator of the basic disputes that plagued the Middle East.

Eisenhower retreated a bit from this position, however, when in May, 1960, the United States offered to supply Israel with advanced radar and communications equipment ("of a quality possessed by only a few nations"), costing some six to ten times more than any previous United States military transaction with Israel.[11]

In August, Secretary of State Christian Herter wrote to Ben Gurion that the United States would not be willing to provide Israel with the advanced Hawk missile air-defense system. He was more direct, however, than the President had been in March, in reminding Ben Gurion that the U.S. government annually provided an enormous *indirect* subsidy to the Israeli defense budget:

> Our view has been that legitimate defense needs are only one facet of an economy which our Government studies in assessing a country's eligibility, under our criteria, for economic assistance. . . . there can be little doubt that the substantial assistance which our Government has extended to Israel since its birth—in the neighborhood of $700,000,000—has contributed greatly to Israel's ability to shoulder its defense burden, including the purchase of its principal military requirements elsewhere.[12]

Herter refrained from pointing out to Ben Gurion that the federal tax-deductible status of U.S. private contributions to Israel—which far exceeded the amount of official assistance—constituted a further indirect subsidy to Israel's defense budget.

It was in the summer of 1960, during this give-and-take about U.S. supply of conventional arms for Israel, that the CIA first reported to the President that what was being constructed in the Negev was not a textile plant or a pumping station, but a large nuclear reactor with the potential for producing fissionable material in quantities sufficient to produce nuclear weapons—about 1.2 bombs per year. Adding to the U.S. concern was the fact that in that same year, the West Germans developed a process for separating fissionable material from spent reactor fuel using a gas centrifuge. The German process was simple and cheap enough to enable small countries—such as Israel—to produce nuclear weapons without constructing a plutonium separation plant. More important, the gas centrifuge was smaller and could be more easily hidden than a separation plant.[13]

In December 1960, Secretary of State Herter called in the Israeli Ambassador in Washington and posed eight questions in an attempt to learn "officially" whether Israel was or was not building a large reactor. The Israeli government responses were not very convincing, resulting in pressure on Ben Gurion from Eisenhower to be more forthright. Finally, the State Department publicly disclosed on its own that Israel, with French assistance, was building a reactor, resulting in considerable embarrassment to both of the latter governments. Trying to keep at least the other half of the cat in the bag, Ben Gurion went before the Knesset on December 21, 1960, to admit that a second Israeli reactor was indeed being built, but stated that, like the first, this one was "for peaceful purposes" only.[14]

Ben Gurion's leftist opposition was enraged by the revelation, in particular by the manner in which it had been elicited. The Knesset members had not been consulted on the Dimona reactor project, and thought it odd that they had to learn about it from the U.S. State Department. Moreover, it is unlikely that Ben Gurion's new assurances about "peaceful purposes" satisfied the Eisenhower administration, which no doubt recalled the Prime Minister's solemn assurances in 1953 that Israeli troops had not attacked Kibya, and his promise in October, 1956, that Israel was not preparing to attack Egypt.

At the time—December, 1960—the President and his staff were meeting periodically with President-elect Kennedy and his staff to discuss transition matters. A background brief was prepared for the December 6 meeting, outlining the manner of discovery of the Dimona project and the Eisenhower administration's concern for its military implications and the possible Arab reaction. It was one more problem to be passed to the new administration. Kennedy termed the situation "highly distressing."[15]

EISENHOWER'S NONPOLICY ON NONPROLIFERATION (1953–1960)

It would be misleading to imply that Israel's decisions in 1957 to build Dimona, and in cooperation with the French to embark upon a nuclear weapons development program, were made in the face of a clear-cut Eisenhower administration policy against the proliferation of nuclear weapons. This was simply not the case. In fact, certain of the U.S. policies in those years on the spread of nuclear weapons and nuclear technology may have inadvertently had the effect of encouraging Israel to opt for nuclear weapons.

In December of 1953, Dwight Eisenhower launched his

Atoms for Peace campaign in a major address before the United Nations General Assembly. He called for the establishment of an international uranium stockpile to be controlled and dispensed by a new international atomic energy agency. The idea was to spread the benefits of peaceful uses of atomic energy to then nonnuclear countries, and at the same time to ensure international inspections that would limit diversion of the shared material and technology for weapons production.

There was at the time in the Eisenhower administration a kind of boyish enthusiasm that surrounded the proposal. A State Department Instruction that went out to U.S. Embassies just after the speech gushed that the President's purpose was

> . . . to make meaningful to people in every country the significance of atomic energy and research in their daily lives. . . . the task of the information program concerning the proposal is greater than any undertaken for several years past and any in prospect.[16]

In retrospect it is easy to see how naïvely inconsistent were the twin objectives of the spread of nuclear technology and the limitation of nuclear weapons proliferation. One observer recently pointed out that under Atoms for Peace, 26 American research reactors were installed in other countries, and that

> Between 1954 and 1979 some 13,456 foreign researchers have received training in the United States. Of these, some 3,532 were from nations that did not sign the 1968 Nuclear Non-Proliferation Treaty.[17]

In 1954–1956 Eisenhower compounded the ambivalence of U.S. policy on nuclear weapons by repeatedly opposing proposals (notably by Indian Prime Minister Nehru) for a nuclear test ban treaty, declaring that the United States would only accede to such an agreement in the larger context of comprehensive disarmament. In October, 1956, Eisenhower rejected a USSR proposal to stop testing with the statement that

> We must continue—until a properly safeguarded international agreement can be reached—to develop our strength in the most advanced weapons—for the sake of our own

national safety, for the sake of all free nations, for the sake of peace itself.[18]

David Ben Gurion may have been listening. Six years later, in 1962, the Prime Minister was again trying to reassure the Knesset that Israeli atomic research was being conducted for peaceful purposes only. Communist and Mapam (leftist) Knesset members had proposed a resolution that advocated the establishment of a nuclear-weapons-free zone covering Israel and the Arab states. Ben Gurion responded by recalling that his government backed the "Basic Principles" approved by the Knesset in 1959 that advocated total regional disarmament, including the abolition of all armed forces,

. . . on condition that constant and unhampered mutual control of this agreement is assured and that the borders and sovereignty of all these States are not affected.[19]

But there were other Eisenhower administration policies with respect to nuclear weapons that may have had an even more direct impact upon the Israel government. In 1956, a plan of several years' standing for the sharing with NATO allies of information about nuclear weapons use, and related troop-deployment tactics, was extended to Baghdad Pact nations. A generally selective U.S. policy toward nonproliferation was one thing, but when countries like Iraq and Pakistan—both Baghdad Pact members—were included among the select few to receive U.S. assistance, the matter began to directly touch Israeli national security interests.

In April of 1956 the Commander of U.S. Armed Forces in Europe proposed to the Pentagon that courses should be provided for Baghdad Pact military planners, covering the following subjects:

a) principles of atomic weapons (basic physics)
b) medical and psychological effects
c) weapons effects and target analysis
d) radiation and decontamination
e) ground tactics
f) air tactics[20]

In December, 1956, the JCS Joint Middle East Planning Committee recommended that the Atomic Energy Act of 1954 be amended to permit "the execution of an agreement between the Baghdad Pact powers and the United States for cooperation regarding atomic information."[21]

And less than six months later, Israel signed a secret agreement with then NATO member France, to cooperate in a program of nuclear research that would make Israel the world's sixth country to possess nuclear weapons. Even here there may have been an indirect, unintended helping hand from the Eisenhower administration. In 1958, the U.S. enraged Charles de Gaulle by opposing French acquisition of nuclear weapons while publicly acknowledging that a special nuclear relationship existed between the United States and Britain.

In this period, the late 1950's, U.S. policies on nonproliferation of nuclear weapons were selective and ineffective, but the public, stated attitude toward an Israeli weapons program was consistent—the Eisenhower administration was "agin it." In later years and other presidential administrations, however, this would change. U.S. assistance for the development of an Israeli bomb would be neither indirect nor unintended.

A COMPANY IN PENNSYLVANIA (1957–1960)

In early 1957, as the Israelis and French were negotiating their agreement, a small corporation began to do business in Apollo, Pennsylvania. The Nuclear Materials and Equipment Corporation, known as NUMEC, described itself in its public relations releases as a "leading manufacturer of nuclear materials, equipment and radio isotopes." The stated purpose of NUMEC in its articles of incorporation was to

> . . . manufacture, construct, sell, repair, deal in, and conduct research in respect to all kinds of personal property, including, but not limited to nuclear reactor fuels, controls, shielding, moderating and cladding materials, apparatus, and products.[22]

Initially, NUMEC's mix of contracts did include, among others, some private consulting, analytical work performed in its laboratories, and production of exotic materials such as uranium oxide for nearby reactors in Pennsylvania. Increasingly, however, NUMEC specialized in contracts for the processing of nuclear fuel and the reprocessing of nuclear material from other companies' scraps, left over from the production of fuel for reactors. A 1968 FBI report described how the system was supposed to work:

> [Excised]* companies are authorized by the Atomic Energy Commission (AEC) to possess and process nuclear materials and these companies draw the nuclear material needed for their manufacturing process from the AEC, Oak Ridge, Tennessee. [Excised] they then process the material into fuel to be used in reactors with most of the nuclear material used in the fuel. However, the balance of the nuclear material will be retained in scraps left over from the manufacturing process, which have to be reprocessed to recover the remaining nuclear material. [Excised] this nuclear material is normally uranium and in some cases plutonium. [Excised] that the scraps are then sent to reprocessing companies, like NUMEC, where the nuclear material is recovered and returned to AEC, Oak Ridge. [Excised] normally the reprocessing companies have 60 days to reprocess the scraps and return the recovered material to AEC or they are charged a penalty of four per cent interest.[23]

NUMEC had certain advantages in competing for the AEC and other U.S. government contracts it was awarded. All three of its founders had previously worked for AEC. Dr. Zalman Shapiro, the company's President, had worked for seven years, before forming NUMEC, in AEC's Bettis plant, operated by Westinghouse Electric Corporation. The Vice-President of the new company, Dr. Frederick Forscher, had also worked at Bettis. A third NUMEC founder, Dr. Leonard Pepkowitz, had worked for the Knolls Atomic Power Laboratory (operated by General Electric for AEC) before joining the Apollo, Pennsylvania, company.[24]

And NUMEC did prosper. Gross revenues in 1957, the first (partial) year of operation, were $27,000. The gross in 1958, the company's first full year, was $246,000, and in 1959, $800,000.

---

*The excisions in the cited report appear to have been made to protect an FBI source— "Mr. Smith said . . ."

Shapiro, interviewed by *The New York Times* in 1960, estimated $2 million in gross revenues for that year.

It was in 1960 that unusual things first began to be noticed at NUMEC. The New York Operations Office of the AEC wrote to Shapiro in October, following an inspection at the Apollo plant, that "you did not have adequate control over the nuclear material both licensed and accountable and Government-owned."[25] Thus began one of the strangest relationships between a private company and a government agency in the history of the United States—a six-year period in which hundreds of pounds of weapons-grade enriched uranium would disappear, many hundreds of thousands of dollars in fines would be paid, but the AEC would simply be unable to determine for certain whether or not a diversion to a foreign country was occurring.

IN ISRAEL: NUCLEAR DEVELOPMENT AND A DEBATE (1961)

The next year—1961—was to be an important one in the process of the nuclearization of the Middle East. In January, David Ben Gurion informed the Israeli Knesset and the rest of the world that the Dimona reactor was in fact not a textile plant or a pumping station, but "a scientific institute for research in problems of arid zones and desert flora and fauna." A new American president, John Kennedy, was not amused. In May, Kennedy and Ben Gurion met in New York at the Waldorf-Astoria Hotel. Kennedy had already written to Ben Gurion expressing his extreme concern about the Dimona project, and suggesting regular inspections by the International Atomic Energy Agency. In New York, Ben Gurion agreed to a compromise—(approximately) annual inspections by U.S. scientists at times and on terms to be determined by the Israeli Defense Ministry.

Later, Meyer Feldman, Kennedy's aide for Middle East matters, would reveal that in return for the periodic U.S. inspections, Ben Gurion had exacted a promise of provision of advanced Hawk ground-to-air missiles.[26] There is no reason to doubt Kennedy's seriousness in wanting to track Israeli nuclear research and forestall weapons development, but whether annual inspections under the terms indicated achieved this result is, as we shall see, open to question.*

In July, Israel launched a multistaged, solid fuel "weather rocket" to a height of 50 to 80 miles. Shavit II, as the missile was called, was actually the culmination of a rocket development program that had begun in the late 1950's, involving research on electronic guidance systems, studies of the upper atmosphere, and, most important, observation of French tests of a similar rocket in Saharan Algeria. Shavit II was given some publicity by the IDF, but Shavit III (launched in October) and later, longer-range versions were not.[27] Israel was working on a delivery system for nuclear warheads.

And there were other options. France agreed in 1961 to the sale of 72 Mirage III-C fighter-bombers capable of carrying nuclear weapons. Added to the extensive purchases of various versions of the Mystère jet fighter, Israeli orders of planes from France were now such an important factor in the French aircraft industry that the Israeli government began to demand that the major company involved, Dassault, contract certain of the support systems, such as jettisonable fuel tanks, for manufacture in Israel. The orders from Dassault were significant enough, in economic terms, to constitute a major balance-of-payments problem for Israel.[28]

In November, news of German scientists working in Egypt on "the Arab rocket" raised a great hue and cry. Ben Gurion personally vilified the Germans, and launched an international media campaign that assumed what one observer called "a violently anti-German tenor." Israeli intelligence had of course known about Nasser's Germans for years, and in 1954 had even managed to place an agent in Cairo posing as a German engineer, who obtained plans of the rocket's design.† The Affair of the German Scientists, as this came to be known in Israel, posed both problems and opportunities for the government:

> Ben Gurion and his team found themselves in a dilemma. The affair of the German scientists was useful in that it

* According to Jabber, op. cit., the inspections commenced shortly after the New York meeting in the spring of 1961, and occurred more or less annually thereafter until June of 1967, with the exception of 1963.

† See Chapter 5 above, concerning the exploits of Israeli spy Auraham Seidenwerg, alias Avri El-Ad.

gave good reasons for speeding up the nuclear program as the only deterrent to Nasser's preparations to annihilate Israel. On the other hand, the campaign gained a momentum which endangered the continuation of the massive German support for Israel's economy, rearmament and scientific research which, in Ben Gurion's eyes, largely outweighed whatever the German scientists were doing in Egypt.[29]

The problem was that during the public brouhaha in Israel about Egypt's Germans, the West German press revealed that Prime Minister Ben Gurion and Chancellor Konrad Adenauer had concluded a secret agreement the previous year whereby Germany agreed to supply the IDF with $80 million worth of tanks, torpedo boats, antitank guns, and fighter-bombers.*

The Affair of the German Scientists had an aura of fundamental public dishonesty about it that lingered in Israeli public life for over a year. Together with a spy scandal involving a close associate of Ben Gurion's, and the continuing controversy of the Lavon Affair, it ultimately contributed to Ben Gurion's ignominious resignation from the position of Prime Minister in June of 1963.

At the end of 1961, Israel witnessed the formation of a small anti–nuclear weapons movement, centered on the Committee for the Denuclearization of the Israeli-Arab Conflict. The organization included many prominent Israeli scholars and scientists, including two, Professor P. Olendorf of the Haifa Technion and Professor S. Sambursky of the Hebrew University of Jerusalem, who had been Commissioners of the IAEC prior to the mass resignation in 1957.[30]

The committee was a crystallization, an institutionalization of the doubts shared by many Israelis and prominent world Jewish figures about the decisions taken in 1954–1957. On the occasion of the 13th anniversary of *Ma'ariv*, a large Israeli evening daily newspaper, a symposium had been held in March, 1961. Dr. Nahum Goldmann, President of the World Zionist Organization and the World Jewish Congress, participated in the affair. Dr. Goldmann stated that atomic weapons would not improve

*The Soviet press had at the time charged collaboration between Israeli and German nuclear scientists. The Soviets were ill placed to point the finger at the Germans, for 1961 was also the year in which the Soviet-built 2,000-kilowatt reactor at Inshass in Egypt "went critical," i.e., began operations. However, it was, they would no doubt have responded, too small to produce militarily significant quantities of plutonium.

Israel's security situation, and that no country had "the moral right to produce an atomic bomb." The moderator challenged:

> Some think that once the Chinese obtain the bomb it will find its way to the Arabs.

Dr. Goldmann responded:

> According to that logic, since America has the bomb, it may find its way to Israel too.[31]

A WARNING TO NUMEC (1962)

It was in the following year, 1962, that the U.S. government began to suspect that NUMEC and its President, Dr. Zalman Shapiro, might be intentionally manipulating records to make it difficult for AEC inspectors to trace losses of "strategic nuclear materials," i.e., enriched uranium. For at least two years (1960–1962) AEC regional offices in New York and then in Oak Ridge, Tennessee, had repeatedly drawn to Shapiro's attention their concern about poor record keeping and sloppy procedures at NUMEC.[32] But what concerned the AEC—at least some people at the AEC—a great deal more were the security problems and the seemingly constant flow of alien visitors. J. A. Waters, Director of the Division of Security at the AEC, wrote in February, 1962:

> Security inspections at NUMEC have disclosed numerous security discrepancies attributable to lack of effort on the part of NUMEC management to establish and maintain an adequate and effective security program. Coupled with this is . . . an agreement with Israel under which NUMEC serves as technical consultant and training and procurement agency for Israel in the U.S.[33]

What specifically concerned the Security Division were frequent instances of "unauthorized access to classified material" at a work site (NUMEC) that received "R and D reports and a few weapons data documents" that had the "atomic weapons data stamp."[34] An AEC inspection report that year stated that if security discrepancies "continue to develop, classified weapons work may be withheld from NUMEC."[35] A letter from the office of the AEC Chairman finally warned NUMEC (i.e., Shapiro) that failure to strictly control the access of the aliens who visited the plant could amount to a violation of the espionage laws.[36]

PEACEFUL INTENTIONS (1962–1964)

In October of 1962, Israeli Foreign Minister Golda Meir addressed the United Nations General Assembly on the subject of Israel's attitude toward nuclear weapons. She said:

> Israel watches with special concern the growing nuclear arming and it is our declared policy to support every effort to remove the awful dangers to humanity arising out of the continuation of this process. Israel therefore supports every means that may limit and decrease weapons in the world.[37]

Alas, these peaceful intentions required that the Dimona reactor undergo yet another transformation. In January, 1963, Israel's Deputy Defense Minister Shimon Peres declared that the Defense Ministry—which, it will be recalled, controlled every aspect of the country's atomic development—was planning the desalination of a billion cubic meters of seawater annually, for the irrigation of the Negev Desert. This was too much for Aharon Wiener, the Director of Tahal, the Israel Water Company, who was obliged to respond that Peres's remarks were "unfounded."[38]

Several U.S. government agencies were beginning to doubt in 1963 that fresh water was all that was planned at Dimona. (The reactor was still under construction, and would go critical in 1964). In February, the Secretary of Defense drafted a memorandum for the President in which it was stated that Israel would "likely" become the world's sixth nation to possess nuclear weapons. After reviewing the reasons why most nations with the capability to produce nuclear weapons chose nevertheless not to do so (high cost, international repercussions, and so on), the memo stated:

The pressures for possession: prestige, coersive and deterrent value, and military utility, have overridden inhibitions, apart from the two superpowers, only in the case of the UK, France, almost certainly China, and probably, Israel.[39]

The next month, March, 1963, the Chairman of the Board of National Estimates at the CIA, Sherman Kent, wrote a lengthy memorandum (eight pages) to the agency's Director on the subject "Consequences of Israeli Acquisition of Nuclear Capability." For the purposes of this internal memorandum,* Kent defined "acquisition" by Israel as either (a) a detonation of a nuclear device with or without the possession of actual nuclear weapons, or (b) an announcement by Israel that it possessed nuclear weapons, even without testing. Kent's primary conclusion was that an Israeli bomb would cause "substantial damage to the U.S. and Western position in the Arab world." The memorandum was very strong and decidedly negative in its conclusions:

> Even though Israel already enjoys a clear military superiority over its Arab adversaries, singly or combined, acquisition of a nuclear capability would greatly enhance Israel's sense of security. In this circumstance, some Israelis might be inclined to adopt a moderate and conciliatory posture. . . . We believe it much more likely, however, that Israel's policy toward its neighbors would become more rather than less tough. [Israel would] seek to exploit the psychological advantages of its nuclear capability to intimidate the Arabs and to prevent them from making trouble on the frontiers.

In dealing with the United States, Kent estimated, a nuclear Israel would

> . . . make the most of the almost inevitable Arab tendency to look to the Soviet Bloc for assistance against the added

---

*It is perhaps significant that the memorandum was not drafted as a formal national intelligence estimate, which would have involved distribution to several other agencies of the government. No formal NIE was issued by CIA on the Israeli nuclear weapons program until 1968.

Israeli threat, arguing that in terms of both strength and reliability Israel was clearly the only worthwhile friend of the U.S. in the area. It would use all the means at its command to persuade the U.S. to acquiesce in, and even to support, its possession of nuclear capability.[40]

Years later, FBI inquiries at the Energy Research and Development Administration (ERDA) would retroactively point to 1963 as the year in which diversions of enriched uranium to Israel might have begun to occur from a small company near Pittsburgh, Pennsylvania. Samuel C. T. McDowell, a scientist at ERDA, was interviewed by an FBI official, who

> . . . asked what technique might be available to determine whether enriched uranium, if such can be obtained from the Israelis, could be traced to the NUMEC facility during the 1963–1965 timeframe.[41]

In Israel in 1963, the new government of Prime Minister Levi Eshkol, who succeeded David Ben Gurion, tried in its first days to assuage concerns about the country's nuclear program. The Director of the IDF's development program, Shimon Yiftak, announced in a news conference that Israel would not construct a plutonium separation plant to process the plutonium obtained at Dimona.[42] And in August, 1963, Israel signed the Nuclear Test Ban Treaty.

These were of course public statements. Less well publicized, in late 1963, was a new contract between the Defense Ministry and the Dassault aircraft company in France for development by the company and purchase by Israel of the surface-to-surface Dassault MD-620 missile. The initial contract was for $100 million. The finished missiles would cost almost $1 million each— far too much to be used effectively with conventional warheads. Deliveries were initially scheduled for 1968.[43]

Perhaps the most significant development of 1963 for the Israeli nuclear weapons program, however, occurred on November 22 on a plane flying from Dallas to Washington, D.C., Lyndon Baines Johnson was sworn in as the 36th President of the United States, following the assassination of John F. Kennedy.

In the early years of the Johnson administration the Israeli nuclear weapons program was referred to in Washington as "the delicate topic." Lyndon Johnson's White House saw no Dimona, heard no Dimona, and spoke no Dimona when the reactor went critical in early 1964. The administration was not afraid to put its foot down with the Israelis, however. When the bilateral agreement for U.S. inspection of the tiny, U.S.-supplied Nahal Soreq reactor expired, the U.S. Assistant Secretary of State for Near Eastern Affairs informed the Chargé d'Affaires of the Israeli Embassy in Washington that the extension of IAEA safeguards to the reactor "represented a firm U.S. policy position."[44]

The U.S. government did apparently send a team of scientists to Dimona in 1964, continuing the secret arrangement for annual inspections originated in 1961 by Kennedy and Ben Gurion. The visit was made, of course, at a time and to areas of the plant predetermined by the Israeli hosts. When the scientists returned to Washington, they indicated they were "reassured" that Israel was not contemplating weapons production in the near term. They had seen, they said, no sign of a plutonium separation plant.[45] There is no declassified record indicating whether the American scientists inquired about the existence of a concealed gas-centrifuge process, or if they probed to determine whether there might be another, more distant source of enriched uranium from which bombs could, in fact, more easily be made than from plutonium.

In May the State Department asked the U.S. Ambassador in Cairo to warn Nasser against proceeding with his missile development program. But the Ambassador was instructed to be careful not to convey the wrong impression:

> We particularly want you to emphasize mischievous role of UAR missile program in pushing arms rivalry to new and dangerous levels, as covered in previous guidelines. We recognize of course thin line between ensuring Nasser understands and appreciates nature of this escalation and on other hand giving him impression Israel about to go nuclear with our understanding and tacit support. We therefore leave to you best means of convincing Nasser this is game he cannot win because of Israel's technological development and access to outside financial sources.[46]

In November *The New York Times* raised the question of

safeguards at Dimona in an editorial. Trying to avoid embarrassment to the Israeli government, the State Department made no
mention of the recent inspection, and reminded the *Times* that
both Ben Gurion and Eshkol had "affirmed that Dimona [was]
to be utilized solely for peaceful purposes." A circular was sent
around the department explaining the administration's official
position on the matter. It ended with the sentence "Department
will respond to further inquiries in similar vein."[47]

In the following year, 1964, Israeli military officials participated in further testing of French nuclear devices in the Sahara.
When they were asked, the U.S. Atomic Energy Commission
declined to say whether they had detected an explosion.[48]

A MISSILE FOR THE WARHEAD
(1964–1967)

Reportedly, the Saharan exercises also included tests of a
surface-to-surface missile built jointly by the French and Israelis,
and in the ensuing months, the Israeli missile began increasingly
to look like a delivery system for "unconventional" warheads.

In March of 1965, the National Military Command Center in
the Pentagon received a three-page-long, cabled intelligence report from the U.S. Air Attaché in Tel Aviv. A "usually reliable
source," a senior Israeli military official vacationing in Israel
from a tour of duty in Paris, "having frequent contacts" with the
Attaché and his family, painted the following picture:

> Source confirmed that testing of French-designed SSM
> [surface-to-surface missile] for Israel has already begun on
> Isle de Levant. Initially "the missile had some troubles but
> appears satisfactory now." According to the source, the
> mobile SSM's will not be useful; there is no need to make
> Israel's SSM's mobile due to small topographic size of
> country and fact that enemy targets are known and fixed,
> thus Israel will concentrate on fixed launching positions.

French-Israeli collaboration was by no means limited to missile
development, extensive as that was:

> Small things produced a big picture. There are now so
> many Israeli "diplomats" in Paris, there are not enough

cigarettes in duty-free shops to supply cigarettes for all of
them. More Israelis there now than Americans. . . . Air
Force Chief Ezer Weizman must be in France. . . . Chief of
French Intelligence arriving Israel approx. 21–22 March 65
with those French aircraft. . . .

The Air Attaché commented to his headquarters that since the
25 Ouragan aircraft destined for Israel would have already transited before that date, he assumed that "those French aircraft"
referred to by his source meant the new Mirage III-B's due to
arrive soon. The Attaché did not fail to follow up on the subject
he knew most interested Air Force Headquarters:

> To counter argument that Israel's SSM would not be mate-
> rially significant with conventional warhead, source blurts
> out: "Don't worry, when we need the right kind of war-
> head, we will have it . . . and after that, there will be no
> more trouble in this part of the world." . . . To elicitor's
> worries that tension in [Middle East] increasing steadily
> and good possibility entire area could explode shortly,
> source countered: "You don't have to worry about any-
> thing before six to nine months. After that there will be
> time of peace. Israel will have something that will scare
> everybody."

The Air Attaché commented that his impression was that the
source was referring to "acquisitions in equipment" in making
this last statement. At the end of his telexed report, the Attaché
added that since returning to Israel the source had conferred "at
some significant length" with IAF Chief General Ezer Weizman,
IAF Deputy Chief Colonel "Monty" Had, Acting IDF Director
of Intelligence Colonel Carmon, Deputy Minister of Defense
Shimon Peres, and, for almost a full morning's session, Moshe
Dayan, then in temporary retirement.[49]
   The Israeli missile development program was one of the
worst-kept secrets in the Middle East. In January of 1966, *The
Times* of London (January 8) and *Aviation Week and Space
Technology* (January 17) in the United States carried articles de-
scribing the program in some detail. Nevertheless the Israeli
government continued for years to deny the existence of the
missile that emerged, in 1965–1967, from the extensive French-

Israeli collaboration. Eventually, it would be named Jericho.

To the continued frustration of the Johnson White House, the Israelis persisted in trying to mislead the administration about the matter, even in secret briefings with White House staffers. In September of 1967, some two and a half years after the Air Force Intelligence report cited above, Hal Saunders recounted for Walt Rostow such an instance, following a visit to Washington by General Ezer Weizman (who in the interim had become IDF Chief of Staff):

> As you know, we have been after the Israelis and the Egyptians since about 1964 to persuade them not to introduce more sophisticated weapons into the Middle East arms race.
>
> We decided before General Weizman came that we ought to use his visit as an occasion for continuing this dialogue. We had U.S. Ambassador to Israel Wally Barbour warn him that we wanted to hear his views on this subject, and Weizman presumably cleared his position with Eshkol before coming.
>
> In sum, his answer to our probing was that Israel is merely keeping itself in a position to go into missiles, if it has to, to counter a similar Arab move. But Weizman insisted that "nothing is imminent."[50]

Dimona had only gone critical in 1964, and had hardly begun to produce the plutonium with which Israel could, with a hidden separation plant or a gas centrifuge, produce fissionable, weapons-grade nuclear material. Nevertheless, within a few months of receiving the Air Attaché's report on the Israeli missile program, U.S. intelligence authorities had a pretty good idea where Israel might be obtaining the "stuff" to produce numerous atomic warheads—they were getting it from the United States. Specifically, they were getting it from Apollo, Pennsylvania.

DELIBERATE COLLUSION
(1965–1966)

During the first eight years of its operations, the vast majority of NUMEC's business involved U.S. government contracts, in particular the reprocessing of nuclear materials for the Atomic Energy Commission itself. During that period the AEC, which was also the nation's policeman responsible for the monitoring and security of all nuclear materials in the United States, had had to repeatedly bring to NUMEC's attention shortcomings regarding accounting, security procedures, and the handling of "strategic nuclear materials." Several of the firms that did business with NUMEC had been forced to sue the company to obtain compensation for losses occurring during this period.[51] Yet over these eight years, NUMEC continued to receive new contracts for reprocessing, from the AEC and its subsidiary organizations.

In 1962 one of those subsidiaries, Westinghouse Astro Nuclear Laboratory (WANL), had entered into a reprocessing contract with NUMEC that was to terminate on January 28, 1965. Any uranium unaccounted for, i.e., not returned to Westinghouse reprocessed or located in filters, scraps, and the like, was under the contract to be charged to NUMEC after a period of grace of 90 days following contract termination. In March, Frederick Forscher of NUMEC informed Westinghouse that his company simply did not have the uranium to return, to meet NUMEC's contractual obligations. After two months of extensions, Westinghouse informed the AEC, which sent personnel from its Oak Ridge Operations office to take inventory at the Apollo plant. It was the beginning of a long and bizarre investigation.

Over the next year, there would be numerous meetings between NUMEC and the AEC staff, and two full-scale inventories of nuclear material at the Apollo facility. Checks of filters, waste pits, and such revealed only a small fraction of the missing uranium. About 93 kilograms of enriched uranium was missing from the Westinghouse contract alone, with total losses running close to 178 kilograms. The AEC was obliged to bill NUMEC $1,134,800 for the missing material.[52]

It was difficult if not impossible for AEC inspectors to establish NUMEC's total liability because, according to the FBI investigators:

- The company had for years mixed material from different contracts, in effect robbing Peter to pay Paul, by borrowing from recently received material to meet obligations on terminating contracts.

- NUMEC's records keeping had been so bad for so long that it was difficult to reconstruct missing balances.
- A fire had somehow started in NUMEC's vaults a year earlier, destroying some records. Others had been mistakenly destroyed at about the same time in an over-zealous clean-up of the company's offices.[53]

In an AEC-NUMEC meeting held in August, 1965, Dr. Shapiro expressed confidence that the missing material would be accounted for if not recovered. He noted that in earlier years NUMEC had had to pay "up to $1 million for material losses."[54] This was apparently separate from and prior to that material unaccounted for (or MUF) which was the subject of the 1965 meetings and inventories. All told then, since 1957, NUMEC may have lost or otherwise not accounted for somewhere between 178 and 270 kilograms of enriched uranium, depending upon whether or not the previous fines were paid against the "total" loss which was finally established in the November, 1965, AEC inventory, or was part of a separate, previous accounting with AEC. Working from the AEC records of this period that have been released, it is difficult to determine just how much enriched uranium went astray.

In November of 1965, one member of the AEC inspection team, James Lovett, quit and joined the staff of NUMEC one day after the investigation fieldwork was completed. While still in the employ of the AEC, but after being hired by NUMEC, he had attended at least one commission meeting at which the NUMEC matter was apparently discussed. The Department of Justice investigated the matter and determined that it "did not warrant prosecutive action." And when, in early 1966, the AEC knew that it was dealing with the largest single instance of MUF in the history of the AEC safeguards program, the commission's general counsel, over the protest of the investigators, ordered them not to take any written statements in their investigations.[55] Another member of the AEC senior staff specifically advised the commission members against involving the FBI in an investigation of NUMEC. Finally, in the spring of 1966, after Congress's Joint Committee on Atomic Energy had asked the General Accounting Office to investigate NUMEC, and with all of the AEC's own investigations pending, the commission selected NUMEC for the largest plutonium fuel-processing contract ever given to a U.S. private firm—2,900 kilograms over three years!

What was going on here? Was the AEC, as one informed journalist has said, possibly sabotaging its own investigation?[56] And why was all this new "strategic material" being placed in NUMEC's hands while the AEC's investigations of previous MUF's were being stalled? Where was the FBI and why were NUMEC and its corporate officers not being prosecuted? The answers to these questions seem to lie in NUMEC's foreign connections.

In May of 1966, Assistant General Manager Howard Brown sent a memorandum to Chairman Glenn Seaborg and the other AEC Commissioners on the subject of NUMEC. Specifically, Brown addressed a growing worry on the part of one or two of the Commissioners: that some or all of the missing material might have been shipped overseas, possibly to Israel. Having done his own investigation of the problems at NUMEC, Brown was generally reassuring about the possibility of diversion, but he offered one small caveat:

> NUMEC has sufficient internal control on shipments which when properly implemented should, in the absence of deliberate collusion, ensure that the quantities reported on the transfer documents were those quantities shipped.
>
> As the Commission is aware, the AEC presently makes no independent verification of special nuclear material quantities shipped overseas prior to the time of the shipment. A report is in preparation which will set forth measures which the AEC may wish to institute to provide this protection.[57]

THE ISORAD CONNECTION (1964–1965)

In 1965, NUMEC had established a subsidiary corporation in Israel of which the co-owner (50–50) was the government of Israel. The company was to be known as Israeli NUMEC Isotopes and Radiation Enterprises (ISORAD) and was to experiment in the irradiation of citrus fruit and other agricultural products to inhibit spoilage. For this purpose NUMEC would supply ISORAD with cylindrical irradiation tanks, or Neutron Pacs as

NUMEC called them, containing plugs of irradiation source material such as cobalt-60.

When the AEC learned that NUMEC was negotiating with the IAEC to establish this joint venture, it contacted the Department of Justice as a matter of course to determine whether NUMEC or ISORAD or both should be registered as agents of a foreign principal under the Foreign Agents Registration Act. The Justice Department responded that since NUMEC, an American corporation, was merely doing business on its own behalf on the basis of an export license duly granted by the Department of Commerce, it did not appear to require registration.[58]

The NUMEC Neutron Pac or howitzer, as it was also called, was no doubt a viable portable unit for irradiating oranges, fruit flies, small animals, and seeds. It was also a virtually undetectable means for the illegal exportation of highly enriched uranium. Given AEC's "honor system" for foreign shipments, which depended upon end-user certificates to match quantities sent and quantities received, the NUMEC–Neutron Pac–ISORAD system was a perfect means of circumventing the Atomic Energy Act, which controlled the export of "strategic nuclear materials." All that was needed, in Howard Brown's words, was a little "deliberate collusion."

Was this the way it happened? Years later, in 1967 or 1968, the CIA monitored uranium traces around the Dimona plant in Israel and determined that a nuclear weapons program at the facility was in advanced stages. Recalling NUMEC's MUF problems and the numerous connections between NUMEC and Israel, the agency asked the FBI to undertake surveillance of Dr. Shapiro and to conduct interviews at the Apollo facility. One such interview that was declassified in 1981 contains the following passage:

> [Excised] learned that NUMEC had sustained unaccountable losses of nuclear material, and since, that this might possibly have been diverted [excised] to Israel, [excised] that about the same period of time that NUMEC sustained the unaccountable losses of U-235 [excised] advised that at least one large irradiator was manufactured, and a number of smaller units called "Howitzers" were manufactured and sent to Israel. Source was of the opinion that had U-235 or

any other nuclear material been available for shipment to Israel, it would have been a simple matter of placing large quantities of the material in these food irradiator units and shipping to Israel with no questions asked.[59]

As part of its 1968 investigation, the FBI placed a tap on Dr. Shapiro's telephone, only to discover that the man used an encoded phone device to communicate directly with the office of the Israeli Commercial Attaché at the consulate in New York City.[60] At the time, Shapiro was traveling frequently in the United States to recruit Jewish scientists to go to live and work at Dimona in Israel.*

On February 18, 1969, FBI Director J. Edgar Hoover sent to William T. Riley, the AEC's Director of Security, a detailed summary report some 56 pages in length. On the basis of its assessment of the evidence, the FBI recommended termination by the AEC of all classified contracts with NUMEC. Prosecution of Dr. Shapiro presented certain problems, however, since the Atomic Energy Act provided the death penalty for anyone who violated AEC regulations "with the intent to secure advantage to any foreign nation."[61]

It was as if a stone had been dropped into a deep well. There was no response from the AEC to the FBI for six months. In August, the AEC advised that it did not "contemplate further action in this matter at this time." That was it. Attorney General John Mitchell informed the CIA that the Justice Department was closing the case against Shapiro and NUMEC. Shapiro was, however, stripped of his security clearance.

In 1979 Joseph Hendrie, the Chairman of the Nuclear Regulatory Commission (a successor agency to the AEC), was asked whether he thought a diversion had occurred at NUMEC in the mid-1960's. His response was that circumstantial evidence "points one way, but not enough to go out and indict someone."[62]

---

*On February 5, 1967, the *Jerusalem Post* had carried an article describing a "Home-to-Dimona" call issued to "Israeli physicists working in the United States." The *Post's* source of information about the project was said to be Mr. Abraham Ben Zvi of the "Bureau for Israeli Professionals" in New York City.

SOME TENTATIVE CONCLUSIONS

In April and May of 1966, Prime Minister Levi Eshkol took a series of measures that appeared to constitute a freeze on Israel's nuclear weapons program. Professor Ernst Bergman, the hawkish Chairman of the IAEC who alone among the Commissioners had not resigned after the 1957 French-Israeli agreement was signed, was fired. The IAEC itself was entirely reformed and was transferred out from under the Ministry of Defense into the Prime Minister's office. Eshkol himself assumed the chairmanship of the new IAEC. New commission members were appointed whose backgrounds related primarily to civilian uses of nuclear energy. They came from the Israeli Electric Company, the National Water Authority, the petroleum industry, and research institutes of agriculture and medicine. On their face, the actions taken represented a clear shift from military to civilian priorities in the Israeli nuclear program.[63]

These moves occurred just before and just after Prime Minister Eshkol's statement in the Knesset on May 18, 1966, in which he promised that Israel would not be the first to introduce nuclear weapons into the region. Eshkol also said that day that Israel did not possess a nuclear weapon, and he supported the concept of mutual inspection (of Egypt and Israel) though he was not specific on how or under what aegis such inspection would take place. The Prime Minister stated that Israel supported a balance of conventional arms in the Middle East, and generally presented a picture of an Israel that would in the near future rely on conventional deterrents. And the next day, May 19, his government announced an agreement with the United States that would supply Israel with significant numbers of A-4 Skyhawk planes and Sherman tanks—the first major agreement for U.S. arms supplies in the history of the State of Israel.[64] In fact, the agreement exceeded in dollar value the cumulative total of all U.S. arms supplied to Israel in the period 1948–1965.

The standard interpretation of these statements and actions is that Eshkol was genuinely departing from Ben Gurion's previous policy of actively seeking the nuclear option, partially in response to a substantial offer from the Johnson administration of sufficient conventional arms to ensure Israel's security at a time when the Russians were furiously supplying the Egyptians.[65] Eshkol did say in his speech to the Knesset that his government reserved the right to continue research and training at Dimona, but the atomic bomb development program had been terminated. A corollary of this conventional wisdom is that, since Israel had not constructed a plutonium separation plant at Dimona, she could not, prior to the 1967 war, have reached the stage of being able to assemble bombs for her Mirages or warheads for her Jericho (i.e., Dassault) missiles.

The other, stronger possibility is that the Israeli Defense Ministry had already, in mid-1966, both the elements needed to construct a nuclear weapon and the planes and/or rockets to deliver it to a target. Prime Minister Eshkol might have been permitted the largesse of forswearing nuclear weapons because Israel already had one, or at least the "last wire" capability to assemble one in a short time, if it was needed. It is a safe assumption that Israel had nuclear weapons and the ability to deliver them at the beginning of the Six-Day War in 1967. The ingredients were there, hence the bomb was ready.

Looking at the first 20 years of Israel's history, there is simply no factual basis upon which to presume discretion or restraint in matters of military development. None. Within about 25 minutes of the time Israel could have developed an atomic weapon, Israel did develop an atomic weapon.

True, the CIA had not yet detected the traces of enriched uranium that led the agency in 1968 to request an FBI investigation of Shapiro and NUMEC. But then the CIA had no reason to monitor for such a program in Israel, as all AEC investigations of the NUMEC-ISORAD connection in 1965–1966 had blandly concluded that no diversions of weapons-grade material could be proven or had likely occurred. There were also periodic reassuring statements by the AEC officials who were permitted, in 1961, 1962, 1964, 1965, 1966, and 1967, to inspect Dimona, or at least that part of it which the Israelis wished them to see.

In 1965 and 1966, the conclusions of the AEC engineers who participated in these "secret" inspections were somehow leaked to the press. In March, 1965, an article appeared on the front page of *The New York Times* that concluded:

> On the basis of the inspections, American officials have come to the tentative conclusion that Israel is not now

using the relatively large research reactor for the production of plutonium for atomic weapons.[66]

And 15 months later in the same newspaper, another article appeared:

> The United States has quietly re-inspected a closely guarded Israeli atomic power plant and affirmed its tentative conclusion that the plant was not being used for making atomic weapons.
>
> The inspection, which took place recently, was the third by Atomic Energy Commission engineers to the Dimona plant in the Negev near Beersheba.[67]

The author of these pieces, John W. Finney, was apparently unaware of the U.S. "visits" to Dimona that had occurred in 1961 and 1962 at the urging of then President John F. Kennedy. Finney wrote similar articles in July of 1967 ("U.S. officials have no indication that the reactor is being used for anything besides civilian research into atomic power technology"[68]) and again in January of 1969 ("The American officials also do not believe that the Israeli Government . . . has made a decision to build an atomic bomb"[69]). Finney seemed over this entire period to have remarkable access to AEC officials on a very sensitive subject, and to rely on them heavily, to the exclusion of a great deal of evidence that might have pointed, at least circumstantially, to an Israeli nuclear weapons program in a very advanced stage indeed, even before the Six-Day War.*

In fact, an enterprising reporter in mid-1967 might have discovered quite a bit of circumstantial evidence indicating who Israel's silent partner was in developing the "Jewish" bomb:

1. In the late 1940's and early 1950's financial support was provided to the Weizmann Institute on defense-related projects by the U.S. Defense Department and the National Institutes of Health.
2. All three of NUMEC's founding corporate officers had

---

*John Finney was also the first U.S. journalist to write about the NUMEC investigation, though without naming the company. On September 18, 1966, an article by Finney appeared in *The New York Times* disclosing the discovery by an AEC official that strategic nuclear materials had been "lost" by a "fuel fabricating concern in the vicinity of Pittsburgh." Finney's AEC sources, usually very forthcoming, would not reveal the name of the company, however.

worked for AEC-funded and -operated laboratories, just prior to NUMEC's incorporation. Several members of NUMEC's original Board of Directors had had previous experience in classified AEC-funded projects.

3. NUMEC's first major contract, the one that established its commercial viability and first provided access to large amounts of weapons-grade strategic material, came from the AEC. During 1961–1966 a high percentage of the strategic material in NUMEC's possession came directly from the AEC.

4. And yet, during this same period, 1961–1966, the AEC's own field inspection reports raised numerous questions about NUMEC's poor record keeping, violations of health standards, sloppy materials-handling procedures, and inadequate security arrangements for safeguarding classified documents and procedures from foreign visitors.

5. No FBI investigation (in fact, no formal AEC Security Division investigation) occurred in 1966, when there was already substantial evidence of violation of the Atomic Energy Act by NUMEC personnel.

6. In the midst of all of the above, in 1966, NUMEC was awarded the largest contract for plutonium processing ever given by the U.S. government to a private firm.

7. In the midst of all of the above, James Lovett of the AEC inspection staff left the government and joined NUMEC. Before leaving, however, and while already employed by NUMEC, he attended meetings in which NUMEC matters were discussed.

8. In spite of all of the above, combined with detailed U.S. intelligence about the Dimona reactor and the Israeli-French SSM (surface-to-surface missile) project, no formal national intelligence estimate had been done on the Israeli nuclear weapons program, thus avoiding interagency circulation of such an estimate, and the leaks and questions re U.S. government involvement that an NIE might have caused.

9. No reference was apparently made, in any of the informal secret briefings to Finney by the AEC "inspectors" of the Dimona reactor, to the NUMEC-ISORAD connection. Instead, there was a curious preoccupation with the irrelevant question of the evidence for and against a plutonium separation plant.

As of this writing the case has not been conclusively made for a diversion of enriched uranium to Israel from NUMEC. Nor can such a case be made on the basis of the AEC, FBI, and CIA documents that have been declassified to date.* In fact, there may never be such evidence, given the unbelievably naïve and superficial system the AEC maintained, in 1963–1966, for checking shipments to foreign contractors. There simply is no paper trail to follow. Hence the CIA's inquiries in 1976 at ERDA (one of the AEC's successor agencies) to determine if technical means existed to compare the uranium tracings detected in Israel in 1967–1968 with mass spectrometer data from the NUMEC materials produced in 1963–1965, when the diversion likely took place.

One thing is certain: if the case is eventually made, then the revealed record will leave little doubt that the AEC played a direct role in facilitating the diversion. The circumstantial evidence for that conclusion already is flat and overwhelming.

In August of 1966 the Joint Committee on Atomic Energy of the U.S. Congress held hearings on "uranium enrichment services criteria and related matters." One of the people to testify at these hearings was Dr. Zalman Shapiro. Time limitations prevented Dr. Shapiro from responding to all of the committee's questions, so certain of them were submitted in writing, and these, together with Dr. Shapiro's responses, were included in the written report on the hearings. Among the questions and answers included in that record:

Q. Do you believe that AEC's licensees are currently maintaining records and other controls pertaining to special nuclear material which are adequate for the purpose of safeguarding against diversion of such material to unauthorized uses?

A. We believe that, by and large, the records and other controls maintained by AEC's licensees are, and have been, effective in safeguarding against the diversion of special nuclear material to unauthorized purposes.[70]

By and large, it was an honest answer.

---

*In mid-1983, the FBI was preparing to release, under the Freedom of Information Act, over 200 pages of reports and summary reports on their 1962–1967 Shapiro-NUMEC investigations.

—8—

America Chooses Sides

A U.S. POLICY THAT HELPED, or at least permitted, Israel to build atomic devices from enriched uranium stolen in the United States appears implausible until one examines other strange dimensions in U.S.-Israeli relations in the mid-1960's. Between 1964 and 1967, the Johnson administration found the parameters of U.S. public support for Israel's security and territorial integrity to be too confining, and a new, unprecedented, covert military-security relationship was forged, of which the assistance to Israel's nuclear weapons program was only one aspect.

In a period in which the Johnson White House was becoming increasingly obsessed with the war in Vietnam, Israel's military leaders offered to impose stability upon the peoples and countries of the Middle East—it was to be a "Pax Hebraeca." There were, of course, costs involved for America. The United States would have to take the initial steps toward becoming what three previous Presidents had said we never would be—Israel's major arms supplier. We would also at least temporarily forfeit our role as primary mediator of the multifaceted Arab-Israeli dispute. The new arrangement would necessitate throwing our long-standing nuclear nonproliferation policy to the winds, the 1968 treaty to the contrary notwithstanding. Perhaps most important, U.S. national security interests in the region would become merged with Israel's to a degree that was, and is to this day, unique in the history of U.S. foreign relations. Inevitably, this new relationship would involve the U.S. directly—operationally—in the Six-Day War of 1967. But I am getting ahead of my story.

THE "KENNEDY DOCTRINE"

In December of 1962, Israeli Foreign Minister Golda Meir traveled to Palm Beach, Florida, to meet with President John Kennedy. It was a 70-minute, candid exchange of views on which a lengthy (eight-page) memorandum of conversation was later done by Phillips Talbot, Assistant Secretary of State for Near Eastern Affairs. Mrs. Meir spoke to the President of "an identity in the kind of developments the U.S. and Israel would like to see in the Middle East." She carefully reviewed each bilateral relationship her country had with neighboring Arab states, explaining the Israeli position on individual disputes. Frequently, she returned to the theme of Israel's vulnerability in the face of Arab hatred, Russian weapons, and Nasser's new missiles built "with German help."

Kennedy then delineated the depth, and the limitations, of America's relationship with Israel as he saw it:

> The United States, the President said, has a special relationship with Israel in the Middle East really comparable only to that which it has with Britain over a wide range of world affairs. But for us to play properly the role we are called upon to play, we cannot afford the luxury of identifying Israel—or Pakistan, or certain other countries—as our exclusive friends. . . .

The best way for the United States to effectively serve Israel's national security interests, Kennedy said, was maintain and develop America's associations with the other nations of the region. Our influence could then be brought to bear as needed in particular disputes to ensure that Israel's essential interests were not compromised. "If we pulled out of the Arab Middle East and maintained our ties only with Israel this would not be in Israel's interest," Kennedy said.

The President then discussed specific issues in which direct Israeli action made it difficult for the United States to both maintain good relations with the Arabs and also support Israel: diversion of the Jordan River waters, retaliation raids in border areas, and the continuing Palestinian refugee problem. These matters, together with U.S. sale to Israel of advanced Hawk missiles, were putting severe strains upon American relations with the Arab countries. There would of necessity be differences, Kennedy said, between the U.S. and Israeli approaches on certain matters. For example, he felt that greater use should be made of the UN in dealing with border problems, whereas "Israel probably thinks that the UN actions are too slow."

The President then pointed out to Mrs. Meir the distinction between U.S. and Israeli national security interests. They were not always the same.

> We know that Israel faces enormous security problems but we do too. We came almost to a direct confrontation with the Soviet Union last spring and again recently in Cuba. . . . Because we have taken on wide security responsibilities we always have the potential of becoming involved in a major crisis not of our own making, e.g. in the event of a coup in Iran or of the Sino-Indian affair. Our security problems are, therefore, just as great as Israel's. We have to concern ourself with the whole Middle East.

Mrs. Meir could read between the lines. Kennedy was not really thinking of Iran or India. He continued:

> We would like Israeli recognition that this partnership which we have with it produces strains for the United States in the Middle East. . . . when Israel takes such actions as it did last spring, whether right or wrong, those actions involve not just Israel but also the United States.

The President was referring to a large-scale retaliation raid into Syria about which the Soviets had been extremely concerned, and for which Israel had been condemned by the UN Security Council.

Kennedy repeatedly assured Mrs. Meir of America's commitment to Israel's security and prosperity, but he asked in return that Israel should consider the interests of the United States. "Our relationship," he said, "is a two-way street."[1]

It was a remarkable exchange, and the last time for many, many years in which an American president precisely distinguished for the government of Israel the differences between U.S. and Israeli national security interests.

John Kennedy's Middle East policy was activist on the matter of the resolution of the basic issues dividing Arab and Jew, as he had promised in the 1960 presidential campaign. He sought to involve the United States with both sides at once. Agreeing with Israeli concerns about Soviet rearmament of the United Arab Republic (and hoping to check the Israeli nuclear weapons program), he initiated the sale of Hawk missiles to Israel. Concurrently aid to the UAR, particularly food aid, was greatly expanded. The Kennedy administration quickly accorded diplomatic recognition to the UAR-backed Republican regime in Yemen, but he also brought constant pressure to bear on Nasser to withdraw Egyptian troops from that country. With the UAR as with Israel, Kennedy wanted relations with the United States to be a "two-way street."

Shortly after assuming office, Kennedy addressed letters to the Arab heads of state, seeking to determine how the United States could involve itself in each country's disputes with Israel. He was disappointed in the essentially negative responses he received to these letters, but he kept pushing American diplomats into the region with proposals for conflict resolution, particularly on the Palestinian refugee problem. In all of this, as one Israeli writer has noted, he proceeded from a basic understanding and sympathy for both the Jewish and the Arab national liberation movements, and from a profound inner conviction that the Arab-Israeli conflict *could* be solved.

> While searching for a solution, Kennedy understood that the first and foremost thing was "to make it crystal clear that the U.S. meant what it said in the Tripartite Declaration of 1950—that we will act promptly and decisively against any nation in the Middle East which attacks its neighbor."[2]

The other essential tenets of the "Kennedy Doctrine" were an international effort to halt the arms race in the region, combined with "the realization that if this is not accomplished, we shall not permit an imbalance to exist which threatens the right of any country to self-defense."[3]

American Middle East policy during the Kennedy administration was more interventionist, more oriented toward crisis prevention than it had been in previous administrations. But in its essentials, it was not fundamentally different from Truman's warm diplomatic support of Israel combined with a strict arms embargo of the region, nor from Eisenhower's balanced insistence upon Israel's right of passage in the Strait of Tiran on the one hand, and Israeli withdrawal from Egyptian territory captured in the Suez War on the other. All three Presidents based their Middle East policies on the Tripartite Declaration of 1950.

There were of course differences. Kennedy, for example, did not share Eisenhower's preoccupation with pacts and regional defense organizations as a means of halting Soviet "penetration" of the Middle East. Resolution of the Arab-Israeli conflict would itself, he felt, achieve this goal.*

In a practical sense, Israel's security through the early years of its existence rested upon the Tripartite Declaration, for it had no legal borders. The armistice agreements of 1949 merely created armistice lines between Israel and its neighboring states, and froze the concerned parties in a technical state of war. With the Tripartite Declaration, however, the United States, Britain, and France made themselves guarantors of the armistice agreements and most particularly of the territorial integrity of the states party to those agreements, as defined by the armistice lines.[4]

The Tripartite Declaration of 1950, which had nearly succumbed during the Suez War, died finally in November, 1963, at the Parkland Hospital in Dallas, Texas. Lyndon Johnson's presidency would bring a fundamental turning point in U.S.-Israeli relations.

LYNDON JOHNSON: A MORE "RESPONSIVE" PRESIDENT

John Kennedy's assassination occurred during one of those cyclical depressions in U.S.-Israeli relations that he himself had

*In August of 1961, Kennedy even told Amos Elon, Washington correspondent of the Israeli daily *Haaretz* that he would be pleased to see a neutralist Israel, in terms of the East-West conflict, if this would lead to improved relations with the Soviet Union, and through the Soviets, to improved relations between Israel and the Arab world. The interview with Elon, which was apparently off the record, was not published until after Kennedy's death. (*Haaretz*, November 24, 1963.) Had John Foster Dulles known that a sitting American president was saying such things to an Israeli journalist, he might well have had cardiac arrest.

forecast in his 1962 meeting with Golda Meir. The point of difference in November, 1963, happened to be U.S. sponsorship of a resolution in the UN General Assembly that provided a formula for resolution of the Palestinian refugee problem. Israel much preferred to deal with each Arab country individually on the matter of refugees, without the intercession of the UN, because in direct negotiations Israel could support her positions with force, whereas the Arab country concerned could not. For this reason among others, every Arab government involved had vehemently opposed direct negotiations, leaving the matter at an impasse, which of course was exactly where the Israeli government wanted it left.

The U.S. Embassy in Tel Aviv informed the State Department:

> The assassination of President Kennedy caught the Israeli press protest campaign against the U.S. refugee resolution at the UNGA in midstream. Articles and editorials immediately became eulogies of the late President.[5]

The Israeli press was by contrast unreservedly enthusiastic about the prospect of a Johnson presidency. *Omer,* the periodical of the Histadrut, the major Israeli labor federation, anticipated expanded and deepened relations with the United States in the new administration. A number of Israeli newspapers, the U.S. Embassy noted,

> . . . suggested that President Johnson might be more responsive than his predecessor to appeals from sympathizers of Israel in the U.S., particularly now, with the 1964 elections approaching; HERUT and HABOKER [major Israeli dailies] called for stepped-up efforts to mobilize these sympathizers.[6]

Another major Israeli paper, *Yediot Ahoronot,* noted that Lyndon Johnson would have to overcome what it felt was State Department anti-Israel bias ("U.S. policy in the Middle East is laid down by the U.S. Department of State in accordance with what suits U.S. interests as interpreted by the Department"). Under Lyndon Johnson however, *Yediot* felt, the issue of "U.S. interests" would not be so much of an impediment as it had been previously:

But there is no doubt that, with the accession of Lyndon Johnson, we shall have more opportunity to approach the President directly if we should feel that U.S. policy militates against our vital interests.[7]

In Washington, the American Israel Public Affairs Committee, the central Israeli lobby, agreed with these assessments. On November 26, 1963, AIPAC's director, I. L. Kenen, sent a memo to his executive and national committees ("Not for Publication or Circulation") hailing what it described as Lyndon Johnson's "front-rank pro-Israel position" on a number of recent issues, including the Eisenhower administration's withholding of U.S. aid during the 1953 Jordan River diversion dispute and threat of sanctions following Israel's refusal to withdraw from the Sinai in 1956–1957, and the 1959 Morse Amendment to the foreign aid bill, which would have eliminated aid to countries (such as Israel) that discriminated against the Americans on the basis of race or religion.

AIPAC's and the Israeli press's assessment of the likely change in U.S. Middle East policy was soon confirmed by another source—Gamal Abdel Nasser. The CIA country station in Cairo reported to headquarters in March of 1964 that Nasser had informed Assistant Secretary of State Phillips Talbot that "the U.S. had shifted its policy into more active support of Israel."[8]

Over the next few years—the first three years of the Johnson administration—that support would change both qualitatively and quantitatively. U.S. government assistance to Israel in FY 1964, the last budget year of the Kennedy administration, stood at $40 million. This was substantially reduced from the levels of assistance in previous years. In FY 1965, this figure rose to $71 million, and in FY 1966, to $130 million. More significant, however, was the change in the composition of that assistance. In FY 1964, virtually none of the official U.S. assistance for Israel was military assistance; it was split almost equally between development loans and food assistance under the PL 480 program. In FY 1965, however, 20 percent of U.S. aid was military in nature, and in FY 1966, fully 71 percent of all official assistance to Israel came in the form of credits for purchase of military equipment.

Moreover, the nature of the weapons systems we provided

had changed. In FY 1963, the Kennedy administration agreed to sell five batteries of Hawk missiles valued at $21.5 million. This however was an air defense system. The Johnson administration, in FY 1965–1966, provided Israel with 250 modern (modified M-48) tanks, 48 A-1 Skyhawk attack aircraft, communications and electronics equipment, artillery, and recoilless rifles. Given the configuration of the IDF (discussed in Chapter 6), these were anything but defensive weapons. The $92 million in military assistance provided in FY 1966 was greater than the total of all official military aid provided to Israel, cumulatively, in all the years going back to the foundation of that nation in 1948.[9]

By the end of calendar 1965, the Tripartite Declaration of 1950 was effectively dead, buried, and forgotten . . . at least as an element of United States policy toward the countries of the Middle East.

The totals of Israel's arms purchases from France in this period were still far greater than those from the United States, and the French only sold arms on a cash basis. The United States provided loans to Israel for arms sales, often at concessionary rates. Not surprisingly, then, in spite of the largesse of the Johnson administration, Israel refused to provide information about hard-currency obligations for acquisition of the French equipment, leading U.S. Ambassador Walworth Barbour in Tel Aviv to plead with Secretary of State Dean Rusk to try to pry this information from Prime Minister Eshkol during the latter's May, 1964, visit to Washington.[10] Israel's assumed posture of vulnerability vis-à-vis her Arab neighbors was much easier to take while the Johnson White House was being kept in the dark about the "French connection." And the Israeli government understandably did not want to purchase from the French what it could obtain on a concessionary basis from the United States.*

Israel's heavy foreign arms purchases could not forever be paid from donations, i.e., from Zionist fund-raising in the United States and Europe, and from German reparations. The

---

*Arms purchases for hard currency constituted a considerable burden for Israel in 1960–1965—11.3 percent of GNP. Israel's economy was strong during this period, with an annual GNP growth rate of 10.7 percent. But her economy was also heavily leveraged: the debt of the Israeli central government amounted to a staggering 65 percent of GNP. (U.S. Agency for International Development tables prepared for President Zalman Shazar's visit to Washington in August, 1966.)

latter were in any event scheduled to terminate in 1965. In an effort to boost export earnings, Israel began in the mid-1960s to develop markets for what would eventually become the largest single sector in her economy—arms sales.

One of the first indications that the Johnson administration had of this new enterprise came, not from the Israelis themselves, but from the American Embassy in Port-au-Prince, Haiti. In late June of 1964, a group of rebels apparently trained in the neighboring Dominican Republic were put ashore during the night, near Saltron, Haiti. Their intent was to overthrow the regime of President for Life "Papa Doc" Duvalier. The position of the U.S. government in this matter was neutral, more or less. In the following month, the Secretary of State cabled the U.S. Ambassador in Santo Domingo, Dominican Republic:

> We are naturally repulsed by unconfirmed reports of atrocities committed by the Duvalier regime. But our policy is to avoid intervention in Haiti's internal affairs. [The U.S. government] did not finance or otherwise aid rebels. . . . In our opinion it would not be in interests of [the government of the Dominican Republic] to become involved in rebel activities in Haiti.[11]

Thus, a mildly dissatisfied U.S. government refused, when asked by the Duvalier government, to license the export from the United States of small arms and replacement parts for Haiti's aging T-28 trainer planes.[12]

The government of Israel, however, was apparently less repulsed by the reports of Papa Doc's atrocities, and arranged to covertly send from Israel *through the United States* some $800,000 in small arms in cases labeled "shoe manufacturing material and spare parts." The deal, according to a "Confidential" telegram from the U.S. Ambassador in Port-au-Prince to Secretary Rusk, was arranged by Nathan Abramowitz, "former honorary Haitian consul in Israel," and was carried off by a Sidney Shine and a gentleman by the name of Stern (first name unknown) "of Miami and New York." Shine had previously arranged for the shipment of the T-28 spares, presumably in a similar fashion.[13]

A MILITANT ZION

If Israel's military involvements were worldwide in scope by 1964–1967, they were nonetheless concentrated in the Middle East, and there the image that Israel projected was far from that of the supplicating, threatened, vulnerable small state that was shown at Zionist fund-raisers in New York.

In September of 1963, Deputy Minister of Defense Shimon Peres addressed the Knesset following the resignation of David Ben Gurion. Like Moshe Dayan, Peres was less than pleased to see the moderate Levi Eshkol succeed Ben Gurion, and a situation developed not unlike that which had existed a decade earlier during Moshe Sharett's administration. Peres's Knesset speech painted a hellfire and brimstone picture of the Arab hostility surrounding Israel, and the steps that he thought needed to be taken to meet this threat.

National unity and the friendship of other nations was important, Peres said, but this alone would not ensure the security of Israel in a region being flooded with Russian weapons. Nor would defensive weapons ("one-dimensional help") suffice, such as the Hawk missile systems provided by the Kennedy Administration. Independent strength was the answer, produced by a combination of fund-raising in the Diaspora and arms purchases in Europe. Even in September of 1963, Peres said, Israel was well along this road.

> I do not believe that our main duty is to impress a world public opinion that there is an eventuality that Israel can be destroyed. Such talk has a negative effect. . . . I would prefer that we emphasize the other danger, no less unfortunate, of the threat to peace in the Middle East. We are capable of scoring a victory in war, and we are doing what we can to ensure our ability to do so in the future, under new conditions.[14]

A leading Israeli journalist of the time, Simha Flaphan, wrote a long, thoughtful article using Peres's speech to describe what was happening to the IDF and what he thought would be the long-term implications for Israel. For while Peres did not at

the time speak for the Mapai party, he did fairly represent the
attitudes of Israel's "defense" establishment. Flaphan said:

> The acquisition of arms, more arms and better arms, from
> whatever source, at whatever price, whatever the implica-
> tions, are the alpha and omega of the theory Israel's Dep-
> uty Prime Minister advocates.

Flaphan did not disagree with the need to develop an IDF sufficiently strong to deter Arab aggression but there were, he said,
two concepts of deterrence: a defense-oriented army capable of
protecting the homeland, and a strike force designed for "preventive war," i.e., for a first strike:

> These two concepts involve completely different implica-
> tions. The first calls for a combination of political and mili-
> tary strategy in which the political is predominant and in
> which the military means are organized for defense (and
> counteroffense when necessary). The second concept leads
> to the domination of military over political considerations
> and the overwhelming predominance of offensive weapons
> in the military sphere. The first implies an avoidance of mil-
> itary conflict and attempts to localize clashes and to relax
> tension, while the second utilizes local clashes in order to
> increase tension and seeks opportunities to deliver a
> "crushing blow."

Indirectly, Flaphan foretold what this renewed commitment to
belligerence would mean for Israel's allies—notably for the
United States—in the coming years. Peres's definition of "deterrence" meant the fostering of alliances with countries prepared
"to undertake common action" against Israel's enemies, as opposed to seeking out countries willing and able to cultivate
friendship with Arabs and thus able to mediate the basic conflict. There were implications for domestic politics as well:

> Armaments have become a substitute for foreign policy and
> instead of being a means of defense have become an end in
> themselves to which all other aspects—economic, political
> and international—must be subservient. This is the funda-
> mental error of Mr. Peres' approach, and from this fallacy

he goes on from error to error, misstating certain facts, ignoring others, in order to make reality fit his theory.[15]

I have quoted extensively from Flaphan's analysis because Peres's "strike force" concept of deterrence, so deftly described therein, contributed in 1965 to the split-off of the militarist faction of the Mapai party, resulting in the formation of the Rafi party. The leading figures in this movement—Ben Gurion, Dayan, and Peres—used the platform of Rafi to vilify Prime Minister Eshkol, accusing him of "selling out" Israel's security when, for instance, he advocated reining in the country's nuclear weapons program. (See Chapter 7.) When, in the early days of June, 1967, Eshkol bowed to public pressure and appointed Moshe Dayan Minister of Defense, "preventive war" was inevitable. Years later, the Rafi faction merged again with Mapai, but the defense and foreign policies described above predominated in the resulting Israel Labor party coalition. And when, in 1977, Menahem Begin formed Israel's seventh government, the spirit of Rafi was merged with the spirit of the Irgun, and the "strike force" concept of national security was doctrine, as it is to this day.

In 1964 and 1965, Israel applied her military superiority over neighboring Arab states in practical ways. In early 1964 a major national conduit to carry the waters of Lake Tiberias to the Negev was completed. Sustained pumping began in the summer. The Arab states had long since said they would oppose by force such a unilateral diversion, but these were empty threats, as they had not the military strength to intervene. When Syria began a diversion project near B'not Yaakov (some three kilometers inside its borders) in March, 1965, however, Israel immediately fired on the project with artillery and tanks.[16]

Secretary of State Rusk had asked Ambassador Barbour in Tel Aviv to intercede with the Israelis to prevent military action against the Syrian diversion project, and had even threatened "application of U.S. economic pressures and action in the UN" in the event.[17] But Lyndon Johnson was not Dwight Eisenhower, and the Israelis knew it. When the Israelis attacked, U.S. Consul General Evan Wilson in Jerusalem reported:

Many informed observers ruddering [wondering?] at what point humiliation caused Syrians by failure reply in kind to repeated Israeli attacks may overcome restraint based so far on appreciation realities of military power.[18]

Simha Flaphan, it will be recalled, described such tactics by the IDF as "local clashes in order to increase tension."

Another area of practical application of IDF force involved the control of the demilitarized zones between Israel and Syria—again, a dispute with a long history. In July of 1964, however, the U.S. Consulate in Jerusalem reported that brute force was beginning to carry the day.

> Arabs concerned selves basically with preservation situation envisioned in [the UN armistice agreements] while Israel consistently sought gain full control. Even this aspect struggle visibly cooling during past eight years, with Israel emerging victorious largely because UN never able oppose aggressive and armed Israeli occupation and assertion actual control over such areas, and Arab neighbors not really prepared for required fighting. If end justifies means, Israel's reliance on force and threat using it seemed proving successful.

The report continued:

> Most UN observers accord certain amount credit to Syrians for restraint over long period in face Israel seizure control in [the demilitarized zones] by force or constant threat using it. They believe frequently expressed Syrian disappointment at failure UNTSO effectively restrain Israeli inroads in [demilitarized zones] being translated into action against Israel by low-level Syrian military. . . . they fear escalation and spread because no change Israel pressures discernible.[19]

Simha Flaphan had said the IDF, in addition to endeavoring to increase tension, would seek "opportunities to deliver a 'crushing blow.'" The opportunity was to come soon.

PREPARING THE BLITZ

The third major Middle East war was inevitable from around 1965 until it occurred in June of 1967, and the outcome of that war was absolutely certain. What of Arab unity? It was formally proclaimed in an intergovernmental statement, it is true, in April, 1963. William Brubeck, White House Executive Secretary, summarized U.S. intelligence estimates on the matter for McGeorge Bundy a month later:

True Arab unity will not be achieved for many years, if then. . . . this federation would not detract from Israel's military superiority over the Arabs.[20]

Israeli military might was not a secret to the Arabs. The June 9, 1964, CIA "Trends in the World Situation Report" stated:

[The Arabs] continue to recognize the danger of forceful action against the Israelis. They respect Israeli military power, and some at least realize that the West would prevent them from destroying Israel, even if they could.

And what about the dangerous Egyptian-German missile program? In 1964, Acting Secretary of State George Ball prepared a background memorandum for the President in connection with the upcoming visit to Washington of Prime Minister Eshkol, in which he addressed this subject:

Our assessment is that Israel will continue to enjoy its present military superiority over the Arabs for the next several years. Despite exaggerated Israeli claims for the foreseeable future, the U.A.R. missile capability will remain primarily a psychological threat and the U.A.R. nuclear capability nil.

Ball urged President Johnson to press Prime Minister Eshkol "to prevent stimulation of the Near East arms race by Israeli acquisition of missiles or nuclear weapons."[21]

But Israel was preparing these and other forms of escalation.

In May of 1965, Ambassador Avraham Harman in a meeting at the State Department asked for early delivery of the M-48 tanks. At the time, Israel was moving tanks into the Israel-Syrian demilitarized zone with impunity, and was repeatedly firing upon Syrian civilian irrigation projects, trying to goad the Syrian Army into war. Assistant Secretary of State Phillips Talbot described the situation as "explosive," and reminded Ambassador Harman of the United States' opposition to "the use of force on the water issue." It seemed a bit odd for Israel to be asking for early delivery of more tanks when they were countering U.S. policy and endangering Middle East peace with the ones they had. The meeting ended on a cool note.[22]

The next month, June of 1965, the undaunted Ambassador Harman asked the State Department for authorization to purchase F-4 Phantom aircraft, which were far superior at the time to anything the Russians had, let alone anything they had supplied to the Arabs. The F-4 had been operational for less than a year at the time of the request, and would in 1965 have constituted a quantum escalation of the Middle East arms race. The answer to the Israeli request was no, but as we shall see, when the time came, the Israelis were not only given their Phantoms, but U.S. pilots to fly them as well.

During 1966, the White House and the National Security Council followed Israel's "security position" very closely. Several U.S. intelligence analyses at the time indicated that Israel's armed strength was superior to that of the Arabs combined, and the Joint Chiefs' assessment was that relatively, the Israeli position was improving.[23]

By April of 1967, Israeli strength had grown to the point that they could flaunt it in the Arabs' faces. A planned celebration in Jerusalem of Israeli Independence Day was to include a huge military parade, prominently featuring the newly arrived American tanks and other equipment. The display seemed designed to arouse Arab anger against the United States, and Secretary of State Rusk made a point of instructing the U.S. Ambassador in Tel Aviv, Walworth Barbour, not to attend the ceremonies.[24]

THE WITHDRAWAL OF THE UNEF:
A CEREMONIAL MATING DANCE

In early 1967, both Israel and the UAR accused each other of troop buildups on the Syrian border. Like brightly plumed birds strutting on a breeding ground, Gamal Abdel Nasser and various Israeli government representatives described in lurid detail the threatening moves being made by the other side, and warned of the dire consequences for peace in the region. One curious aspect of this display was that it was pure fabrication on both sides.* UN Secretary-General U Thant reported to the Security Council on May 19:

> Reports from UNTSO Observers have confirmed the absence of troop concentrations and significant troop movements on both sides of the line.

In his speech U Thant also attributed to "high Israeli officials" statements "so threatening as to be particularly inflammatory." Neither Nasser nor any of the "front-line" Arab leaders could continue to back away from such verbal attacks, whether the troop concentrations were there or not. And finally, on May 16, Nasser reacted. The Egyptian Chief of Staff requested the withdrawal of the United Nations Emergency Force (UNEF) contingent separating Israeli and Egyptian troops along their common border, including the fortifications at Sharm al-Sheikh overlooking the Strait of Tiran. Within hours of this request, Nasser had confirmed his intention to close the strait to Israeli shipping (a violation of the 1957 agreement under which Israel withdrew from the Sinai) and U Thant had confirmed that he would comply with the Egyptian request, and withdraw the UNEF. The stage was set for the "crushing blow."

In the days and weeks that followed, Israeli and American leaders termed Nasser's actions "acts of war" and U Thant was characterized as a weak international bureaucrat who had acted

---

*Randolph S. and Winston S. Churchill, in *The Six Day War* (Boston: Houghton Mifflin Company, 1967), maintain (p. 28) that the Russians precipitated the crisis by lying to Nasser about the Israeli troop concentrations. The Churchills do not reveal who might have lied to the Israelis.

too hastily in agreeing to remove the UN troops. Strangely, no
one seemed to notice the section in his subsequent May 27 address that explained the legal basis for his actions:

> It may be relevant to note here that UNEF functioned ex-
> clusively on the United Arab Republic side of the line in a
> zone from which the United Arab Republic had voluntarily
> stayed away for over 10 years. It was this arrangement
> which allowed UNEF to function as a buffer and as a re-
> straint on infiltration. . . . If UNEF had been deployed on
> both sides of the line as originally envisaged in pursuance
> of the General Assembly Resolution, its buffer function
> would not necessarily have ended. However, its presence
> on the Israel side of the line has never been permitted.

The UN Secretary-General went on to explain that Israel's
refusal to accept the UN force was a perfectly justifiable exercise
of its sovereign rights, and that in exactly the same way,
Nasser's request for the force's removal was a valid reassertion
of the UAR's sovereignty. Out of consideration for good diplomatic manners, U Thant did not say in his address to the Security Council that two Secretaries-General, Dag Hammarskjöld
in 1957 when the UNEF went in, and he himself in the first few
days of the then current crisis, had pleaded with the Israeli government to accept UN troops on their side of the border . . . to
no avail.

To be sure, Nasser had deepened the crisis by suddenly demanding that the UNEF be withdrawn, and even before the
physical departure of the UN troops from the border, a new
issue—Israel's right of passage in the strait—had been raised.
Almost immediately the Johnson White House began to examine the various possible means of dealing with the second issue,
i.e., sending the U.S. aircraft carrier *Intrepid* through the canal
to demonstrate our concern, submission of the issue (the UAR's
claim of sovereignty in the strait) to the World Court, and forming an allied naval "regatta" to force Nasser to allow free passage.

Lost in all of this is the obvious question "Yes, but why
didn't Israel agree to accept the UNEF on her soil, if only temporarily, until the crisis could be resolved?" Then there is the
ancillary question "And why didn't Israel's major ally, the

United States, urge such a course upon Israel?" The obvious answer—indeed it is self-evident—is that neither Israel nor the United States wanted a UN buffer force between Israel and the UAR.*

Israel went to great lengths to convince the United States that the Arabs were preparing for war. In the last week of May, Mossad's Director contacted the CIA station chief in Tel Aviv and gave him information purporting to show frightful Arab troop concentrations near Israel's border. High-altitude aerial reconnaissance failed, however, to find the concentrations, and the CIA so informed President Johnson.[25] Israel appeared to be endeavoring to force the United States to take sides.

On May 25, Israeli Foreign Minister Abba Eban traveled to Washington to meet with President Johnson, ostensibly to determine whether the latter's very public efforts to mediate the maritime rights crisis, and/or force Nasser to capitulate through the allied regatta, were likely to succeed. That evening, Eban had a preliminary meeting with Secretary of State Rusk. The Israeli Foreign Minister again claimed to have evidence of advanced preparations for a two-front, Egyptian-Syrian attack upon Israel. Rusk commented on that point in his note the next morning to the President. "Our intelligence," Rusk said, "does not confirm this Israeli estimate."[26]

Rusk also told Johnson that at a time when the Israelis seemed to be making preparations for war, the administration would appear to have two choices: either to "let the Israelis decide how best to protect their own national interests . . . i.e., to 'unleash' them," or, second, to actively, prominently mediate a resolution to the crisis while holding the armies of both sides at bay. Rusk advocated the second course to the President, adding:

> Pre-emptive action by Israel would cause extreme difficulty
> for the United States. In our position of world leadership,

---

*In March, 1983, the author asked Walt Rostow in an interview in Austin, Texas, why the United States had not—strongly—suggested the obvious solution to Israel. The answer from Rostow, who was Lyndon Johnson's closest foreign-policy adviser in 1967, was "That's a very good question." Mr. Rostow was kind enough to verify for me with C. V. Narasimhan, who was Undersecretary-General for General Assembly Affairs in June, 1967, that Israel had in fact twice been urged to accept a UN force and had flatly refused. Michael Bar Zohar, in *Embassies in Crisis* (Englewood Cliffs, N.J.: Prentice-Hall, 1970), says (pp. 106–107) that Walt Rostow's brother, Eugene, who was Undersecretary of State in June, 1967, had in fact raised with Israeli Ambassador Harman the idea of Israel's accepting UN troops on her side. Bar Zohar does not, however, indicate that Eugene Rostow received any response.

the American people would do what has to be done if "the fault is on the other side and there is no alternative." Therefore, the question of responsibility for the initiation of hostilities is a major problem for us.[27]

THE GREAT MIDDLE EAST TURKEY SHOOT

There was a third possible course of action open to the administration, and that was to publicly seek to resolve the dispute peacefully, while covertly "unleashing" the Israelis. And this was precisely what happened.

During the meeting with Abba Eban on May 26, a written statement was used that strongly committed the United States both to the territorial integrity of the nations of the Middle East and to a "vigorous pursuit" of the available diplomatic means of resolving the dispute peacefully. In regard to the first point, Johnson said that the territorial integrity and political independence of *all* of the countries of the Middle East were one of two principles that he called "vital national interests of the United States" (the other being freedom of the seas). In regard to the question of the avoidance of conflict, Johnson was equally strong. The written statement, which one week later was sent to Prime Minister Eshkol in a letter from the President, contained the following passage:

> I must emphasize the necessity for Israel not to make itself responsible for the initiation of hostilities. Israel will not be alone unless it decides to go alone. We cannot imagine that it will make this decision.[28]

Johnson later embellished his account of the discussion with Eban on this part of the written statement. His memoirs recall:

> "The central point, Mr. Minister," I told him, "is that your nation not be the one to bear the responsibility for any outbreak of war." Then I said very slowly and positively: "Israel will not be alone unless it decides to go alone." He was quiet, and I repeated the statement once more.[29]

Dramatic, but perhaps a bit disingenuous. On the afternoon of June 3, when Walt Rostow transmitted to the President for his signature the final draft of the letter to Levi Eshkol, Rostow added in his transmittal note the comment: "It may be urgent that we put this letter on record soon."[30]

An opportunity existed, if the Israelis were "unleashed," to achieve a number of administration objectives in the Middle East at one stroke:

- Embarrass the Soviets in the Middle East by thoroughly smashing the armies of states that they had been heavily arming over the previous three to four years.
- Destroy the bulk of the equipment the Soviets had sent to the Middle East, and in the process examine the performance of U.S. and other weapons systems against the counterpart Soviet systems.
- Discredit Gamal Abdel Nasser and, just possibly, bring down his government.
- Enable the Israelis to capture territory with which finally, after 19 years, they might be able to bring the front-line Arab states to the bargaining table to seriously negotiate the basic issues that separated Arab and Jew in the Middle East.

One fundamental prerequisite for achieving all of this was of course a quick, clean Israeli victory on the field. Lyndon Johnson made very certain of this. In a meeting of the National Security Council at noon on May 24, Johnson asked for a "new reading on Israeli capability." In fact, the President had been pressing Director of Central Intelligence Richard Helms for some days before the meeting for estimates of the capacity of the Israelis to withstand a combined attack of the Arabs, and had already been told that Israel would win a war against one or all of the Arab countries, whichever struck the first blow, in about a week. Richard Helms, in the oral history prepared for the Lyndon Baines Johnson Library, recalls that "We predicted almost within the day of how long the war would last if it began."[31]

Nevertheless, at the NSC meeting on May 24, Johnson asked the CIA, NSA, and State Department to again update and revise their strength estimates. The result, prepared by all three

agencies, was a report that was delivered to the President on
May 26, and not only confirmed the previous CIA estimates, but
indicated in some detail just how the victory would come—a
quick, heavy Israeli air strike accompanied by armored penetration in the Sinai, toward the Suez Canal.[32]

Was there any possibility that the fighting would go the other
way? Were the Israelis taking any risks? None at all. Nicholas
Katzenbach, Under Secretary of State, who in 1967 was heavily
involved in Middle East matters, responded to such a question
in his oral history interview for the Johnson Library:

> *Interviewer:* What about contingencies if the fighting had
> gone the other way? I know you have con-
> tingency plans for all sorts of alternatives, but
> were any of them seriously considered at the
> Presidential level as far as you know?
> *Katzenbach:* No, I think that *nobody* expected *any*
> possibility of the fighting going the other way.
> *Interviewer:* In other words, this was such a far-fetched
> alternative . . .
> *Katzenbach:* The intelligence was absolutely flat on the
> ` fact that the Israelis would in essence do just
> what they did. That is, that they could mop
> up the Arabs in no time at all. And so we
> really never decided what it is we could do if
> it went the other way.[33]

There were other forms of assistance from the U.S. government required by the Israelis—not to win the war, which they
could easily have done on their own, but to achieve the territorial objectives that they had established from the outset.

First, the Israelis needed to be sure that the Soviets would
not intercede in what they knew from the outset would be very
one-sided fighting. On the morning of June 5, when the air attacks on four Arab countries were launched, Eshkol sent a message to Johnson specifically asking that the U.S. protect Israel,
should the Russians intervene. And on June 10 that became necessary. Israel's full-scale invasion of Syria on the morning of
June 9, after Nasser had formally accepted the UN cease-fire (in
the name of the United Arab Republic, which included Syria),
was simply too much for Soviet Premier Aleksei Kosygin, who
utilized the Moscow-Washington hot line the next morning to

inform Johnson that the Israelis had gone too far, and that Russia would now have to intervene directly. After a brief meeting at the White House of the President's Middle East action task force, orders were given for the entire Sixth Fleet to turn and head for the eastern Mediterranean. It was a provocative act, fraught with risks as far as the Soviet reaction was concerned, but it was taken promptly when the need arose. The IDF would be permitted to finish the job in Syria.

Later, senior presidential assistant Harry McPherson would say:

> The American Jewish Community believed that Johnson had done nothing for them; that he was in effect prepared to see Israel suffer terribly. The opposite was the case, but we were in a terrible situation. We couldn't say anything about the fact that the Sixth Fleet had been turned East, aimed at the Russian fleet. . . . we couldn't say what we had said on the Hot Line about the necessity for Russia to keep its mitts off the Middle East, because of our relations with the Russians and because we were trying to settle the Middle Eastern situation.[34]

Second, there were forms of material assistance required by Israel. On May 23, Johnson authorized an emergency air shipment of armored personnel carriers, tank spare parts, spare parts for the Hawk missile air defense system, bomb fuses, artillery ammunition, and gas masks, among many other items.[35] (Parts of the list have been excised.) These items were packed and sent just prior to the June 5 invasion, in preparation for it, at a time when President Johnson had publicly declared an arms embargo on all items going to the Middle East. One almost wonders whether there might not have been two Lyndon Johnsons in the White House in early June, 1967.*

Third, the IDF needed time. Predictably, the calls for a cease-fire imposed by the UN Security Council began almost as soon as the fighting. By the evening of June 6, a cease-fire resolution had been passed. But during those first two critical days of furious bargaining on the matter, the U.S. delegation, led by

---

*On June 5, Arthur Krim, who was the Chairman of the New York State Democratic party and an active Zionist, informed Johnson that certain of the "armed shipments" due to leave that day by chartered airline had been delayed. He told Johnson it would be "most helpful if these could be released." A note to this effect is, believe it or not, in the National Security File in the Lyndon Baines Johnson Library.

Ambassador Arthur Goldberg, resisted any cease-fire resolution that would (a) brand Israel as the aggressor or (b) include a demand for a troop withdrawal to the June 4 borders. This in spite of the fact that the Johnson White House knew well that Israel had carried out a massive sneak attack that had, in the case of Egypt, destroyed 300 planes on the ground in the first 170 minutes, as Israel's armored units swept into the Sinai.[36]

Asking the Arab states to accept a cease-fire resolution without these two elements was tantamount to asking them to formally approve the attack and the new territorial status quo. As Goldberg and Soviet UN Delegate Nicolai T. Federenko wrangled on June 5 and 6 about the wording of the cease-fire resolution, the IDF gobbled up territory in Jordan and in Egypt.

The Soviet UN delegation caved in under U.S. and European pressure on June 6, and approved the U.S. version of the cease-fire, to the shock of the Arabs.[37] As they were losing on the battlefield, the Arabs had no alternative but to accept the terms of the U.S.-supported cease-fire, and they reluctantly did so—Jordan on the evening of June 7 and the UAR on the afternoon of June 8.

And on June 8, Ambassador Goldberg formally proposed to the UN Security Council President a resolution calling upon the parties to the conflict to negotiate what Goldberg called "the basic political issues which have fed the fires of conflict in this Region for decades." These negotiations would be conducted, of course, upon the basis of the new territorial status quo, the new cease-fire lines. In the short period of 72 hours, the IDF in the field and the U.S. delegation to the UN in New York had completely altered the basis for resolving the 19-year-old Arab-Israeli dispute. Israel now had enormous new bargaining chips in any future negotiations with Jordan or Egypt. And following a similar sequence of events in the days after the June 9 invasion of Syria, new territorial conditions also revised the basis for future Israeli-Syrian negotiations.

The Johnson White House was not exactly unaware of the long-term implications of the events described above; in fact it would appear that it was from the White House that they were being orchestrated.*

*There is some evidence that the White House staff wished to specifically exclude the State Department from the group of "orchestrators." When, in the early days of the crisis, a special committee was established in the White House to meet regularly on the matter, McGeorge Bundy wrote the President before one meeting that "With a number

On June 4, Walt Rostow sent to Secretary of State Rusk and Secretary of Defense Robert McNamara by "long distance Xerox" what he called "scenarios" for the coming events in the Middle East.[38] On the following day, in the evening, Rostow sent to the President an intelligence report on the first day's fighting. His transmittal note was the following:

Mr. President:
Herewith the account, with a map, of the first day's turkey shoot.

W.W. Rostow[39]

On the afternoon of June 6, Rostow sent Johnson another transmittal note, covering a report from the U.S. mission to the UN in New York. It said:

Mr. President:
Herewith Nat Davis' report on the situation in New York. If the Israelis go fast enough, and the Soviets get worried enough, a simple cease-fire might be the best answer.
This would mean that we could use the *de facto* situation on the ground to try to negotiate not a return to armistice lines but a definitive peace in the Middle East.

W.W. Rostow[40]

And on the next morning, June 7, Rostow sent the President "some thoughts" on, among other things, "the Israeli situation and bargaining position." It appeared, he said, that Israel would end up controlling the West Bank of the Jordan, all of Jerusalem and the whole of the Sinai peninsula, including the east bank of the Suez Canal. Moreover, depending ("but not much") upon how fast the Soviets replaced destroyed Arab aircraft, "the Israelis for the moment are in a position to dominate militarily the region." It was, Rostow felt, a perfect time for U.S. diplomatic initiatives to encourage the Arabs and Israelis to resolve their problems on a regional basis: *

---

of Dean Rusk's staff present, you may not wish to discuss organizational assignments for the special committee's work." (Note dated June 7, 1967, in National Security File, NSC History of the Middle East Crisis, etc., Volume 7, Appendix 1.)
*Most interestingly, within days of the end of the fighting, the Israeli government called for "direct negotiations" with the Arabs. This remained the Israeli position for 11 barren years until Jimmy Carter convinced Menahem Begin to participate in some very indirect negotiations at Camp David in 1978.

The UN role should be to set a framework within which these things become possible but not to become excessively involved in detail.[41]

Rostow detailed in the memorandum the objectives he hoped to achieve by giving the Arabs an offer they could not refuse. These included a transition from Arab radicalism to moderation, the development of regional pride to supplant the Arab sense of defeat and humiliation, regional development cooperation, and even regional arms control arrangements, "optimally to be worked out within the region itself."[42] These latter "arrangements" would of course have frozen the Israelis in a state of total military dominance of the Middle East for many years to come.

Was all of this merely naïve and simplistic, or was it something else—part of a "scenario" in which the Israelis were "unleashed," the map of the Middle East effectively redrawn, and the Arabs then forced to negotiate the region's future from a position of weakness?

The answer to that question depends, of course, upon whether Rostow and the Johnson White House were merely reacting to the events of the war, or had a hand in planning them, even participated in them.

RAMSTEIN, WEST GERMANY

In the early morning hours of June 3, the pilots of the 38th Tactical Reconnaissance Squadron of the 26th Tactical Reconnaissance Wing, U.S. Air Force, were rousted out of bed. Their planes were quickly prepared. They were to fly to Morón, Spain, they were told, for what they assumed would be a NATO fair-weather training exercise.

Their planes were RF-4C's, modified versions of the F-4 Phantom jet fighter. In June of 1967, the RF-4C was state-of-the-art military reconnaissance equipment that had only been operational for three years. It utilized cameras of various focal lengths and forward and side-looking radar (SLR) to provide both low- and high-altitude reconnaissance. Using the radar, and infrared sensors, which provided a thermal map of the area under reconnaissance, the RF-4C could operate day or night. An advanced correlator-processor could process the SLR imagery on board the plane. The RF-4C carried new types of navigational systems and altimeters, and was equipped with a high-frequency radio that enabled the pilot to communicate with the plane's base from any point in its "performance envelope." The RF-4C was a very modern military aircraft.

Four of these "birds" winged off from Ramstein on the morning of June 3, headed for the U.S. air base at Morón. Another plane was headed for Morón that morning, a big C-141 cargo plane from Upper Heyford, outside Oxford in England. The plane's belly contained a complete WS 430a photo reconnaissance system—two photo cubes, two processing cubes, a center cube, two generators, two cubes of processed film, and two of made duplications.* With the equipment were nine photo technicians from the 17th Tactical Reconnaissance Squadron of the 66th Tactical Reconnaissance Wing at Upper Heyford. Like their colleagues from Ramstein, they had been rudely chased from their beds that morning, and were wondering why a training exercise was so important. It was not even the right time of year for an exercise—fair-weather training at Morón or Wheelus (Libya) or one of the other Mediterranean area bases was normally done in the fall.

MORÓN, SPAIN

This was not a training exercise. At Morón the planes were taxied to a remote end of the base. There was plenty of room—Morón had originally been built for B-52's and had 10,000-foot runways. The base was very spread out. Pilots and technicians were hustled into a hangar for briefings, but at different times—the 17th and 38th were given separate briefings. They were told they would be going to a remote section of the Negev Desert to provide tactical reconnaissance support for the IDF against the Arabs. The mission was to be top secret. Pilots from the 38th Squadron (Ramstein) were to go with the technicians and equipment from the 17th (Upper Heyford). The cover for the RF-4C's and their pilots was that they were in Morón on IRAN (inspection

---

*"Cubes" here refers to portable aluminum enclosures 8 feet high and ranging in area from 8 by 12 to 20 by 12. They are used to transport photo-processing and other equipment. At the site in a "dispersed" mission (i.e., one set up quickly in a remote area) the cubes become shelter and work space.

and repair as necessary). The 17th's planes, which were RF-101's—less advanced in design than the RF-4C's—were to stay in Morón and fly training missions, photographing miles of sand and scrub hills in Spain. This would be their cover.

Those who would be going on the mission itself were issued civilian passports and manuals on lab operations in plastic binders. The manuals had been printed by Aero-Tec Corporation in Dallas–Fort Worth. This was to be their cover. They would be U.S. civilian contract employees hired by the Israeli government, if anything went wrong. It was at about this time that the seriousness of what they were doing dawned on some of the men who would participate in the operation.

Military ID's, keys, coins and clothes were all collected and new, plain fatigues were issued. The men were allowed to take their shoes and socks along. The briefing and clothes exchange took two hours, and then the men were told they could rest for a few hours. That same afternoon several C-130 turboprop cargo planes would take them to Israel. The RF-4C's were painted over with a white Star of David on a blue background on the rear fuselage. New tail numbers were painted on, corresponding to actual inventory numbers in the Israeli Air Force.

NEAR BEERSHEBA, ISRAEL

About half of the photo equipment was left in Morón. The C-130's departed that evening and landed at a small, remote, abandoned airfield in the Negev, southeast of the big IAF air base at Beersheba, and southwest of Dimona. The French Air Force had used this base on an earlier top-secret mission—when French Mystères and Thunderstreaks had been used to provide air cover for Israel during the Suez War.

The RF-4C's arrived at about dark on June 4, just as the technicians had finished assembling the cubes. They were ready. Early the next morning, June 5, the air to the northwest was filled with sights and sounds, as the IAF launched the largest coordinated air attack ever undertaken in the Middle East. The war was on.

The operation began that morning, with the RF-4C's overflying bombed and burning air bases in Egypt, Syria, and Jordan.

Forward and side oblique as well as panoramic cameras were used to record the damage. Eight to ten sorties a day were flown, at both low and high altitudes. Each plane shot about 500 feet of film per sortie, which was developed in long strips back at the desert base. In-flight data-recording equipment automatically printed date, time, altitude, latitude, longitude, heading, pitch, roll, drift angle, and squadron and mission numbers on the film frames.

At the base, U.S. crews serviced and maintained the planes between sorties, but virtually all of the photo interpretation was done by Israelis, about 60 of whom were kept busy analyzing the thousands of feet of exposed film brought back daily by the planes. Four copies were made of all the pictures taken—one was turned over immediately to the Israelis, one was kept by the American technicians and only turned over to the Israelis at the end of the mission (June 12), and two were picked up at the base each day by couriers who arrived and departed by light plane or helicopter. The men were told that these copies went back to the United States.

At night, the men slept in tents. The food was, they were told, typical IDF field rations. On the third day, the Israelis brought a treat—some local beer and wine. But overall, there was little fraternization between the Americans and the Israelis. The operation was all business. The Americans had the impression that the Israeli photo interpreters were very good at what they did.

The base itself was little to see—a few rusted auxiliary buildings with peeling paint. There were no airplane hangars. One auxiliary building was used as a communications center, and one housed a contingent of Israeli guards. There was a storage building. All power was generated on site. Water was trucked in daily, which was important, for it was needed for photo processing as well as drinking and "bodily functions." The men were told it was distilled water from the atomic power plant at Dimona. At midday, the heat was terrible, and the technicians had to overpaint their olive-drab photo cubes, giving them a light, sandy color to reflect the sun's rays.

On the third or fourth day of the operation, the men were told to afix phosphorus grenades to the aluminum photo cubes. If they were detonated, the grenades would burn the cubes to a crisp. The men assumed these precautions were intended to enable them to abandon the site quickly, leaving no identifiable trace, if the operation was detected or overrun.*

At about the same time, June 8 or 9, the operation's mission changed somewhat. In the early hours of the war, the Israeli Air Force concentrated on destroying as many Arab planes and airfields as possible, leaving the Arab armies to fight planes with tanks in the open desert. The RF-4C's thus concentrated in the early stages on photographing and assessing damage done to the Arab air bases. Both day and night sorties were required for this, though primarily the former. Once the Arab air forces had been demolished on the ground, however, the Arabs were forced to move their troops and equipment at nighttime, to avoid as much as possible the attacks from Israeli planes, which they no longer could oppose in the air. Thus, the primary mission of the Negev reconnaissance operation switched to night sorties ferreting out Arab movements, to permit devastatingly accurate Israeli air attacks early the following morning. The night reconnaissance on June 8 and 9 also enabled IDF commanders to accurately assess the Jordanian and Egyptian strength that remained and thus facilitated decisions about which units could be sent north to undertake the attack upon Syria, and exactly when these units could be safely moved.

Different reconnaissance equipment was utilized for the night work. The RF-4C's used infrared sensors to detect the heat produced by moving trucks and tanks. The side-looking radar was also used, producing an imagery that could be photographically recorded on the strips of film. While not as precise as regular photography, images of troop movements or placements could be obtained at night or even through clouds. In 1967, the Israeli Air Force had no night reconnaissance capability whatever.

Once the battle had been joined in Syria, the mission changed again to close-in tactical reconnaissance of Syrian positions, in and just north of the Golan Heights.

*Later, at their debriefing at Morón, the men would learn of Arab accusations, in the early days of the war, of U.S. operational assistance to the Israelis in the form of tactical air support by U.S. planes flying from Sixth Fleet aircraft carriers. The Arabs had, quite coincidentally, the right idea but the wrong operation. No U.S. planes from the Sixth Fleet or elsewhere fired weapons for the Israelis. But the accusations enraged the Arabs in capital cities throughout the region, resulting in attacks upon U.S. Embassies and installations. President Johnson was obliged to publicly deny that any assistance in any form was being provided the Israelis, thus making the operation herein described even more sensitive than it had been when first mounted.

And then on June 12 it was over. The C-130's swooped in and landed, the cubes were packed up and loaded, and the men flew back to Morón for debriefing.

TO MORÓN AND HOME

It was an ultrasecret exercise. Each man on the operation, pilot or technician, was debriefed individually and in groups. The political implications of their mission were made carefully, painfully clear, and the men were told that they were never, under any circumstances, to reveal what they had been doing the previous week. They were not even to talk about the mission among themselves, when they returned to Ramstein and Upper Heyford. The men had never seen the debriefers before, and had the impression that they had been flown in from Washington especially for the job. Fatigues, Aero-Tec manuals, passports, and the like were piled on one side of the hangar, and the men walked naked to the other side to retrieve their military ID's and uniforms, and pick up mail (rerouted to Morón during the week's "training exercise"). The men assumed their former identities. Nothing but nothing was brought out of Israel—no "happy" snapshots, no souvenirs. Nothing.

There was one more job to do at Morón, and it was dull indeed in comparison to the previous week. For two days, the technicians from the 17th Squadron developed the photographs taken by their own planes, the RF-101's that had been left back in Spain. Thousands of feet of Spanish hills and plains. It had, after all, been a training exercise.

And then they returned to their home bases—the pilots of the 38th to Ramstein, Germany, and the technicians and pilots of the 17th to Upper Heyford, England. The two units had no further contact, but they did share one other common experience. The men who participated in the mission all received early promotions.*

---

*The principal source for this story claims to have been a participant in the operation described. The author has verified the story circumstantially; that is, by checking Air Force unit histories, commanders' names, technical details, and so forth. Furthermore, certain of the details provided by the source would have been very difficult to learn other than by participation in such a mission in Israel. Nevertheless, efforts to confirm this story either through contacts with other individuals who might have participated in such an operation, or through senior officials in the Pentagon, White House, and State De-

WHOSE IRRESPONSIBILITY WAS THIS?

The aerial reconnaissance assistance that the United States provided to Israel during the Six-Day War was not a factor in the Israeli victory. The IDF did not need any help to win the war. But like the diplomatic delaying tactics used by Ambassador Goldberg in the UN Security Council, the aerial reconnaissance did help the Israelis to achieve certain territorial objectives within a very finite, limited time. U.S. and Israeli strategists knew well before the commencement of the fighting that diplomatic pressures for a cease-fire would be enormous. It was important for the IDF to capture certain strategic ground in a very short time, before the cease-fire lines were frozen. In this respect, the U.S. tactical reconnaissance assistance was not only important, it was critical.

Was the aerial reconnaissance the only form of operational assistance provided by the United States? The author has been told of other forms, most specifically signals intelligence assistance, whereby U.S. Army personnel and equipment aided the Israelis in jamming and "cooking" Arab battlefield communications. But it has not been possible to verify this assistance positively, nor to obtain the details of the operation.

Michael Bar Zohar in *Embassies in Crisis* maintains that the U.S. Joint Chiefs of Staff developed, in late May, 1967, contingency plans for direct U.S. military intervention in the then-expected war, should the fighting go badly for Israel. Two possible scenarios were developed, one involving a large-scale paratroop drop and naval bombing in the Sinai peninsula, and the other envisaging the flying of mobile U.S. forces directly into Israel, providing a buffer around the Israeli civilian population, which would "collapse" to the center of the country. This contingency-planning exercise was abandoned in its early stages, Bar Zohar says, when it became apparent to the JCS that the U.S. intelligence

---

partment, have not met with success. During the course of these efforts at verification (July-September, 1983) Air Force Intelligence has contacted several former members of the 17th Tactical Reconnaissance Squadron, reminding them of their obligations to maintain silence on any previous intelligence missions in which they may have been involved.

services were unanimous in their estimates that there was no chance whatever of the Arabs winning the war or even stringing it out. It is possible, then, that the aerial reconnaissance described above was originally intended as one element of a larger plan for U.S. intervention, and that when the larger plan was abandoned, the reconnaissance (and possibly signals intelligence) elements were allowed to proceed.

Were Rostow and Johnson aware of the painted-over RF-4C's in the Negev? Most probably so, as a maverick conspirator in the JCS or U.S. Air Force or CIA would have been committing career suicide by allowing such an operation to proceed on its own without approval from the "highest authority," particularly after the Arab accusations of U.S. operational assistance on the first day of the war, and the President's flat disclaimers.

The great likelihood is that the President and certain trusted White House staff members were well aware of the operation I have described, and that it was part of a much larger "scenario" to embarrass the Soviets by enabling the Israelis to smash the Arab armies and capture sufficient Arab land to provide them a bargaining chip that would force the Arabs to negotiate directly on the larger, more basic issues in the 19-year Arab-Israeli dispute. Did the scheme work? I leave the reader to judge.

Lastly, even in an age when we have become blasé about government abuse of authority, it is perhaps worth noting that those who authorized this operation and carried it out were, without the knowledge of Congress or the American people, taking enormous risks with American lives and property in the Arab world. Had the reconnaissance assistance been discovered at a time when Arab soldiers and civilians were dying by the thousands under the Israeli blitzkrieg, one can imagine the revenge that would have been taken against Americans across the Middle East. And given Israel's total military superiority over the Arabs in June of 1967, plus the CIA's and Department of Defense's detailed knowledge of that superiority, one wonders why such risks were taken.

—9—

"Remember the Liberty. . . .*"*

NOW, YEARS LATER, it is obvious that the ship should never have been sent there in the first place. Even at the time, which was May and June, 1967, there were many people involved in the ship's mission who were very concerned for her safety.

The ship was the U.S.S. *Liberty*. Her naval designation was AGTR-5—the fifth ship in a series undertaking "Auxiliary General Technical Research." The *Liberty* was in fact a World War II victory ship refitted by the National Security Agency for use as a signals intelligence (SIGINT) "platform"—a floating listening post.

The official Pentagon description of the *Liberty*'s mission stated that it was to conduct

> . . . technical research operations in support of U.S. Navy electronic research projects which include electromagnetic propagation studies and advanced communications systems such as moon relay and satellite communications.[1]

And the classified, in-house Pentagon mission statement or "cover statement," which has never been previously published, was the following:

> To provide shipborne COMINT [communications intelligence] and ELINT [electronic intelligence] platforms to intercept and exploit foreign electromagnetic radiations in those areas of the world where suitable shore based intercept stations do not exist.

In less elliptical terms, the *Liberty* could intercept virtually any form of wireless communication, including short- and long-distance military and diplomatic traffic, telemetry data, rocket guidance, and satellite control, among others. The ship could decode and process these messages, and then relay them back to the NSA at Fort Meade, Maryland, via shortwave radio or through a very special communication system called TRSSCOM, using a 10,000-watt microwave signal bounced off the surface of the moon.[2] It was, then, a very advanced spy ship.

On May 23, 1967, the day after Gamal Abdel Nasser announced his decision to bar Israeli ships from the Gulf of Aqaba, the NSA ordered the *Liberty* to proceed as quickly as possible from the Gulf of Benin off the coast of West Africa, to Rota, Spain, and thence to the eastern Mediterranean. One senior NSA official later recalled that from the moment the ship was ordered into what was fast becoming a war zone, he intended it to stay well away from the coastlines of Syria, Israel, and Egypt. But somehow these intentions were never transformed into orders. In fact, *Liberty*'s "operations area" was to be just outside Egyptian territorial waters off the northern coast of the Sinai, and about midway between Tel Aviv and Cairo. The ship was ordered to execute a dogleg pattern at slow speed in what would obviously be (to anyone watching her) a surveillance mode.

When full-scale war finally did break out, on the morning of June 5, the *Liberty* was about halfway between Spain and Israel, steaming straight for the conflict. The officers and crew of the ship, who for days had questioned the wisdom of sending a virtually unarmed spy ship into an area of high tensions and sporadic fighting, now assumed that senior Defense Department officials would reconsider the ship's assignment. But it did not happen. So on the evening of June 5, the *Liberty* radioed Admiral William Martin, Commander of the Sixth Fleet (COMSIXTHFLT), requesting a destroyer escort to accompany the ship into the war zone.[3] In a separate message, Captain William McGonagle pointedly reminded Admiral Martin that "self defense capability limited to four .50 caliber machine guns and small arms."[4]

On June 6 Martin responded, denying the request because the *Liberty* was, he said, a clearly marked United States ship in international waters, was not a participant in the conflict, and therefore was "not a reasonable subject for attack by any nation."[5] Martin would later tell a JCS fact-finding team set up to investigate the performance of the Defense Department communications network in the affair, that he had expected on June 5 when the war broke out that "higher authority" would have modified the *Liberty*'s orders "in the interest of her safety."[6]

And the next day, more worry. Even though the *Liberty* had technically been under Sixth Fleet command since its passage through the Strait of Gibraltar, on the afternoon of June 6 the ship received a message from CINCUSNAVEUR (Commander in Chief, U.S. Naval Forces, Europe) in London formally transferring command to Admiral Martin of the Sixth Fleet, to facilitate "any possible requirement for protection during Mideast hostilities." In turn Martin, who had just denied the ship an armed escort, shot a gratuitous message off to the *Liberty* warning it to maintain a "high state of vigilance" against attack.[7] Like many other messages sent to the *Liberty* in the days that followed, this one was misrouted and never reached the ship.

From Washington to London to the Mediterranean, the various command echelons of the U.S. Navy were busy warning each other about the *Liberty*'s vulnerability. But through June 6 and into June 7, the ship continued, alone and virtually unarmed, toward a war zone in which naval and air battles were being fought with planes and rockets and real guns. Captain McGonagle, the ultimate link in the chain of command, refused to content himself with the sending of messages during these hours. He declared a "Modified Condition of Readiness Three" on the ship, in which the forward gun mounts were manned continuously. Repeated General Quarters and other drills were conducted.

By late afternoon on June 7, the Department of Defense was beginning to have second thoughts about sending the world's most sophisticated spy ship to stalk the shores of Egypt and Israel. At 5:04 P.M. Eastern daylight time—just after 11 P.M. ship time—the National Security Agency contacted the JCS Joint Reconnaissance Center (JRC) to ask that the word be passed through the various levels of command (in Europe and on the flagship of the Sixth Fleet) to change the *Liberty*'s planned area of operations to "Op Area 2," farther from the eastern Mediterranean coastline.[8] About an hour and a half later, at 6:30 P.M. EDT, the JRC responded with a message to USCINCEUR

(Commander in Chief, U.S. Armed Forces, Europe), asking that the *Liberty* be notified that its assigned operating area was "for guidance only and may be varied as local conditions dictate." The *Liberty* was to be instructed, however, that it was to stay 20 nautical miles from the coast of Egypt, and 15 nautical miles from Israel.[9] (Previous instructions had set the minimum distances at 12.5 and 6.5 miles, respectively.)

It was a fairly routine change of orders prompted, according to the JCS fact-finding team, by a question raised by the Chief of Naval Operations concerning the prudence of sending the *Liberty* to a position so close to the area of hostilities. This message was assigned a "priority" precedence, as was usually the case in changes of operational orders under "normal" circumstances. Finally, worry had crystallized into resolve, and the Navy was taking steps to move the *Liberty* out of harm's way.* But this effort was now overtaken by circumstances.

THE WARNING

Sometime in the late afternoon or early evening of June 7, probably just after the routine "move" order was given, the NSA learned, from an intelligence report emanating from the Office of the U.S. Defense Attaché in Tel Aviv, that Israel was planning to attack the *Liberty* if her course was not changed.† The NSA reacted quickly, initiating through the JCS Joint Reconnaissance Center an extraordinary effort to warn and reposition the *Liberty*. The NSA and or the Chief of Naval Operations contacted Captains Merriwell Vineyard and Sam Rorex, Jr., at JCS-JRC, who in turn ordered Major Breedlove in their office to phone U.S. Naval Headquarters in Europe to get the ship moved. This time, the *Liberty* was to stay 100 nautical miles away from the coasts of Israel, Syria, and Egypt.[10]

In several respects this action was unusual. First, the order followed by only 1 hour and 20 minutes a previous order to reposition the ship. Second, it employed voice communications to

---

*The JCS-JRC released this message to the Army Communications Center at the Pentagon at 6:30 P.M. But it was not actually sent on to USCINCEUR until 8:55 the next morning!

†Further details about this report, and about testimony on it subsequently presented to the Defense Subcommittee of the House Committee on Appropriations, are provided later in this chapter.

initiate an action, contrary to the normal procedures requiring a written (i.e., telexed) message-order. Third, the phoned order was passed from Captains Vineyard and Rorex (both of whom were in the Navy) straight to the Navy headquarters in Europe, and not—initially, at least—to the office of USCINCEUR.

Forty minutes later, at 8:30 P.M. EDT, the JCS-JRC followed up by phone with USCINCEUR to find out if action had been taken on the previous oral "order." And 40 minutes after this call, the JCS telexed to USCINCEUR to confirm the oral order.[11] This message was assigned an "immediate" precedence, and like the earlier "priority" move order was copied directly to *Liberty* and to the Commander of the Sixth Fleet. And at ten minutes past midnight EDT, Naval Headquarters in Europe repeated the JCS-JRC pattern of actions: it phoned the Commander of the Sixth Fleet in the Mediterranean to pass along the order to move the ship, and followed that with a proper, written message to him.[12]

But by now some five hours and five minutes had elapsed since Major Breedlove had first picked up the phone to call the U.S. Navy in Europe and get that ship moved. Why? The JCS fact-finding team later attributed the delay to a large volume of high-precedence traffic, related to a NATO communications exercise to relay numerous press extracts as part of the Foreign Broadcast Intercept System (FBIS) of the CIA, and to transmission of many messages related to a press conference held on the morning of June 8 by Secretary of Defense McNamara.[13] The *Liberty*'s genuine emergency simply got lost in a bureaucratic jumble of essentially routine messages.

From there on, thing got worse. The Sixth Fleet Commander was sent the formal move order at 12:55 A.M. EDT, or 6:55 A.M. his time (and *Liberty*'s time) on the morning of June 8.[14] It then required 4 hours and 22 minutes for a message-order to be sent on from the Sixth Fleet flagship U.S.S. *Little Rock* to the U.S.S. *Liberty*.[15] Why? The Committee on Appropriations of the U.S. House of Representatives later determined that the routing clerk on the *Little Rock* had misplaced the information sheet indicating which naval communications station was to be used to relay messages to the U.S.S. *Liberty*, so he had simply sent the ship's move order to a relay station that *Liberty* was not monitoring at the time.[16]

Even more difficult to understand is the fact that whatever

had happened to the action copies of all of these messages, the *Liberty* had been sent information copies of most of them, any one of which would have told her of the urgent need to move the ship. She received none of these, either. Four years later, the House Armed Services Committee summed up the situation this way:

> In implementing [the decision to move the *Liberty*] a series of five messages from JCS and U.S. commanders in the European Command were directed to *U.S.S. Liberty* and other addressees. None of those messages had reached *Liberty* by 1200 Z hours on June 8th, 13½ hours after the first message was released for transmission. The circumstances surrounding the misrouting, loss and delays of those messages constitute one of the most incredible failures of communications in the history of the Department of Defense.[17]

THE REASON FOR CONCERN

As spectacularly inept as they were, the efforts of the Defense Department to move the *Liberty* were truly extraordinary. Beginning around 7 to 8 P.M. EDT on June 7, procedures were just thrown to the wind. Orders were duplicated. Voice communications were used where telexes were required. Orders were transmitted on a watch-to-watch basis, sometimes without verification from the proper authority. All of which leads to one obvious question: why, one might wonder, did the NSA and the Joint Chiefs of Staff react with such a sense of urgency to a report of a planned attack on a U.S. ship in international waters by a supposed ally? Surely the report was incorrect. In a general sense, the answer to that question is that American intelligence and military officials were collectively aware of the policies and events that have been the subject of the first nine chapters of this book.

But there were other, more immediate reasons why an attack by the IDF upon the U.S.S. *Liberty* on June 7 and 8, 1967, was entirely plausible. The White House, Defense and State departments, and U.S. intelligence community were fully aware of these factors, and reacted accordingly. It had to do with an "understanding" that the Johnson administration had with the gov-

ernment of Israel—about the scope of the war and about
territorial expansion.

One fundamental tenet of U.S. foreign policy in the Middle
East, to which every administration had been committed since
the signing of the Tripartite Declaration of 1950, was that of the
territorial integrity of all of the states of the region. Eisenhower's insistence after the Suez War that Israel physically quit
the Sinai in return for international guarantees of right of passage through the Strait of Tiran was an example of the depth of
this commitment. Ike's stance had been immensely unpopular at
home, involving five months of bitter wrangling with David Ben
Gurion, but he had held his ground and, in March of 1957, the
IDF had withdrawn from Egyptian territory.

In late May, 1967, with tensions mounting dangerously in the
Middle East, President Johnson addressed the nation and the
world in a conscious effort to clearly state American policy on
the multifaceted Arab-Israeli dispute. In the Fish Room at the
White House he spoke for nine minutes, reading a speech that
for weeks afterward was referred to by White House staffers as
a "basic" policy statement. Johnson was particularly emphatic
that evening on the matter of territorial integrity:

> To the leaders of all the nations of the Near East, I wish to
> say what three American Presidents have said before me—
> that the United States is firmly committed to the support of
> the political independence and territorial integrity of all the
> nations in that area.

In actual fact, as subsequent events were to demonstrate, the
Johnson administration was committed to nothing of the sort.
But in the last days of May and the first days of June, 1967,
there certainly *appeared* to be a clear policy on this matter.
There is reason to believe that the government of Israel, at
least, took the President at his word. Within hours after the devastating Israeli air attacks commenced on June 5, Foreign Minister Abba Eban asked to see U.S. Ambassador Barbour in Tel
Aviv. He previewed a letter that Prime Minister Eshkol was preparing to send President Johnson rationalizing Israel's attack
upon its neighbors in terms of Article 51 of the UN Charter (the
"inherent right of self-defense"), but most specifically reassuring

Johnson on the matter of territorial integrity. Ambassador Barbour elaborated:

> Letter will add that [government of Israel] has no, repeat no, intention taking advantage of situation to enlarge its territory, that hopes peace can be restored within present boundaries, that it also hopes conflict can be localized and in this regard asks our help in restraining any Soviet initiative.[18]

As the IDF demolished from the air unit after unit of the armies of Egypt and Jordan in the first two days of fighting, however, some of Israel's resolve to restore peace "within present boundaries" began to wane. On June 7, Secretary of State Rusk informed a meeting of the National Security Council that

> At the beginning it seemed that Israel was not seeking territorial acquisition, but Ambassador Barbour feels they will want Sharm el-Sheikh and straightened-out borders.[19]

But Israel wanted and intended to take a good deal more than that. Later on that same day, June 7, the administration received a hint, in the traditional way, of the rapidly expanding horizons of Israel's territorial ambitions. David Brody, Director of the Anti-Defamation League of the B'Nai B'Rith, came to the White House to speak with Larry Levinson and Ben Wattenberg of the President's staff. The Jewish community of America, he said, was concerned that the administration not force Israel to "lose the peace" after it had won the war, as had been the case with Eisenhower after the Suez War. Brody suggested that in future public statements on the war, the President ought to stress the "peace, justice and equity theme," and should specifically *not* mention "territorial integrity." In a memo to the President, Levinson and Wattenberg allowed that this was good advice:

> It would neutralize the "neutrality" statement and could lead to a great domestic political bonus—and not only from Jews. Generally speaking, it would seem that the Mid-East crisis can turn around a lot of anti-Vietnam, anti-Johnson

feeling, particularly if you use it as an opportunity to your advantage.[20]

There is no evidence in the memorandum that Levinson and Wattenberg queried why the Anti-Defamation League might be interested in the question of the territorial integrity of the states of the Middle East.

At about the time Brody, Levinson, and Wattenberg were meeting, the Hashemite Kingdom of Jordan formally accepted the cease-fire that had been proposed the day before by the UN Security Council. But the Israelis continued to fight on all fronts, consolidating their military positions in Jerusalem and on the West Bank. Another sign.

On the previous day, June 6, U.S. Ambassador to Jordan Findley Burns, Jr., had telexed the Secretary of State that only isolated elements of the Jordanian Army were still fighting. The Jordanian Air Force had been destroyed by Israel in the sudden air attacks in the early morning hours of June 5. The Syrians were doing virtually nothing to assist the Jordanians, who were carrying on with hand-to-hand fighting in the streets of Jerusalem and in several West Bank areas, particularly Jenin. Ambassador Burns added:

> IDF Air Force yesterday and again today hit many civilian targets on West Bank where there absolutely no military emplacements.[21]

The following day, June 7, Ambassador Burns reported that Radio Amman had been announcing the government of Jordan's acceptance of the UN cease-fire for several hours, in the face of continued IDF military action. Burns "respectfully" urged President Johnson to telephone Prime Minister Eshkol to bring a cease-fire into effect "soonest," and added:

> I recognize IDF goal may well be total destruction of Jordanian Army. I consider that JAA destruction, if achieved, would have disastrous effect on this regime and on area stability as a whole. I am gravely concerned about resultant effects on public order and on safety large American community still in Kingdom.[22]

This telegram was logged into the White House communication center at 3:11 P.M. on June 7.

Later that afternoon, the Jordanian Permanent Delegate to the UN, Muhammad el-Farra, speaking before the UN Security Council, accused Israel of preventing a UN cease-fire by continuing the fighting "in order to seize more territory."* In Jerusalem, even as the fighting still progressed, Israeli Defense Minister Dayan told reporters that the IDF would never again leave Jerusalem: "We have returned to this, most sacred of our shrines, never to part from it again." A few days later Dayan declared that Jerusalem had been "reunited" under Israeli control. This generated howls of protest, even from the Israeli Minister of Interior and from Teddy Kollek, the Mayor of Jewish Jerusalem.† But Moshe Dayan would not be denied. The IDF was on a roll.

On June 7 and 8, rumors began to circulate that King Hussein had abdicated in the face of the continuing IDF onslaught, and had flown to Rome. Ambassador Burns in Amman was not alone in viewing these developments with concern—*The New York Times* quoted "informed British diplomatic sources" who were puzzled and worried at the IDF drive for total victory. If Hussein was driven from power and his Army destroyed, they said, he would doubtless be replaced by more xenophobic and pro-Nasser elements in Jordan. The British failed to see what the Israelis could hope to gain, in the long run, from such a development:

> It would be very short-sighted by the Israelis to risk that kind of political change in Jordan for a few more miles of territory.[23]

But in Jordan and in the Sinai, "a few more miles of territory" was exactly what the IDF had in mind.

As the fighting continued in Jordan into the eighth of June, Israel's diplomatic position in the Security Council debates be-

---

*UN Secretary-General U Thant had reported to the Security Council earlier that morning that he had personally forwarded to the government of Israel a message from Jordanian Foreign Minister Ahmad Toukan accepting the terms of the cease-fire. Shortly thereafter, he said, the headquarters of the Israeli-Jordanian Mixed Armistice Commission had been seized by the IDF. (*The New York Times*, June 8, 1967, 17:7.)
†Dayan gives this version of his de facto annexation of Jerusalem in his autobiography. (*My Life*, Chapter 22.)

came increasingly difficult to sustain. On June 7, Foreign Minister Eban had explained before the UN body that while Jordan had accepted the cease-fire, the United Arab Republic had not, and he said, "as the Security Council no doubt knows," Jordan and UAR had a unified command. Eban added somewhat defensively, "This is not simply a question of theory." [24]

On the afternoon of June 8, this argument was voided when the UAR also accepted the UN cease-fire. But Dayan's and the IDF's objectives had not been achieved in the West Bank, as the Jordanian Army continued to resist, fighting house by house, building by building. Combat was particularly heavy in the area south of Damiya Bridge, and the IDF even carried out heavy bombing raids at Mafraq, far from the front lines. When UN Truce Supervisor Odd Bull transmitted a Jordanian complaint about the fighting and bombing on June 8 to the Israeli Foreign Ministry, he was informed—at least with respect to the bombing—that the IDF had found it necessary "because Iraqi troops and planes were in the Mafraq area." [25]

And the IDF had other unfinished business on the Golan Heights, in Syria. Since the outbreak of the war on June 5, Syrian artillery and Israeli planes and artillery had engaged in sporadic exchanges of fire, but neither side had moved troops across the border. On June 8, however, with the scale of the fighting greatly reduced on other fronts where cease-fires were in effect, the IDF prepared to launch an offensive to capture the Golan area. Until this time, Dayan had opposed such an attack because, according to Gideon Raphael, "he feared that it would create serious international complications." [26] He was correct. At about 3:30 P.M. local time on June 8, U.S. Consul General Evan Wilson in Jerusalem informed Secretary of State Rusk by "flash"* telegram that Israel had that morning, according to General Bull, the UNTSO Supervisor, launched an "intensive air and artillery bombardment" of Syrian positions that Wilson assumed was an "apparent prelude to large scale attack." [27]

Dean Rusk was furious, and one hour later shot the following telegram (also with "flash" precedence) to U.S. Ambassador to Israel Barbour:

> UNTSO report reftel [in the referenced telegram] deeply disturbing. You should urgently approach [the Israeli For-

---

*"Flash is the highest precedence designation for State or Defense Department messages.

eign Ministry] at highest level to express deep concern this new indication military action by [government of Israel]. If reported bombardment correct, we would assume it prelude to military action against Syrian positions on Syrian soil. Such a development, following on heels Israeli acceptance [Security Council] cease-fire resolution would cast doubts on Israeli intentions and create gravest problems for [U.S. government] representatives in Arab countries. You should stress we must at all costs have complete cessation Israeli military action except in cases where clearly some replying fire is necessary in self-defense.[28]

Ambassador Barbour, no doubt feeling that his side was being unfairly singled out for criticism by the Secretary, responded that Syrian shelling from the heights had been "continuous and incessant," and reminded the Secretary that the Syrians, as of 9:45 P.M. local time, had not accepted the UN cease-fire.

Later that night the Syrians, who were doubtless aware of the troops and planes being massed for the attack, did accept the cease-fire, which under UN supervision went into effect at 5:20 A.M. local time on June 9. Dayan, who had postponed the attack to allow for the redeployment of elements of his Army from the Egyptian and Jordanian fronts, ordered the invasion of Syria to proceed at 11:30 A.M. local time on June 9. In New York at the UN, the attack generated a barrage of charges by the Arab states and the Soviet Bloc countries that in Syria, as in Jordan and Egypt, Israel was flagrantly violating the cease-fire. Nikolai Federenko of the Soviet Union went further, charging that Israel, with the tacit assent of the United States, was actually using the UN cease-fire to enable it to deal more efficiently with the Arab countries it had attacked, one by one, stabilizing one front with a cease-fire and then moving its forces to the next.

Exasperated at the charges and countercharges, and unable to effectively supervise the cease-fire in effect in the various war zones with the meager personnel available to UNTSO and to the various UN mixed armistice commissions, Secretary-General U Thant called on June 10 for the reactivation of the UN Observer Corps, which had patrolled the armistice lines in the Middle East after the 1948 war.

In Washington, however, the National Security Agency had

a very complete picture of the progress of the war and the countries that might be violating one or another UN cease-fire, for unlike the UN, the NSA did not have to depend upon field observers to get its information. Using ground-based intercept stations as far away from the action as Scotland and as near as Ethiopia and Iran, the NSA could listen in on the many forms of wireless communication that accompany military operations. Supplementing these efforts, Navy EC-121 and EA-3B planes flew regularly out of Athens, in June, 1967, crisscrossing the eastern Mediterranean. This information could be cross-referenced with satellite photographic intelligence to give the Defense Department a good idea of what all parties and observers—but most particularly the Soviet Navy and military aid missions in the region—were doing.

But the *pièce de résistance* of this network at the beginning of the 1967 war was the seagoing electronic intelligence "platform" called the U.S.S. *Liberty*. In the six years prior to the war, the Navy had commissioned seven ELINT vessels, of which the *Liberty*, along with the U.S.S. *Belmont*, was the latest, the largest, and the most advanced.

A COURSE CHANGE LEFT

It was just after dinner on the evening of June 7, 1967. William McGonagle sat down to write out his Captain's Night Orders. Outside, the sea was relatively calm, the skies clear. The *Liberty* was steaming due south on a line between the western coast of Cyprus and Port Said, Egypt, and had reached a point about 30 miles from the Egyptian coast. The page was a mimeographed form filled out each evening by the Captain for the guidance of the night-duty deck officers. Opposite "Nature and type of operation:" McGonagle wrote, "Steaming independently from Rota, Spain to operations area in accordance with CINCUSNAVEUR movement order, 7/67." Then, opposite "Course:" and "Speed:" he wrote, "180 degrees," and "10 knots." Finally he filled in "Instructions:," writing, "At 072039 Bravo [local time] change course to 090; at 080300 Bravo, change course to 123 degrees."[29]

Without realizing it, McGonagle may at that moment have sealed the fate of his ship and forever changed the lives of his officers and crew. After completing the form, he retired. At the bridge, the officer of the deck was Lieutenant Malcolm Watson. And precisely at 8:39 P.M. local time, as instructed, Watson ordered, "come left to course 090." The *Liberty,* still steaming at ten knots, hove left to a course due east, more or less parallel to the coastline. As the skies darkened, the lights from Port Said appeared in the distance off the starboard side.

At the IDF Central Coastal Command in Tel Aviv, aerial reconnaissance reported the change in the *Liberty's* course, which was duly noted on the control table. The ship was represented by a green symbol, indicating a neutral craft. Strictly speaking, that was true. But the ship's markings, GTR-5, ten feet high on both sides of her bow, identified her in *Jane's Fighting Ships* as a signals intelligence ship. The *Liberty* was now steaming on a course toward a point on the Israeli coast midway between Tel Aviv and the naval base at Ashdod.

The IDF command did not have to consult *Jane's Fighting Ships* to learn the eavesdropping capabilities of the *Liberty.* Modiin—Israeli military intelligence—had close working relationships with the CIA and the U.S. Defense Department. The Israelis knew well that close in, the *Liberty* could intercept tactical communications, such as:

- Messages to and from the brigade and division headquarters of IDF units still fighting in Jerusalem and the West Bank, in violation of a UN cease-fire that had just gone into effect.
- Movement orders for units that, on the evening-morning of June 7–8, were being rushed from the Sinai and Jordanian fronts to the northern Galilee border with Syria, in preparation for an invasion that would widen the war and enrage Israel's European and American allies.
- Side-looking radar emissions, and radio communications in a peculiar idiomatic English, between specially equipped night-flying RF-4C's and the "abandoned" French airbase in the Negev not far from Dimona.

It was dark now around the *Liberty* as she steamed on due east, engines thumping. Most of the crew had turned in. On the ship's forecastle, seamen still manned the forward gun tubs, peering into the night. "Modified Condition of Readiness 3." Lieutenant Watson moved to and fro on the brightly lit bridge.

At about 10:00 P.M., the ship's "research department" detected jets—identified as Israeli by *Liberty*'s sophisticated radar-sensing equipment—circling the ship in the night distance.

Strangely, fire-control radar was being directed at the ship. The planes were homing their rockets in on the *Liberty*. A small group gathered in the communications center and, playfully, employed the ship's electronic countermeasure (ECM), or "spoof," equipment to distort her radar image and send it back to the planes, making the ship appear a fraction of its size one time, several times its size the next.* For form's sake, the communications technicians filled out a contact report, but it was never sent on to NSA Headquarters by the officers in the research center. First Class Petty Officer Charles Rowley remembers that no one took the contact very seriously. The planes, after all, were Israeli, and they were only playing games.

But they were not playing games. At about the time this small group gathered around the *Liberty*'s radar screen, the Office of the U.S. Defense Attaché in Tel Aviv sent a startling message back to U.S. Army Communications Center in Washington by code telegram: the IDF was planning to attack the *Liberty* if the ship continued to move closer to the Israeli coast! This "bomb" arrived at the NSA either just before or just after the NSA Director dispatched message 2104Z† to the JCS requesting that the *Liberty* be moved west "to satisfy technical requirements." [30] At the time (11:40 P.M. ship time), it will be recalled, the ship was steaming east, toward Tel Aviv and Ashdod. Had the JCS been able (and they were not) to relay the message to the *Liberty* as requested by the NSA, the ship would have had to turn 180 degrees and proceed due west into the coastal waters of Alexandria, Egypt's largest naval port. The idea, clearly, was just to get it away from Israel.

It was at this point (2230Z) that the JCS Joint Reconnaissance Center initiated the two transatlantic telephone calls and two messages, "immediate" precedence messages, all within the space of two and a half hours, in a frantic effort to move the ship away from coastal areas. Technical requirements indeed.

---

*The *Liberty*'s ECM equipment was of the latest, most sophisticated type, designated AN/SSR-20, and was operated off the 5-foot dish on the ship's forecastle.

†Z denotes Greenwich mean time, i.e., two hours earlier than *Liberty* (or Israeli) local time in its position on June 7 and 8, 1967. This is the third time zone mentioned in the chapter and this may be somewhat confusing to the reader. In the interest of accuracy, however, the author has decided to indicate the zones.

But all messages and all copies of messages to the *Liberty* from the JRC, CINCUSNAVEUR, USCINCEUR, and even COMSIXTHFLT, only a few hundred miles from the *Liberty,* were misrouted or delayed in the hopelessly convoluted channels and procedures of the Defense Department's Worldwide Communications system.

Dawn on the morning of June 8 brought another beautiful, clear day in the eastern Mediterranean, with light breezes and a calm sea. The aerial reconnaissance of the ship began at 6:00 A.M. local time.* A lumbering Israeli Nord 2501 Noratlas circled the ship slowly, while on the bridge Ensign John Scott studied the plane with binoculars. At 7:20 A.M., Lieutenant James Ennes replaced Scott as Officer of the Deck. A new flag, measuring five by eight feet, was ordered for the ship's tripod mainmast, as the high-speed trip from Rota had badly sooted the old one. Every person on the bridge—for that matter, every person on the ship—was well aware that the *Liberty* was in a war zone and was being examined very, very carefully.

At 9:00 A.M. the *Liberty*'s operating orders required her to make a sharp right-hand turn, reduce speed to five knots, and double back in a westerly direction, roughly parallel to the Egyptian coast north of El Arish. As Ennes ordered the turn, the *Liberty* was 25 miles from Gaza and less than 30 miles from the nearest point on the Israeli coast. And as the turn was being made, another plane—this time a jet aircraft—reconnoitered the ship at a distance. And again at 10:00 A.M., two rocket-armed, delta-winged jets circled the ship three times, this time close enough for officers on the bridge to see the pilots in the cockpits with binoculars. Curiously, the jets did not seem to have any markings.

By now the sun was high and off-duty crew members began to accumulate on the forward decks on blankets and lawn chairs. Sunbathing was the order of the day. Thus it was that a great many crew members saw the Noratlas flying boxcar return, circle the ship, and then pass directly over the *Liberty* at a "very

---

*The account of the intense aerial reconnaissance during the hours from 6:00 A.M. to 1:00 P.M. is taken mainly from Jim Ennes's book, *Assault on the Liberty,* pp. 50–60. Ennes was Officer of the Deck on the ship during this entire period and personally witnessed each overflight and later verified his recollections in interviews with several other crewmen. Seaman George Wilson, who was looking out on the bridge and forecastle during this watch, verified Ennes's account of the reconnaissance in a telephone interview with the author.

low level, probably not more than 200 feet."[31] The plane was clearly marked with the Star of David. Crewmen on the deck and the pilots in the cockpit could see the features on each other's faces. Lieutenant Commander Dave Lewis was on deck at the time, and remembers that crew members and pilots waved at each other. *Liberty* crewmen were used to such close inspections. Because of the huge antennae, including the 32-foot dish for the TRSSCOM system, the ship was frequently an object of curiosity for passing ships and planes.

From this point on until about 12:45 P.M. local time, the same Israeli Noratlas returned every 30 to 40 minutes to examine the ship. Lookout George Wilson, who was on the bridge at the time with Lieutenant Ennes, remembers several "very low level" passes by the Noratlas, in addition to the one just described, which occurred at 10:30 A.M. local time. The ship's flag stood out in an eight-knot relative breeze. The sky was clear. The *Liberty* was moseying along at five knots. The letters GTR-5 were clearly visible on both sides of the bow, painted in white letters ten feet high, and on both sides of the stern, in letters three feet high. The Israelis had obviously identified the ship several times over. What else did they want?

At 1:10 P.M., with the noon meal completed, the *Liberty* conducted a series of drills that took a total of about 40 minutes to complete, including fire, damage control, and gas attack. Afterward, Captain McGonagle addressed the ship's officers and crew, complimenting them on the job done in the drills, but cautioning them about the ship's proximity to the war that was in progress amid smoke and fire on the clearly visible shoreline. By way of reassurance, he reminded the men that the repeated overflights by "friendly" forces at least assured that the *Liberty* had been identified and, he seemed to imply, there could be no mistaken attacks.

FRIENDLY FIRE

The off-duty crew was looking forward to a resumption of sunbathing after the business of the drills when three planes appeared on the radar. This time, there was no circling. At high speed, the delta-winged Mirages came straight for the ship, hardly giving those on the bridge a chance to reach for their binoculars. The first rockets took out one of the forward gun tubs and toppled several of the ship's antennae.

Over the next 20 to 25 minutes, the *Liberty* was attacked continuously from the air. The three Mirages were soon joined by several Mystère fighters, which were slower and more efficient for strafing and for the dropping of napalm.* Before it was finished the *Liberty* had some 821 holes in her sides and decks, including over 100 rocket holes six to eight inches wide.

Two aspects of the air attack are particularly interesting. First, the planes that carried it out were unmarked. The *Liberty*'s radioed early call for help to COMSIXTHFLT, sent minutes after the commencement of the air attack, referred to the attacking forces as "unidentified jet aircraft." Not until armed helicopters appeared on the scene, some 1 hour and 15 minutes later, did those on the bridge—or anywhere else on the ship— know for sure the identity of the attacking forces. In spite of scores of strafing runs by the planes, no one on the bridge or deck at the time remembers markings on the planes. Nor were any reported in messages at the time; nor was any testimony regarding markings on the attacking planes given to the naval court of inquiry. At the inquiry, Captain McGonagle did suddenly remember seeing an Israeli flag flown on one of the motor torpedo boats that later appeared, but his own messages during or after the attack itself contain no hint of an identification. COMSIXTHFLT's fourth situation report, message 081447Z, was the following:

1. Following from *Liberty* (no DTG):
   Quote: We are unable to identify the aircraft or surface vessels. Believe to be Israeli helicopters that circled the ship under attack. Positive identification not made. Will have to be made from ship's photographs.

In sum, the *Liberty* was attacked by forces that were trying to disguise their identity. Why disguised? The answer to that is perhaps best provided by asking other questions. If the *Liberty* had gone down with all hands before sending the above message,

*The ship's doctor, Richard Kiepfer, has confirmed to the author that napalm was used, and that he treated numerous napalm burns. Those who were topside during the air attack remember that "several" canisters were dropped. Ensign David Lucas managed to collect a sample of unburned jelly and took it with him to the naval court of inquiry subsequently held on the attack.

i.e., before the helicopters arrived, who would have known for
sure whom the attackers were? Would the Israeli government
have acknowledged and apologized, as they subsequently did
do? Might not all concerned, including the Johnson administration, have found it much easier to blame the attack on the Egyptians?

A second interesting aspect of the attack is that participating
planes and/or shore-based units in the operation were jamming
the *Liberty*'s radios throughout. Chief Radioman Wayne Smith
recalls that five of the *Liberty*'s six shore circuits were being
jammed, and that whoever was doing it "went searching" for
the last circuit. It was on this last circuit that Smith got a message out to the Sixth Fleet Commander. He also frantically tried
to reach what he thought were the nearest friendly forces . . .
the Israeli naval base at Ashdod.[32]

About 30 minutes after the air attack began, the planes suddenly disappeared . . . just as the ship's radar sighted three
motor torpedo boats approaching at high speed. Again, there
was no hesitation in the attack, though one of the boats did signal something as it sped toward the *Liberty*. Altogether, the Israeli MTB's fired five torpedoes at the ship, one of which struck
amidships, accounting for 25 of the 34 men eventually killed in
the attack.

After the torpedo hit, with the ship now listing 9 degrees, the
motor torpedo boats began circling the ship slowly, firing at the
bridge and at any activity they could see on deck. The boats
trained their 40-millimeter cannon on the ship's waterline in an
apparent effort to explode her boilers.* Petty Officer Charles
Rowley, one of the ship's communications technicians, had been
wounded and moved to the ward room for treatment. He dis-
tinctly remembers the incessant firing from the motor torpedo
boats for a "long time" after the torpedo struck, for the armor-
piercing shells were passing through the ward room itself as he
lay exposed on a table waiting for treatment, until someone
mercifully pushed him off the tabletop onto the floor.

Finally, when an order to "Prepare to abandon ship!" came
over the ship's loudspeaker system, and lifeboats were lowered

---

*A description of the firing by the MTB's after the torpedo explosion is contained in
Ennes, op. cit., pp. 91–96. The author has interviewed several *Liberty* survivors who
vividly remember the incessant machine-gun fire of the MTB's, as they were belowdecks
at this time and were awaiting a second torpedo hit.

into the water, the motor torpedo boats moved in closer and shot the lifeboats out of the water with their cannon. Several *Liberty* crewmen witnessed this, and Petty Officer Rowley also noticed the concentration of Israeli machine-gun fire on the lifeboats stored on deck. After the attack he carefully photographed the shredded boats, thinking that one day the pictures would help tell a story. "They didn't want *anyone* to live," he maintains. And then it was over; the motor torpedo boats suddenly wheeled and departed in the same high-speed V formation in which they had first appeared.

It was 3:05 P.M. local time.* The *Liberty* had been under constant attack for over an hour. She had no engines, no rudder, no power, and no lights. Nine of the officers and crew were known dead. Another 25 were missing and presumed dead, submerged in the now-flooded compartments that had taken the torpedo explosion. One hundred seventy-one of the officers and crew were wounded. Not all of these men were incapacitated, however, and they, together with the 90 men on the ship who were not dead, missing, or wounded, set about collecting bodies, dressing wounds, fighting fires, controlling flooding, buttressing walls and bulkheads, stringing lights and hand-operated phone sets, and repairing engines.

Something else had happened at 3:05 P.M. ship time, just before the Israeli MTB's departed. COMSIXTHFLT had sent the following message via plain-language radio:

> Your flash traffic received. Sending aircraft to cover you. Surface units are on the way. Keep [situation reports] coming.†

Was the MTB withdrawal pure coincidence? Perhaps. But there would be others.

There now began a period of intense, armed reconnaissance of the *Liberty*. Even before the motor torpedo boats had receded from view, a large Israeli SA-321 Super Frelon helicopter appeared and began to slowly circle the ship. And then another.

*The time of the termination of the attack is verified in CINCUSNAVEUR message 151003Z, June, 1967, a chronology of the events surrounding the attack on the *Liberty* prepared for the Secretary of the Navy. This message was declassified on March 19, 1982.

†This message, COMSIXTHFLT 081305Z, was not received by the *Liberty,* as she temporarily had no electricity and was off the air at the time. (See Ennes, op. cit., p. 238.)

The cargo bay doors were open, and *Liberty* crewmen could see that the helos were crammed with armed troops in full battle gear. A mounted machine gun pointed from each of the cargo bays. Large blue Stars of David marked each helicopter. The *Liberty*'s general announcing system blared, "Stand by to repel boarders." "They've come to finish us off," yelled one hysterical, but logical, sailor.[33]

But the helicopters only passed close by the *Liberty*'s decks, and then they too receded into the distance.

For the next hour, as the officers and crew of the ship tried desperately to get her under way again, there were repeated visitors. At 3:36 P.M. local time, the MTB's returned, and later came two unidentified delta-winged jets, causing panic among the crew, who were expecting a resumption of the air attacks.[34] Understandably, some were also beginning to wonder when or whether they might begin to see U.S. planes or ships responding to the *Liberty*'s many calls for assistance.

At 4:14 P.M. local time, quite unknown to the *Liberty,* the Office of the U.S. Defense Attaché in Tel Aviv informed the White House that the U.S. Naval Attaché had been called to the Foreign Liaison Office of the IDF to receive a report that Israeli aircraft and MTB's had "erroneously attacked U.S. ship at 08/1200Z." It was "maybe Navy ship."* The Israelis, said the Defense Attaché, "send abject apologies and request info of other U.S. ships near war zone coasts."[35]

There is no indication in the message exactly when the Naval Attaché had been called to the Foreign Liaison Office—probably a very few minutes before the dispatch of this message at 4:14 P.M., local time. At 3:16 P.M., however, Carrier Task Force 60 had sent a message to the carriers *America* and *Saratoga,* ordering them to launch eight aircraft to assist the *Liberty* and to "destroy or drive off any attackers."[36] At 3:20 P.M. COM-SIXTHFLT had informed the Commander of U.S. Armed

---

*What was truly unusual about this, the first official acknowledgment by the government of Israel of responsibility for the attack, was that after a full morning and afternoon of aerial reconnaissance, some of it at very close distance, scores of strafing runs by warplanes, almost two hours of close-in "work" by MTB's, and visits at spitting distance by two helicopters, the IDF still claimed to be uncertain that the *Liberty* was a Navy ship. Speaking to a reunion of *Liberty* survivors 15 years later in Washington, D.C., Admiral Thomas Moorer, former JCS Chairman, stated that he had "never been willing to accept the Israeli explanation that it was a case of mistaken identity." He could not accept that Israeli pilots "don't know how to identify ships . . . and therefore there must have been some other motive which [he was] confident some day will be made public." (Reunion speech at Hotel Washington in Washington, D.C., on June 5, 1982.)

Forces in Europe that aircraft were being deployed.[37] And at 3:39 P.M. local time (also Israeli time), COMSIXTHFLT had informed the Chief of Naval Operations in Washington of the actions being taken.[38] Estimated flight time from the Sixth Fleet to the *Liberty* by A-4's and A-1's, the types of aircraft that were launched by the *America* and *Saratoga,* was approximately 30 minutes.

QUESTIONS OF PRIORITIES

If the Defense Department experienced delays in communicating a warning to the *Liberty* once the plans for the attack were known, such delays were not experienced after the attack had occurred. The first rocket that struck the *Liberty* fused the senior levels of the Defense Department in a matter of minutes into a determination that no U.S. aircraft would be thrust into an adversary role with the IDF, whatever the implication for the struggling U.S.S. *Liberty.* And suddenly, there were no delays, no communications snafus. The system worked perfectly, as a closer look at the rescue-launch sequence will reveal.

The first attempt to assist the *Liberty* was a reflexive one. Captain Joseph Tully on the bridge of the U.S.S. *Saratoga* was informed of the attack within eight minutes of the first strafing run. Radioman Smith, using the one unjammed shore circuit, reached the *Saratoga*'s communications center almost before the first plane had completed the first pass. At the time, 2:00 P.M., the *Saratoga* was conducting an exercise and had four A-1's launch-ready on its decks. Navigator Max Morris on the *Saratoga* received the *Liberty*'s first urgent calls for help and discussed them with Tully on the bridge, who immediately ordered the *Saratoga* to head into the wind, and launched the A-1's. Thus, less than 15 minutes after Israel attacked the *Liberty,* armed U.S. planes were in the air, headed toward the scene.

As the planes winged off to the southeast, Captain Tully informed Sixth Fleet Commander Admiral Martin of the *Liberty*'s predicament and Tully's response, over the fleet's Primary Tactical Maneuvering Circuit radio network. Martin's immediate reaction was to use that same circuit to order both the *Saratoga* and the *America,* the other carrier in Carrier Task Force 60, to launch planes to protect the *Liberty.* The *America,* however, was not at the same state of alert or readiness (vis-à-vis armed planes, suited pilots, and steam to the catapults) and was unable to ready planes in time for launch before the whole affair was canceled. Within minutes of the *Saratoga*'s launch, Rear Admiral Lawrence R. Geis, Commander of Carrier Task Force 60, issued an order to recall the planes, and minutes after that, the planes were back on the *Saratoga*'s decks. Thus ended the one rescue effort that might have provided timely assistance to the *Liberty*.

For the next hour and a half, while planes and MTB's savaged the *Liberty,* the Defense Department (and presumably the White House) discussed a second rescue effort. Finally a decision was taken and a launch made (from both the *Saratoga* and the *America* this time) just minutes before the formal admission and apology was received from the government of Israel in Tel Aviv. And again a recall order was issued,, and again the planes responded within minutes. By this time, the *Liberty* was floating dead in the water, trying to repair her vital systems, and awaiting the coup de grâce that, mercifully, never came.

Night would fall and another day would dawn before the *Liberty* would see its first help from the Sixth Fleet. Sixteen hours passed in which the *Liberty* saw no U.S. plane or ship, and was not even checked at a distance with a flyby. The Russians offered help, though. At midnight on June 8, a Soviet guided-missile destroyer drew alongside the *Liberty* and sent a message by flashing light:

—Do you need help?
—No, thank you.
—I will stand by in case you need me.[39]

If the Defense Department's actions to recall the rescue planes were fast and efficient, they were nothing compared to the speed with which officials in Washington, and particularly in Congress, began to "explain" the attack on the U.S.S. *Liberty* to the American people. The message from the U.S. Defense Attaché's Office in Tel Aviv stating that the government of Israel had reported an "erroneous" attack on a U.S. ship ("maybe Navy ship") was sent to Washington at 10:14 A.M. EDT. Naturally, there were no casualty figures available at this time, for no U.S. forces had yet reached the ship, and the *Liberty* still considered herself to be under attack. (The feinted attacks by the motor torpedo boats continued until approximately 11:15 A.M. EDT.)[40] The *Liberty* was just too busy trying to stay alive to begin to assess and report, until almost noon Washington time.

The first report on casualties from the ship itself was relayed back to Washington in COMSIXTHFLT situation report 8, contained in COMSIXTHFLT message 081621Z, i.e., at 12:21 A.M. Washington time. The report said, among other things:

> Casualties (approximate): four dead, three severely wounded, 50 wounded.

Obviously this was a first, rough estimate of casualties and a gross underestimate at that.

The Defense Department's Assistant Secretary for Public Affairs, Philip Goulding, issued the first official word on the attack to the American people in press release 542-67, which, after stating that the Israeli government had "informed" the United States that the attack had been made in error, and had apologized, went on to estimate casualties at 4 dead and 53 wounded. The Defense Department has informed the author that this release was made at 11:50 A.M. EDT, but that seems unlikely, in view of the fact that COMSIXTHFLT situation report 8 was not received in Washington until 12:21 A.M. EDT.

The House of Representatives convened at noon on June 8. After a speaker or two addressed the subject of saline water, Representative Roman Pucinski from Illinois asked the consent of the House to speak for one minute. He said:

> Mr. Speaker, it was with heavy heart that we learned a little while ago of the tragic mistake which occurred in the Mediterranean when an Israeli ship mistakenly attacked an American ship and killed four boys and injured and wounded 53 others.
>
> These are the tragic consequences of armed conflict; such mistakes happen frequently in Vietnam.
>
> It would be my hope that this tragic mistake will not obscure the traditional friendship we in the United States have with the people of Israel. The Israeli Government already has apologized. . . .[41]

Pucinski went on to add a few hopes that hostilities would cease. When *The Congressional Record* printed the proceeding of that day, Pucinski's speech was appropriately entitled "Tragic Mistake."

At about the same time that Pucinski spoke, 12:30 P.M., Senator Jacob Javits was committing a similar act on the floor of the Senate. The first five paragraphs of Javits's "remarks" on that day contained five separate references to the accidental nature of the attack. He even explained how such a mistake could occur:

> Mr. President, I must say that it is a great tribute to the valor of the troops of Israel that this morning I have heard Senator after Senator say that while they were terribly dismayed and saddened by this accident, they understood how it could take place under the terrible stress which the forces of Israel have been under in these last few weeks.[42]

FOREKNOWLEDGE AND FOREWARNING

About a week after the attack on the ship, Secretary of State Rusk attended a meeting of NATO Foreign Ministers in Luxembourg. Rusk was genuinely disturbed at the events surrounding the *Liberty* affair, and spoke candidly, though privately, to NATO Secretary-General Manlio Giovanni Brosio and to several others in attendance. After Rusk's departure from Europe, U.S. NATO Ambassador Harlan Cleveland cabled to Undersecretary of State Eugene Rostow:

> Quite apart from Newsweek Periscope item, Secretary's comments to Brosio and several foreign ministers at Luxembourg about Israeli foreknowledge that *Liberty* was a U.S. ship piqued a great deal of curiosity among NATO delegations. Would appreciate guidance as to how much of this curiosity I can satisfy, and when.[43]

The *Newsweek* "Periscope" item to which Cleveland referred had appeared on the newsstands about three to four days previously, and included the following passage:

Although Israel's apologies were officially accepted, some high Washington officials believe the Israelis knew the *Liberty*'s capabilities and suspect that the attack might not have been accidental. One top-level theory holds that someone in the Israeli armed forces ordered the *Liberty* sunk because he suspected it had taken down messages showing that Israel started the fighting.[44]

In all likelihood, it was not messages already taken down by the *Liberty,* but rather messages that might in the future be intercepted, which on June 8, 1967, posed an unacceptable risk to the IDF high command. Otherwise, the item was strikingly close to the truth.

In retrospect, one wonders why more American journalists did not pursue the question of what had really happened to the U.S.S. *Liberty*. To be sure, it would not have been easy for an investigative journalist of the time to pry the matter open. Secretary of Defense McNamara informed the media on June 14, 1967, that "Until the Court [of inquiry] has had an opportunity to obtain the full facts, the Department of Defense will have no further comment."[45] For the *Liberty* officers and crew, this meant that nothing, but nothing, was to be said to reporters about the affair. Rear Admiral Isaac Kidd, who was appointed to preside over the court of inquiry, elaborated somewhat upon this gag order a few days later, instructing *Liberty* crewmen to

Refer all questions to the commanding officer or executive officer or to Admiral Kidd. Answer no questions. If somehow you are backed into a corner, then you may say that it was an accident and that Israel has apologized. You may say nothing else.[46]

A skeptic might have seen in this some prior indication as to how the court of inquiry would find, on the question of the intentional nature of the attack. The court's final report was completed on June 18, and was classified "Top Secret." A 28-page unclassified summary of the proceedings was released by the Defense Department ten days later. The summary indicated that the court had had

insufficient information before it to make a judgment on
the reasons for the decision by Israeli aircraft and motor
torpedo boats to attack.

And later in the text:

In as much as this was not an international investigation, no
evidence was presented on whether any of these aircraft
had identified *Liberty* or whether they had passed any information on *Liberty* on to their own higher headquarters.

The summary was also careful to explain that the fact of the
appointment of the court did not mean that anyone in the Defense Department was at fault:

Convening of such an inquiry is a normal procedure, com-
monly employed after any serious accident or incident resulting in substantial loss of life or damage to a ship. The
fact of its convening does not, of itself, indicate an assumption by the Navy that anyone in the Navy is at fault.[47]

There was another branch of the U.S. government, however,
that was little interested in the international implications of the
affair, or in "covering ass" within the Defense Department. The
Defense Subcommittee of the House Committee on Appropriations was charged with responsibility for defense budget
allocations, including those for the department's Worldwide
Communications network. Certain aspects of the *Liberty* affair
seemed to the subcommittee, in the days after the attack, to
have implications for the effectiveness of that communications
network.

Within the Defense Subcommittee as it was constituted in
the 90th Congress, a group of five members constituted the intelligence working group, dealing more or less informally with
appropriations pertaining to defense intelligence matters, including communications.* Over time, the working group and its staff
had developed a procedure for dealing with intelligence-related

---

*These five members were George H. Mahon, Texas, Chairman; Robert L. F. Sikes,
Florida; Jamie L. Whitten, Mississippi; Frank T. Bow, Ohio; and Glenard P. Lipscomb,
California. In later years, the informal intelligence working group would evolve into a
formal standing subcommittee within the Committee on Appropriations.

incidents that had systemic and/or appropriations implications for defense intelligence—they would quickly take testimony, as soon as possible after the event, and before the administration, the Pentagon, and others were able to develop a position with respect to that incident.

And so it was with the incident involving the U.S.S. *Liberty*. A very few days after the attack, even before the naval court of inquiry had completed its report, the intelligence working group met and took testimony on, among other things, what events or information had led the NSA and JCS to move with such urgency on June 7 to try to reposition the *Liberty*, why these efforts were unsuccessful, and what improvements in the Defense Department communications system would be necessary to ensure that in the future the system would not break down as it clearly had this time.

Representative Robert L. F. Sikes was particularly interested in the *Liberty* matter, as it seemed to him to be a perfect example of the potential human cost of Defense Department communications dysfunctions. Sikes recalls that a representative of the Central Intelligence Agency testified to the working group that the frantic efforts by the NSA and JCS to move the ship on the evening of June 7 were prompted by an intelligence report from the Office of the U.S. Defense Attaché in Tel Aviv. The report indicated that the IDF planned to attack the *Liberty* if she continued to operate in Israeli coastal waters.[48]

On the basis of this and other testimony given to the working group, the full House Appropriations Committee on August 14, 1967, asked its Surveys and Investigations Staff to "examine the effectiveness of the DOD worldwide communications system." The staff then produced a two-volume study entitled "A Report to the Committee on Appropriations—U.S. House of Representatives on the Effectiveness of the Worldwide Communications Systems and Networks of the Department of Defense." This document is still classified "Top Secret," but according to Representative Sikes and other committee sources, it includes the CIA testimony described above.[49]

"THE CIRCUMSTANCES UNDER
WHICH THESE PEOPLE DIED . . ."

When American servicemen are killed in combat, certain amenities are observed by the United States government. Over the years, these amenities have assumed the importance of traditions. Families are informed in a certain way. The President sends a letter of condolence. Those dead who performed meritoriously in combat are honored in ceremonies that have become part of the ritual of warfare.

Like the *Liberty* survivors who had witnessed a deliberate, determined, total attack on their ship by a presumed ally, the *Liberty* dead posed certain problems for their government, in the wake of the Six-Day War. White House aide James Cross, writing to senior White House aide Harry McPherson, described those problems:

> 31 [sic] Navy personnel were killed aboard the *U.S.S. Liberty* as the result of the accidental attack by Israeli forces. The attached condolence letters, which have been prepared using basic formats approved for Vietnam war casualties, strike me as inappropriate in this case. Due to the very sensitive nature of the whole Arab-Israeli situation and the circumstances under which these people died, I would ask that you review these drafts and provide me with nine to ten different responses which will adequately deal with this special situation.[50]

McPherson responded to Cross a few days later, agreeing that many of the paragraphs in the Vietnam letters were "inappropriate for those who died on the *U.S.S. Liberty*." He suggested certain thoughts that would be more fitting for the sacrifices made by the men of the *Liberty*, thoughts that did not unduly emphasize the combat, the adversary, or the sacrifice itself. He suggested that the President draw attention to the "contribution to the cause of peace" made by the *Liberty* dead and to the "hope that from the ashes of war in the Middle East may arise a new opportunity for peace." The President should add, McPherson said, that "We sought to avert that war."[51]

The Joint Chiefs of Staff knew about the planned attack by Israel on the U.S.S. *Liberty* before it occurred and presumably informed the White House. When the early reports of the attack arrived, those who had known of the plan had a choice: either take retaliatory action against Israel, or become an accessory after the fact to the attack by promoting the fiction that it was somehow an accident.

The men of the *Liberty* never stood a chance, but they made the best of a bad situation. They were virtually unarmed, and had been denied the protection they had requested from their own government. Their attackers, when they came, were disguised and tried to jam their communications, to prevent calls for help from reaching the Sixth Fleet. Somehow, through cannon fire, rockets, napalm, and torpedoes, the *Liberty* stayed afloat and did get a message through. An abortive air assistance effort was mounted as a purely reflexive action by naval line officers who were not aware that the ship was being attacked by an ally, and would not have cared had they known. The air assistance was canceled and a cover story for the attack later propagated by politicians who dishonored the *Liberty* dead and wounded, and by senior U.S. military officers who dishonored the uniforms they wore.

These are the circumstances under which 34 men of the U.S.S. *Liberty* died.

No attempt is made in this chapter to recount or to reconcile the many official inquiries, studies, and reports that have been done on the *Liberty* Affair, though they have been used and occasionally cited in the chapter's preparation.

In the United States, in addition to the naval court of inquiry transcript, which is now declassified and available, there has been a major study by the Joint Chiefs of Staff and several detailed chronologies and compilations of official messages related to the attack. Both the NSA and the CIA have completed and released studies, large portions of which have had to be excised to protect the intelligence mission and capabilities of the ship, and to preserve good relations between the United States and Israel. The thrust of the American studies has been to explain why no assistance was sent to the ship during and just after the attack. Ultimately, of course, there can be no explanation, no justification.

Two major Israeli studies of the *Liberty* Affair are available—a preliminary inquiry report completed by a judge shortly after the attack and transmitted to the Department of State in August, 1967, and a more detailed study by the IDF History Department completed in 1982, which, at least as of this writing, is "the official version of the State of Israel."* The Israeli studies are inconsistent, one with the other, in several respects, and they tend to dwell on such absurd propositions as the "fact" that the *Liberty* flew no flag and had no identifying markings. Like the American courts and agencies, the Israeli officials concerned have been faced with the task of explaining the unexplainable, and these studies must be seen in this tolerant if not understanding light.

All of the official versions of the *Liberty* Affair, with the probable exception of the unreleased portions of the reports of the two U.S. intelligence agencies, have for political reasons had to proceed from the pleasant fictional premise that the attack was an accident. Now, foreknowledge of the planned attack, by both the U.S. and (obviously) the Israeli governments, is established by this book, thanks to recently declassified State Department documents, and to candor from Congressmen and congressional staffers who took testimony in executive session on the *Liberty* Affair within days after the attack. One would hope that both governments will henceforth cease their dissembling about flags and wind speed and such irrelevancies, and will be willing and able to focus upon the matter of individual and collective responsibility for this unspeakably squalid operation.

There are unresolved obligations here, to the families and friends of the *Liberty* dead as well as to the surviving officers and crew. Both are debtors: the "friendly" government that attacked the ship, and the other government that abandoned it.

---

*The Israeli "preliminary inquiry" has not been formally released by the State Department, though it is unclear to the author whether it was ever actually classified. It has, however, been mistakenly sent to at least one researcher, and through him, made available to the author.

—10—

Final Thoughts

IN THE YEARS 1948–1963, America was perceived by all of the governments in the Middle East as a major power that acted upon the basis of its own, clearly defined national self-interest. Moreover, U.S. Middle East policy was just that—Middle East policy; it was not an Israeli policy in which Arab countries were subordinate actors. In the years 1948–1963, Presidents Truman, Eisenhower, and Kennedy firmly guaranteed Israeli national security and territorial integrity, but just as firmly guaranteed those of Jordan, Lebanon, and the other nations of the region. That was what the Tripartite Declaration of 1950 was all about.

For successive Israeli governments in this period, the boundary line between U.S. and Israeli national security interests was drawn frequently, and usually decisively. Truman's policies on arms exports to the Middle East, Eisenhower's stands on regional water development and on territorial integrity during the Suez Crisis, and Kennedy's candor with Mrs. Meir—all of these were markers on this boundary line.

Nevertheless, during this time U.S. financial support for Israel far exceeded that given any other nation in the world, on a per capita basis. And U.S. diplomatic support for Israel in the UN and elsewhere was no less generous. But the limits to U.S. support for Israel were generally understood by all of the countries of the region, and it was precisely these limits that preserved America's ability to mediate the various issues that composed the Arab-Israeli dispute.

Then, in the early years of the Johnson administration, 1964–1967, U.S. policy on Middle Eastern matters abruptly

243

changed. It would perhaps be more accurate to say that it disintegrated. America had a public policy on the nonproliferation of nuclear weapons, but suddenly had a covert policy of abetting Israel's nuclear weapons program. We had a public policy on arms balance in the region, but secretly agreed, by the end of 1967, to become Israel's major arms supplier. Officially, the United States was "firmly committed to the support of the political independence and territorial integrity of all the [Middle Eastern] nations," while consciously, covertly, the Johnson "Middle East team" set about enabling Israel to redraw to her advantage virtually every one of her borders with neighboring Arab states.[1]

It was, of course, a policy without principle, without integrity. But it was also ineffective, in the sense that Israel steadily continued to act in ways that ignored U.S. national security interests. In a sense the Eshkol government could not be blamed, for although Israel and America were now close "security" allies, at least covertly, there was very understandable confusion on the part of the Israelis regarding just what America did and did not conceive to be her essential national security interests in the Middle East.

For example, the Johnson administration had approved a limited war against Egypt, but expected Israel to abide by U.S. judgment about the timing and the territorial limits of the fighting. Meanwhile, U.S. financial and military assistance gave Israel the military power to invade any or all of the Arab countries at any time and any place she chose, without fear of the outcome. After the war, in a meeting at the White House, Johnson would whine to Foreign Minister Eban:

> . . . he regretted that the advice he had given in his last meeting with the Foreign Minister had been ignored. While there may seem to be victory now for the Israelis, in the long term he was not sure anyone had gained. It had been a difficult moment, and the President must say that the most awesome decisions he had taken since he came into office resulted from [the threatened Soviet intervention in the] crisis. The President said he thought at the time that Israeli action [to invade Syria] was unwise. He still thought so.[2]

Similarly, Walt Rostow had written the President in the early stages of the war that swift Israeli victory and the enormous territorial gains that came with it would lead to an unparalleled opportunity for peace negotiations on basic issues, and thus for the fulfillment of long-term U.S. objectives in the region. In the months after the war, however, it was apparent that Israel did not intend to bargain for negotiations . . . in fact, did not want negotiations at all. What she wanted was land, which she had plenty of, as of June 11, 1967. So there was more American whining. In September, 1967, the State Department instructed Ambassador Barbour in Tel Aviv "to make the following points clear" to Abba Eban:

> There is growing concern among governments friendly to Israel at indications Israeli objectives may be shifting from original position seeking peace with no repeat no territorial gains toward one of territorial expansionism. Israel's refusal to authorize the return of all refugees desiring to resume residence on the West Bank, reported breaking off of West Bank banking negotiations and statements by senior Israeli officials quoted in American press give rise to impression that Israeli Government may be moving toward policy of seeking security simply by retaining occupied areas rather than by achieving peaceful settlement with Arabs. . . . Ability of U.S. to work for more realistic position on part of Arabs depends to great degree on assumption among Arabs and in world community generally that Israel sincerely wishes peaceful settlement above all.[3]

Ambassador Barbour had a difficult job. Quite obviously, very little was "clear" to the Israelis. Particularly unclear was just what limits the United States was prepared to place upon the use of Israeli force in the Middle East even, it seemed, when that force was used on a ship of the U.S. Navy.

"A TERRIBLE WAY TO GET"

If the cause of Middle East peace and/or U.S. national security interests had not been very well served by the business of pandering to Israel, it should be said in partial defense of Johnson's Middle East team that that was not entirely the purpose of the exercise. There were other considerations, such as the 1966

mid-term congressional elections, and the prospect of a 1968
presidential election campaign. Aid to Israel had its impact in
these areas also.

In September of 1966, two months before the midterm elections, Walt Rostow wrote the President about the "timing of
Israeli aid moves" so as to achieve maximum "public attention."[4] Then just before the election itself, the White House
staff was asked to produce a summary of "U.S. Help for Israel,
1964–1966." It probably had the desired effect with the U.S.
Jewish community, as it was an impressive document. In addition to "important sales to Israel of tanks and combat aircraft in
1965 and 1966," the summary estimated that official U.S. aid
composed 59 percent of all Israeli expenditures on agriculture
development, 35 percent of all improvement of telephone services, 58 percent of railway development, and 64 percent of all
Israeli government expenditures on construction of schools.
These figures did not include the indirect subsidies provided by
the U.S. tax-deductible status of Israeli development bonds.[5]

In September, 1967, one of the President's closest aides,
Harry McPherson, wrote Johnson several memos about the generous efforts of "Eppie" Evron, who was the number two man
in the Israeli Embassy in Washington at the time.* Evron was a
close friend of Johnson's and had seen him frequently before
during and after the June war to "coordinate" matters pertaining to that event. Now, in September, "Eppie" had offered to
assist the President of the United States politically with certain
of his own constituents. McPherson wrote:

> [Evron] is encountering a great deal of suspicion and doubt
> in the Jewish community about the Administration's posi-
> tion before June 5. He has tried to counter it, but he finds
> that people who have talked to State get a much more cau-
> tious view of what American policy was in the pre-war
> weeks; not enough sense of your commitment has gotten
> through.[6]

*In 1954, Evron had been one of the Modiin (Israeli military intelligence) case officers
for the Lavon group, which had fire-bombed the U.S. cultural centers in Cairo and
Alexandria. McPherson, a few years later in his LBJ Library oral history interview,
described himself as "the staff semi-Semite." When asked by the interviewer what this
entailed, he said, for the record, ". . . a continuing relationship with B'nai B'rith, the
Anti-Defamation League, to some extent the Zionist organization, and others who want
various things." (Tape 1, p. 31, Harry McPherson interview, LBJ Library Oral History
Project.)

Evron's government was also encountering certain "obstacles" in dealing with the U.S. government, which made it appear that the administration was trying to pressure Israel to be a bit less intransigent vis-à-vis the Arabs. "Eppie" was certain this was not the case, McPherson said, but help would be appreciated. The State Department was holding up export licenses for the sale of 18 Piper Cub airplanes to Israel, and for $3 million in spare parts for "attack aircraft" (presumably the A-1 Skyhawks). The U.S. Army was also being difficult, and had been refusing to make training materials available to the IDF.

McPherson thought that the deal being offered was one that should be accepted:

> I remember Dean Acheson saying in 1960 that the U.S. should have handled Castro, not by denunciation and threat, but by lousing up the customs and visa and commercial processes—getting that point across by studied bureaucratic inaction and bumbling. Maybe that's what we were doing now. If that's the case, it's having its effect; and my antennae tell me that it ought not to be prolonged beyond the point where it becomes politically damaging.[7]

Several years later, in another of his interviews with the Lyndon Baines Johnson Library Oral History Project, Harry McPherson reflected upon this kind of "service" to an American president:

> [In the White House] you tend to view everything in terms of whether it hurts your Administration, your President and that sort of thing; or helps. You look at almost nothing from the point of view of whether it's true or not. It's only the sort of PR sense: what effect it will have on public support or lack or support for your Administration. And that's a terrible way to get. It makes you very efficient. You become very quick. And you become very good at offering advice on what your principal should do instantly. But you may miss the boat badly, because you haven't really understood and taken in what the concern of the country is.[8]

Lyndon Johnson's Middle East team simply lost sight of the distinction between U.S. and Israeli national security interests.

It was a perceptual failure. By late 1967, the administration was feeling enormous political pressure from the American public on the question of U.S. involvement in Vietnam. There was a fear of being overextended in Southeast Asia and a corresponding tendency to "let Israel do it" in the Middle East. And Israel, as we have seen, drove a very hard bargain indeed.

Conversely, Prime Minister Eshkol and the rest of the Israeli leadership never lost sight for a moment of the difference between Israeli and U.S. national security interests. Ironically, it is on the subject of Vietnam that this can best be demonstrated.

VIETNAM PATHETIQUE

For Lyndon Johnson, Israel, like practically everything else, was occasionally viewed through the distorting prism of the U.S. war effort in Southeast Asia. Johnson could never understand why a people and a country that had suffered from aggression could not support the "free-world effort" in South Vietnam. We were after all only defending a small country from Communist aggression. And Israel, in 1965 and 1966, just steadfastly refused to join the "free-world effort."

Initial contacts on this subject were made in 1965, when it was suggested to the Israeli government that surgical-medical or rural health teams might be sent to help in Vietnam.[9] In early 1966, the Thieu government, at U.S. urging, transmitted official requests to the Israelis for establishment of diplomatic relations between the two countries, and for various forms of aid in the war effort. The State Department asked the U.S. Ambassador in Tel Aviv to urge Foreign Minister Eban to consider these requests favorably, and added:

> Israel would rightly be the first to be frightened if the U.S. were to "cut and run" in Vietnam. You should note that U.S. is being most helpful to Israel currently, and that reciprocal gestures would be well received in Washington.[10]

To ensure that Israel got the point, the State Department informed the Israelis of a Radio Hanoi broadcast on February 26, 1966, expressing support for the Palestine Liberation Organization, and attacking U.S. tank sales to Israel. The answer from Israel was no. In March, the Israeli government informed the

Republic of Vietnam that no aid mission would be sent. Nor would there be any diplomatic exchange between the two countries.[11]

In April, U.S. Assistant Secretary of State Raymond Hare traveled to Israel to meet with Prime Minister Eshkol to again bring up the question of Israeli-Vietnamese relations. Hare told Eshkol that the Vietnam problem was "now the touchstone of American foreign policy," and that the U.S. government considered closer relations between Israel and the Thieu government to be "important." The Israeli Prime Minister was very candid, very firm in his response:

> [Eshkol's] reaction was to emphasize obstacles in way of positive Israeli action. He pointed out that Israel was small nation which [was a] gateway to Asia and that Israeli relations with Asian and African developing nations would suffer by Israel's support for Vietnam.[12]

Foreign Minister Eban, who was also present, expanded upon this, pointing out that the evident political disarray in South Vietnam was causing increasing doubts about the U.S. war effort there. Public opinion in Israel, members of the Knesset, and even cabinet ministers shared these doubts. Eban added that the voices of dissent in the U.S. itself, particularly among intellectuals, had considerable influence with the Israeli body politic.

What Prime Minister Eshkol and Foreign Minister Eban were gently saying to Ambassador Hare, and through him to President Johnson, was that the establishment of diplomatic relations with the Thieu regime would damage the essential national security interests of Israel. They were simply drawing the line, setting the boundary post. It was a point of view that President Kennedy would have clearly understood. "Thanks, but no thanks."

To Johnson, to presidential assistants Walt Rostow and McGeorge Bundy, and to the others who dealt with Middle East matters, this response seemed outrageous. Having themselves repeatedly fudged the line between U.S. and Israeli interests, having in fact forgotten where that line was, they considered the Israelis to be ungrateful. Harry McPherson later quoted the President as saying, "Dammit, they want me to protect Israel, but they don't want me to do anything in Vietnam."[13]

In the summer of 1966 Israel did finally agree to assist the "free-world effort" in Vietnam. They agreed to accept eight Vietnamese trainees in dry-land farming. And there was a condition. The U.S. government had to ensure that there would be no publicity about the matter.[14] It appears from the documentation that the State Department agreed. It was not a proud moment in the history of American foreign policy.

By June of 1967, for a variety of reasons that prominently included "domestic political considerations," Lyndon Johnson and his team of foreign-policy advisers had completely revised U.S.-Israeli relations. To all intents and purposes, Israel had become the 51st state. I do not mean to imply, in the account of failed U.S. efforts to promote Israeli-Vietnamese relations, that there were no benefits at all to the United States in this new security alliance with Israel. In July of 1967, *The New York Times* reported that Israel was offering to sell or barter to the U.S. examples of up-to-date Soviet weapons captured during the June war, including artillery, electronic gear, rockets and launchers, tanks, and planes.[15]

The offer was, however, made to Britain and West Germany as well as the United States, and the Israelis did want something in return. The *Times* reported that Israel was seeking to use the Soviet weapons as an "inducement" to obtain purchasing rights for advanced U.S. weapons. It may have worked. Less than 12 months later, the United States agreed to sell Israel the F-4 Phantom, a plane whose capabilities the Israelis had come to appreciate during the Six-Day War . . . at an abandoned French air base outside Beersheba in the Negev.

While the Johnson administration may have lost sight of the line separating U.S. and Israeli national security interests, the government of Israel most certainly had not. Walt Rostow and his colleagues would have done well to study and to some degree follow Israel's somewhat more careful, more sophisticated approach to its foreign affairs.

A TURNING POINT

U.S.-Israeli relations would never be the same again. The pattern established in 1964–1967 has continued more or less intact down to the present day.

In all respects except one, Israel has become America's client state. Only in the case of the Republic of Vietnam, in the decade spanning the late 1960's and early 1970's, has the United States had such a relationship—one in which we provide the daily sustenance for virtually every single human being in the country. From 1946 to 1983, we have provided over $27 billion in official economic and military aid to Israel. This amounts to over $7,700 for every man, woman, and child living in Israel at the present time—over $38,000 for each family of five. During the last three fiscal years (1981–1983), U.S. official assistance has averaged over $3,400 *each year* for each Israeli family of five. These figures do not include private gifts and donations, or the sale of Israeli development bonds.

Seventy percent of all U.S. official assistance to Israel has been military. America has given Israel over $17 billion in military aid since 1946, virtually all of which—over 99 percent—has been provided since 1965. The United States has given, in this period, almost three times the military assistance to Israel alone than we have given to the other 19 Middle Eastern states combined, even including the assistance provided to Iran during the time of the Shah.[16]

This is the public face of our relationship. There is another one, less well known. The United States and Israel have for many years cooperated closely on civilian intelligence matters. The current Director of Mossad (the equivalent of our CIA), for example, Yitzhak Hoffi, attended the U.S. Army Command and General Staff College in the mid-1960's, at an earlier, less civilian phase of his career.[17] In a 1978 article in *The New York Times Magazine,* Seymour Hersh maintained that it was the CIA that transferred "technical information" to the Israeli nuclear weapons program in the "mid-1960's."[18] When I appealed, in 1982, the CIA's refusal to release to me a document concerning the 1967 war, which I had located at the LBJ Library, I was informed by letter that the CIA's Information Review Committee

> . . . determined that the only unclassified portion of the document is the subject line: "The Arab-Israeli War: Who Fired the First Shot." The remainder of the document continues to be classified.

Cooperation between Israel and America on military intelligence is particularly close. Following the 1973 war in the Mid-

dle East, the Pentagon and the IDF established joint, high-level
"data acquisition teams" as part of the work of the Defense Department's Weapons Systems Evaluation Group (WSEG). The
purpose of the WSEG, according to its Director, Vice Admiral
E. C. Waller, was to

> . . . undertake the task of systematic collection, organiza-
> tion and distribution of data having to do with the details of
> the interactions between opposing weapons and weapons
> systems utilized in the October, 1973 Middle East War.[19]

In other words, the WSEG studied the performance of various
Soviet and U.S. weapons systems when used in opposition to
each other.

On the Israeli side, the senior participant in this effort was
Brigadier General Uzi Eilam, Chief of Research and Development for the IDF. The WSEG's reports carry the following classification stamp: SECRET: NOFORN EXCEPT ISRAEL. This means
"Secret: no dissemination to any foreign national except an Israeli with U.S. security clearance." It was by 1973 a relationship
unique in American history, and perhaps unique in the modern
history of nation-states.

Not surprisingly, those who point out the closeness of this
curious U.S.-Israeli security relationship, and its inherent risks,
do so at their own peril. A Defense Department official published an article in 1977 in the *Armed Forces Journal International* in which he examined the latest Israeli military buildup
and the magnitude of Israeli requests for U.S. military assistance
into the mid-1980's—requests that the Congress has since
granted. The official estimated that these weapons would give
Israel the capability to launch lightning offensives against any or
all of the Arab States before the United States or the other
"powers" had a chance to intervene. The number of medium
tanks Israel had requested from the United States, for example,
for the decade 1976–1986, nearly equaled the total number deployed by the U.S. military within NATO. On its publication,
the article was attacked by the Anti-Defamation League of the
B'Nai B'Rith as "anti-Israel and anti-Jewish."[20]

It will also be no surprise to the reader of the first nine chapters of this volume that extensive U.S.-Israeli cooperation on
security matters has not prevented repeated efforts by the latter

to spy upon the former. The CIA's March, 1979, report entitled "Israel: Foreign Intelligence and Security Services" contains the following passage:

> Israel's program for accelerating its technological, scientific and military development as rapidly as possible has been enhanced by exploiting scientific exchange programs. Mossad plays a key role in this endeavor. In addition to the large scale acquisition of published scientific papers and technical journals from all over the world through overt channels, the Israelis devote a considerable portion of their covert operations to obtaining scientific and technical intelligence. This had included attempts to penetrate certain classified defense projects in the United States and other Western nations.[21]

TOWARD A SELF-RESPECTING RELATIONSHIP

On July 15, 1982, George W. Ball read a statement to the Foreign Relations Committee of the United States Senate. He was appearing, he said, in a "purely personal capacity." Nevertheless, his views reflected his experience as Undersecretary of State from 1961 to 1966, and as United States Permanent Representative to the UN in 1968.

He began: "The burden of my comments this morning is that our country urgently needs to recast its relations with Israel." Repeatedly in the last quarter century, said Ball, the Israeli government had taken matters into its own hands in the Middle East, "secretly launching military adventures without regard to their effect on America's plans or concerns." He ticked off the instances he had in mind—the invasions in 1956 and 1967, a bombing raid on an Iraqi nuclear reactor in 1981, the savage bombing of residential areas of Beirut only one month later, and the invasion of Lebanon that was still proceeding as he spoke that day.

Such a protracted sequence of events has established a pattern so routine as to be taken for granted. First, Israel embarks secretly on a military adventure at a carefully chosen time when America's attention is focused elsewhere. Second, our government responds, if at all by mild threats both sides know will never be carried out. Third, when the Israeli Government reacts in anger at our threats, we appease it by providing more planes, guns, tanks and economic help.

It had been 25 years, said Ball, since an American president had had the political fortitude to use this country's "influence" to make Israel back down from these aggressive adventures—when Dwight Eisenhower had forced the withdrawal from Sinai after the Suez War. One price we had paid for this lack of courage was that the UN had been rendered impotent in fulfilling its peacekeeping functions in the region, even when we strongly backed its actions there. Ball cited the example of the tattered UN Security Council Resolution 242 of 1967, which, *inter alia,* called for Israel to withdraw from the occupied territories. Since 1967, he reminded the Senators, America had stood mute while Israel established its capital city in captured Jerusalem, annexed the Golan Heights, and settled 40 percent of the West Bank of the Jordan.

In U.S. foreign relations since 1967, Israel seemed to be the exception to every rule, every principle America stood for. When Turkey invaded Cyprus in 1974, we suspended all military assistance to the aggressor for two years because the Turks illegally used weapons we had given or sold to them for self-defense. When Israel invaded Lebanon eight years later, however, in an action far costlier of innocent civilian lives, America—in particular the U.S. Congress—seemed to have misplaced its last copy of the Arms Export Control Act. Our response was to promise delivery to Israel of 75 more advanced F-16 fighter planes.

One problem with current U.S. policy in the Middle East was that it was based upon a patently false premise:

Our first step in shaping a Middle East policy that will advance and protect our indispensable national interests is to acknowledge that Israel is no longer a weak, beleaguered state menaced by powerful enemies on all sides. Yet we

have never seriously tried to adjust our policies to this
change in circumstances. . . .*

All too often when Americans discuss possible resolutions to
the problems of the Middle East, said Ball, someone tries to
terminate the discussion with the comment that "Israel would
never agree to that."

> It is a habit we should break. United States Middle East
> policy has marched to an Israeli drum far too long.

Ball's statement that July morning in 1982 was a heavy dose
of reality and common sense for the Senate Foreign Relations
Committee. It is my hope that this book, covering the period
1948–1967, and one to follow that will deal with 1968 to the
present, will contribute to public discussion of the need for a
thorough reexamination and recasting of our relations with Israel.

Amos Oz, an Israeli novelist, wrote an article in 1967 in
which he asked the rhetorical question "Why Israel?" His answer was direct and powerful:

> Because there is no other part of the world to which the
> Jews would have come in their masses to establish a Jewish
> country in it. . . . Our justification in respect of the Arab
> inhabitants of the country cannot base itself on our age-old
> longings. We have no other objective justification than the
> right of one who is drowning and grasps the only plank he
> can.[22]

There is however, he said, an important moral difference between the drowning man who grasps a plank and makes room by
pushing the others who sit on it aside, and the one who pushes
the others on the plank into the sea.

My objections to Israel's militarism (and to America's role in
its development) are both moral and pragmatic. We should not
lose sight of the fact that it simply has not worked. Who can
look at Israel today, and at its posture in the Middle East and
the world, and see a secure Jewish homeland?

*If I have one fault to find with George Ball's thesis it is that, as the foregoing pages
amply document, the State of Israel in fact never was a "weak, beleaguered state. . . ."

True, the militarists have seemingly won, in the sense that the compassion of Nahum Goldmann and the wisdom of Moshe Sharett have for the time being been discredited by leaders with embittered perspectives on Israel and the world. But will men like Menahem Begin and Ariel Sharon secure Israel's future with a mailed fist? Does truth really come from the barrel of a gun? Will Israel be a safe Jewish homeland in the Middle East as an independent state with normalized political and economic relations with its neighbors, or will it finally have to become a formal dependency of the United States, deriving its economy and security from that relationship? That is a question that the leaders of both countries will have to answer in the near future.

Gradually, over the time span that is the focus of this book, and most particularly in the last three years before the 1967 war, America took sides—not with Israel as such, but with the militarists within that country whose vision of the future never allowed space for the others who were clinging to the plank. With American support and assistance of a different kind, there might yet be a future for all who wish to call Israel *and* Palestine their home.

Acknowledgments

THE EARLY STAGES of my research involved a scan of published sources, much of which was done at Norwich University Library in Northfield, Vermont. The staff there, in particular Ann Turner, Paul Heller, Margaret Partlow, Jacqueline Painter, and Wilma and Bruce Coon, provided constant assistance in many ways. In the age of the computerized interlibrary loan system, the helpfulness, patience, and persistence of the staff are far more important than the size of the library.

The next phase took me to Washington, and particularly to the National Archives. Archivist Wilbert Mahoney of the Modern Military Branch and Archivist William Lewis at the National Records Center in Suitland, Maryland, spent many hours helping me to locate documents and, more than that, suggesting fruitful avenues of inquiry on their own.

The mysteries of the federal Freedom of Information Act were explained to me by Tonda Rush at the FOI Service Center in the offices of the Reporters' Committee for Freedom of the Press, and I found it necessary to contact her frequently thereafter. Pursuing FOIA requests takes an enormous amount of hard-nosed persistence, and I am not sure I could have stuck with it without Tonda's encouragement and advice.

My contacts with the Dwight D. Eisenhower Presidential Library in Abilene, Kansas, were by mail and telephone, and mostly with Archivist Jim Leyerzapf, who responded to requests with astonishing speed. The finding aides at the Eisenhower Library are the finest I have seen anywhere. I was able to travel to the Lyndon Baines Johnson Library in Austin, Texas, where my chief contact was Archivist David Humphrey. Together with the Archivists of the reading room there in Austin, David helped me to understand what important national resources the presidential libraries and materials centers are.

On individual chapters, I have received invaluable assistance from John Fialka of *The Wall Street Journal,* William Broad of *The New York Times,* Tom Cochran of the Natural Resources Defense Council, and most particularly James Ennes, Jr., and numerous former shipmates of Jim's on the U.S.S. *Liberty.*

Of necessity, the controversial nature of this book has meant adversarial relationships with some agencies of the U.S. government, and at such times I have invariably had advice, assistance, and competent legal counsel from Mark Lynch and Susan Shaffer of the National Security Project at the American Civil Liberties Union in Washington, D.C.

Throughout the research and writing, I have received advice and reactions from two individuals who know far more about the Middle East than I—John P. Richardson, a former colleague of mine, and Clyde Mark of the Congressional Research Service.

There were times when it appeared that the controversy might actually terminate the project, and in those moments I drew upon the calm strength and moral support of my editor at William Morrow and Company, Bruce Lee, who several times convinced me that I could do something when I *knew* I couldn't.

There are others whom I would like to thank but cannot, as this might prove embarrassing to them in their current positions, or in their present or past associations.

Finally, but most important, I owe a debt of gratitude to my wife, who typed, corrected, chastised, occasionally smiled, and otherwise made these past 27 months bearable.

Notes

CHAPTER 2

Classification designations in quotation marks below indicate merely the *previous* designations. Virtually all documents used have been declassified, many of them at the specific request of the author.

1. "Confidential" letter to Col. Fred Pillet from Col. E. P. Archibald, dated December 19, 1949, Israel Air Attaché Branch Station File, Record Group 341, Records of Headquarters USAF, National Archives.

2. "Confidential" letter to Col. Fred Pillet from Col. E. P. Archibald, dated January 14, 1949, Israel Air Attaché Branch Station File, Record Group 341, Records of Headquarters USAF, National Archives.

3. "Confidential" message MAI 177 from U.S. Military Attaché, Tel Aviv, to Army Intelligence (CSGID), dated August 23, 1949, Confidential and Secret Messages, Records of the Cable Section, Office of the Assistant Chief of Staff, G-2, Record Group 319, Records of the Army Staff, National Archives.

4. Message MAI 213 from U.S. Military Attaché, Tel Aviv, to Army Intelligence (CSGID), dated October 20, 1949, Confidential and Secret Messages, Records of the Cable Section, Office of the Assistant Chief of Staff, G-2, Record Group 319, Records of the Army Staff, National Archives.

5. "Top Secret" JCS paper 1684/11, dated March 31, 1948, copy in Decimal File 1946–1948, Plans and Operations Division, 091 Palestine TS (Section IIA, Case 6), Record Group 319, National Archives.

6. Dispatch 224, from American Consul General, Cairo, to Secretary of State, dated November 26, 1947, Top Secret Cairo Legation and Embassy Files, Record Group 84, National Archives.

7. J. Bowyer-Bell's *Terror out of Zion* (New York: Avon Books, 1977), Part 5, contains a detailed and well-researched account of the *Altadena* incident, though both Begin and Ben Gurion cover the affair in their own autobiographies.

8. "Restricted" dispatch 315 from American Embassy, Warsaw, to Secretary of State, dated May 20, 1948, copy in Jerusalem Consular Files, Series 800 Israel, Record Group 84, National Archives.

9. "Restricted" dispatch 239 from American Embassy, Tel Aviv, to Secre-

tary of State, dated October 5, 1949, Tel Aviv Embassy Files, Series 350.21, Record Group 84, National Archives.

10. Gideon Raphael in *Destination Peace: Three Decades of Israeli Foreign Policy* (New York: Stein and Day, 1981), p. 7.

11. "Restricted" airgram 1758 from American legation, Beirut, to Secretary of State, dated June 2, 1948, in Project Decimal Files, 1946–48, Office of the Assistant Chief of Staff, Intelligence, G-2, Record Group 319, National Archives.

12. "Top Secret" telegram NIACT MARTEL 134 from Secretary of State George C. Marshall to Undersecretary Robert Lovett, dated November 15, 1948, in Carrolton Press Declassified Documents Reference System, 1975/721E.

13. "Secret" telegram 26 from U.S. Consulate General, Jerusalem, to Secretary of State, dated January 7, 1948, Jerusalem Consular Files, Series 800 Palestine, Record Group 84, National Archives.

14. "Restricted" telegram 301 from U.S. Consulate General, Jerusalem, to Secretary of State, dated March 12, 1948, in Jerusalem Consular Files, Series 800 Palestine, Record Group 84, National Archives.

15. J. Bowyer-Bell, op. cit., p. 371.

16. *The New York Times,* April 14, 1948, 6:2.

17. "Confidential" telegrams 439 and 455 from U.S. Consulate General, Jerusalem, to Secretary of State, dated respectively April 15 and 17, 1948, Jerusalem Consular Files, Series 800 Palestine, Record Group 84, National Archives.

18. *The New York Times,* May 23, 1948, 1:5.

19. This statement is based upon telephone interviews conducted with both of the individuals, Robert B. Houghton and Stuart W. Rockwell.

20. "Secret" military attaché report 273-48 from USMA/Baghdad to Assistant Chief of Staff, G-2, dated July 2, 1948, U.S. Army "ID File," Record Group 319, National Archives.

21. "Secret" memorandum for the President from R. H. Hillenkoetter, Director of Central Intelligence, dated July 8, 1948, Israel Air Attaché Branch Station File, Record Group 341, Records of Headquarters USAF, National Archives.

22. "Secret" report ORE 38.48 by the Central Intelligence Agency, dated July 27, 1948, in *Foreign Relations of the United States,* 1948, Volume 5, pp. 1240–1248.

23. "Top Secret" memorandum for the President from George C. Marshall, Secretary of State, dated August 16, 1948, in *Foreign Relations of the United States,* 1948, Volume 5, pp. 1313–1314. See Appendix, Document 1.

24. "Top Secret" telegram 70 from Special Representative of the United States in Israel (McDonald) to President Truman, dated August 24, 1948, in *Foreign Relations of the United States,* 1948, Volume 5, pp. 1337–1339.

25. "Secret" telegrams 1357 and 1411 from U.S. Consulate General, Jerusalem, to Secretary of State, dated respectively September 30 and October 21, 1948; and "Secret" memorandum A-109 from Acting Secretary of State Robert Lovett to American Consul, Jerusalem, dated October 18, 1948, Jerusalem Consular Files, Series 800 Israel, Record Group 84, National Archives.

26. "Top Secret" memorandum, dated October 12, 1948, in the Diaries of James Forrestal, Operational Archives, U.S. Naval History Division, p. 2567.

27. "Secret" telegram 1335 from U.S. Consulate General, Jerusalem, to

Secretary of State, dated September 24, 1948, in Jerusalem Consular Files, Series 800 Palestine, Record Group 84, National Archives.

28. Ibid.

29. "Top Secret" JCS paper 1877/4, dated July 1, 1948, Plans and Operations Division, Decimal File 1946–1948, 091 Palestine TS (Section 2B, Case 7), Record Group 319, National Archives.

30. "Secret" telegram 1413, from U.S. Consulate General, Jerusalem, to Secretary of State, dated October 22, 1948, Jerusalem Consular Files, Series 800 Palestine, Record Group 84, National Archives.

31. "Confidential" telegram DELGA 1053, repeated London as 1422, dated December 4, 1948, London Embassy Files, Series 800 Palestine, Record Group 84, National Archives.

32. "Secret" memorandum of conversation by Secretary of State George C. Marshall, dated October 5, 1948, in *Foreign Relations of the United States, 1948*, Volume 5, pp. 1452–1453.

33. Hal Lehrman in "Gathering Storm in U.S.-Israeli Relations," *Commentary*, October, 1949, p. 327.

34. "Confidential" letter to Director of Intelligence, USAF, from Col. E. P. Archibald, dated September 29, 1949, Israel Air Attaché Branch Station File, Record Group 341, Records of Headquarters USAF, National Archives.

CHAPTER 3

1. "Secret" weekly intelligence report 87 from the Office of the Director of Intelligence, OMGUS, dated January 10, 1948, copy in Publications File, Records of the Document Library Branch, Office of the Assistant Chief of Staff, G-2, Record Group 319, National Archives.

2. "Secret" weekly intelligence report 112 from the Office of the Director of Intelligence, OMGUS, dated July 3, 1948, copy in Publications File, Records of the Document Library Branch, Office of the Assistant Chief of Staff, G-2, Record Group 319, National Archives.

3. Ibid.

4. "Secret" weekly intelligence report 113 from the Office of the Director of Intelligence, OMGUS, dated July 10, 1948, copy in Publications File, Records of the Document Library Branch, Office of the Assistant Chief of Staff, G-Z, Record Group 319, National Archives. See Appendix, Document 2.

5. "Confidential" summary of information, dated March 25, 1948, file 091.7141 Palestine, Decimal Correspondence Files, Office of the Assistant Chief of Staff, G-2, Record Group 319, National Archives.

6. "Confidential" summary of information dated April 27, 1948, file 091.7141 Palestine, Decimal Correspondence Files, Office of the Assistant Chief of Staff, G-Z, Group 319, National Archives.

7. "Secret" agent report, entitled "Recruiting of Reserve Officers for Haganah Forces by Unknown Persons in the Department of the Army," dated May 20, 1948, file 091.7141 Palestine, Decimal Correspondence Files, Office of the Assistant Chief of Staff, G-2, Record Group 319, National Archives.

8. "Secret" agent report by Lyman G. White, dated April 28, 1948, in "ID Files," Records of the Document Library Branch, Office of the Assistant Chief of Staff, G-2, Record Group 319, National Archives.

9. "Secret" memorandum from Col. John Kaylor to Director of Intelligence, U.S. Army, dated June 3, 1948, file 091.7141 Palestine, Decimal Cor-

respondence Files, Office of the Assistant Chief of Staff, G-Z, Record Group 319, National Archives.

10. A. Joseph Heckleman in *American Volunteers and Israel's War of Independence* (New York: KTAV Publishing House, 1974), p. 254.

11. "Secret" telegram 442 from U.S. Embassy, London, to Secretary of State, dated February 5, 1948, in London Post Files, Record Group 84, National Archives.

12. "Confidential" telegram 131 from American Consulate, Haifa, to Secretary of State, dated July 31, 1948, repeated Jerusalem as 131, Jerusalem Consular Files, Series 800 Israel, G-2, Record Group 84, National Archives.

13. "Restricted" memorandum for the record, subject: "Request of Belgian Military Attache for Samples of Stocks of Toxic Ammunitions," dated June 3, 1948, Plans and Operations Division, Decimal File 4648, 400 Belgium (Case 4), Record Group 319, National Archives.

14. "Secret" military attaché report R-239-48 from USMA/Mexico City, dated June 7, 1948, document 470505, "ID Files," Records of the Document Library Branch, Office of the Assistant Chief of Staff, G-2, Record Group 319, National Archives.

15. "Confidential" dispatch 332 from U.S. Embassy, Helsinki, to Secretary of State, dated July 15, 1948, document 0479376, "ID Files," Records of the Document Library Branch, Office of the Assistant Chief of Staff, G-2, Record Group 319, National Archives.

16. "Confidential" intelligence report R-38-48 from Military Attaché, Lebanon, to U.S. Army Intelligence Division, document 440533, "ID Files," Records of the Document Library Branch, Office of the Assistant Chief of Staff, G-2, Record Group 319, National Archives.

17. Golda Meir in *My Life* (New York: G. P. Putnam's Sons, 1975), p. 231.

18. Message 512-25 from USMA/Prague to U.S. Army Intelligence and to European Command, dated March 25, 1948, Confidential and Secret Messages, Records of the Cable Section, Mail and Records Branch, Office of the Assistant Chief of Staff, G-2, Record Group 319, National Archives.

19. "Secret" message 525-02 from USMA/Prague to Army Intelligence (CSGID), dated April 2, 1948, Records of the Cable Section, Office of the Assistant Chief of Staff, G-2, Record Group 319, National Archives.

20. "Secret" military attaché report from Maj. E. H. Whitaker, Jr., dated April 13, 1948, document 457997, "ID Files," Records of the Document Library Branch, Office of the Assistant Chief of Staff, G-2, Record Group 319, National Archives.

21. "Secret" memorandum from Admiral R. H. Hillenkoetter, Director of Central Intelligence, to President Truman, dated April 12, 1948, in Carrolton Press Declassified Documents Reference System, 1979/341B, C. See Appendix, Document 3.

22. Message 738-19 from USMA/Prague to Army Intelligence (CSGID), dated July 19, 1948, Top Secret Messages, Records of the Cable Section, Office of the Assistant Chief of Staff, G-2, Record Group 319, National Archives.

23. "Top Secret" memorandum from Admiral R. H. Hillenkoetter, Director of Central Intelligence, to President Truman, dated August 5, 1948, in Carrolton Press Declassified Documents Reference System, 1979, number 341C.

24. "Secret" military attaché report IR-32-48 from U.S. Air Attaché/Prague to Air Force Intelligence Directorate, dated October 7, 1948, copy in

"ID File," Office of the Assistant Chief of Staff, G-2, Record Group 319, National Archives.

25. "Secret" military attaché report IR-66-48 from U.S. Air Attaché/ Prague to Air Force Intelligence Directorate, dated November 15, 1948, copy in "ID File," Office of the Assistant Chief of Staff, G-2, Record Group 319, National Archives. See Appendix, Document 4.

26. "Secret" military attaché report IR-98-48 from U.S. Air Attaché/ Prague to Air Force Intelligence Directorate, dated December 27, 1948, copy in "ID File," Office of the Assistant Chief of Staff, G-2, Record Group 319, National Archives.

27. "Secret" summary of information from 117th CIC Detachment, New York Field Office, NYPE, dated December 28, 1948, copy in Decimal File 091.112 Czechoslovakia, Decimal Correspondence Files, Office of the Assistant Chief of Staff, G-2, Record Group 319, National Archives.

28. "Top Secret" memorandum of information 493, entitled "Certain Evidence Given to the Anglo-American Committee of Inquiry on Palestine," dated May 3, 1946, American-British Conversations File, 092.3 Palestine, Record Group 165, National Archives.

29. "Secret" memorandum for the Assistant Director, Reports and Estimates, CIA, dated November 13, 1947, copy in Decimal File 350.09 Palestine, Decimal Correspondence Files, Office of the Assistant Chief of Staff, G-2, Record Group 319, National Archives.

30. "Secret" telegram "INFOTEL from Secretary of State," dated May 14, 1948, 800 Daily File, Jerusalem Consular Files, Record Group 84, National Archives.

31. "Secret" memorandum for the Chief of Staff, Department of the Army, entitled "Implications of a New Truce in Palestine," dated July 16, 1948, Decimal File 350.05 Palestine, Decimal Correspondence Files, Office of the Assistant Chief of Staff, G-2, Record Group 319, National Archives.

32. Message A-32, from U.S. Embassy, Tel Aviv, to Secretary of State, dated January 31, 1949, Confidential and Secret Messages File, Records of the Cable Section, Office of the Assistant Chief of Staff, G-2, Record Group 319, National Archives.

33. Military attaché report MAI 109 to U.S. Army Intelligence (CSGID), dated May 10, 1949, Confidential and Secret Messages File, Records of the Cable Section, Office of the Assistant Chief of Staff, G-2, Record Group 319, National Archives.

34. "Top Secret" Tab. A to memorandum for the record dated March 14, 1952, Army Chief of Staff Decimal File 1951–1952, file 091 Israel, Record Group 319, Records of the Army Staff, National Archives.

CHAPTER 4

1. Hal Lehrman in "Kibya, Jerusalem and the River Jordan," *Commentary*, April, 1954, p. 321.

2. "Secret" memorandum for the President from Walter B. Smith, dated October 21, 1953, Box 10, folder Israeli Relations 1951–1957, Dulles Papers Subject Series, Dwight D. Eisenhower Presidential Library, declassified August 31, 1981.

3. "Classified" memorandum to Dr. Horace S. Craig from N. C. Debevoise, Operations Coordination Board, President's Science Advisory Com-

mittee, dated October 29, 1953, OCB Miscellaneous Memos, Box 1, Dulles Papers Subject Series, Dwight D. Eisenhower Presidential Library, declassified September 21, 1979.

4. Hal Lehrman in "Washington Comes to Israel's Economic Rescue," *Commentary,* October, 1952, p. 300.

5. Ibid., p. 303.

6. *The New York Times,* March 23, 1953, 12:6.

7. Abba Eban in *Abba Eban: An Autobiography* (New York: Random House, 1977), pp. 172–173.

8. Moshe Dayan in *Story of My Life* (New York: William Morrow, 1976), p. 173.

9. *The New York Times,* October 19, 1953, 1:5. All of the events recounted in this paragraph were reported in *The New York Times* on October 16–19, 1953.

10. The Mizrachi speech and Ambassador Eban's statement were covered in *The New York Times,* October 19, 1953, 8:5.

11. *The New York Times,* October 21, 1953, 13:2.

12. *The New York Times,* October 23, 1953, 2:3.

13. "Restricted" memorandum of conversation, entitled "Economic Sanctions Against Israel and Related Matters Affecting U.S.-Israeli Relations," dated October 26, 1953, Box 10, folder Israeli Relations, 1951–1957, Dulles Papers Subject Series, Dwight D. Eisenhower Presidential Library.

CHAPTER 5

1. *The New York Times,* January 5, 1954, 75:2.

2. Entry in Moshe Sharett's *Personal Diary* dated May 26, 1955, quoted in Livia Rokach, *Israel's Sacred Terrorism* (Belmont, Mass.: Association of Arab-American University Graduates, 1980), p. 44. The force estimates cited earlier in this section are from an article by Hanson Baldwin in *The New York Times,* October 27, 1953, 8:3.

3. Miles Copeland in *The Game of Nations* (London: Weidenfeld and Nicolson, 1969), p. 56.

4. Jean and Simonne Lacouture in *Egypt in Transition* (New York: Criterion Books, 1958), pp. 232–233.

5. Wilbur Crane Eveland in *Ropes of Sand* (New York: W. W. Norton and Company, 1980), pp. 84–90.

6. "Secret" telegram 1400 from U.S. Consulate, Jerusalem, to Secretary of State, dated October 15, 1948, Jerusalem Consular Files, Series 800-TC-Israel, Record Group 84, National Archives.

7. *The New York Times,* December 12, 1952, 9:3.

8. *The New York Times,* March 30, 1953, 5:3.

9. Nahum Goldmann in *The Jewish Paradox* (New York: Fred Jordan Books–Grosset and Dunlap, 1978). Goldman's account of his efforts at mediation appear on pp. 203–204, and his comment on Jewish people as negotiators, on p. 61.

10. Lacouture, op. cit., p. 233.

11. "Confidential" telegram 1185 from U.S. Embassy, Tel Aviv, to Secre-

tary of State, dated May 11, 1954, Cairo Embassy Files, Box 255, Record Group 84, National Archives.

12. *The New York Times,* September 2, 1954.

13. Raphael, op. cit., p. 44.

14. The quotations in this section appear in Avi Shlaim, *Conflicting Approaches to Israel's Relations with the Arabs: Ben Gurion and Sharett, 1953–1956* (Washington, D.C.: International Security Studies Program, Woodrow Wilson International Center for Scholars, Smithsonian Institution, 1981), pp. 13–14.

15. Raphael, op. cit., p. 32.

16. Moshe Sharett in *Personal Diary* entry dated March 18, 1954, pp. 2398–2400, quoted in Rokach, op. cit., p. 28.

17. Donald Neff in *Warriors at Suez* (New York: Linden Press/Simon and Schuster, 1981), pp. 54–55.

18. Moshe Sharett in *Personal Diary* entry dated January 10, 1955, p. 639, quoted in Rokach, op. cit., p. 40.

19. Olshan-Dori Commission findings quoted in Avri El-Ad, *Decline of Honor* (Chicago: Henry Regnery Company, 1976), p. 197.

20. Enclosure to "Top Secret" memorandum for Brig. Gen. Chester V. Clifton, Military Aide to the President, from Allen W. Dulles, Director of Central Intelligence, dated February 8, 1961, declassified December 7, 1978. See Appendix, Document 5.

21. The political aftershocks of the Lavon Affair are covered in some detail in the Clyde Mark memorandum of December 21, 1972, entitled "The Lavon Affair," prepared for the Congressional Research Service, pp. 6–9, and in the issues of *New Outlook Magazine* dated March, 1961, and May, 1964.

22. Enclosure to memorandum from Allen W. Dulles, dated February 8, 1961, pp. 2–3.

23. Entry in Moshe Sharett's *Personal Diary* dated January 9, 1954, p. 637, quoted in Rokach, op. cit., p. 40.

24. Neff, op. cit., p. 33.

25. "Top Secret" NSC policy paper 155/1, entitled "A Report to the National Security Council by the Executive Secretary on United States Objectives and Policies with Respect to the Near East," dated July 14, 1953, Ann Whitman File, NSC Policy Papers Series, Records of OSANSA, Dwight D. Eisenhower Library, declassified December 10, 1981.

26. "Top Secret" telegram 874 from U.S. Embassy, Beirut, to Secretary of State, dated April 18, 1954, declassified May 5, 1982. See Appendix, Document G.

27. "Top Secret" telegram 1072 from U.S. Embassy, Tel Aviv, to Secretary of State, dated April 17, 1954, declassified May 5, 1982. See Appendix, Document 7.

28. "Confidential" telegram 153 from U.S. Consulate General, Jerusalem, to Secretary of State, dated April 3, 1954, copy in Cairo Embassy Files, Box 255, Record Group 84, National Archives.

29. "Top Secret" telegram 160 from U.S. Embassy, Tel Aviv, to Secretary of State, dated April 17, 1954, declassified May 5, 1982. With one exception (footnote 28) the telegrams cited in the preceding section were obtained by the author under the Freedom of Information Act and are still in the possession of the Department of State, i.e., they have not yet been deposited with the National Archives.

30. The account of the series of Ben Gurion–Sharett cabinet battles in 1955–56 is drawn largely from Shlaim, op. cit., pp. 17–35. In turn, Professor Shlaim's work is drawn largely from Moshe Sharett's *Personal Diary.*

31. Based upon personal telephone interviews with Ambassador Byroade in late 1982.

CHAPTER 6

1. "Top Secret" memorandum of conversation at the White House by John Foster Dulles, dated January 11, 1956, Papers of John Foster Dulles, Box 10, Dwight D. Eisenhower Library.

2. "Secret" memorandum for Admiral Arthur Radford (Chairman, JCS) from Col. George T. Powers, dated February 27, 1956, Plans and Operations Division, file 091 Palestine, Record Group 319, National Archives.

3. Appendix C to "Top Secret" memorandum for the Commander in Chief, U.S. Naval Forces, Eastern Atlantic and Mediterranean, from Captain Richard H. Phillips (for the JCS), dated April 27, 1956, Records of the United States Joint Chiefs of Staff, file 381 EMMEA (1H9-47), National Archives.

4. "Top Secret" memorandum for the Secretary of Defense from Admiral Arthur Radford, Chmn. JCS, dated August 28, 1956, Records of the United States Joint Chiefs of Staff, file CCS 092 Palestine, Record Group 218, National Archives.

5. "Top Secret" memorandum JCS 912389, dated October 29, 1956, Records of the Joint Chiefs of Staff, file 381 EMMEA (1H9-47), National Archives.

6. Neff, op. cit., pp. 379–380.

7. Hugh Thomas in *Suez* (New York: Harper and Row, 1966), pp. 66, 69.

8. "Secret" memorandum for the Chairman, JCS, from Rear Admiral Edwin T. Layton, Deputy Director for Intelligence, dated October 12, 1955, Records of the United States Joint Chiefs of Staff, Record Group 218, National Archives.

9. "Personal and Confidential" memorandum for the President from Secretary of State John Foster Dulles, dated May 22, 1956, Papers of John Foster Dulles, White House Memo Series, Dwight D. Eisenhower Library.

10. Raphael, op. cit., pp. 55–56.

11. Mohamed Heikal in *The Cairo Documents* (New York: Doubleday and Company, 1973), pp. 62–63.

12. Neff, op. cit., p. 276.

13. Ibid., p. 283.

14. Thomas, op. cit., p. 64.

15. Dayan, op. cit., p. 183.

16. "Secret" memorandum for Brigadier General Richard Collins, JCS, from General G. B. Erskine, Assistant to the Secretary of Defense, dated August 17, 1956, Records of the United States Joint Chiefs of Staff, file 091 Palestine (June 56–December 56), Record Group 218, National Archives. See Appendix, Document 9.

17. Dayan, op. cit., pp. 202–208.

18. *The New York Times,* October 26, 1956, 4:4.

19. *The New York Times,* October 31, 1956, 5:1.

20. "Top Secret" telegram JCS 912463 to Commanders in Chief of various

U.S. domestic and foreign bases, dated October 30, 1956, in Records of the United States Joint Chiefs of Staff, Record Group 218, file 381 EMMEA (11-19-47) SW 47 RB, National Archives.

21. "Official Use Only" telegram 650 from U.S. Embassy, Tel Aviv, to Secretary of State, dated November 23, 1956, declassified October 29, 1982, in response to a federal Freedom of Information Act request.

22. "Confidential" telegram 2665 from U.S. Embassy, Paris, to Secretary of State, dated November 29, 1956, declassified October 29, 1982, in response to a federal Freedom of Information Act request.

23. "Top Secret" memorandum for the Chairman, JCS, from the Joint Middle East Planning Committee, dated March 20, 1956, Records of the United States Joint Chiefs of Staff, 091 Palestine file, Record Group 218, National Archives.

24. "Confidential—Personal and Private" letter from U.S. Ambassador to the UN Henry Cabot Lodge to Secretary of State John Foster Dulles, dated March 29, 1956, Papers of John Foster Dulles, Subject Series, Dwight D. Eisenhower Library.

25. "Top Secret—Personal and Private" memorandum to William Rountree, Assistant Secretary of State for Near Eastern Affairs, from John Foster Dulles, Papers of John Foster Dulles, Subject Series, file Israeli Relations 1951–1957, Dwight D. Eisenhower Library.

26. "Top Secret" memorandum for Rear Admiral R. A. Currie from Major General Oliver Picher, Deputy Director, JCS Joint Staff, dated April 4, 1956, Records of the United States Joint Chiefs of Staff, file CCS 381 EMMEA (11-19-47) (SCC 29), Record Group 218, National Archives.

27. "Top Secret" memorandum for Admiral Radford (Chairman, JCS) from "Hedding," dated May 25, 1956, Records of the United States Joint Chiefs of Staff, file CCS 381 EMMEA (11-19-47) (SCC 39), Record Group 218, National Archives.

28. "Secret—Personal and Private" memorandum for the President from Secretary of State John Foster Dulles, dated September 28, 1956, Papers of John Foster Dulles, White House Memo Series, Dwight D. Eisenhower Library.

29. Two memorandums of conversations with the President by Secretary of State John Foster Dulles, dated October 2 and 3, 1956, Papers of John Foster Dulles, White House Memo Series, Dwight D. Eisenhower Library.

30. "Secret" record of decision re Israel, memorandum for Colonel A. J. Goodpaster, the White House, from Fisher Howe, Director, Executive Secretariat, Department of State, dated November 11, 1956, in White House Central Files, Confidential File, Box 82, Folder: Suez Canal Crisis, Dwight D. Eisenhower Library.

31. Neff, op. cit., p. 383

32. Enclosures to "Unclassified" memorandum from Commander, Transport Amphibious Squadron Six, to Commander, Amphibious Force, U.S. Atlantic Fleet, dated November 6, 1956, in U.S. Naval Archives, Washington Navy Yard, Washington, D.C.

33. Scripps-Howard Newspapers interview with General Randolph Pate, quoted in "Confidential" message JCS 915748 to U.S. Commands and Bases from JCS, dated January 3, 1957, and "Top Secret" memorandum DM-190-56 for General Everest, etc., from Vice Admiral B. L. Austin, Director, JCS Joint Staff, dated December 28, 1956; both in Records of the United States Joint Chiefs of Staff, file CCS 381 EMMEA (11-19-47) (SCC 53), Record Group 218, National Archives.

34. Edgar O'Ballance in *The Sinai Campaign of 1956* (New York: Frederick A. Praeger, 1959), p. 194.

35. Ibid., p. 46.

36. Dayan, op. cit., p. 173.

37. O'Ballance, op. cit., p. 141.

38. Dayan, op. cit., p. 243.

39. O'Ballance, op. cit., pp. 152–155, 158.

40. Ibid., p. 186.

41. Peter Woods of the *London Daily Mirror,* quoted in *The New York Times,* November 7, 1956, 33:6.

42. *The New York Times,* November 10, 1956, 8:3.

43. *The New York Times,* November 25, 1956, 24:1.

44. *The New York Times,* November 11, 1956, 29:1.

45. *The New York Times,* November 15, 1956, 3:5.

CHAPTER 7

1. Fuad Jabber in *Israel and Nuclear Weapons* (London: Chatto and Windus, 1971), pp. 15–17. Written for the International Institute of Strategic Studies in London. Jabber's work was the first book-length analysis of this subject and even today remains, in the author's opinion, an excellent source on the Israeli nuclear weapons program prior to the October War.

2. Sylvia Crosbie in *A Tacit Alliance: France and Israel from Suez to the Six Day War* (Princeton, N.J.: Princeton University Press, 1974), p. 115.

3. Quoted in Crosbie, op. cit., pp. 216–217. General Gaston Jean Lavaud is the senior French military official cited by Ms. Crosbie regarding the cost-saving estimate.

4. Aubrey Hodes in *Dialogue with Ishmael: Israel's Future in the Middle East* (New York: Funk and Wagnalls, 1968), p. 230.

5. *Haaretz,* December 21, 1960, and the London *Times,* December 20, 1960, among other sources quoted in Crosbie, op. cit., p. 162.

6. Crosbie, op. cit., p. 162.

7. Yair Evron in "Israel and the Atom: The Uses and Misuses of Ambiguity, 1957–1967," *Orbis,* Volume 17 (Winter, 1974), p. 1331.

8. Crosbie, op. cit., p. 111. Ms. Crosbie notes as well that such collaboration was not new—the Israelis had made several suggestions for design modifications in the French Mystère airplane, following extensive use of the plane by the IAF in the Suez War.

9. Clyde R. Mark in "Israel and the Treaty on the Non-Proliferation of Nuclear Weapons," a study done for the Library of Congress Legislative Reference Service, February 6, 1969, p. 4.

10. "Secret" memorandum of conversation between Prime Minister Ben Gurion of Israel and the President, dated March 10, 1960, in Record of the W.H. Office, Office of the Staff Secretary, Box 8 of the International Series, Folder: Israel, Dwight D. Eisenhower Library.

11. "Personal and Confidential" letter from Secretary of State Christian Herter to Prime Minister David Ben Gurion, dated August 4, 1960, in Christian Herter Papers, Box 9, Folder Title: August 1960, Dwight D. Eisenhower Library.

12. Ibid.

13. Crosbie, op. cit., p. 163.

14. Simha Flaphan in "Nuclear Power in the Middle East," *New Outlook Magazine,* July, 1974, p. 50.

15. Memorandum for the record dated December 6, 1960, Ann Whitman File, Transition Series, Memos of the Staff re Change of Administration, Dwight D. Eisenhower Library.

16. "Confidential" Department of State instruction USIA CA-352, dated December 24, 1953, in White House Central Files (Confidential File), Box 7, Folder: Atomic Energy and Bomb, Dwight D. Eisenhower Library.

17. David Hoffman, quoted in Shai Feldman's *Israeli Nuclear Deterrence: A Strategy for the 1980s* (New York: Columbia University Press, 1982), p. 196.

18. Quoted in William Bader's *The United States and the Spread of Nuclear Weapons* (New York: Pegasus, 1968), p. 25.

19. Victor Cigielman in "Rockets Now—What Next?," *New Outlook Magazine,* September, 1962, p. 7.

20. "Top Secret" telex EC 9-2165 from USCINCEUR, Paris, France, to OCSOP DEPTAR, Washington, D.C., dated April 11, 1956, Records of the United States Joint Chiefs of Staff, file CCS 381 EMMEA (11-19-47) Section 30, Record Group 218, National Archives.

21. "Top Secret Note by the Secretaries to the JCS on U.S. National Atomic Disclosure Policies Within the Middle East Area," JCS 2220/113, dated December 3, 1956, in Carrolton Press Declassified Documents Reference System, 1980/270A.

22. "Secret" FBI report file 97-123, dated July 1, 1970, p. 4 (bureau file number 117-2564), prepared by the Pittsburgh field office.

23. "Confidential" FBI report (the identifying file number is excised, as is the subject), dated July 25, 1968, prepared by the Pittsburgh field office.

24. *The New York Times,* September 25, 1960, 24:4.

25. "Official Use Only" case history, "Enriched Uranium," undated, RO-1, Nuclear Materials Division of Babcock and Wilcox Company, SNM-145, Docket 70-135, released by the Energy Resources Development Administration in 1976, p. 32.

26. See Jabber, op. cit., p. 124.

27. Ibid., p. 95, and Crosbie, op. cit., pp. 160–161.

28. Crosbie, op. cit., pp. 154–155.

29. Simha Flaphan in "Nuclear Power in the Middle East," Part Two, *New Outlook Magazine,* October, 1974.

30. Ibid.

31. "Symposium: The Atom Bomb in Israel," in *New Outlook Magazine,* March–April, 1961.

32. "Official Use Only" undated ERDA case history released in 1976, p. 34.

33. "Secret" memorandum from J. A. Waters, Director, Division of Security (AEC), to Brig. Gen. A. W. Betts, USA, Director of Military Application, dated February 27, 1972, released by ERDA in 1976.

34. "Official Use Only" undated ERDA case history released in 1976, p. 34.

35. "Confidential" FBI report (number and subject excised), dated May 29, 1968, pp. 8–9, prepared by the Pittsburgh field office.

36. John J. Fialka in "The American Connection: How Israel Got the Bomb," *The Washington Monthly,* January, 1979, p. 54.

37. Mark, "Israel and the Treaty on the Non-Proliferation of Nuclear Weapons," p. 16.

38. Dr. Gavriel Stein in "Technological Considerations and Nuclear Development in Israel," *New Outlook Magazine,* February, 1964. Both Peres's speech and Wiener's response were reported in *Davar* on January 3, 1963.

39. "Secret" memorandum for the President from the Secretary of Defense, dated February 12, 1963, subject: "The Diffusion of Nuclear Weapons with and Without a Test Ban Agreement," in Carrolton Press Declassified Documents Reference System, 1978/49B.

40. "Secret" memorandum for the Director, CIA, from Sherman Kent, Chairman, Board of National Estimates, dated March 6, 1963, in Carrolton Press Declassified Documents Records System, 1979/352B.

41. "Confidential" memorandum for the files from Samuel C. T. Mc-Dowell, Division of Safeguards and Security, AEC, dated May 25, 1976, released by ERDA in 1976. See Appendix, Document 10.

42. Jabber, op. cit., p. 122.

43. Crosbie, op. cit., p. 158–159.

44. "Confidential" memorandum of conversation, subject: "U.S.-Israel Agreement on Civil Uses of Atomic Energy," dated March 26, 1964, in NSF Country File—Israel, Box 138, Lyndon Baines Johnson Library.

45. Hodes, op. cit., p. 232.

46. "Top Secret" telegram 5592 to American Embassy, Cairo, from Undersecretary of State George Ball, dated May 30, 1964, in Carrolton Press Declassified Documents Reference System, 1976/184A.

47. "Confidential" circular 887, dated November 10, 1964, in Carrolton Press Declassified Documents Reference System, 1977/62F.

48. *The New York Times,* December 8, 1964, 23:6.

49. "Secret" telegram from Air Attaché, Tel Aviv, to Air Force Headquarters, Washington, DTG 0312152 March 1965, NSF Country File—Israel, Volume IV, Cables 2/65 to 11/65, Lyndon Baines Johnson Library. See Appendix, Document 11.

50. "Secret" memorandum from Harold Saunders to Walter Rostow, dated September 13, 1967, NSF Country File—Israel, Volume VI, Memos 12/66 to 7/67, Lyndon Baines Johnson Library.

51. "Confidential" FBI report dated July 25, 1968, p. 3.

52. "Confidential" AEC summary notes of briefing held in the Washington, D.C., office on February 14, 1966, obtained from the Department of Energy under the federal Freedom of Information Act.

53. "Confidential" FBI summary report dated February 18, 1969, Field Office File 97-123, prepared by the Pittsburgh field office. Also Fialka, op. cit., p. 55.

54. "Official Use Only" summary notes of an AEC-NUMEC meeting held in Germantown, Md., on August 10, 1965, p. 1060, obtained from the Department of Energy under the federal Freedom of Information Act.

55. David Burnham in "The Missing Uranium," *The Atlantic Monthly,* April, 1979, p. 80.

56. Ibid.

57. "Official Use Only" memorandum to the AEC from Howard C. Brown, Jr., Assistant General Manager, dated May 10, 1966, obtained from the Department of Energy under the federal Freedom of Information Act.

58. "Confidential" FBI summary report dated February 18, 1969, pp. 12, 14.

59. "Confidential" FBI report (number and subject excised) dated January 20, 1969, completed by the Pittsburgh field office.

60. Fialka, op. cit., p. 56.

61. Ibid.

62. *The New York Times,* June 12, 1979, B9:3

63. Flaphan, op. cit., pp. 51–52.

64. Mark, "Israel and the Treaty on the Non-Proliferation of Nuclear Weapons," p. 18.

65. See for example Hodes, op. cit., pp. 235–236, and Feldman, op. cit., p. 211. Also Flaphan, op. cit., p. 51, and Mark, op. cit., p. 18.

66. *The New York Times,* March 14, 1965, 1:4.

67. *The New York Times,* June 28, 1966, 8:1.

68. *The New York Times,* July 6, 1967, 10:4.

69. *The New York Times,* January 11, 1969, 3:7.

70. Hearings before the Joint Committee on Atomic Energy (89th Congress) on "Uranium Enrichment Services Criteria and Related Matters," August 2, 3, 4, 16, and 17, 1966, pp. 234–235.

CHAPTER 8

1. "Secret" Department of State memorandum of conversation, subject: "Conversation with Israel Foreign Minister Meir," dated December 27, 1962, in Carrolton Press Declassified Documents Reference System, 1979/193A.

2. Ze'ev Katz in "Kennedy and the Middle East," *New Outlook Magazine,* January, 1964, p. 5.

3. Quoted in ibid.

4. See Safran, op. cit., p. 166.

5. "Confidential" airgram A-434 from U.S. Embassy, Tel Aviv, to the Department of State, dated December 17, 1963, in Carrolton Press Declassified Documents Reference System, 1977/62D.

6. Ibid.

7. Ibid.

8. "Unclassified" CIA intelligence information cable, dated March 5, 1964, in Carrolton Press Declassified Reference System, 1976, 12B.

9. The information in the previous paragraphs is derived from data sheets prepared by the United States Agency for International Development, and attached to "Secret" background papers prepared in conjunction with the informal visit of Israeli President Zalman Shazar to Washington in August of 1966. A number of the background papers have been declassified and issued as part of the Carrolton Press Declassified Documents Reference System.

10. "Secret" State Department telegram DEPTEL 963 from U.S. Embassy, Tel Aviv, to Secretary of State, dated May 15, 1964, in Carrolton Press Declassified Documents Reference System, 1979/193C.

11. "Secret" Department of State telegram 87 from Secretary of State to U.S. Embassy, Santo Domingo, dated July 31, 1964, in Carrolton Press Declassified Documents Reference System, 1979/433C.

12. "Secret" Department of State telegram 86 from Secretary of State to U.S. Embassy, Port-au-Prince, dated August 4, 1964, in Carrolton Press Declassified Documents Reference System, 1979/433D.

13. "Confidential" Department of State telegram 174 from U.S. Embassy, Port-au-Prince, to Secretary of State, dated July 25, 1964, in Carrolton Press Declassified Documents Reference System, 433B.

14. Deputy Defense Minister Shimon Peres's entire address to the Knesset

on June 25, 1963, is quoted in full in "Outlines for an Israeli Foreign Policy," *New Outlook Magazine,* September, 1963, pp. 14–19.

15. Simha Flaphan in "Wonderful Logic—All Wrong," *New Outlook Magazine,* September, 1963, p. 26.

16. "Confidential" Department of State telegram 325 from U.S. Consulate, Jerusalem, to Secretary of State, dated May 14, 1965, NSF Country File—Israel, Volume 4, Cables 2/65 to 11/65, Lyndon Baines Johnson Library.

17. "Secret" State Department circular telegram from Secretary of State to, *inter alia,* U.S. Embassy, Tel Aviv, dated March 18, 1965, NSF Country File—Israel, Volume 4, Cables 2/65 to 11/65, Lyndon Baines Johnson Library.

18. "Confidential" Department of State telegram 325.

19. "Secret" Department of State telegram 29 from U.S. Consulate, Jerusalem, to Secretary of State, dated July 21, 1964, NSF Country File—Israel, Volume 2, Cables 4/64 to 8/64, Lyndon Baines Johnson Library. See Appendix, Document 12.

20. "Secret" White House memorandum for McGeorge Bundy from William H. Brubeck, dated May 9, 1963, in Carrolton Press Declassified Documents Reference System, 1979/193B.

21. "Secret" memorandum for the President from Acting Secretary of State George Ball, subject: "Visit of Israeli Prime Minister Eshkol," undated, in Carrolton Press Declassified Documents Reference System, 1979/193D.

22. "Secret" Department of State memorandum of conversation by H. Earle Russell, Jr., dated May 19, 1965, NSF Country File—Israel, Volume 4, Memos and Miscellaneous 2/65 to 11/65, Lyndon Baines Johnson Library.

23. "Secret" memorandum for the President from Robert W. Komer, dated January 18, 1966, NSF Country File—Israel, Volume 5, Memos 12/65 to 9/66, Lyndon Baines Johnson Library.

24. "Unclassified" State Department telegram 3419 from U.S. Embassy, Tel Aviv, to Secretary of State, dated April 28, 1967, NSF Country File—Israel, Volume 6, Memos 12/66 to 7/67, Lyndon Baines Johnson Library.

25. Memorandum for the President from Walt Rostow, dated May 25, 1967, National Security File, NSC History—Middle East Crisis, May 12—June 19, 1967, Volume 2, tabs 31–42, Lyndon Baines Johnson Library.

26. "Secret" memorandum for the President from Secretary of State Dean Rusk, dated May 26, 1967, NSF Country File—Israel, Container 142, Volume 12, Lyndon Baines Johnson Library.

27. Ibid.

28. "Secret" letter from President Lyndon B. Johnson to Prime Minister Levi Eshkol, dated June 3, 1967, National Security File, NSC History—Middle East Crisis, May 12–June 19, 1967, Volume 3, Lyndon Baines Johnson Library.

29. Lyndon B. Johnson in *The Vantage Point* (New York: Holt, Rinehart, and Winston, 1971), p. 293.

30. "Secret" note to the President from Walt Rostow, dated June 3, 1967 (2:50 P.M.), National Security File, NSC History—Middle East Crisis, May 12–June 19, 1967, Volume 3, Lyndon Baines Johnson Library.

31. Lyndon Baines Johnson Library Oral History Project, interview number 1 with Richard Helms, recorded April 4, 1969.

32. Michael Bar Zohar, *Embassies in Crisis* (Englewood Cliffs, N.J.: Prentice-Hall, 1970), pp. 114–115.

33. Lyndon Baines Johnson Library Oral History Project, interview number 3 with Nicholas Katzenbach, recorded December 11, 1968.

34. Lyndon Baines Johnson Library Oral History Project, interview number 1 with Harry McPherson, recorded December 5, 1968.

35. "Top Secret" note and attached table from Harold Saunders to Lois Nivens, dated May 23, 1967. Also note from Marvin Watson to the President, dated June 5, 1967. Both are in National Security File, NSC History—Middle East Crisis, May 12–June 19, 1967, Volume 1, Lyndon Baines Johnson Library.

36. The figures on Egyptian plane losses are from Winston and Randolph Churchill, *The Six Day War* (Boston: Houghton Mifflin Company, 1967), p. 85.

37. *The New York Times,* June 7, 1967, 1:1.

38. "Secret" long-distance Xerox from Walt Rostow to both Secretary of State Dean Rusk and Secretary of Defense Robert McNamara, dated June 4, 1967, National Security File, NSC History—Middle East Crisis, May 12–June 19, 1967, Volume 3, tabs. 96–110, Lyndon Baines Johnson Library.

39. "Secret" note to the President from Walt Rostow, dated June 5, 1967, National Security File, NSC History—Middle East Crisis, May 12–June 19, 1967, Volume 4, Tabs. 111–127, Lyndon Baines Johnson Library.

40. "Confidential" note to the President from Walt Rostow, dated June 6, 1967, National Security File, NSC History—Middle East Crisis, May 12–June 19, 1967, Volume 4, Tabs. 111–127, Lyndon Baines Johnson Library. See Appendix, Document 13.

41. "Secret" memorandum to the President from Walt Rostow, dated June 7, 1967, National Security File, NSC History—Middle East Crisis, May 12–June 19, 1967, Volume 4, Tabs. 128–150, Lyndon Baines Johnson Library.

42. Ibid.

CHAPTER 9

1. Quoted in Phil G. Goulding, *Confirm or Deny* (New York: Harper and Row, 1970), p. 93. At the time of the *Liberty* Affair, Goulding was Assistant Secretary of Defense for Public Affairs.

2. James Bamford in *The Puzzle Palace* (Boston: Houghton Mifflin, 1982), p. 219.

3. James M. Ennes, Jr., in *Assault on the Liberty* (New York: Random House, 1979), p. 38.

4. U.S.S. *Liberty* message 062036Z, June, 1967, included under tab 34 in "Top Secret Report of the JCS Fact Finding Team, USS Liberty Incident, 8 June 1967," declassified in May, 1982, in response to an FOIA request by the author. The copy of the report obtained by the author is undated, but was delivered to the Joint Chiefs by fact-finding team leader Major General Joseph R. Russ in late June, 1967.

5. Ennes, op. cit., pp. 38–39.

6. "Report of the JCS Fact Finding Team," p. 14.

7. Ibid., Tab. 36, COMSIXTHFLT message 062349Z, June, 1967.

8. Ibid., Tab. 41, NSA message DTG 072104Z, June, 1967.

9. Ibid., Tab. 42, JCS message 072230Z, June, 1967.

10. Ibid., Tab. 43, JCS telecom 072350Z, June, 1967.

11. Ibid., Tab 45, JCS message 070110Z, June, 1967.

12. Ibid., Tab. 47, USNAVEUR telecom 080410Z, June, 1967.

13. Ibid., pp. 26, 27, 42.

14. Ibid., Tab. 48, CINCUSNAVEUR message 080455Z, June, 1967.

15. Ibid., Tab. 53, COMSIXTHFLT message 080917Z, June, 1967.

16. "Department of Defense Appropriations for 1969, Hearings Before a Subcommittee of the Committee on Appropriations, House of Representatives, Part 4, Operations and Maintenance," April 8, 1968, p. 396.

17. "Review of Department of Defense Worldwide Communications, Phase I: Report of the Armed Services Investigating Subcommittee of the Committee on Armed Services," May 10, 1971, p. 6.

18. "Secret" State Department telegram 3928 from U.S. Embassy, Tel Aviv, to Secretary of State, dated June 5, 1967, declassified at the request of the author on December 13, 1982, under the federal Freedom of Information Act. See Appendix, Document 14.

19. Memorandum for the record, subject: "NSC Meeting, Wednesday, June 7, 1967," dated January 7, 1969, document 55, National Security File, NSC History—Middle East Crisis, Volume 2, Lyndon Baines Johnson Library.

20. "Confidential" memorandum for the President from Larry Levinson and Ben Wattenberg, dated June 7, 1967, White House Central Files (CO126 ND19/CO1-6), Lyndon Baines Johnson Library.

21. "Secret" State Department telegram 4098 A from American Embassy, Amman, to Secretary of State, dated June 6, 1967, in NSF Country File, Middle East Crisis, Vol. 4, Box 107, Lyndon Baines Johnson Library.

22. "Secret" State Department telegram 4125 from American Embassy, Amman, to Secretary of State, dated June 7, 1967, in NSF Country File, Middle East Crisis, Vol. 4, Box 107, Lyndon Baines Johnson Library.

23. The New York Times, June 8, 1967, 12:1.

24. The New York Times, June 8, 1967, 18:4.

25. The New York Times, June 9, 1967, 16:1.

26. Raphael, op. cit., p. 162.

27. "Confidential" State Department telegram 1053 from American Consulate, Jerusalem, to Secretary of State, dated June 8, 1967, in NSF Country File, Middle East Crisis, Vol. 4, Box 107, Lyndon Baines Johnson Library.

28. "Secret" State Department telegram 209182 from Secretary of State to American Embassy, Tel Aviv, dated June 8, 1967, in NSF Country File, Middle East Crisis, Vol. 4, Box 107, Lyndon Baines Johnson Library. See Appendix, Document 15.

29. The author obtained a copy of the Captain's Night Orders for the Liberty for June 7–8, 1967, from James M. Ennes, Jr., author of Assault on the Liberty.

30. Taken from a chronology prepared by CINCUSNAVEUR, in naval message 132105Z, June, 1967, from CINCUSNAVEUR to USCINCEUR, declassified and released on November 24, 1982, by the Naval Security Group, Department of the Navy, in response to a federal Freedom of Information Act request. The chronology indicates that the NSA message wanted Liberty to proceed west "to satisfy technical requirements." It is hard to imagine how moving 180 degrees away from all of the fighting then ongoing would have achieved this.

31. Ennes, op. cit., p. 55.

32. Chief Radioman Wayne Smith's testimony on the jamming appears in the official record of the naval court of inquiry. The jamming during the attack was established as a "finding of fact" by the court. Other details were obtained in a personal telephone interview with Mr. Smith.

33. This scene is described in Ennes, op. cit., p. 96.

34. From chronology in CINCUSNAVEUR 151003Z, June, 1967.

35. "Report of the JCS Fact Finding Team," Tab 65, USDAO message 081414Z, June, 1967.

36. Ibid., Tab. 59, CTF 60 message 081316Z, June, 1967.

37. COMSIXTHFLT message 081320Z, June, 1967.

38. "Report of the JCS Fact Finding Team," Tab. 61, COMSIXTHFLT message 081339Z, June, 1967.

39. The foregoing account of help never quite sent the *Liberty* is taken from Ennes's *Assault on the Liberty*, pp. 98–116, and from Ennes's more recent article on the subject in the *U.S.S. Liberty Newsletter*, Volume 1, No. 1, August, 1981, pp. 5–6.

40. From chronology in CINCUSNAVEUR 151003Z.

41. *Congressional Record–House*, June 8, 1967, p. 15131.

42. *Congressional Record–Senate*, June 8, 1967, p. 15261.

43. "Secret" State Department telegram 20317 from American Embassy, Paris, to Secretary of State, dated June 17, 1967, National Security File, Middle East Crisis, "Liberty File," Lyndon Baines Johnson Library, declassified February 16, 1983, in response to a request from the author. See Appendix, Document 16.

44. *Newsweek*, June 19, 1967.

45. Goulding, op. cit., p. 130.

46. Ennes, op. cit., p. 143.

47. DOD news release 594-67, dated June 28, 1967, p. 1.

48. Based upon telephone interviews with Representative Robert L. F. Sikes. The information provided by Representative Sikes has been corroborated by other committee sources who do not wish to be identified.

49. This report is cited in a study by the Central Security Service of the National Security Agency entitled, "United States (Excised) —Attack on (Excised) the U.S.S. Liberty (Excised)." Portions of the title are still classified, along with much of the study itself. But the NSA segregated and released portions of the study in early 1983.

50. Memorandum for Harry McPherson from James U. Cross, dated June 20, 1967, document 40c, Office Files of Harry McPherson, Lyndon Baines Johnson Library.

51. Memorandum for Jim Cross from Harry C. McPherson, Jr., dated June 26, 1967, document 40, Office Files of Harry McPherson, Lyndon Baines Johnson Library.

CHAPTER 10

1. Press statement by the President on the Near East situation, delivered in the Fish Room, the White House, 6:10 P.M. EDT, May 23, 1967.

2. "Secret" memorandum of conversation dated October 24, 1967, National Security File—Israel, Volume 12 (1965–1968), Box 142, Lyndon Baines Johnson Library. See Appendix, Document 17.

3. "Secret" State Department telegram from Secretary of State to U.S.

Embassy, Tel Aviv, dated September 14, 1967, in Carrolton Press Declassified Documents Reference System, 1980/201A.

4. "Secret" memorandum for the President from Walt Rostow, dated September 2, 1966, National Security File—Israel, Volume 6, Memos 12/66–7/67, Lyndon Baines Johnson Library.

5. Paper entitled "U.S. Help for Israel, 1964–1966," National Security File—Israel, Volume 6, Memos 12/66–7/67, Lyndon Baines Johnson Library.

6. Memorandum for the President from Harry McPherson, dated September 20, 1967, National Security File—Israel, Volume 6, Memos 12/66–7/67, Lyndon Baines Johnson Library.

7. Ibid.

8. McPherson LBJ Library Oral History Project interview.

9. "Confidential" State Department telegram 860 from Secretary of State Dean Rusk to U.S. Embassy, Tel Aviv, dated March 28, 1965, National Security File—Israel, Volume 4, Cables 2/65–11/65, Lyndon Baines Johnson Library.

10. "Secret" State Department telegram 818 from Secretary of State Dean Rusk to U.S. Embassy, Tel Aviv, dated February 23, 1966, National Security File—Israel, Volume 4, Cables 12/65–9/66, Lyndon Baines Johnson Library.

11. "Secret" letter from Secretary of State Dean Rusk to Vice-President Hubert Humphrey, dated March 31, 1966, National Security File—Israel, Volume 5, Memos 12/65–9/66, Lyndon Baines Johnson Library.

12. "Secret" Department of State telegram 889 from U.S. Embassy, Tel Aviv, to Secretary of State, Washington, dated April 26, 1966, National Security File—Israel, Volume 5, Cables 12/65–9/66, Lyndon Baines Johnson Library.

13. McPherson LBJ Library Oral History Project interview.

14. "Secret" background paper prepared for the informal visit to Washington of President Zalman Shazar of Israel, undated, in Carrolton Press Declassified Document Reference System, 1978/82C.

15. The New York Times, July 25, 1967, 1:1.

16. Paper entitled "U.S. Foreign Assistance to the Middle East and North Africa: Programs, Rationale and Amounts, FY 78–FY 82 (Proposed)," prepared by Shirley Zebroski, Research Fellow, Congressional Research Service, Library of Congress, June 22, 1981. The author was able to update the figures given in this paper in telephone conversations with staff members of the CRS.

17. "Secret" CIA report entitled "Foreign Intelligence and Security Services—Israel," dated March, 1979, p. 46.

18. The New York Times Magazine, June 25, 1978, p. 15.

19. "Secret" memorandum from Vice Admiral E. C. Wallen, USN, to Director, Defense Research and Engineering, Department of Defense, dated September 22, 1975, obtained by the author from the Defense Intelligence Agency under the federal Freedom of Information Act.

20. Seth P. Tillman in The United States in the Middle East (Bloomington, Ind.: Indiana University Press, 1982), pp. 154–155.

21. "Secret" CIA report entitled "Foreign Intelligence and Security Services—Israel," pp. 21–22.

22. Amos Oz in "Meaning of Homeland," New Outlook Magazine, December, 1967, p. 11.

List of Acronyms

AEC (U.S.) Atomic Energy Commission

AGO Adjutant General's Office

AGTR Auxiliary General Technical Research (ship)

AIPAC American Israel Public Affairs Committee

CARE Cooperative for American Relief Everywhere

CEA (French) Commissariat of Atomic Energy

CID (British) Criminal Investigation Division

CINCUSNAVEUR Commander in Chief, U.S. Naval Forces, Europe

COMINT communications intelligence

COMSIXTHFLT Commander, Sixth Fleet

CSA Czechoslovak Airlines

DMZ demilitarized zone

DOD (U.S.) Department of Defense

DP displaced person

ECM electronic countermeasure

EDT Eastern daylight time

ELINT electronic intelligence

ERDA (U.S.) Energy Research and Development Administration

FBIS (CIA) Foreign Broadcast Intercept System

FOIA (U.S.) Freedom of Information Act

FY fiscal year

IAEA International Atomic Energy Agency

IAEC Israel Atomic Energy Commission

IAF Israeli Air Force

ID (U.S. Army) Intelligence Division—also known as G-2

IDF Israeli Defense Forces

IRAN inspection and repair as necessary

ISORAD (Israeli NUMEC) Isotopes and Radiation Enterprises

JCS (U.S.) Joint Chiefs of Staff

JIG (Pentagon) Joint Intelligence Group

JRC (JCS) Joint Reconnaissance Center

MTB motor torpedo boat

MUF material unaccounted for

NIE national intelligence estimate

NSC (U.S.) National Security Council

NSA (U.S.) National Security Agency

NUMEC Nuclear Materials and Equipment Corporation

OMGUS Office of the Military Government for Germany—U.S.

RCC (Egyptian) Revolutionary Command Council

SCUA Suez Canal Users' Association

SIGINT signals intelligence

SLR side-looking radar

SSM surface-to-surface missile

UAR United Arab Republic

UJA United Jewish Appeal

UNEF United Nations Emergency Force

UNGA United Nations General Assembly

UNRWA United Nations Relief and Works Agency

UNSCOP United Nations Special Committee on Palestine

UNTSO United Nations Truce Supervision Organization

UNCINCEUR Commander in Chief, U.S. Armed Forces, Europe

WANL Westinghouse Astro Nuclear Laboratory

WSEG (Pentagon) Weapons Systems Evaluation Group

Appendix

Document #1—as cited in Chapter 2, Note 23.

"Top Secret" memorandum for the President, from George C. Marshall, Secretary of State, dated August 16, 1948, in *Foreign Relations of the United States*, 1948, Volume 5, pp. 1313–1314.

AUG 16 1948

~~TOP SECRET~~

MEMORANDUM FOR THE PRESIDENT

Subject: Proposed Representations to Provisional Government of Israel Regarding Maintenance of Peace in Palestine.

Information from a wide number of sources causes the Department increasing concern over the apparent tendency of the Provisional Government of Israel to assume a more aggressive attitude in Palestine.

Following the termination of the British mandate on May 15 and the establishment of a Jewish State, the Israeli authorities were quick to respond to United Nations efforts to stop the fighting in Palestine. After the termination of this four-week truce on July 9, hostilities were resumed and it soon became apparent that Israel had materially improved its military position during the period of the earlier truce. Nevertheless, both the Government of Israel and the Arab States agreed to accept the Security Council's order of July 15 for a cease-fire and truce of indefinite duration in Palestine. The demilitarization of Jerusalem was included in the Security Council's resolution and was accepted by the Government of Israel and the Arab States in principle. In recent weeks, however, a new and aggressive note has become manifest, and the readiness of Israel to maintain the truce has become subject to doubt.

The Department has noted evidence of hostility of Israelis in Palestine toward the military observers serving under Count Bernadotte; the inflammatory speeches of the Israeli Foreign Minister, Mr. Shertok, with regard to alleged "rights" of Israel in Jerusalem; the military occupation by Israel of much of the Jerusalem area; and the refusal of the Israeli military governor in Jerusalem to cooperate with Count Bernadotte in discussions regarding the demilitarization of Jerusalem. The Department has likewise noted increasing evidence of systematic violations of the United Nations truce by the forces of Israel, including forward movement of Israeli forces from agreed truce positions, continued sniping and firing against Arab positions; and conclusive evidence of the organized transport of arms shipments to Palestine from France, Italy and Czechoslovakia. Furthermore, the Israeli Foreign Minister has officially proclaimed that Israel will not accept, pending

negotiation

- 2 -

negotiation of a final peace settlement, the return of the approximately 300,000 Arab inhabitants of that part of Palestine now comprising the Jewish State who fled from their homes and are now destitute in nearby Arab areas.

The Foreign Minister of Great Britain, in a conversation with our Ambassador on August 6, expressed grave concern over the situation in Palestine. He was fearful not only that the USSR would take advantage of this situation to foment trouble in Iraq and Iran but also that within "the next few days" the Jews, on grounds of some Arab provocation, real or manufactured, would reopen their offensive with the objective of seizing more territory - probably Transjordan. Mr. Bevin thought that the Palestine situation was as serious as Berlin. "If the United States and United Kingdom go slack (in Palestine), we lose."

The Department, in light of these developments, feels that it would be wise to call in Mr. Eliahu Epstein, the Representative of the Provisional Government of Israel, and discuss frankly our concern with him. We would tell Mr. Epstein that, as he undoubtedly knows, the United States is the best friend of Israel. We have recognized that State and desire to see it continue in existence and prosper as a peaceful member of the community of nations. We have now before us the question of de jure recognition of the Provisional Government of Israel, support for Israel's membership in the United Nations, and the application from Israel for a loan from the Export-Import Bank. We should like to see all these matters arranged in a manner satisfactory to both governments but we should find it exceedingly difficult, for example, to advocate a loan to Israel if that country is likely to resume hostilities. Similar difficulties would arise concerning membership in the United Nations.

As a friend of Israel we deem it of paramount importance that this new republic not place itself before the bar of world opinion and the United Nations in the role of an aggressor. We should like to tell Mr. Epstein for the information of his government that we shall be not less zealous in the Security Council to oppose aggression from the Israeli side as we were when the attack was launched by the Arab side.

From the wider political aspect and not for the information of Mr. Epstein, it is obvious that it would be most injurious to the interests of the United States if hostilities should be opened by Israel against Transjordan with the result that the United Kingdom would automatically honor its commitments to Transjordan under its existing treaty with that country. This would bring forth an outcry in the United States for the lifting of our arms embargo in favor of Israel,

with the

-3-

with the result that the two great Anglo-Saxon partners would be supplying and aiding two little states on the opposite sides of a serious war, from which only the Soviet Union could profit.

With your concurrence the Under Secretary of State proposes immediately to discuss these matters with Mr. Epstein.

G. C. MARSHALL

MEMORANDUM FOR THE PRESIDENT

Subject: Proposed Representations to Provisional Government of Israel Regarding Maintenance of Peace in Palestine

Information from a wide number of sources causes the Department increasing concern over the apparent tendency of the Provincial Government of Israel to assume a more aggressive attitude in Palestine.

Following the termination of the British mandate on May 15 and the establishment of a Jewish State, the Israeli authorities were quick to respond to United Nations efforts to stop the fighting in Palestine. After the termination of this four-week truce on July 9, hostilities were resumed and it soon became apparent that Israel had materially improved its military position during the period of the earlier truce. Nevertheless, both the Government of Israel and the Arab States agreed to accept the Security Council's order of July 15 for a cease-fire and truce of indefinite duration in Palestine. The demilitarization of Jerusalem was included in the Security Council's resolution and was accepted by the Government of Israel and the Arab States in principle. In recent weeks, however, a new and aggressive note has become manifest, and the readiness of Israel to maintain the truce has become subject to doubt.

The Department has noted evidence of hostility of Israelis in Palestine toward the military observers serving under Count Bernadotte; the inflammatory speeches of the Israeli Foreign Minister, Mr. Shertok, with regard to alleged "rights" of Israel in Jerusalem; the military occupation by Israel of much of the Jerusalem area; and the refusal of the Israeli military governor in Jerusalem to cooperate with Count Bernadotte in discussions regarding the demilitarization of Jerusalem. The Department has likewise noted increasing evidence of systematic violations of the United Nations truce by the forces of Israel, including forward movement of Israeli forces from agreed truce positions, continued sniping and firing against Arab positions; and conclusive evidence of the organized transport of arms shipments to Palestine from France, Italy, and Czechoslovakia. Furthermore, the Israeli Foreign Minister has officially proclaimed that Israel will not accept, pending negotiation of a final peace settlement, the return of the approximately 300,000 Arab inhabitants of that part of Palestine now comprising the Jewish State who fled from their homes and are now destitute in nearby Arab areas.

The Foreign Minister of Great Britain, in a conversation with our Ambassador on August 6, expressed grave concern over the situation in Palestine. He was fearful not only that the USSR would take advantage of this situation to foment trouble in Iraq and Iran but also that within "the next few days" the Jews, on grounds of some Arab provocation, real or manufactured, would reopen their offensive with the objective of seizing more territory—probably Transjordan. Mr. Bevin thought that the Palestine situation was as serious as Berlin. "If the United States and United Kingdom go slack (in Palestine), we lose."

The Department, in light of these developments, feels that it would be wise to call in Mr. Eliahu Epstein, the Representive of the Provisional Government of Israel, and discuss frankly our concern with him. We would tell Mr. Epstein that, as he undoubtedly knows, the United States is the best friend of Israel. We have recognized that State and desire to see it continue in existence and prosper as a peaceful member of the community of nations. We have now before us the question of *de jure* recognition of the Provisional Government of Israel, support for Israel's membership in the United Nations, and the application from Israel for a loan from the Export-Import Bank. We should like to see all these matters arranged in a manner satisfactory to both governments but we should find it exceedingly difficult, for example, to advocate a loan to Israel if that country is likely to resume hostilities. Similar difficulties would arise concerning membership in the United Nations.

As a friend of Israel we deem it of paramount importance that this new republic not place itself before the bar of world opinion and the United Nations in the role of an aggressor. We should like to tell Mr. Epstein for the information of his government that we shall be not less zealous in the Security Council to oppose aggression from the Israeli side as we were when the attack was launched by the Arab side.

From the wider political aspect and not for the information of Mr. Epstein, it is obvious that it would be most injurious to the interests of the United States if hostilities should be opened by Israel against Transjordan with the result that the United Kingdom would automatically honor its commitments to Transjordan under its existing treaty with that country. This would bring forth an outcry in the United States for the lifting of our arms embargo in favor of Israel, with the result that the two great Anglo-Saxon partners would be supplying and aiding two little states on the opposite sides of a serious war, from which only the Soviet Union could profit.

With your concurrence the Under Secretary of State proposes immediately to discuss these matters with Mr. Epstein.

G. C. MARSHALL

Document #2—as cited in Chapter 3, Note 4.

"Secret" weekly intelligence report 113 from the Office of the Director of Intelligence, OMGUS, dated July 10, 1948, copy in the Publications File, Records of the Document Library Branch, Office of the Assistant Chief of Staff, G-Z, Record Group 319, National Archives.

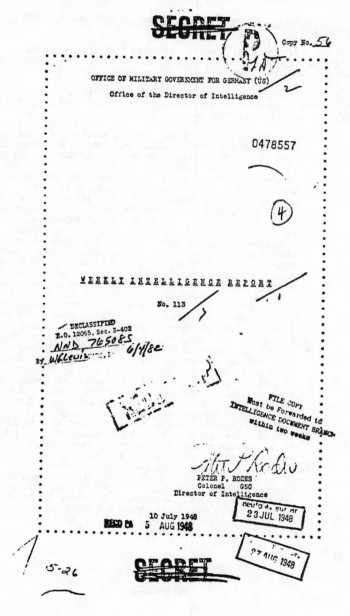

are aware of the fact that continued border crossings on a large
scale will eventually have serious effects on the Germany economy,
especially since the currency reform. Military Government does not
prefer charges in Military Government courts against those individuals
for violation of border regulations.

3. Jewish Recruitment Involves Use of Terrorist Tactics.   (CLASSIFICATION:
    CONFIDENTIAL)

        Continuing instances of pressure tactics in recruiting
volunteers for Palestine are assuming SOP proportions with more and
more DP camps reporting the use of these methods.

        The following report from Traunstein, Bavaria, is the newest
received and supports the trend as reported in ODI "Weekly Intelligence
Report" No. 112, Item S & D 1:

        "Since the founding of Israel, about a dozen men have
    left the Jewish DP Camp, Kriegslazerett, in Traunstein as
    volunteers. These volunteers are called "Ghuis". Six or
    seven of these men returned to camp on 11 June for a few
    days' leave. During their stay in camp they terrorized
    other camp inmates who are reluctant to go to Israel. Katz
    and Feldmann, Camp Leader and Chief of Police respectively,
    in no way interfered with the 'Ghuis' actions. Since the
    State of Israel came into existence, the Palestina Amt has
    organized an active terror group among camp inhabitants to
    encourage emigration to Israel. The Palestina Amt members
    encouraged the 'Ghuis' to put pressure on reluctant persons
    in camp. Aaron Stanner, clerk in the IRO camp office was
    removed by force from his office on 4 June by this terror
    organization. Members of the Palestina Amt include: Mendel
    Grunspan, Mayer Czuthovic, Mayer Glicner, and Zupnik.

        "At about 0130 hours, 14 June, a group of six to eight
    'Ghuis' entered the room of Aaron Stanner and assaulted the
    six occupants of the room, allegedly because one of Stan-
    ner's sons refused to enter the Jewish Army. During this
    time, the camp police had put a cordon around the building
    to prevent anyone from entering or leaving. Feldmann, chief
    of police, was on duty at the main gate at this time. About
    this same time, Josef Fisch, another DP, entered the camp
    and was going to his room in the same building. The 'Ghuis'
    were just leaving the building as he arrived. Thinking
    Fisch was going to the aid of the Stanners, they beat him
    into unconsciousness. At about 0200 hours, Stanner tried
    to put through a call to Military Government Traunstein but
    was unable to get past the camp switchboard.

        "As 14 June was a Jewish holiday of mourning, camp in-
    habitants who were not willing to go to Israel were warned
    not to enter the synagogue because they would be forced to
    leave. Most of the people warned did remain at home, and

S & D 6

nothing happened until 1130 hours when three 'Ghuis'
entered Hermann Jakubovic's room. There they tore
pictures from the wall, threw things around, and tried
to wreck the room in general. When Jakobovic entered
his room, they tore up a telegram he had received the
same day from the Funk Kaserne in Munich. In the telegram,
he and his brother were invited by a screening team to come
to Munich prior to emigrating to the United States. Both
brothers were maltreated during this time.

"During all of these happenings, neither the camp police
nor the camp leader tried in any way to stop them. During
the first incident, the police actually aided the terrorists.
Further investigation of these matters is being conducted...."

3. *Jewish Recruitment Involves Use of Terrorist Tactics. (CLASSIFICATION: CONFIDENTIAL)*

Continuing instances of pressure tactics in recruiting volunteers for Palestine are assuming SOP proportions with more and more DP camps reporting the use of these methods.

The following report from Traunstein, Bavaria, is the newest received and supports the trend as reported in ODI "Weekly Intelligence Report" No. 112, Item S & D 1:

"Since the founding of Israel, about a dozen men have left the Jewish DP Camp, Kriegslazerett, in Traunstein as volunteers. These volunteers are called "Ghuis". Six or seven of these men returned to camp on 11 June for a few days' leave. During their stay in camp they terrorized other camp inmates who are reluctant to go to Israel. Katz and Feldmann, Camp Leader and Chief of Police respectively, in no way interfered with the 'Ghuis' actions. Since the State of Israel came into existence, the Palestina Amt has organized an active terror group among camp inhabitants to encourage emigration to Israel. The Palestina Amt members encouraged the 'Ghuis' to put pressure on reluctant persons in camp. Aaron Stanner, clerk in the IRO camp office was removed by force from his office on 4 June by this terror organization. Members of the Palestina Amt include: Mendel Grunspan, Mayer Czuthovic, Mayer Glicner, and Zupnik.

"At about 0130 hours, 14 June, a group of six to eight 'Ghuis' entered the room of Aaron Stanner and assaulted the six occupants of the room, allegedly because one of Stanner's sons refused to enter the Jewish Army. During this time, the camp police had put a cordon around the building to prevent anyone from entering or leaving. Feldmann, chief of police, was on duty at the main gate at this time. About this same time, Josef Fisch, another DP, entered the camp and was going to his room in the same building. The 'Ghuis' were just leaving the building as he arrived. Thinking Fisch was going to the aid of the Stanners, they beat him into unconsciousness. At about 0200 hours, Stanner tried to put through a call to Military Government Traunstein but was unable to get past the camp switchboard.

"As 14 June was a Jewish holiday of mourning, camp inhabitants who were not willing to go to Israel were warned not to enter the synagogue because they would be forced to leave. Most of the people warned did remain at home, and nothing happened until 1130 hours when three 'Ghuis' entered Hermann Jakubovic's room. There they tore pictures from the wall, threw things around, and tried to wreck the room in general. When Jakobovic entered his room, they tore up a telegram he had received the same day from the Funk Kasorno in Munich. In the telegram, he and his brother were invited by a screening team to come to Munich prior to emigrating to the United States. Both brothers were maltreated during this time.

"During all these happenings, neither the camp police nor the camp leader tried in any way to stop them. During the first incident, the police actually aided the terrorists. Further investigation of these matters is being conducted. . . ."

Document #3—as cited in Chapter 3, Note 21.

"Secret" memorandum from Admiral R. H. Hillenkoetter, Director of
Central Intelligence, to President Truman, dated April 12, 1948, in Carrolton Press 1979, Declassified Documents Reference Service, 341B, C.

ER 3862

CENTRAL INTELLIGENCE AGENCY
WASHINGTON 25, D. C.

12 April 1948

1979 / 341 B+C

MEMORANDUM FOR: THE PRESIDENT
                 THE SECRETARY OF STATE
                 THE SECRETARY OF DEFENSE

Subject: Clandestine air transport operations in Europe

Incidents involving the clandestine transport of munitions by aircraft into foreign areas of extreme political sensitivity, such as
Northern Italy and Palestine, are increasing. U.S.-owned aircraft and
U.S. crews are directly participating in these activities. It appears
that no effective U.S. controls are exercised outside of the U.S. in
restraint of such operations.

Examples of clandestine operations include the following: (a) a
C-46 transport aircraft, owned by a non-scheduled U.S. airline, was
cleared by the State Department for a flight to Italy where it was
allegedly to be converted to civilian passenger use. This aircraft
landed on 11 March at Genova where its contents were observed to include
small arms. The aircraft departed the same day for Rome, but was finally
reported to have been located, completely empty and apparently abandoned
by the crew, at an airfield near Perugia, Italy. (b) an American-owned
C-54 four-engine transport aircraft landed on 31 March at the Prague
airport. The plane was immediately surrounded by secret police and subsequently loaded with a number of very heavy crates. The aircraft took
off without obtaining the required clearance, and protests by Czech airport officials were overruled by the senior secret police officer who
stated that the flight was a government operation. The plane returned the
next day to Prague where the American crew, after attempting to evade
interrogation, finally admitted that they had flown a cargo of "surgical
instruments and hand tools" to a small village in Palestine. They further
asserted that the owner of the aircraft had been unaware of the operation;
(c) the Czechoslovak airline (CSA) requested OMGUS early in March for
clearances to operate two flights weekly for a total of six weeks into
Italy via Munich and Innsbruck for the purpose of hauling "cut timber."
The aircraft were to land at an airfield situated on the Italian coast
between Genoa and the French border. (No Italian customs officials are
stationed at this airfield and the location is such that trans-shipment
of air cargo to ocean shipping could be effected.) Although none of these
flights appears to have taken place with the above itinerary, there is reason
to believe that several operations into Northern Italy have been completed
covertly. (For further information on the above examples, see attachment.)

DECLASSIFIED
CIA LTR., JUSTICE DEPT. LTR. 2-2P-79
PROTECT NLT 77-PD
By NLTHG NARS on 3-24-79

It is apparent that further irresponsible activities of privately-owned U.S. aircraft and U.S. unscheduled airlines (operating on charter basis only) can have the following unfavorable effects on the U.S. national security: (a) increase in the potential of the Italian Communists, particularly in Northern Italy; (b) embarrassment to the U.S. through smuggling of arms to either side in the current Palestine hostilities; (c) objections by friendly governments; and (d) furtherance of the objectives of unfriendly nations in activities over which the U.S. has no control.

R. H. HILLENKOETTER
Rear Admiral, USN
Director of Central Intelligence

Attachment

COPY

Example (a): The C-46 transport aircraft reported to have landed in Italy after departing from Geneva on 11 March with a cargo of small arms was located at Castiglione de Largo on the same day. At this airfield the pilot turned over the aircraft to an Italian company, Societa Aeronautica Italiana, for conversion and use as a passenger plane. Although the aircraft and crew were examined by Italian customs officials dispatched to the field in advance by the Italian Director of Civil Aviation, the nature of the cargo, which was presumably removed at this time, has not been reported. The pilot has stated that upon his arrival at destination, Italian officials assured him that the required notification would be given to the proper air authorities. American officials, however, were not officially informed of the plane's arrival. Flight clearances and all documents for the aircraft were found to be in order. USMA, Rome, reports that all the crew numbers were apparently Jewish and suspects that the flight may have some connection with the Jewish underground movement although he points out that it is also possible that the crew simply engaged in the sale of contraband as a sideline to their legitimate business. Although A-2 cabled a request for full information concerning the cargo, the MAA Rome gives no indication in his reply that he interrogated the pilot on this matter.

The C-46 is owned by an American non-scheduled carrier, Service Airlines, Inc. (owned by a group of US veterans, Martin Bellefond, President, and William Burr, Jr., Vice President, formerly a New York State airline operator) and is the first of a number of C-46's for which this company is obtaining flight clearances through the Department of State for delivery to the Italian Aviation company mentioned above. The F.B.I. became suspicious of the activities of Service Airlines last January during the course of an investigation of the export of explosives by boat from the port of Newark, New Jersey. Some of the personalities involved in this illicit export operation appear to be involved also in financing the transport of arms and ammunition by air to Europe. The principal figure under investigation is a man named Wiseman, whose activities have been followed and whose name appears on numerous checks for very large sums of money. (He is reported to have at his disposal a fund of some 2½ million dollars.) Service Airlines was engaged by a group of individuals, including Wiseman, who met one night in January in the offices of the Pratt Steamship Company in New York. Service Airlines, which is based in Burbank, California, agreed to arrange with the Lockheed Corp. for the purchase and reconditioning of three Constellations. It has also acquired a total of twelve C-46's. Meanwhile, a subsidiary company was established in Panama under the name of Aereas de Panama and a number of C-46's and one of the Constellations have been flown to Panama where they are now registered as Panamanian aircraft. The US Civil Aeronautic Authority was duly notified and these air transports have been dropped from the list of US aircraft and have now acquired foreign status. The US Government automatically grants transit permits to aircraft registered in foreign countries with which it has reciprocal air agreements. Service Airlines, thus, has been able to obtain such transit permits calling for specified stops in the US en route to South America, points in the Carribbean, or Europe. The cargo manifests or bills of lading for such aircraft are usually cleared without question, nor is

the actual cargo examined even in cases where an export license is required.
Service Airlines appears to have complied with all existing requirements and, in
spite of abundant indications of illegal operations, the present evidence available appears to be insufficient to warrant prosecution for illegal activities.
The F.B.I. investigation is continuing, however. The Italian Government
apparently has cooperated closely with Service Airlines, but the behavior of
minor Italian officials in failing to report the C-46 incident to American
authorities in Italy may indicate that the cargo of arms was unloaded and disposed of with their knowledge and perhaps collusion. (Active cooperation may be
expected between left wing Italians and members of the Jewish underground inasmuch as the USSR is still sponsoring the partition of Palestine.)

     Example (b): On 31 March, an American C-54 transport plane arrived in
Prague. It was immediately surrounded and isolated by Czech security police and
two large trucks drove up from which 35 heavy cases were loaded onto the aircraft.
The plane took off immediately without making the necessary clearances with airport officials. Their protests, however, were overruled by the Chief of Security
Police who stated that this was a government operation. The aircraft returned
the following day and representatives of the US Embassy and the Military Attache
interrogated the pilot and crew. In a sworn statement, Seymour Lerner admitted
being in charge of the flight and revealed that the plane is owned by Ralph Cox
of New York who operates a charter airplane service under the name of Ocean Trade
Airways. The plane was chartered in Paris by Lerner to a British subject named
Cooper, without the knowledge, but under the general authority given by Cox to
Lerner to carry freight from Prague to various destinations. At Prague, the
plane loaded 14,000 pounds, stated on the manifest to be "hand tools and surgical
instruments" and took off for a non-stop flight to Beit Darras, Palestine. After
unloading the cargo at its destination, the plane returned to Prague. US Ambassador Steinhardt believes that the facts sworn to above are substantially correct,
but that the cases probably contained small arms and/or ammunition. (Beit Darras
is an Arab village not far from the coast of Palestine but, due to the fluid
situation existing in the area, it is not known whether the cargo was delivered
to Arab or Jewish agents.)

     Investigation of this irregular airline in the US has developed the follow-
ing information: Ocean Trade Airways operates out of an airfield at Laurinburg-
Maxton, North Carolina, about twenty-five miles from Pope Field (USAF base).
Mr. Cox and most of the operating personnel are employed by American Airlines on
a part-time basis. When operating for Ocean Trade Airways, crews wear American
Airlines uniforms with the company insignia removed. The airline apparently has
a heavy schedule of commitments and is flying DC-3's as well as the C-54's on
missions both to South America and Europe.

Example (c): No firm information has been received concerning the operations of Czech Airlines (CSA) in a series of special flights to Villanova d'Albegna near the Italian coast between Genoa and the French border. (Villanova d'Albegna has a recently established air service to Trieste, via Milan and Venice. Scheduled flights are operated three times weekly.) USAFE reported, however, that on 2 April a Czechoslovak aircraft with identification letters OAJ overflew Munich, apparently en.route to Nice, France. No clearance over the US zone was sought or granted.

R Hillenkoitter

CENTRAL INTELLIGENCE AGENCY
WASHINGTON 25, D.C.

12 April 1948

MEMORANDUM FOR: THE PRESIDENT
                        THE SECRETARY OF STATE
                        THE SECRETARY OF DEFENSE

Subject: Clandestine air transport operations in Europe

Incidents involving the clandestine transport of munitions by aircraft into foreign areas of extreme political sensitivity, such as Northern Italy and Palestine, are increasing. U.S.-owned aircraft and U.S. crews are directly participating in these activities. It appears that no effective U.S. controls are exercised outside of the U.S. in restraint of such operations.

Examples of clandestine operations include the following: (a) a C-46 transport aircraft, owned by a non-scheduled U.S. airline, was cleared by the State Department for a flight to Italy where it was allegedly to be converted to civilian passenger use. This aircraft landed on 11 March at Geneva where its contents were observed to include small arms. The aircraft departed the same day for Rome, but was finally reported to have been located, completely empty and apparently abandoned by the crew, at an airfield near Perugia, Italy; (b) an American-owned C-54 four-engine transport aircraft landed on 31 March at the Prague airport. The plane was immediately surrounded by secret police and subsequently loaded with a number of very heavy crates. The aircraft took off without obtaining the required clearance, and protests by Czech airport officials were overruled by the senior secret police officer who stated that the flight was a government operation. The plane returned the next day to Prague where the American crew, after attempting to evade interrogation, finally admitted that they had flown a cargo of "surgical instruments and hand tools" to a small village in Palestine. They further asserted that the owner of the aircraft had been unaware of the operation; (c) the Czechoslovak airline (CSA) requested OMGUS early in March for clearances to operate two flights weekly for a total of six weeks into Italy via Munich and Innsbruck for the purpose of hauling "cut timber." The aircraft were to land at an airfield situated on the Italian coast between Genoa and the French border. (No Italian customs officials are stationed at this airfield and the location is such that transshipment of air cargo to ocean shipping could be effected.) Although none of these flights appears to have taken place with the above itinerary, there is reason to believe that several operations into Northern Italy have been completed covertly. (For further information on the above examples, see attachment.)

It is apparent that further irresponsible activities of privately-owned U.S. aircraft and U.S. unscheduled airlines (operating on charter basis only) can have the following unfavorable effects on the U.S. national security: (a) increase in the potential of the Italian Communists, particularly in Northern Italy; (b) embarrassment to the U.S. through smuggling of arms to either side in the current Palestine hostilities; (c) objections by friendly governments; and (d) furtherance of the objectives of unfriendly nations in activities over which the U.S. has no control.

R. H. HILLENKOETTER
Rear Admiral, USN
Director of Central Intelligence

Attachment

Example (a): The C-46 transport aircraft reported to have landed in Italy after departing from Geneva on 11 March with a cargo of small arms was located at Castiglione de Largo on the same day. At this airfield the pilot turned over the aircraft to an Italian company, Societa Aeronautica Italiana, for conversion and use as a passenger plane. Although the aircraft and crew were examined by Italian customs officials dispatched to the field in advance by the Italian Director of Civil Aviation, the nature of the cargo, which was presumably removed at this time, has not been reported. The pilot has stated that upon his arrival at destination, Italian officials assured him that the required notification would be given to the proper air authorities. American officials, however, were not officially informed of the plane's arrival. Flight clearances and all documents for the aircraft were found to be in order. USMAA, Rome, reports that all the crew members were apparently Jewish and suspects that the flight may have some connection with the Jewish underground movement although he points out that it is also possible that the crew simply engaged in the sale of contraband as a sideline to their legitimate business. Although A-2 cabled a request for full information concerning the cargo, the MAA Rome gives no indication in his reply that he interrogated the pilot on this matter.

The C-46 is owned by an American non-scheduled carrier, Service Airlines, Inc. (owned by a group of US veterans, Martin Bellefond, President, and William Burr, Jr., Vice President, formerly a New York State airline operator) and is the first of a number of C-46's for which this company is obtaining flight clearances through the Department of State for delivery to the Italian Aviation company mentioned above. The F.B.I. became suspicious of the activities of Service Airlines last January during the course of an investigation of the export of explosives by boat from the port of Newark, New Jersey. Some of the personalities involved in this illicit export operation appear to be involved also in financing the transport of arms and ammunition to Europe. The principal figure under investigation is a man named Wiseman, whose activities have been followed and whose name appears on numerous checks for very large sums of money. (He is reported to have at his disposal a fund of some 2½ million dollars.) Service Airlines was engaged by a group of individuals, including Wiseman, who met one night in January in the offices of the Pratt Steamship Company in New York. Service Airlines, which is based in Burbank, California, agreed to arrange with the Lockheed Corp. for the purchase and reconditioning of three Constellations. It has also acquired a total of twelve C-46's. Meanwhile, a subsidiary company was established in Panama under the name of Aereas de Panama and a number of C-46's and one of the Constellations have been flown to Panama where they are now registered as Panamanian aircraft. The US Civil Aeronautic Authority was duly notified and these air transports have been dropped from the list of US aircraft and have now acquired foreign status. The US Government automatically grants transit permits to aircraft registered in foreign countries with which it has reciprocal air agreements. Service Airlines, thus, has been able to obtain such transit permits calling for specified stops in the US en route to South America, points in the Caribbean, or Europe. The cargo manifests or bills of lading for such aircraft are usually cleared without question, nor is the actual cargo examined even in cases where an export license is required. Service Airlines appears to have complied with all existing requirements and, in spite of abundant indications of illegal operations, the present evidence available appears to be insufficient to warrant prosecution for illegal activities. The F.B.I. investigation is continuing, however. The Italian Government apparently has cooperated closely with Service Airlines, but the behavior of minor Italian officials in failing to report the C-46 incident to American authorities in Italy may indicate that the cargo of arms was unloaded and disposed of with their knowledge and perhaps collusion. (Active cooperation may be expected between left wing Italians and members of the Jewish underground inasmuch as the USSR is still sponsoring the partition of Palestine.)

Example (b): On 31 March, an American C-54 transport plane arrived in Prague. It was immediately surrounded and isolated by Czech security police and two large trucks drove up from which 35 heavy cases were loaded onto the aircraft. The plane took off immediately without making the necessary clearances with airport officials. Their protests, however, were overruled by the Chief of Security Police who stated that this was a government operation. The aircraft returned the following day and representatives of the US Embassy and the Military Attache interrogated the pilot and crew. In a sworn statement, Seymour Lerner admitted being in charge of the flight and revealed that the plane is owned by Ralph Cox of New York who operates a charter airplane service under the name of Ocean Trade Airways. The plane was chartered in Paris by Lerner to a British subject named Cooper, without the knowledge, but under the general authority given by Cox to Lerner to carry freight from Prague to various destinations. At Prague, the plane loaded 14,000 pounds, stated on the manifest to be "hand tools and surgical instruments" and took off for a non-stop flight to Beit Darras, Palestine. After unloading the cargo at its destination, the plane returned to Prague. US Ambassador Steinhardt believes that the facts sworn to above are substantially correct, but that the cases probably contained small arms and/or ammunition. (Beit Darras is an Arab village not far from the coast of Palestine but, due to the fluid situation existing in the area, it is not known whether the cargo was delivered to Arab or Jewish agents.)

Investigation of this irregular airline in the US has developed the following information: Ocean Trade Airways operates out of an airfield at Laurinburg-Maxton, North Carolina, about twenty-five miles from Pope Field (USAF base). Mr. Cox and most of the operating personnel are employed by American Airlines on a part-time basis. When operating for Ocean Trade Airways, crews wear American Airlines uniforms with the company insignia removed. The airline apparently has a heavy schedule of commitments and is flying DC-3's as well as the C-54's on missions both to South America and Europe.

Example (c): No firm information has been received concerning the operations of Czech Airlines (CSA) in a series of special flights to Villanova d'Albegna near the Italian coast between Genoa and the French border. (Villanova d'Albegna has a recently established air service to Trieste, via Milan and Venice. Scheduled flights are operated three times weekly.) USAFE reported, however, that on 2 April a Czechoslovak aircraft with identification letters OAJ overflew Munich, apparently en route to Nice, France. No clearance over the US zone was sought or granted.

Document #4—as cited in Chapter 3, Note 25.

"Secret" military attaché report IR-66-48 from U.S. Air Attaché/Prague to Air Force Intelligence Directorate, dated November 15, 1948, copy in "ID File," Office of the Assistant Chief of Staff, G-2, Record Group 319, National Archives.

REPORT NO. IR-66-48
PAGE NO. 2

Additional information given State by a student pilot training for the ISRAEL Air Force in CZECHOSLOVAKIA confirms previous report written on same subject. Included in his report are the following:

1. Corrected list of students named.
2. Expected termination of JEWISH training in CZECHOSLOVAKIA.
3. Name and address of Recruiting Officer in PRAGUE.

The informant (a Christian) has been attempting to find a way to leave CZECHO other than through the U. S. Zone of Germany, and was told by a Jewish friend, a student pilot, of the possibility of joining the HAGANNAH Air Force. He was directed to report to the .I.A.S. office No. 7 JOSEPHOFSKA (same building where American Joint Distribution Committee has its offices). There he was interrogated by a GARY FRIED, American Jew who speaks fluent Czech. Organization is believed to be a Jewish Welfare (H.I.A.S.) Organization, believed by source to be affiliated with JOINT. FRIED is a civilian in charge of recruiting and reported to commute every two (2) weeks between PRAHA and ISRAEL.

Upon acceptance as a student pilot, the source was ordered to report to General ANKLSON, the ISRAEL Commander of training at OLOMOUC. There he joined a group of fifty-six (56) student pilots (one eventually was killed in a training crash). Twenty (20) of the above students, including the source, were recruited in CZECHOSLOVAKIA. (The list of students is included in Appendix).

Source claims between 4,000 - 5,000 students are taking part in the training program on Czechoslovakian soil. Of this number, there are 1,500 Infantry troops and 500 women training as nurses and auxiliaries at VELKA STREBNA (near HRANICE). The remaining forces are distributed as follows:

Radio and Telegrapher students - LIBEREC
Electromechanics and Radio Operators - PARDUBICE
Tank Troops and Parachutists - CESKE BUDEVICE

A few days ago, prior to a flight training course, source was told to report immediately to a meeting of all pilot students. At this meeting the Commanding Officer stated that the Czechoslovak Government had directed the Jewish Organization to terminate all training on Czechoslovak land. Consequently, approximately 4,000 - 5,000 students are being given leave and ordered to report to the KARLOVY VARY staging area for evacuation by air and land to ISRAEL. The Commanding Officer added that he believed that the Czechoslovak Government feared to continue this training due to "spies and informers" in their midst who had notified Western powers of their activities. The Commanding Officer further stated he hoped to obtain permission to continue this program later in another country - possibly POLAND or RUSSIA.

Source claims that final stage of training was to be conducted in SPITFIRES at the CESKE BUDEVICE Airdrome; however, this stage has been eliminated due to the latest change in orders.

COMMENTS: A recent field trip conducted by a member of this office showed no sign of activity in CESKE BUDEVICE. Further investigation, however, will be conducted between 15 November and 19 November 1948. There are no known SPITFIRES left in CZECHO (See IR-52-48 and IR-66-48.)

0210382

DISTRIBUTION: USAFE
* H.I.A.S. = HEBREW IMMIGRANTS' AID SOCIETY
No USAF NOTE.

NOTE: This document contains information affecting the national defense of the United States within the meaning of the Espionage Act, 50 U.S.C. 31 and 32, as amended. Its transmission or the revelation of its contents in any manner to an unauthorized person is prohibited by law.

A P P E N D I X

LIST OF STUDENTS

PETER MUNK (USA, Ohio)

STEPAN POLLAK (Sydney, Australia)

JURAJ BOSKOVIC (Russian)

TIBOR SAJO (Czech)

LADISLAV SAJOVIC (Czech)

LADISLAV BERGMAN (Czech)

IRWIN FEDER (Czech - Former NAV. with RAF)

HERBERT CATER (USA)

MIROSLAV FISHER (Sub-Capt., UKR)

HUGO MAJSL (English - RAF)

LARRY LAUFER (Czech)

MILAN FING (Czech)

LADISLAV KAFKA (Czech)

COSTA (Brazil)

FLACEK (Czech)

LEBOVIC (Sub-Capt., UKR)

MILOS JELINEK

ZSURAN (Israel) - Killed in training

Additional information given State by a student pilot training for the IS-RAEL Air Force in CZECHOSLOVAKIA confirms previous report written on same subject. Included in this report are the following:

1. Corrected list of student names.
2. Expected termination of JEWISH training in CZECHOSLOVAKIA.
3. Name and address of Recruiting Officer in PRAGUE.

The informant (a Christian) has been attempting to find a way to leave CZECHO other than through the U.S. Zone of Germany, and was told by a Jewish friend, a student pilot, of the possibility of joining the HAGANNAH Air Force. He was directed to report to the H.I.A.S. office No. 7 JOSEPHOFSKA (same building where American Joint Distribution Committee has its offices). There he was interrogated by a GARY FRIED, American Jew who speaks fluent Czech. Organization is believed to be a Jewish Welfare (H.I.A.S.) Organization, believed by source to be affiliated with JOINT. FRIED is a civilian in charge of recruiting and reported to commute every two (2) weeks between PRAHA and ISRAEL.

Upon acceptance as a student pilot, the source was ordered to report to General ANKLSON, the ISRAEL commander of training at OLOMOUC. There he joined a group of fifty-six (56) student pilots (one eventually was killed in a training crash). Twenty (20) of the above students, including the source, were recruited in CZECHOSLOVAKIA. (The list of students is included in Appendix).

Source claims between 4,000-5,000 students are taking part in the training program on Czechoslovakian soil. Of this number, there are 1,500 Infantry troops and 500 women training as nurses and auxiliaries at VELKA STREBNA (near HRANICE). The remaining forces are distributed as follows:

Radio and Telegrapher students—LIBEREC
Electromechanics and Radio Operators—PARDUBICE
Tank Troops and Parachutists—CESKE BUDEVICE

A few days ago, prior to a flight training course, source was told to report immediately to a meeting of all pilot students. At this meeting the Commanding Officer stated that the Czechoslovak Government had directed the Jewish Organization to terminate all training on Czechoslovak land. Consequently, approximately 4,000-5,000 students are being given leave and ordered to report to the KARLOVY VARY staging area for evacuation by air and land to ISRAEL. The Commanding Officer added that he believed that the Czechoslovak Government feared to continue this training due to "spies and informers" in their midst who had notified Western powers of their activities. The Commanding Officer further stated he hoped to obtain permission to continue this program later in another country—possibly POLAND or RUSSIA.

Source claims that final stage of training was to be conducted in SPITFIRES at the CESKE BUDEVICE Airdrome; however, this stage has been eliminated due to the latest change in orders.

COMMENTS: A recent field trip conducted by a member of this office showed no sign of activity in CESKE BUDEVICE. Further investigation, however, will be conducted between 13 November and 17 November 1948. There are no known SPITFIRES left in CZECHO (See IR-62-48 and IR-65-48.

A P P E N D I X

LIST OF STUDENTS

PETER MUNK (USA, Ohio)

STEPAN POLLAK (Sydney, Australia)

JURAJ MOSKOVIC (Russian)

TIBOR SAJO (Czech)

LADISLAV SAJOVIC (Czech)

LADISLAV BERGMAN (Czech)

IRWIN FEDER (Czech—Former NAV. with RAF)

HERBERT CATER (USA)

MIROSLAV FISHER (Sub-Capt., UKR)

HUGO MAJSL (English—RAF)

LARRY LAUFER (Czech)

MILAN FING (Czech)

LADISLAV KAFKA (Czech)

COSTA (Brazil)

PLACEK (Czech)

LEBOVIC (Sub-Capt., UKR)

MILOS JELINEK

ZSURAN (Israel)—Killed in training

Document #5—25 as cited in Chapter 5, Note 20.

Enclosure to "Top Secret" memorandum for Brig. Gen. Chester V. Clifton, Military Aide to the President, from Allen W. Dulles, Director of Central Intelligence, dated February 8, 1961, declassified December 7, 1978.

CENTRAL INTELLIGENCE AGENCY
WASHINGTON 25, D. C.

OFFICE OF THE DIRECTOR

1979/ 352 A   February 8, 1961

MEMORANDUM FOR: Brig. Gen. Chester V. Clifton
                 Military Aide to the President

        Attached is a memorandum regarding the present governmental crisis in Israel, the position of Ben-Gurion, and the so-called "Lavon Affair", which I felt might be of interest to the President.

        I would appreciate it if this report could be returned when it has served its purpose.

                                        Allen W. Dulles
                                             Director

Enclosure

7 February 1961

MEMORANDUM

SUBJECT: Prime Minister Ben-Gurion's Resignation

1. Ben-Gurion's resignation is the culmination of long-standing intra-party quarrels of a personal and ideological nature which reached their climax during the months of December 1960 and January 1961. The tensions released by the "Lavon Affair", characterized in the censored Israeli press as a serious "security mishap" damaging to the vital interests of Israel, were intensified at the height of the controversy by the unexpected expose in the British and American press of a sizable second nuclear reactor under construction near Beersheba and Ben-Gurion's criticism of western Jews in the diaspora* because of their unwillingness to immigrate to Israel. The real issue, however, is concerned with government policy in a number of fields, the future leadership of Israel upon the decease or retirement of the aging Prime Minister (he is now 74), and the ideological complexion of the State of Israel.

2. It is the consensus of many well-informed Israelis that the strongest, brightest and most experienced leader in Israel after Ben-Gurion is Pinhas Lavon, former Minister of Defense under Moshe Sharett in 1954 and currently Secretary General of the Histadrut, Israel's extremely powerful trade union organization. Lavon, an old Zionist, builder of the State, and a leading member of Ben-Gurion's political party, Mapai, aspires to the office of the Prime Minister as Ben-Gurion's successor. As spokesman for the Histadrut, which was founded 26 years before the State, he frequently opposed the political, economic and labor policies of the government. But the origins of the so-called "Lavon Affair" go back to 1954.

- - - - - - - - -

*Jews living outside of Israel.

3. During the 13 months from late 1953 to 1954, when Ben-Gurion retired to his desert retreat at Sde Boker, Lavon held the position of Minister of Defense under the prime minister-ship of Moshe Sharett. It was under Sharett's quiet and deft diplo-macy that the first and only link Israel has ever had with Egypt was forged.

He attached major importance to this channel through which he hoped to negotiate a lasting peace between the Arabs and the Jews. Sharett promised that in return for a peace settlement he would bring the full weight of world Zionist support to help Nasser realize his ambitions as undisputed leader of a united Arab world, and Nasser listened with interest. The policy of the Government of Israel at this time was that nothing should be done to disturb the status quo or to antagonize the Arabs in any way.

4. Despite the affirmation of this policy of conciliation, in mid-1954, Brigadier General Benjamin Gibli, a capable career officer with a promising future in the Israel Defense Forces and head of G-2, while serving under Lavon as the Minister of Defense, ran an espionage net into Egypt which was assigned certain intel-ligence targets as well as several political action assignments, one of which is stated to have been the bombing on 14 July 1954 of the USIS libraries in Cairo and Alexandria in order to damage U.S.-Egyptian relations.* The net was rolled up by the Egyptian security service and 13 Jews were arrested and tried. Despite U.S. efforts, upon the request of the Israeli Government, to ameliorate the sen-tences, two were executed, one committed suicide in jail, several were given long prison sentences, and some escaped. The dis-illusioned Nasser, believing that the link had been used to deceive him, ordered a discontinuation of all contacts with the Israelis, leaving bitterness in both camps. After the Israeli net was dis-covered the Egyptians inaugurated a series of armed incursions along the Israeli-Egyptian borders which eventually resulted in the

---

*Note: Egyptian Minister of National Guidance White Paper, "The Story of Zionist Espionage in Egypt", states that the net made an attempt to destroy the USIS libraries.

2

violent Israeli retaliation against Gaza on 28 February 1955. In December 1955, when Mr. Robert B. Anderson (later Secretary of the Treasury) was attempting mediation, President Nasser recalled these incidents stating that his "confidence in the Israelis had been gravely shaken."

findings of Lavon inves Committee

As a result of the findings, which have never been made public, both Lavon and Gibli, though neither was accused of malfeasance, were asked to resign their positions by Mr. Sharett because they had destroyed his peace negotiations. In February 1955, Ben-Gurion returned from retirement and assumed Lavon's portfolio. Lavon was later named Secretary General of the Histadrut in 1956. Gibli, however, continued his military career, being given command of the Northern District of the Israel Defense Forces and subsequently became military attache in London. In November 1955, Ben-Gurion replaced Sharett as Prime Minister and named Sharett Minister for Foreign Affairs.

6. Lavon, realizing that his chances of re-entering the political arena would remain remote so long as his reputation was besmirched by this fiasco, was determined to clear himself of all responsibility. However, Lavon never possessed the means of vindication until 1960 when, on a trip to Europe, he discovered

what?

that General Gibli had perjured himself. Lavon returned to Israel and requested a reopening of the case which was heard by a ministerial committee composed of seven Cabinet members.

3

acceptable to all coalition partners with the exception of Mapam. After testimony that the order had been forged and that General Gibli had perjured himself, the committee announced that their findings completely exonerated Lavon of all responsibility for the "security mishap" of 1954. This decision satisfied Lavon, who stated that he was ready to forget the incident, but it infuriated Ben-Gurion. The latter informed the committee that its procedures were "mistaken and misleading" and "led to unfairness, half-truths and a miscarriage of justice." He then demanded a judicial inquiry (to which Lavon objected) or threatened to resign. Abetted by so-called new evidence uncovered by General Dayan, Ben-Gurion publicly denounced Lavon as a liar and immoral character. At this point the Cabinet and the Mapai Central Committee were shattered. Foreign Minister Golda Meir, who is known to be anti-Dayan and Peres and pro-Lavon, threatened to resign from the Cabinet if Mr. Ben-Gurion pursued the case. She is reported to have felt that the fight was damaging to the country and to the Mapai party, and that nothing was to be gained by its continuance.

7. Ben-Gurion is a unique synthesis of the prophet-statesman and the strong-willed politician who loves intensely and hates passionately. He has attempted on occasion to destroy not only his political opponents but their memories as well. In Lavon he apparently encountered a stubborn opponent. According to an individual close to Ben-Gurion, Lavon had hurt him more deeply than he had ever been hurt before, because he had tarnished Ben-Gurion's historical reputation. Having carried his attacks to the extreme, he left himself no other alternative but resignation.

8. In addition to the personal animus between the two protago-nists, there is also an ideological clash which has become increasing-exacerbated by the changing texture of Israel's political and economic fiber. Since the establishment of the State in 1948, the impact of American Jewry, with its enormous contributions, and the substantial grants and loans of the U.S. Government have profoundly influenced the thinking of the government leaders. In order to replace charity

with solid investments, Ben-Gurion and many leading members
of the Mapai party have made concessions to western and
particularly American Jews by compromising some of their
original ideals. By creating a more palatable political and
economic environment, it is hoped that American Jews can be
induced to immigrate to Israel, a prime tenet of Zionist ideology
and fundamental to the security of the State. These developments
have alarmed the doctrinaires, and especially Lavon, who
deplore the waning of pioneer fervor among Israelis and the
corruption of their socialist ideals. Lavon in a recent interview
stated: "The question is whether older people shall be able . . . .
to build up a group of men and women with technical ability and
scientific training which at the same time remains faithful to
those spiritual forces which made us what we are and made Israel
what it is. It is a fight . . . ., step by step, against the established
powers. But the fight must be continued no matter how powerful
the established interests may be."

9. Ben-Gurion is obsessed by the security of the State and
the ultimate success of the Zionist movement, and he will do his
utmost to reach these objectives. One might even call him a
pragmatic ideologist because he believes that only an ever-increasing
immigration of diaspora Jewry can rebuild Zion and guarantee the
security of the State. Each immigrant, however, must find work
compatible with the State's development. He has therefore placed
every emphasis on science and technology, fields requiring minimal
natural resources but a high quotient of brain power which the Jews
have in abundance. Viewed in this light, and realizing it will be
some years before the population of Israel will be large enough to
permit the country to relax, Ben-Gurion without the knowledge of
his Cabinet, gave the order some time in 1956 to begin construction
of a second nuclear, plutonium-producing reactor which would permit,
if necessary, the manufacture of an atomic bomb. This decision was
revealed to an extremely small circle of confidants. Secrecy was
successfully maintained, at least from the outside world, until mid-
1960's. When the project was finally exposed by the British and
American press, the Israeli Government and people were shaken by

5

the intensity of the U.S. reaction. Almost simultaneously and at the height of the "Lavon Affair", Ben-Gurion publicly denounced diaspora Jewry at the 25th World Zionist Congress in Jerusalem in December 1960 for not immigrating to Israel. His Biblical quotation that religious Jews living outside Israel were considered to have no God evoked widespread protests from American Jews and rocked the foundations of the American Zionist organizations.

10. Though corroborating evidence is lacking, this series of characteristic shock treatments touching the very sinews of Zion may have seriously diminished the confidence which the Cabinet and the leaders of the Mapai party have in the future leadership of Ben-Gurion. Publicly they professed loyalty and urged him not to resign, but their private opinions may very well have influenced his final decision. The most likely candidate to succeed Ben-Gurion to date is believed to be Levi Eshkol, the Minister of Finance, who has displayed talent and leadership both in the diaspora and in Israel and particularly during the "Lavon Affai There is also a possibility that Sharett might be recalled to power, but it should not be entirely excluded that Ben-Gurion himself, as he has many times previously, may be the only one capable of formin a new coalition government.

CENTRAL INTELLIGENCE AGENCY
WASHINGTON 25, D. C.

OFFICE OF THE DIRECTOR

MEMORANDUM FOR: Brig. Gen. Chester V. Clifton
Military Aide to the President

Attached is a memorandum regarding the present governmental crisis in Israel, the position of Ben-Gurion, and the so-called "Lavon Affair", which I felt might be of interest to the President.

I would appreciate it if this report could be returned when it has served its purpose.

Allen W. Dulles
Director

Enclosure

7 February 1961

MEMORANDUM

SUBJECT: Prime Minister Ben-Gurion's Resignation

1. Ben-Gurion's resignation is the culmination of long-standing intra-party quarrels of a personal and ideological nature which reached their climax during the months of December 1960 and January 1961. The tensions released by the "Lavon Affair", characterized in the censored Israeli press as a serious "security mishap" damaging to the vital interests of Israel, were intensified at the height of the controversy by the unexpected exposé in the British and American press of a sizable second nuclear reactor under construction near Beersheba and Ben-Gurion's criticism of western Jews in the diaspora* because of their unwillingness to immigrate to Israel. The real issue, however, is

---

*Jews living outside of Israel.

concerned with government policy in a number of fields, the future leadership
of Israel upon the decease or retirement of the aging Prime Minister (he is now
74), and the ideological complexion of the State of Israel.

2. It is the consensus of many well-informed Israelis that the strongest,
brightest and most experienced leader in Israel after Ben-Gurion is Pinhas
Lavon, former Minister of Defense under Moshe Sharett in 1954 and currently
Secretary General of the Histadrut, Israel's extremely powerful trade union
organization. Lavon, an old Zionist, builder of the State, and a leading member of Ben-Gurion's political party, Mapai, aspires to the office of the Prime
Minister as Ben-Gurion's successor. As spokesman for the Histradrut, which
was founded 26 years before the State, he frequently opposed the political,
economic and labor policies of the government. But the origins of the so-called
"Lavon Affair" go back to 1954.

3. During the 13 months from late 1953 to 1954, when Ben-Gurion retired
to his desert retreat at Sde Boker, Lavon held the position of Minister of
Defense under the prime ministership of Moshe Sharett. It was under Sharett's
quiet and deft diplomacy that the first and only link Israel has ever had with
Egypt was forged.

He attached major importance to this channel through which he hoped to negotiate a lasting peace between the Arabs and the Jews. Sharett promised that
in return for a peace settlement he would bring the full weight of world Zionist
support to help Nasser realize his ambitions as undisputed leader of a united
Arab world, and Nasser listened with interest. The policy of the Government
of Israel at this time was that nothing should be done to disturb the status quo
or to antagonize the Arabs in any way.

4. Despite the affirmation of this policy of conciliation, in mid-1954, Brigadier General Benjamin Gibli, a capable career officer with a promising future
in the Israel Defense Forces and head of G-2, while serving under Lavon as
the Minister of Defense, ran an espionage net into Egypt which was assigned
certain intelligence targets as well as several political action assignments, one
of which is stated to have been the bombing on 14 July 1954 of the USIS
libraries in Cairo and Alexandria in order to damage U.S.-Egyptian relations.*
The net was rolled up by the Egyptian security service and 13 Jews were arrested and tried. Despite U.S. efforts, upon the request of the Israeli Government, to ameliorate the sentences, two were executed, one committed suicide
in jail, several were given long prison sentences, and some escaped. The disil-
lusioned Nasser, believing that the link had been used to deceive him, ordered
a discontinuation of all contacts with the Israelis, leaving bitterness in both
camps. After the Israeli net was discovered the Egyptians inaugurated a series
of armed incursions along the Israeli-Egyptian borders which eventually resulted in the violent Israeli retaliation against Gaza on 28 February 1955. In
December 1955, when Mr. Robert B. Anderson (later Secretary of the Trea-

---

*Note: Egyptian Minister of National Guidance White Paper, "The Story of
Zionist Espionage in Egypt," states that the net made an attempt to
destroy the USIS libraries.

sury) was attempting mediation, President Nasser recalled these incidents stating that "his confidence in the Israelis had been gravely shaken."

As a result of the findings, which have never been made public, both Lavon and Gibli, though neither was accused of malfeasance, were asked to resign their positions by Mr. Sharett because they had destroyed his peace negotiations. In February 1955, Ben-Gurion returned from retirement and assumed Lavon's portfolio. Lavon was later named Secretary General of the Histadrut in 1956. Gibli, however, continued his military career, being given command of the Northern District of the Israel Defense Forces and subsequently became military attache in London. In November 1955, Ben-Gurion replaced Sharett as Prime Minister and named Sharett Minister for Foreign Affairs.

6. Lavon, realizing that his chances of re-entering the political arena would remain remote as long as his reputation was besmirched by this fiasco, was determined to clear himself of all responsibility. However, Lavon never possessed the means of vindication until 1960 when, on a trip to Europe, he discovered

that General Gibli had perjured himself. Lavon returned to Israel and requested a reopening of the case which was heard by a ministerial committee composed of seven Cabinet members, acceptable to all coalition partners with the exception of Mapam. After testimony that the order had been forged and that General Gibli had perjured himself, the committee announced that their findings completely exonerated Lavon of all responsibility for the "security mishap" of 1954. This decision satisfied Lavon, who stated that he was ready to forget the incident, but it infuriated Ben-Gurion. The latter informed the committee that its procedures were "mistaken and misleading" and "led to unfairness, half-truths and a miscarriage of justice." He then demanded a judicial inquiry (to which Lavon objected) or threatened to resign. Abetted by so-called new evidence uncovered by General Dayan, Ben-Gurion publicly denounced Lavon as a liar and immoral character. At this point the Cabinet and the Mapai Central Committee were shattered. Foreign Minister Golda Meir, who is known to be anti-Dayan and Peres and pro-Lavon, threatened to resign from the Cabinet if Mr. Ben-Gurion pursued the case. She is reported to have felt that the fight was damaging to the country and to the Mapai party, and that nothing was to be gained by its continuance.

7. Ben-Gurion is a unique synthesis of the prophet-statesman and the strong-willed politician who loves intensely and hates passionately. He has attempted on occasion to destroy not only his political opponents but their memories as well. In Lavon he apparently encountered a stubborn opponent. According to an individual close to Ben-Gurion, Lavon had hurt him more deeply than he had ever been hurt before, because he had tarnished Ben-Gurion's historical reputation. Having carried his attacks to the extreme, he left himself no other alternative but resignation.

8. In addition to the personal animus between the two protagonists, there is also an ideological clash which has become increasingly exacerbated by the changing texture of Israel's political and economic fiber. Since the establishment of the State in 1948, the impact of American Jewry, with its enormous contributions, and the substantial grants and loans of the U.S. Government have profoundly influenced the thinking of the government leaders. In order to replace charity with solid investments, Ben-Gurion and many leading members of the Mapai party have made concessions to western and particularly American Jews by compromising some of their original ideals. By creating a more palatable political and economic environment, it is hoped that American Jews can be induced to immigrate to Israel, a prime tenet of Zionist ideology and fundamental to the security of the State. These developments have alarmed the doctrinaires, and especially Lavon, who deplore the waning of pioneer fervor among Israelis and the corruption of their socialist ideals. Lavon in a recent interview stated: "The question is whether older people shall be able . . . to build up a group of men and women with technical ability and scientific training which at the same time remains faithful to those spiritual forces which made us what we are and made Israel what it is. It is a fight . . . step by step, against the established powers. But the fight must be continued no matter how powerful the established interests may be."

9. Ben-Gurion is obsessed by the security of the State and the ultimate success of the Zionist movement, and he will do his utmost to reach these objectives. One might even call him a pragmatic ideologist because he believes that only an ever-increasing immigration of diaspora Jewry can rebuild Zion and guarantee the security of the State. Each immigrant, however, must find work compatible with the State's development. He has therefore placed every emphasis on science and technology, fields requiring minimal natural resources but a high quotient of brain power which the Jews have in abundance. Viewed in this light, and realizing it will be some years before the population of Israel will be large enough to permit the country to relax, Ben-Gurion, without the knowledge of his Cabinet, gave the order some time in 1956, to begin construction of a second nuclear, plutonium-producing reactor which would permit, if necessary, the manufacture of an atomic bomb. This decision was revealed to an extremely small circle of confidants. Secrecy was successfully maintained, at least from the outside world, until mid-1960's. When the project was finally exposed by the British and American press, the Israeli Government and people were shaken by the intensity of the U.S. reaction. Almost simultaneously and at the height of the "Lavon Affair", Ben-Gurion publicly denounced diaspora Jewry at the 25th World Zionist Congress in Jerusalem for not immigrating to Israel. His Biblical quotation that religious Jews living outside Israel were considered to have no God evoked widespread protests from American Jews and rocked the foundations of the American Zionist organizations.

10. Though corroborating evidence is lacking, this series of characteristic shock treatments touching the very sinews of Zion may have seriously diminished the confidence which the Cabinet and the leaders of the Mapai party have in the future leadership of Ben-Gurion. Publicly they professed loyalty

and urged him not to resign, but their private opinions may very well have influenced his final decision. The most likely candidate to succeed Ben-Gurion to date is believed to be Levi Eshkol, the Minister of Finance, who has displayed talent and leadership both in the diaspora and in Israel and particularly during the "Lavon Affair" There is also a possibility that Sharett might be recalled to power, but it should not be entirely excluded that Ben-Gurion himself, as he has many times previously, may be the only one capable of forming a new coalition government.

Document #6—as cited in Chapter 5, Note 26.

"Top Secret" telegram 874 from U.S. Embassy, Beirut, to Secretary of
State, dated April 18, 1954, declassified May 5, 1982.

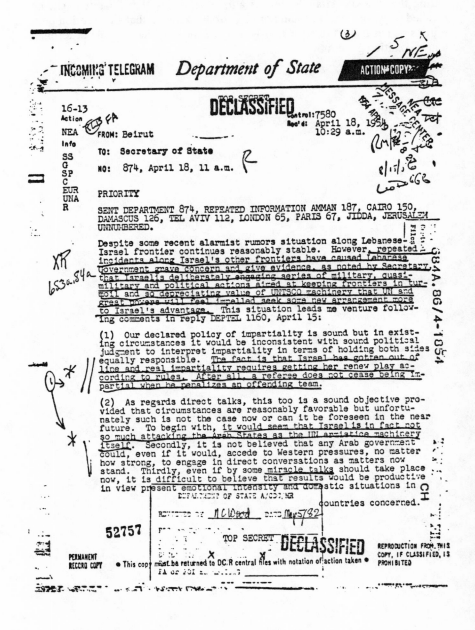

INCOMING TELEGRAM   *Department of State*   ACTION COPY

DECLASSIFIED

16-13
Action

NEA   FROM: Beirut

Info
SS   TO: Secretary of State
G
SP   NO: 874, April 18, 11 a.m.
C
EUR
UNA
R   PRIORITY

Control:7580
Rec'd: April 18, 1954
10:29 a.m.

SENT DEPARTMENT 874, REPEATED INFORMATION AMMAN 187, CAIRO 150,
DAMASCUS 126, TEL AVIV 112, LONDON 65, PARIS 67, JIDDA, JERUSALEM
UNNUMBERED.

Despite some recent alarmist rumors situation along Lebanese-
Israel frontier continues reasonably stable. However, repeated
incidents along Israel's other frontiers have caused Lebanese
Government grave concern and give evidence, as noted by Secretary
that Israelis deliberately engaging series of military, quasi-
military and political actions aimed at keeping frontiers in turmoil and so depreciating value of UNTSCO machinery that UN and
great powers will feel impelled seek some new arrangement more
to Israel's advantage. This situation leads me venture following comments in reply DEPTEL 1160, April 15:

(1) Our declared policy of impartiality is sound but in existing circumstances it would be inconsistent with sound political
judgment to interpret impartiality in terms of holding both sides
equally responsible. The fact is that Israel has gotten out of
line and real impartiality requires getting her renew play according to rules. After all, a referee does not cease being impartial when he penalizes an offending team.

(2) As regards direct talks, this too is a sound objective provided that circumstances are reasonably favorable but unfortunately such is not the case now or can it be foreseen in the near
future. To begin with, it would seem that Israel is in fact not
so much attacking the Arab States as the UN armistice machinery
itself. Secondly, it is not believed that any Arab government
could, even if it would, accede to Western pressures, no matter
how strong, to engage in direct conversations as matters now
stand. Thirdly, even if by some miracle talks should take place
now, it is difficult to believe that results would be productive
in view present emotional intensity and domestic situations in
                                          countries concerned.

DEPARTMENT OF STATE A/CDC MR
REVIEWED BY M C Wood   DATE May 5/82

52757

TOP SECRET   DECLASSIFIED

PERMANENT
RECORD COPY   ● This copy must be returned to DC:R central files with notation of action taken ●

REPRODUCTION FROM THIS
COPY, IF CLASSIFIED, IS
PROHIBITED

RECLASSIFIED

-2-#874, April 18, 11 a.m., from Beirut.

countries concerned.

(3) While reiterating endorsement principles of impartiality
and encouraging direct talks as feasible, it would respectfully
suggest that progress toward solution of Palestine problem may
have been retarded rather than stimulated in past by argument
that Arab-Israel problem is "theirs" not "ours". This is not
fact. Israel came into being as result action by the international community and it will take further action by the international community to settle her as peaceful Near Eastern state.
To be sure the Arab States and Israel have an important share
of responsibility but it is only partial. Furthermore, regardless of responsibility, the task would be beyond Arab-Israeli
capacities in any event. We should not postulate the unrealistic
nor ask the impossible.

(4) It would follow from foregoing that unless and until we and
our major allies, working both within and outside the UN, can
come forward with substantial plans which could be made basis
for effective General Assembly action, it is pointless to seek
maintain policy of seeking "peace" in some other way. Meanwhile,
might it not be more realistic and productive to acknowledge that
all we are seeking for time being is a modus vivendi, which might
even take form of genuinely respected armed truce. If all of us,
that is Arabs, Israelis and international community, could reconcile ourselves to this idea, I believe that there would be better
prospect of working gradually toward final peace.

(5) While the American Government should be prepared to play
vigorous role, it is essential that there should be full cooperation by others, especially our major allies. Unfortunately such
cooperation has not always been up to desired level with result
that we sometimes find ourselves in unnecessarily exposed position.

(6) As regards means for strengthening present truce machinery,
Lebanese-Israeli MAC has had so few problems and worked so well
that we have had little first-hand experience on which to base
specific suggestions other than to endorse helpful ideas in
Cairo's 1309, April 16, and to inquire whether any new thinking
may possibly have been developed regarding an "international police
force" to overcome well-known objections raised when idea was
originally considered.

To summarize, we agree that Palestine crisis indeed serious but
that hope for improvement at this stage does not lie in encouraging
direct negotiations but rather in recognizing that international
community bears important responsibility and in being prepared to
face Near Eastern cold war for some time in anticipation that

52758   eventual peace

TOP SECRET

DECLASSIFIED

TOP SECRET

-3-#874, April 18, 11 a.m., from Beirut.

eventual peace will come either by some new and basic UN action
or by piecemeal adjustment and the passage of time. Meanwhile,
UN supervisory machinery should be strengthened and its authority
imposed with rigid impartiality.

HARE

GB/14

52759

TOP SECRET

PORTIONS DENIED AS INDICATED DECLASSIFIED

SENT DEPARTMENT 874, REPEATED INFORMATION AMMAN 187, CAIRO 150, DAMASCUS 126, TEL AVIV 112, LONDON 65, PARIS 67, JIDDA, JERUSALEM UNNUMBERED.

Despite some recent alarmist rumors situation along Lebanese-Israel frontier continues reasonably stable. However, repeated incidents along Israel's other frontiers have caused Lebanese Government grave concern and give evidence, as noted by Secretary, that Israelis deliberately engaging series of military, quasi-military and political actions aimed at keeping frontiers in turmoil and so depreciating value of UNTSCO machinery that UN and great powers will feel impelled seek some new arrangement more to Israel's advantage. This situation leads me venture. following comments in reply DEPTEL 1160, April 15:

(1) Our declared policy of impartiality is sound but in existing circumstances it would be inconsistent with sound political judgment to interpret impartiality in terms of holding both sides equally responsible. The fact is that Israel has gotten out of line and real impartiality requires getting her renew play according to rules. After all, a referee does not cease being impartial when he penalizes an offending team.

(2) As regards direct talks, this too is a sound objective provided that circumstances are reasonably favorable but unfortunately such is not the case now or can it be foreseen in the near future. To begin with, it would seem that Israel is in fact not so much attacking the Arab States as the UN armistice machinery itself. Secondly, it is not believed that any Arab government could, even if it would, accede to Western pressures, no matter how strong, to engage in direct conversations as matters now stand. Thirdly, even if by some miracle talks should take place now, it is difficult to believe that results would be productive in view present emotional intensity and domestic situations in countries concerned.

(3) While reiterating endorsement principles of impartiality and encouraging direct talks as feasible, it would respectfully suggest that progress toward solution of Palestine problem may have been retarded rather than stimulated in past by argument that Arab-Israel problem is "theirs" not "ours". This is not fact. Israel came into being as result action by the international community and it will take further action by the international community to settle her as peaceful Near Eastern state. To be sure the Arab States and Israel have an important share of responsibility but it is only partial. Furthermore, regardless of responsibility, the task would be beyond Arab-Israeli capacities in any event. We should not postulate the unrealistic nor ask the impossible.

(4) It would follow from foregoing that unless and until we and our major allies, working both within and outside the UN, can come forward with substantial plans which could be made basis for effective General Assembly action, it is pointless to seek maintain policy of seeking "peace" in some other way. Meanwhile, might it not be more realistic and productive to acknowledge that all we are seeking for time being is a modus vivendi, which might even

take form of genuinely respected armed truce. If all of us, that is Arabs, Israelis and international community, could reconcile ourselves to this idea, I believe that there would be better prospect of working gradually toward final peace.

(5) While the American Government should be prepared to play vigorous role, it is essential that there should be full cooperation by others, especially our major allies. Unfortunately such cooperation has not always been up to desired level with result that we sometimes find ourselves in unnecessarily exposed position.

(6) As regards means for strengthening present truce machinery, Lebanese-Israeli MAC has had so few problems and worked so well that we have had little first-hand experience on which to base specific suggestions other than to endorse helpful ideas in Cairo's 1309, April 16, and to inquire whether any new thinking may possibly have been developed regarding an "international police force" to overcome well-known objections raised when idea was originally considered.

To summarize, we agree that Palestine crisis indeed serious but that hope for improvement at this stage does not lie in encouraging direct negotiations but rather in recognizing that international community bears important responsibility and in being prepared to face Near Eastern cold war for some time in anticipation that eventual peace will come either by some new and basic UN action or by piecemeal adjustment and the passage of time. Meanwhile, UN supervisory machinery should be strengthened and its authority imposed with rigid impartiality.

                                                                        HARE

Document #7—as cited in Chapter 5, Note 27.

"Top Secret" telegram 1072 from U.S. Embassy, Tel Aviv, to Secretary
of State, dated April 17, 1954, declassified May 5, 1982.

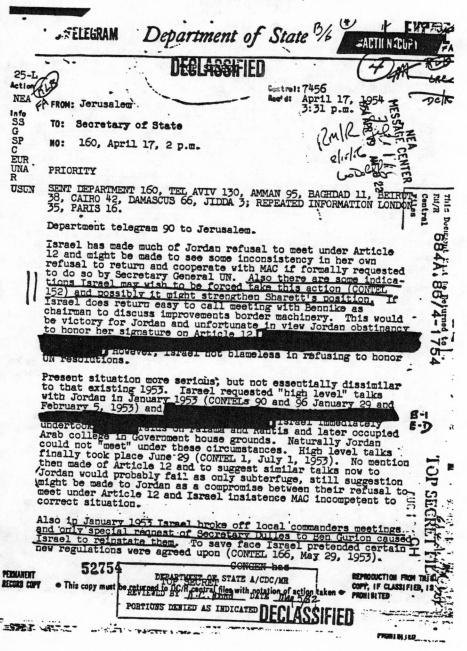

TELEGRAM   *Department of State*

DECLASSIFIED

25-L
Action

NEA   FROM: Jerusalem.

Info
SS   TO: Secretary of State
G
SP   NO: 160, April 17, 2 p.m.
C
EUR
UNA   PRIORITY
R

USUN   SENT DEPARTMENT 160, TEL AVIV 130, AMMAN 95, BAGHDAD 11, BEIRUT
         38, CAIRO 42, DAMASCUS 66, JIDDA 3; REPEATED INFORMATION LONDON
         35, PARIS 16.

Control: 7456
Rec'd: April 17, 1954
3:31 p.m.

Department telegram 90 to Jerusalem.

Israel has made much of Jordan refusal to meet under Article
12 and might be made to see some inconsistency in her own
refusal to return and cooperate with MAC if formally requested
to do so by Secretary General UN. Also there are some indications Israel may wish to be forced take this action (CONTEL
152) and possibly it might strengthen Sharett's position. If
Israel does return easy to call meeting with Bennike as
chairman to discuss improvements border machinery. This would
be victory for Jordan and unfortunate in view Jordan obstinancy
to honor her signature on Article 12.

However, Israel not blameless in refusing to honor
UN resolutions.

Present situation more serious, but not essentially dissimilar
to that existing 1953. Israel requested "high level" talks
with Jordan in January 1953 (CONTELs 90 and 96 January 29 and
February 5, 1953) and

undertook   raids on Falama and Rantis and later occupied
Arab college in Government house grounds. Naturally Jordan
could not "meet" under these circumstances. High level talks
finally took place June 29 (CONTEL 1, July 1, 1953). No mention
then made of Article 12 and to suggest similar talks now to
Jordan would probably fail as only subterfuge, still suggestion
might be made to Jordan as a compromise between their refusal to
meet under Article 12 and Israel insistence MAC incompetent to
correct situation.

Also in January 1953 Israel broke off local commanders meetings
and only special request of Secretary Dulles to Ben Gurion caused
Israel to reinstate them. To save face Israel pretended certain
new regulations were agreed upon (CONTEL 166, May 29, 1953).

CONGEN has

DECLASSIFIED

-2- #160, April 17, 2 p.m., from Jerusalem

CONGEN has always maintained MAC an excellent institution given sincerity both parties, and local commanders meetings best means yet devised to curb infiltration. But Israel has found ▓▓▓▓▓▓▓▓ reasons for denouncing them in past and refusing to agree to improvement in rules of procedure (CONTELs 84, January 21 and 165, May 29, 1953). I feel strongly that we should confront Israel with known facts of her statements calling for easing of border tension as contrasted with her hostile acts of reprisal raids and sabotaging local commanders agreements and rules of MAC procedure which is best method of "nibbling" at border control. Furthermore, Israel makes frequent claims she "knows how to treat Arabs" and therefore, well aware to call for meeting under Article 12 would only irritate Jordan and while giving Israel propaganda advantage it was not in interest of peace or easing border tension. There is also enormous difference between individual acts of infiltrators and group reprisals officially undertaken or condoned by governments. Jordan does punish known infiltrators Israel never punishes those guilty of reprisal raids. CONGEN and UNTSO here in agreement Jordan making sincere effort curb infiltration (Consulate's despatch 160, February 22, 1954 and Amman telegram 394, April 1, 1954). Nor in three years I have been here have I ever had any reasons to suspect infiltration sponsored by Jordan Government. UN states lack of pattern infiltration points to individual or small gang activity. It naturally serves Israel's purpose to claim Jordan Government behind it and Israel must make such claim in order to justify her official reprisal raids.

Entrance Russia into Middle East politics makes Israel's game extremely dangerous and Israel must be made to see danger not only to her own existence but to world and return to MAC and make sincere efforts at working level to ease border tension. Israel once claimed she would be satisfied with partition. Now she has more territory than partition gave her but she does not seem to be satisfied with it leading to possible conclusion that she wants peace but only on her own terms. The patience that caused her to wait 2000 years for Israel to exist must be used if she wants peace. There is no easy way and Israel must begin by being fair to the Arabs within her own borders as well as with those just outside. Otherwise confidence will never be established and peace will never come. To reopen war in hopes of forcing peace seems suicidal. Even if Israel won now forty million Arabs would remember and in end Israel would cease to exist.

▓▓▓▓▓▓▓▓▓▓▓▓▓▓▓▓▓▓▓▓▓▓▓▓▓▓

and lack of

DECLASSIFIED

DECLASSIFIED

-3- #160, April 17, 2 p.m., from Jerusalem

Above reflections not anti-Israel but from belief Israelis not
only key to peace in area but by patience and justice a possible
leader of a democratic Middle East. If Israel
cannot be made to realize the
consequences of her acts she may perish and not impossibly
the world with her. She must be patient and know that we will
support her if she does and that because we disapprove certain
of her acts does not mean we are deserting her. But there is
a limit.

CONGEN fully supports specific recommendations Commander
Hutchison to improve border machinery (CON despatch 163
February 26, 1954.

                                                    TYLER

EB:RSP:HMR/16

52756

DECLASSIFIED
TOP SECRET

SENT DEPARTMENT 160, TEL AVIV 130, AMMAN 95, BAGHDAD 11, BEIRUT 38, CAIRO 42, DAMASCUS 66, JIDDA 3; REPEATED INFORMATION LONDON 35, PARIS 16.

Department telegram 90 to Jerusalem.

Israel has made much of Jordan refusal to meet under Article 12 and might be made to see some inconsistency in her own refusal to return and cooperate with MAC if formally requested to do so by Secretary General UN. Also there are some indications Israel may wish to be forced take this action (CONTEL 152) and possibly it might strengthen Sharett's position. If Israel does return easy to call meeting with Bennike as chairman to discuss improvements border machinery. This would be victory for Jordan and unfortunate in view Jordan obstinancy to honor her signature on Article 12. ████████████████████████

████████████████ However, Israel not blameless in refusing to honor UN resolutions.

Present situation more serious, but not essentially dissimilar to that existing 1953. Israel requested "high level" talks with Jordan in January 1953 (CONTELs 90 and 96 January 29 and February 5, 1953) and ██████████████████
████████████████████████████

████████████████████ Israel immediately undertook ████████ raids on Falama and Rantis and later occupied Arab college in Government house grounds. Naturally Jordan could not "meet" under these circumstances. High level talks finally took place June 29 (CONTEL 1, July 1, 1953). No mention then made of Article 12 and to suggest similar talks now to Jordan would probably fail as only subterfuge, still suggestion might be made to Jordan as a compromise between their refusal to meet under Article 12 and Israel insistence MAC incompetent to correct situation.

Also in January 1953 Israel broke off local commanders meetings and only special request of Secretary Dulles to Ben Gurion caused Israel to reinstate them. To save face Israel pretended certain new regulations were agreed upon (CONTEL 166, May 29, 1953).

CONGEN has always maintained MAC an excellent institution given sincerity both parties, and local commanders meetings best means yet devised to curb infiltration. But Israel has found ████████████████████████████
████████████████████████████

██████████ reasons for denouncing them in past and refusing to agree to improvement in rules of procedure (CONTELs 84, January 21 and 165, May 29, 1953). I feel strongly that we should confront Israel with known facts of her statements calling for easing of border tension as contrasted with her hostile acts of reprisal raids and sabotaging local commanders agreements and rules of MAC procedure which is best method of "nibbling" at border control. Furthermore, Israel makes frequent claims she "knows how to treat Arabs" and therefore, well aware to call for meeting under Article 12 would only irritate

Jordan and while giving Israel propaganda advantage it was not in interest of peace or easing border tension. There is also enormous difference between individual acts of infiltrators and group reprisals officially undertaken or condoned by governments. Jordan does punish known infiltrators Israel never punishes those guilty of reprisal raids. CONGEN and UNTSO here in agreement Jordan making sincere effort curb infiltration (Consulate's despatch 160, February 22, 1954 and Amman telegram 394, April 1, 1954). Nor in three years I have been here have I ever had any reasons to suspect infiltration sponsored by Jordan Government. UN states lack of pattern infiltration points to individual or small gang activity. It naturally serves Israel's purpose to claim Jordan Government behind it and Israel must make such claim in order to justify her official reprisal raids.

Entrance Russia into Middle East politics makes Israel's game extremely dangerous and Israel must be made to see danger not only to her own existence but to world and return to MAC and make sincere efforts at working level to ease border tension. Israel once claimed she would be satisfied with partition. Now she has more territory than partition gave her but she does not seem to be satisfied with it leading to possible conclusion that she wants peace but only on her own terms. The patience that caused her to wait 2000 years for Israel to exist must be used if she wants peace. There is no easy way and Israel must begin by being fair to the Arabs within her own borders as well as with those just outside. Otherwise confidence will never be established and peace will never come. To reopen war in hopes of forcing peace seems suicidal. Even if Israel won now forty million Arabs would remember and in end Israel would cease to exist.

Above reflections not anti-Israel but from belief Israelis not only key to peace in area but by patience and justice a possible leader of a democratic Middle East. If Israel

cannot be made to realize the consequences of her acts she may perish and not impossibly the world with her. She must be patient and know that we will support her if she does and that because we disapprove certain of her acts does not mean we are deserting her. But there is a limit.

CONGEN fully supports specific recommendations Commander Hutchinson to improve border machinery (CON despatch 163 February 26, 1954.

TYLER

Document #8—as cited in Chapter 5, mss. page 111, but not footnoted.

"Limited" Foreign Service dispatch 194 from U.S. Embassy, Cairo, to Department of State, Washington, dated August 3, 1954.

AIR POUCH — LIMITED OFFICIAL USE
PRIORITY — (Security Classification)

DO NOT TYPE IN THIS SPACE

511.741/8-354
XR 124.742
125.1312 774.00

FOREIGN SERVICE DESPATCH

FROM : CAIRO

194

DESP. NO.

TO : THE DEPARTMENT OF STATE, WASHINGTON

August 3, 1954

REF : Cairo's Unclassified telegram #66 dated July 15, 1954; USIS Despatch #5 dated July 21, 1954; USIS Despatch #6 dated July 26, 1954; USIS Despatch #7 dated July 28, 1954.

SUBJECT: USIS LIBRARY FIRES, CAIRO AND ALEXANDRIA, EGYPT

As previously reported, three incendiaries were discovered in the USIS Library, Cairo on the morning of July 15, 1954. These incendiaries were turned over to the Egyptian police force who immediately initiated an investigation. On Tuesday July 27, 1954, Cairo newspapers carried the following communique:

"On July 3, last, fires broke out in two letter boxes in the main Post Office, Alexandria, and a cylindrical parcel, which was found to contain incendiary material was discovered in another letter box near them.

"On the night of July 14, last, fire broke out in the American Library at Alexandria. At the same time two Police officers spotted flames coming out of the American Embassy library in Cairo.

"After the fire had been extinguished an inquiry was opened and three glass cases containing inflammable material were found. It was also found that the fire had been caused by material similar to that used for the attempts at the Post Office.

"The C.I.D. carried out extensive investigations to discover the perpetrators of these outrages and tightened the Police precautions on these buildings.

"On the night of July 23 last a Policeman on the beat by the Rio Cinema, Alexandria, arrested inside the Cinema a person whose clothes were on fire. An officer searched the man and in one of his trouser pockets was found a glass case containing remnants of inflammable material of the same type as that found on the scene of the previous fires.

"The man was found to be a stateless Israeli named Philip Hermann Nathanson. When his house was searched one of the rooms

AUG 3 1954

WASmith:am
REPORTER

LIMITED OFFICIAL USE

ACTION COPY — DEPARTMENT OF STATE

The action office must return this permanent record copy to DC/R files with an endorsement of action taken.

was found to contain large quantities of various chemical ingredients used in making incendiary material.

"On the same night the Police found in both the Radio and Rivoli Cinemas in Cairo glass cases filled with inflammable material similar to that seized in Alexandria. The material in the glass cases had not yet caught fire.

"Investigations disclosed that the accused had two Israeli accomplices. Victor Levi and Robert Nessim Dasa, both of them residents of Alexandria. The former was arrested and the prosecution opened new investigations. The two men held confessed that they had committed all the previous crimes. The Police kept watch for the third accused until he was arrested in Alexandria on his return from Cairo after having committed a number of outrages there.

"All the accused are known for their Zionist activities, of which records exist in the C.I.D. offices."

On Monday, August 2, Major General Abdul Aziz Sufwat, Commandant of Cairo Police, asked Regional Security Officer W. Angie Smith, III, to come to his office to discuss the arrests made by the Egyptian police in this case. General Sufwat stated that he felt that we should have the following story since it would possibly be some time before a detailed report could be prepared. General Sufwat's story of the arrests is as follows:

On the night of July 23 a policeman arrested one Philip Hermann Nathanson at the Cinema Rio in Alexandria. Nathanson came to the attention of the arresting officer after his clothes caught fire at the entrance to the cinema. Nathanson was taken to the hospital and searched and two incendiaries of the type used in the USIS fires were found on him. The police immediately raided Nathanson's home and were told by his father that his son had an accomplice by the name of Victor Levi. Levi was arrested and large amounts of incendiary chemicals were discovered in Levi's room.

Nathanson and Levi both stated that they had a third accomplice known as Robert Nessim Dasa. On the morning of July 24 a valise stored in the Cairo Railroad Station burned. A detailed search was made of the Cairo cinemas since Nathanson and Levi had stated that Dasa was to burn the Cinema Radio and the Cinema Metro on the night of July 23. One incendiary was found in the Cinema Radio by a police officer who carried it to the ticket window. As he laid it on the ticket window, however, the incendiary burned.

LIMITED OFFICIAL USE

A second incendiary was found in the Cinema Rivoli. This was
recovered without burning. Dasa was arrested later that day
when he arrived in Alexandria by bus from Cairo. All three
have confessed to placing the incendiaries. They state that
four incendiaries were placed in USIS Cairo and one incendiary
was placed in USIS Alexandria. General Sufwat stated that the
newspaper account that these men were known Zionists is incorrect.
All three are Egyptian subjects. Levi and Dasa have no police
record. Nathanson, however, has a police record identifying him
as a past Communist. Mr. Smith questioned the general concerning
the newspaper account and his only statement was "That is all a
mistake."

Levi is supposedly a chemist and works for a chemical firm
in Alexandria. According to the general, Nathanson and Levi
claim they learned how to make the incendiaries in Paris, France
approximately seven months ago. They stated that they had copied
the formula from a book. The formula was discovered by the
Egyptian police when they raided Levi's rooms. Later in his
conversation, General Sufwat became worried over some of the
information that he had given and requested that it be kept in
the strictest of confidence since he evidently realized that he
was giving information contrary to the official communiques.

General Sufwat promised that as soon as a detailed report
is completed from the parquet in Alexandria it will be turned
over to the Regional Security Headquarters at this Embassy.

                                        Jefferson Caffery

As previously reported, three incendiaries were discovered in the USIS library, Cairo on the morning of July 15, 1954. These incendiaries were turned over to the Egyptian police force who immediately initiated an investigation. On Tuesday July 27, 1954, Cairo newspapers carried the following communique:

"On July 3, last, fires broke out in two letter boxes in the main Post Office, Alexandria, and a cylindrical parcel, which was found to contain incendiary material was discovered in another letter box near them.

"On the night of July 14, last, fire broke out in the American Library at Alexandria. At the same time two Police officers spotted flames coming out of the American Embassy library in Cairo.

"After the fire had been extinguished an inquiry was opened and three glass cases containing inflammable material were found. It was also found that the fire had been caused by material similar to that used for the attempts at the Post Office.

"The C.I.D. carried out extensive investigations to discover the perpetrators of these outrages and tightened the Police precautions on these buildings.

"On the night of July 23 last a Policeman on the beat by the Rio Cinema, Alexandria, arrested inside the Cinema a person whose clothes were on fire. An officer searched the man and in one of his trouser pockets was found a glass case containing remnants of inflammable material of the same type as that found on the scene of the previous fires.

"The man was found to be a stateless Israeli named Philip Hermann Nathanson. When his house was searched one of the rooms was found to contain large quantities of various chemical ingredients used in making incendiary material.

"On the same night the Police found in both the Radio and Rivoli Cinemas in Cairo glass cases filled with inflammable material similar to that seized in Alexandria. The material in the glass cases had not yet caught fire.

"Investigations disclosed that the accused had two Israeli accomplices. Victor Levi and Robert Nessim Dasa, both of them residents of Alexandria. The former was arrested and the prosecution opened new investigations. The two men held confessed that they had committed all the previous crimes. The Police kept watch for the third accused until he was arrested in Alexandria on his return from Cairo after having committed a number of outrages there.

"All the accused are known for their Zionist activities, of which records exist in the C.I.D. offices."

On Monday, August 2, Major General Abdul Aziz Sufwat, Commandant of Cairo Police, asked Regional Security Officer W. Angie Smith, III, to come to his office to discuss the arrests made by the Egyptian police in this case. General Sufwat stated that he felt that we should have the following story since it would possibly be some time before a detailed report could be prepared. General Sufwat's story of the arrests is as follows:

On the night of July 23 a policeman arrested one Philip Hermann Nathanson at the Cinema Rio in Alexandria. Nathanson came to the attention of the arresting officer after his clothes caught fire at the entrance to the cinema. Nathanson was taken to the hospital and searched and two incendiaries of the type used in the USIS fires were found on him. The police immediately raided Nathanson's home and were told by his father that his son had an accomplice by the name of Victor Levi. Levi was arrested and large amounts of incendiary chemicals were discovered in Levi's room.

Nathanson and Levi both stated that they had a third accomplice known as Robert Nessim Dasa. On the morning of July 24 a valise stored in the Cairo Railroad Station burned. A detailed search was made of the Cairo cinemas since Nathanson and Levi had stated that Dasa was to burn the Cinema Radio and the Cinema Metro on the night of July 23. One incendiary was found in the Cinema Radio by a police officer who carried it to the ticket window. As he laid it on the ticket window, however, the incendiary burned. A second incendiary was found in the Cinema Rivoli. This was recovered without burning. Dasa was arrested later that day when he arrived in Alexandria by bus from Cairo. All three have confessed to placing the incendiaries. They state that four incendiaries were placed in USIS Cairo and one incendiary was placed in USIS Alexandria. General Sufwat stated that the newspaper account that these men were known Zionists is incorrect. All three are Egyptian subjects. Levi and Dasa have no police record. Nathanson, however, has a police record identifying him as a past Communist. Mr. Smith questioned the general concerning the newspaper account and his only statement was "That is all a mistake."

Levi is supposedly a chemist and works for a chemical firm in Alexandria. According to the general, Nathanson and Levi claim they learned how to make the incendiaries in Paris, France approximately seven months ago. They stated that they had copied the formula from a book. The formula was discovered by the Egyptian police when they raided Levi's rooms. Later in his conversation, General Sufwat became worried over some of the information that he had given and requested that it be kept in the strictest of confidence since he evidently realized that he was giving information contrary to the official communiques.

General Sufwat promised that as soon as a detailed report is completed from the parquet in Alexandria it will be turned over to the Regional Security Headquarters at this Embassy.

JEFFERSON CAFFERY

Document #9—as cited in Chapter 6, Note 16.

"Secret" memorandum for Brigadier General Richard Collins, JCS, from General G. B. Erskine, Assistant to the Secretary of Defense, dated August 17, 1956, Records of the United States Joint Chiefs of Staff, file 091 Palestine (June 56—December 56), Record Group 218, National Archives.

OFFICE OF THE SECRETARY OF DEFENSE
WASHINGTON 25, D. C.

6 (16)

MEMORANDUM FOR BRIGADIER GENERAL RICHARD COLLINS, JCS AUG 17 1956

SUBJECT: Emerging Pattern - Arab-Israeli Situation *preventative war "paper*

In reviewing the intelligence on developments in the Middle East, it appears that the dilemma confronting the Israelis has grown more difficult during the current Suez crisis. If Nasr emerges with increased prestige, Pan-Arabism will have been given a powerful boost which could pose an overwhelming threat to the continued existence of Israel.

Ben-Gurion must, under the conditions indicated above, be seriously considering the feasibility of a preventive war aimed at stalling the rate of Arab cohesion. It is my feeling that a forecast on Israel's probable course of action for the short term is required to support policy decisions in the Department of Defense. I would very much appreciate it if the Joint Intelligence Group would undertake to provide such a forecast to support policy decisions of the Secretary of Defense. This paper would be most useful if it discussed the validity of the assumptions indicated above and then addressed itself to the following questions:

a. What is the probability of an Israeli attack?

b. If considered probable, when is this decision likely to be taken?

c. What are the likely objectives of such an attack?

d. What is the probability of U.K. instigation of such an attack?

The forecast along these lines would be particularly useful if it could be made available by Wednesday, 22 August 1956.

SIGNED

G. B. ERSKINE
General, USMC (Ret)
Assistant to the
Secretary of Defense
(Special Operations)

<u>**SECRET**</u>

<u>**ENCLOSURE**</u>

<u>**EMERGING PATTERN - ARAB-ISRAELI SITUATION**</u>

1. Deterring factors to possible aggressive action by the Israelis are the lack of international popular support, the deterrent provisions of the U.N. mandate and the Tri-Partite Agreement, and the fact that Israel would run the risk of having economic sanctions imposed on her by the U.N. In addition, Israel may possibly realize that, in spite of local victories and attainment of her objectives, the war would not end in peace but would continue indefinitely.

2. In view of the various factors regarding the initiation of a "preventive" war by Israel in the short-term it is concluded that:

⌐a. The Suez Canal crisis has substantially increased the⌐
risk of aggressive hostile action by Israel. This is by
virtue of the fact that Nasser's power and prestige will
have reached such heights in the event he is successful
that Israel may eventually be overwhelmed and also because
the major restraining powers are intensely preoccupied
with Egypt and the Canal. It should be noted, in this
connection, that there is a possibility that the United
Kingdom and France may not uphold the Tri-Partite
Declaration of 1950 in this situation.

b. Probable objectives of an Israeli attack on Egypt capable of being attained in the necessarily short blitzkreig type of war are:

(1) To induce the downfall of Nasser and his regime.

(2) To administer a defeat to Egypt to shatter the increased prestige it may have received as a result of the settlement of the Suez crisis.

(3) To reduce the military potential (especially air) of Egypt. (We estimate Israeli superiority until November 1956 after which it swings to the Egyptians).

(4) To refocus the attention of the world on the need for final solution of the Arab-Israel problem.

(5) To gain territorial objectives such as border rectification and expansion limited to the Gaza Strip, West Jordan, and strategic points on the Gulf of Aqaba.

                                        Enclosure

(6) To effect a forced relocation of nearby Arab refugee camps.

c. In the event that the United Kingdom and France become militarily engaged against the Egyptians, there is a definite possibility that Israel, without some form of Western restraint, might attempt to capitalize on the situation by associating herself with Allied actions through concurrent attack on Egypt and Egyptian Allies.

d. There are no indications at present of a large-scale offensive being planned or prepared for by the Israelis in the immediate future; however, the pattern of continuous skirmishes, from which large-scale hostilities could grow, remains unbroken.

e. The probability of United Kingdom instigation is considered small unless the British become hopelessly bogged down militarily in Egypt which is considered unlikely. By such action Britain, in return for a few quick victories, would suffer substantial losses in position and prestige in the long term, particularly in the Arab world.

Enclosure

OFFICE OF THE SECRETARY OF DEFENSE
WASHINGTON 25, D.C.

MEMORANDUM FOR BRIGADIER GENERAL RICHARD COLLINS,
JCS AUG 17 1956

SUBJECT: Emerging Pattern - Arab-Israeli Situation

In reviewing the intelligence on developments in the Middle East, it appears that the dilemma confronting the Israelis has grown more difficult during the current Suez crisis. If Nasr emerges with increased prestige, Pan-Arabism will have been given a powerful boost which could pose an overwhelming threat to the continued existence of Israel.

Ben-Gurion must, under the conditions indicated above, be seriously considering the feasibility of a preventive war aimed at stalling the rate of Arab cohesion. It is my feeling that a forecast on Israel's probable course of action for the short term is required to support policy decisions in the Department of Defense. I would very much appreciate it if the Joint Intelligence Group would undertake to provide such a forecast to support policy decisions of the Secretary of Defense. This paper would be most useful if it discussed the validity of the assumptions indicated above and then addressed itself to the following questions:

    a. What is the probability of an Israeli attack?

    b. If considered probable, when is this decision likely to be taken?

    c. What are the likely objectives of such an attack?

    d. What is the probability of U.K. instigation of such an attack?

The forecast along these lines would be particularly useful if it could be made available by Wednesday, 22 August 1956.

SIGNED

G. B. ERSKINE
General, USMC (Ret)
Assistant to the
Secretary of Defense
(Special Operations)

E N C L O S U R E

EMERGING PATTERN - ARAB-ISRAELI SITUATION

1. Deterring factors to possible aggressive action by the Israelis are the lack of international popular support, the deterrent provisions of the U.N. mandate and the Tri-Partite Agreement, and the fact that Israel would run the risk of having economic sanctions imposed on her by the U.N. In addition, Israel may possibly realize that, in spite of local victories and attainment of her objectives, the war would not end in peace but would continue indefinitely.

2. In view of the various factors regarding the initiation of a "preventive" war by Israel in the short-term it is concluded that:

a. The Suez Canal crisis has substantially increased the risk of aggressive hostile action by Israel. This is by virtue of the fact that Nasser's power and prestige will have reached such heights in the event he is successful that Israel may eventually be overwhelmed and also because the major restraining powers are intensely preoccupied with Egypt and the Canal. It should be noted, in this connection, that there is a possibility that the United Kingdom and France may not uphold the Tri-Partite Declaration of 1950 in this situation.

b. Probable objectives of an Israeli attack on Egypt capable of being attained in the necessarily short blitzkreig type of war are:

(1) To induce the downfall of Nasser and his regime.

(2) To administer a defeat to Egypt to shatter the increased prestige it may have received as a result of the settlement of the Suez crisis.

(3) To reduce the military potential (especially air) of Egypt. (We estimate Israeli superiority until November 1956 after which it swings to the Egyptians.)

(4) To refocus the attention of the world on the need for final solution of the Arab-Israel problem.

(5) To gain territorial objectives such as border rectification and expansion limited to the Gaza Strip, West Jordan, and strategic points on the Gulf of Aqaba.

(6) To effect a forced relocation of nearby Arab refugee camps.

c. In the event that the United Kingdom and France become militarily engaged against the Egyptians, there is a definite possibility that Israel, without some form of Western restraint, might attempt to capitalize on the situation by associating herself with Allied actions through concurrent attack on Egypt and Egyptian Allies.

d. There are no indications at present of a large-scale offensive being planned or prepared for by the Israelis in the immediate future; however, the pattern of continuous skirmishes, from which large-scale hostilities could grow, remains unbroken.

e. The probability of United Kingdom instigation is considered small unless the British become hopelessly bogged down militarily in Egypt which is considered unlikely. By such action Britain, in return for a few quick victories, would suffer substantial losses in position and prestige in the long term, particularly in the Arab world.

Document #10—as cited in Chapter 7, Note 41.

"Confidential" memorandum for the files from Samuel C. T. McDowell,
Division of Safeguards and Security, AEC, dated May 25, 1976, released
by ERDA in 1976.

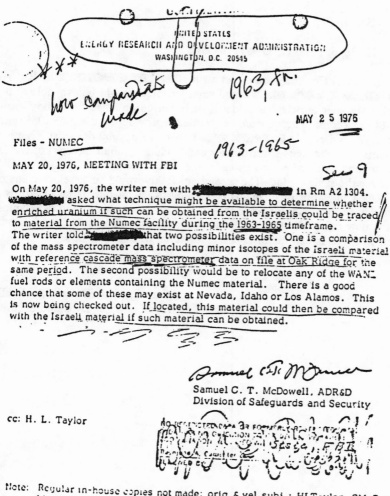

UNITED STATES
ENERGY RESEARCH AND DEVELOPMENT ADMINISTRATION
WASHINGTON, D.C. 20545

how comparison made

1963 fr.

MAY 2 5 1976

Files - NUMEC

MAY 20, 1976, MEETING WITH FBI

1963-1965

See 9

On May 20, 1976, the writer met with ▬▬▬▬▬▬▬ in Rm A2 1304.
▬▬▬▬▬ asked what technique might be available to determine whether
enriched uranium if such can be obtained from the Israelis could be traced
to material from the Numec facility during the 1963-1965 timeframe.
The writer told ▬▬▬▬▬ that two possibilities exist. One is a comparison
of the mass spectrometer data including minor isotopes of the Israeli material
with reference cascade mass spectrometer data on file at Oak Ridge for the
same period. The second possibility would be to relocate any of the WAN
fuel rods or elements containing the Numec material. There is a good
chance that some of these may exist at Nevada, Idaho or Los Alamos. This
is now being checked out. If located, this material could then be compared
with the Israeli material if such material can be obtained.

Samuel C. T. McDowell, ADR&D
Division of Safeguards and Security

cc: H. L. Taylor

Note: Regular in-house copies not made; orig. & yel.subj.; HLTaylor, SMcD read &
file cys made.

NATIONAL SECURITY   EXEMPT FROM GENERAL DECLASSIFICATION SCHEDULE OF

UNITED STATES

ENERGY RESEARCH AND DEVELOPMENT ADMINISTRATION

WASHINGTON, D.C. 20545

Files—NUMEC

MAY 20, 1976, MEETING WITH FBI

On May 20, 1976, the writer met with ██████████████████ in Rm A2 1304. ███████████████████ asked what technique might be available to determine whether enriched uranium if such can be obtained from the Israelis could be traced to material from the Numec facility during the 1963-1965 time-frame. The writer told ██████████████████ that two possibilities exist. One is a comparison of the mass spectrometer data including minor isotopes of the Israeli material with reference cascade mass spectrometer data on file at Oak Ridge for the same period. The second possibility would be to relocate any of the WANI fuel rods or elements containing the Numec material. There is a good chance that some of these may exist at Nevada, Idaho or Los Alamos. This is now being checked out. If located, this material could then be compared with the Israeli material if such material can be obtained.

Samuel C. T. McDowell, ADR&D
Division of Safeguards and Security

Document #11—as cited in Chapter 7, Note 49.

"Secret" telegram from Air Attaché, Tel Aviv, to Air Force Headquarters, Washington, DTG 0312152 March 1965, NSF Country File—Israel, Volume IV, Cables 2/65 to 11/65, Lyndon Baines Johnson Library.

~~SECRET~~

DEPARTMENT OF DE~~FENSE~~
NATIONAL MILITARY COMMAND CENTER
MESSAGE CENTER

4 8 8 1 6

CALL 53337
FOR NMCC/MC
SERVICE

3 03 22 54Z

```
F186/03...JCS681 (R2)
VZCZCIEM019EIA891TEA649
RR RUEKDA
DE RUQMVL 830 03/1339Z            DECLASSIFIED
R 031215Z ZEA                     Authority DOD  9-5-75
FM USAIRA TEL AVIV ISRAEL         By LW , NARS, Date 9-15-75
TO RUEAHQ/CSAF                        air attache in T/A
RUEKDA/DIA
RUEAHQ/1127USAFFLDACTYGP FT BELVOIR VA
INFO RUFLC/USCINCEUR
RUFPBW/CINCUSAFE
RUCJHK/CINCSTRIKE
RUEHCR/DEPT OF STATE WASHDC
RUFGWA/USAIRA PARIS FRANCE
RUGKE/USAIRA ATHENS GREECE
RUEKDA/OSDXISA
BT
```

S E C R E T USAIRA 00030 MAR 1965. CSAF FOR AFNIN.
THIS MESSAGE IN TWO PARTS.
PART I. A USUALLY RELIABLE SOURCE (IS21000018) RETURNED TO
ISRAEL FOR A TWO-WEEK VISIT (18 FEB - 2 MAR 65). DARING
FREQUENT CONTACTS WITH AIRA AND HIS FAMILY, SOURCE DIVULGED
FOLLOWING ITEMS OF INTELLIGENCE INTEREST:
A. (S) SURFACE-TO-SURFACE MISSILE. SOURCE CONFIRMED THAT
TESTING OF FRENCH-DESIGNED SSM FOR ISRAEL HAS ALREADY BEGUN
ON ISLE DE LEVANT. INITIALLY, "THE MISSILE HAD SOME TROUBLES
BUT APPEARS SATISFACTORY NOW". ACCORDING TO SOURCE, THE
MOBILE SSM'S WILL NOT BE USEFUL; THERE IS NO NEED TO MAKE
ISRAEL'S SSM'S MOBILE DUE TO SMALL TOPOGRAPHICAL SIZE OF
COUNTRY AND FACT THAT ENEMY TARGETS ARE KNOWN AND FIXED, THUS
ISRAEL WILL CONCENTRATE ON FIXED LAUNCHING POSITIONS.
B. (S) SSM WARHEAD. TO COUNTER ARGUMENT THAT ISRAEL'S
SSM WOULD NOT BE MATERIALLY SIGNIFICACT WITH CONVENTIONAL WARHEAD,
SOURCE BLURTS OUT: "DON'T WORRY, WHEN WE NEED THE RIGHT KIND OF

```
ACT: DIA-15

    CJCS-1 DJS-3 SJCS-1 J3-8 J5-2 SACSA-5 NMCC-2 SECDEF-5 ISA-9 PA-1

    WHITE HOUSE-3 FILE-1 (56) YS/R
```

                    PAGE 1 OF 3

DEPARTMENT OF DE~~FENSE~~
NATIONAL MILITARY COMMAND CENTER
MESSAGE CENTER

WARHEAD, WE WILL HAVE IT... AND AFTER THAT, THERE WILL BE NO MORE
TROUBLE IN THIS PART OF THE WORLD."
C. (S) TENSION IN MIDDLE EAST. TO ELICITOR'S WORRIES
THAT TENSION IN ME INCREASING STEADILY AND GOOD POSSIBILITY
ENTIRE AREA COULD EXPLODE SHORTLY, SOURCE COUNTERED: "YOU DON'T
HAVE TO WORRY ABOUT ANYTHING BEFORE SIX TO NINE MONTHS. AFTER
THAT THERE WILL BE TIME OF PACE. ISRAEL WILL HAVE SOMETHING THAT
WILL SCARE EVERYBODY." (COMMENT: THOUGH AIRA FAILED GET
AMPLIFICATION, IMPRESSION WAS SOURCE IMPLIED ACQUISITIONS IN
EQUIPMENT, RATHER THAN MAJOR ARAB/ISRAELI CLASH.)
D. (S) ISRAELIS IN PARIS. SOURCE FOUND HIS RECENT EXPERIENCES
IN FRANCE INTERESTING: "SMALL THINGS PRODUCED A BIG PICTURE.
THERE ARE NOW SO MANY ISRAELI 'DIPLOMATS' IN PARIS. THERE ARE
NOT ENOUGH CIGARETTES IN DUTY-FREE SHIPS TO SUPPLY CIGARETTES
FOR ALL OF THEM. MORE ISRAELIS THERE NOW THAN AMERICANS.
E. (C) ISRAELI MILITARY VIP MOVEMENTS. IDF DIR INTEL, ALUF
YARIV, OUT OF COUNTRY TWO-WEEKS RETURNED ISRAEL 1 MAR 65; CHIEF
IDF/AIR FORCE INTEL, SGAN ALUF LERON, NOW OUT OF COUNTRY ON
BUSINESS; AIR FORCE CHIEF EZER WEIZMAN MUST BE IN FRANCE O/A
3 MAR 65.
F. (C) FRENCH INTEL CHIEF. SOURCE STATED THAT "CHIEF OF
FRENCH INTELLIGENCE" ARRIVING ISRAEL APPROX 21-22 MAR 65 WITH
THOSE FRENCH AIRCRAFT." (COMMENT FOR AIRA THENS: ASSUME FROM
YOUR PREVIOUS INFO, ALL 25 FLYABLE FRENCH OURAGAN AIRCRAFT
DESTINED FOR ISRAEL WILL HAVE TRANSITED BEFORE THAT DATE.
POSSIBLE "THOSE FRENCH AIRCRAFT" MAY BE 2-SETA MIRAGE IIIB'S
DUE ISRAEL THIS YEAR. APPRECIATE ANY INFO PERTINENT A/C
MOVEMENTS THRU/OVER GREECE THAT PERIOD.)
G. (C) STRATOCRUISER ATLANTIC CROSSINGS. GOOD POSSIBILITY,
DURING SECOND-HALF 1965, ISRAELI STRATOCRUISERS (C-97 TYPE)
WILL COMMENCE ATLANTIC CROSSING TO US REGULARLY IN SUPPORT
ISRAELI HAWK MISSILE SYSTEM. SOURCE NEEDLED AIRA, "IDF/AF WILL
TRANSPORT YOU ANYTIME YOU WANT, JUST TO SHOW USAF THAT A SMALL

i.e., end
1965

DEPARTMENT OF DEFENSE
NATIONAL MILITARY COMMAND CENTER
MESSAGE CENTER

AF WILL CARRY FOREIGNERS EVEN IF MATS WON'T."
H. (C) INDEPENDENCE DAY PARADE. LAST WEEK SOURCE INFORMED
AIRA, ISRAELI 17TH INDEPENDENCE DAY PARADE TO BE HELD 6 MAY-
HALF IN JERUSALEM, HALF IN TEL AVIV; JERUSALEM: SOME GROUND
FORCES, AIR FORCE CADETS, NO FLY-BY-TEL AVIV: GROUND FORCES
PLUS BIG FLY-BY. (COMMENT: THIS CONFIRMED BY YESTERDAY'S
NEWSPAPERS, STATING, IDF WANTS TO DISPLAY FULL STRENGTH THIS
YEAR: HAWK MISSILES, NEW TANKS AND PLANES. MAIN MILITARY PARADE
IN TEL AVIV IN AM WITH STATE CEREMONY IN JERUSALEM IN PM AUGMENTED
BY SELECTED ARMY UNITS.)
I. (C) NEW MILITARY AIRFIELD. THE NEW AIRFIELD IN THE
BEERSHEVA AREA (SEE MY IR1849006664) WILL BE PARTIALLY OPERATIONAL
IN LATTER PART THIS YEAR, ACCORDING SOURCE. THE IDF/AF FLYING
TRAINING SCHOOL WILL BE TRANSFERRED THERE FROM EQRON AB, AND PROBABLY
ALL THE OURAGAN AIRCRAFT (OTU FUNCTION) WILL TRANSFER THERE FROM
HATZOR AB. SOURCE ADDS THIS AIR BASE WILL NOT BE IN FULL OPERATION
BEFORE 2 - 3 YEARS DUE TO FOLLOW-ON CONSTRUCTION OF BARRACKS, DINING
HALLS, CLASSROOMS, ETC.
PART II. COMMENT: ON PREVIOUS OCCASIONS, INFO RECEIVED FROM
SOURCE HAS BEEN ACCURATE, THUS RATING OF ALL INFO (WITH POSSIBLE
EXCEPTION PART C) IS CONSIDERED "PROBABLY TRUE". PART IC MAY BE
ONLY HIS FIRM OPINION/CONVICTION. ADDITIONALLY,
AIRA KNOWS THAT AMONG MANY ISRAELIS WITH WHOM
HE CONFERRED AT SOME SIGNFICANT LENGTH WERE: AIR FORCE CHIEF
GEN EZER WEIZMAN, AIR FORCE DEP CHIEF, COL "MONTY" HAD, ACTING
IDF/DIR OF INTEL COL CARMON, DEP MOD SHIMON PERES AND MOSHE
DAYAN (FOR ALMOST FULL MORNING SESSION). THUS, ALL INFO CITED
IN PART I SHOULD BE EVALUATED IN LIGHT OF INFO ABOVE CONFEREES
COULD DISCUSS WITH SOURCE. GP-3
BT

THIS MESSAGE IN TWO PARTS.

PART I. A USUALLY RELIABLE SOURCE (IS21000018) RETURNED TO ISRAEL FOR A TWO-WEEK VISIT (18 FEB—2 MAR 65), DARING FREQUENT CONTACTS WITH AIRA AND HIS FAMILY, SOURCE DIVULGED FOLLOWING ITEMS OF INTELLIGENCE INTEREST:

A. (S) SURFACE-TO-SURFACE MISSILE. SOURCE CONFIRMED THAT TESTING OF FRENCH-DESIGNED SSM FOR ISRAEL HAS ALREADY BEGUN ON ISLE DE LEVANT. INITIALLY, "THE MISSILE HAD SOME TROUBLES BUT APPEARS SATISFACTORY NOW". ACCORDING TO SOURCE, THE MOBILE SSM'S WILL NOT BE USEFUL; THERE IS NO NEED TO MAKE ISRAEL'S SSM'S MOBILE DUE TO SMALL TOPOGRAPHICAL SIZE OF COUNTRY AND FACT THAT ENEMY TARGETS ARE KNOWN AND FIXED, THUS ISRAEL WILL CONCENTRATE ON FIXED LAUNCHING POSITIONS.

B. (S) SSM WARHEAD. TO COUNTER ARGUMENT THAT ISRAEL'S SSM WOULD NOT BE MATERIALLY SIGNIFICACT WITH CONVENTIONAL WARHEAD, SOURCE BLURTS OUT: "DON'T WORRY, WHEN WE NEED THE RIGHT KIND OF WARHEAD, WE WILL HAVE IT. . . . AND AFTER THAT, THERE WILL BE NO MORE TROUBLE IN THIS PART OF THE WORLD."

C. (S) TENSION IN MIDDLE EAST. TO ELICITOR'S WORRIES THAT TENSION IN ME INCREASING STEADILY AND GOOD POSSIBILITY ENTIRE AREA COULD EXPLODE SHORTLY, SOURCE COUNTERED: "YOU DON'T HAVE TO WORRY ABOUT ANYTHING BEFORE SIX TO NINE MONTHS. AFTER THAT THERE WILL BE TIME OF PACE. ISRAEL WILL HAVE SOMETHING THAT WILL SCARE EVERYRODY." (COMMENT: THOUGH AIRA FAILED GET AMPLIFICATION, IMPRESSION WAS SOURCE IMPLIED ACQUISITIONS IN EQUIPMENT, RATHER THAN MAJOR ARAB/ISRAELI CLASH.)

D. (S) ISRAELIS IN PARIS. SOURCE FOUND HIS RECENT EXPERIENCE IN FRANCE INTERESTING; "SMALL THINGS PRODUCED A BIG PICTURE. THERE ARE NOW SO MANY ISRAELI 'DIPLOMATS' IN PARIS, THERE ARE NOT ENOUGH CIGARETTES IN DUTY-FREE SHOPS TO SUPPLY CIGARETTES FOR ALL OF THEM. MORE ISRAELIS THERE NOW THAN AMERICANS.

E. (C) ISRAELI MILITARY VIP MOVEMENTS. IDF DIR INTEL, ALUF YARIV, OUT OF COUNTRY TWO WEEKS RETURNED ISRAEL 1 MAR 65; CHIEF IDF/AIR FORCE INTEL, SGAN ALUF LERON, NOW OUT OF COUNTRY ON BUSINESS; AIR FORCE CHIEF EZER WEIZMAN MUST BE IN FRANCE O/A 3 MAR 65.

F. (C) FRENCH INTEL CHIEF. SOURCE STATED THAT "CHIEF OF FRENCH INTELLIGENCE" ARRIVING ISRAEL APPROX 21-22 MAR 65 WITH THOSE FRENCH AIRCRAFT." (COMMENT FOR AIRA THENS: ASSUME FROM YOUR PREVIOUS INFO, ALL 25 FLYABLE FRENCH OURAGAN AIRCRAFT DESTINED FOR ISRAEL WILL HAVE TRANSITED BEFORE THAT DATE. POSSIBLE "THOSE FRENCH AIRCRAFT" MAY BE 2-SETA MIRAGE IIIB'S DUE ISRAEL THIS YEAR. APPRECIATE ANY INFO PERTINENT A/C MOVEMENTS THRU/OVER GREECE THAT PERIOD.)

G. (C) STRATOCRUISER ATLANTIC CROSSINGS. GOOD POSSIBILITY DURING SECOND-HALF 1965. ISRAELI STRATOCRUISERS (C-97 TYPE) WILL COMMENCE ATLANTIC CROSSING TO US REGULARLY IN SUPPORT ISRAELI HAWK MISSILE SYSTEM. SOURCE NEEDLED AIRA, "IDF/AF WILL TRANSPORT YOU ANYTIME YOU WANT, JUST TO SHOW USAF THAT A SMALL AF WILL CARRY FOREIGNERS EVEN IF MATS WON'T."

H. (C) INDEPENDENCE DAY PARADE. LAST WEEK SOURCE INFORMED AIRA, ISRAELI 17TH INDEPENDENCE DAY PARADE TO BE HELD 6 MAY-HALF IN JERUSALEM, HALF IN TEL AVIV; JERUSALEM: SOME GROUND FORCES, AIR FORCE CADETS, NO FLY-BY-TEL AVIV: GROUND FORCES PLUS BIG FLY-BY. (COMMENT: THIS CONFIRMED BY YESTERDAY'S NEWSPAPERS, STATING, IDF WANTS TO DISPLAY FULL STRENGTH THIS YEAR: HAWK MISSILES, NEW TANKS AND PLANES. MAIN MILITARY PARADE IN TEL AVIV IN AM WITH STATE CEREMONY IN JERUSALEM IN PM AUGMENTED BY SELECTED ARMY UNITS.)

I. (C) NEW MILITARY AIRFIELD. THE NEW AIRFIELD IN THE BEER-SHEVA AREA (SEE MY IR1849006664) WILL BE PARTIALLY OPERATIONAL IN LATTER PART THIS YEAR, ACCORDING SOURCE. THE IDF/AF FLYING TRAINING SCHOOL WILL BE TRANSFERRED

THERE FROM EQRON AB, AND PROBABLY ALL THE OURAGAN AIRCRAFT (OTU FUNCTION) WILL TRANSFER THERE FROM HATZOR AB. SOURCE ADDS THIS AIR BASE WILL NOT BE IN FULL OPERATION BEFORE 2–3 YEARS DUE TO FOLLOW-ON CONSTRUCTION OF BARRACKS, DINING HALLS, CLASSROOMS, ETC.

PART II. COMMENT: ON PREVIOUS OCCASIONS, INFO RECEIVED FROM SOURCE HAS BEEN ACCURATE, THUS RATING OF ALL INFO (WITH POSSIBLE EXCEPTION PART C) IS CONSIDERED "PROBABLY TRUE". PART IC MAY BE ONLY HIS FIRM OPINION/CONVICTION. ADDITIONALLY, AIRA KNOWS THAT AMONG MANY ISRAELIS WITH WHOM HE CONFERRED AT SOME SIGNFICANT LENGTH WERE: AIR FORCE CHIEF GEN EZER WEIZMAN, AIR FORCE DEP CHIEF, COL "MONTY" HAD, ACTING IDF/DIR OF INTEL COL CARMON, DEP MOD SHIMON PERES AND MOSHE DAYAN (FOR ALMOST FULL MORNING SESSION). THUS, ALL INFO CITED IN PART I SHOULD BE EVALUATED IN LIGHT OF INFO ABOVE CONFEREES COULD DISCUSS WITH SOURCE. GP-3

BT

Document #12—as cited in Chapter 8, Note 19.

"Secret" Department of State telegram 29 from U.S. Consulate, Jerusalem, to Secretary of State, dated July 21, 1964, NSF Country File—Israel, Volume 2, Cables 4/64 to 8/64, Lyndon Baines Johnson Library.

INCOMING TELEGRAM *Department of State* (19) *Israel*

SECRET

```
NNNNVV   QVA892VV   QMA765JRA887
RR RUEHCR RUEHDT
DE RUQMJR 535 21/1247Z
R 211245Z ZEA
FM AMCONSUL JERUSALEM
TO RUEHCR/SECSTATE WASHDC
INFO RUEHDT/USUN NY
RUQMBE/AMEMBASSY BEIRUT
RUQMDM/AMEMBASSY DAMASCUS
RUQMKG/AMEMBASSY AMMAN
RUQMVL/AMEMBASSY TELAVIV
STATE GRNC
BT
```

Excellent re I. belligerence and A. likely reaction

1254 JULY 21

0 1655 8
AM 10 09

event Sov. arms deals

SECRET (SECTION ONE OF TWO)

ACTION DEPT 29 INFO AMMAN 20 BEIRUT 18 DAMASCUS 20
TELAVIV 22 USUN 21 FROM JERUSALEM JULY 21, 3PM

LIMDIS NOFORN

ISRAEL-SYRIA

FOLLOWING THOUGHTS ON CAUSES AND CURES
CURRENT SURGE BORDER UNREST SUMMARIZES NUMBER
RECENT CONVERSATIONS SENIOR UNTSOP OFFICIALS.
THEY SEE LOW LEVEL SYRIAN MILITARY AS MOST
LIKELY SOURCE TROUBLE. ANALYSIS SITUATION PRESAGES
CFN 29 20 18 20 22 21 21 3PM

PAGE 2 RUQMJR 535 SECRET
GREATER DIFFICULTIES, HOWEVER.

CUSHIONED BY THOUGHT WHOLE THING IMPOSED
BY OUTSIDE FORCES RATHER THAN MILITARY DEFEAT,
ARABS WERE REACHING POINT WHERE LAST UN
PARTITION PLAN COULD BE CITED PUBLICLY AS ACCEPTABLE,
WHILE TERMS GAA·S SUBSTANTIALLY OPERATIVE AS DE FACTO
MODUS VIVENDI WITH ISRAEL. PRINCIPAL CONTINUING
"LUKEWARM WAR" CONCERNED STATUS DEMILITARIZED
ZONES AND AREAS BETWEEN LINES WHERE ARABS CONCERNED
SELVES BASICALLY WITH PRESERVATION SITUATION
ENVISIONED IN GAA·S WHILE ISRAEL CONSISTENTLY
SOUGHT GAIN FULL CONTROL. EVEN THIS ASPECT
STRUGGLE VISIBLY COOLING DURING PAST EIGHT YEARS,

SECRET

-2- 29, JULY 21, 3 P.M. FROM JERUSALEM (SECTION ONE OF TWO)

WITH ISRAEL EMERGING VICTORIOUS LARGELY BECAUSE
UN NEVER ABLE OPPOSE AGGRESSIVE AND ARMED ISRAELI
OCCUPATION AND ASSERTION ACTUAL CONTROL OVER SUCH
AREAS, AND ARAB NEIGHBORS NOT REALLY PREPARED
FOR REQUIRED FIGHTING. IF END JUSTIFIES MEANS,
ISRAEL'S RELIANCE ON FORCE AND THREAT USING IT SEEMED
PROVING SUCCESSFUL.

PAGE 3 RUQMJR 535 S E C R E T
CHANGE IN TREND IS RESULT ISRAEL INITIATIVES,
A VARAB REACTION BASICALLY ONE OF FEAR DERIVED
FROM IMPRESSIONS THAT:

1) LARGE SCALE ISRAELI PUMPING JORDAN
WATERS IS INCURSION ON ARAB RIGHTS SECOND IN
SCALE TO PALESTINE WAR.

2) FOREGOING MAKES POSSIBLE MAJOR INCREASE
ISRAEL POPULATION WHICH IS PRELUDE FURTHER ISRAEL
EXPANSION.

3) ISRAEL PROGRESS IN ATOMIC ENERGY FIELD IS
MORTAL THREAT TO ARAB SECURITY.

4) ISRAEL HAS SUCCEEDED IN GAINING AMERICAN
AND WESTERN SUPPORT FOR FOREGOING, WHICH GREATLY
ENHANCES ISRAELI CHANCES OF SUCCESS.

5) IDENTIFICATION THESE DANGERS BY ARAB
LEADERS SERIOUS ENOUGH TO BRING MAJOR EFFORTS
RECONCILE DIFFERENCES BETWEEN THEM AND COORDINATE
NEW ANTI-ISRAEL INITIATIVES, WHICH CONCEIVED AS
DEFENSIVE DESPITE SPEECHMAKING.

SIMPLE ARAB BEHIND GUN CARRIES ON FROM THERE
CFN 1) 2) 3) 4) 5)

PAGE 4 RUQMJR 535 S E C R E T
WITH TRADITIONAL EASE. IF ARABS ABOUT TO DO SOMETHING
BIG, WHY NOT CONTRIBUTE MY BIT NOW? IF INDIVIDUAL
FORESEES "IMPERIALIST FRUSTRATION ARAB INITIATIVES"
BLIND RAGE AT IMPOTENCE CAN EASILY COMMUNICATE
TWITCH TO TRIGGER FINGER.

SECRET

~~SECRET~~

-3- 29, JULY 21, 3 p.m. FROM JERUSALEM (SECTION ONE OF TWO)

SYRIANS MOST SUSCEPTIBLE THIS LINE REASONING.
THEY NEVER SUFFERED MAJOR MILITARY DEFEATS AND
HAVE FEELING SECURITY FROM TACTICALLY SUPERIOR
POSITIONS. THEY HAVE BEFORE THEM THE DEMILITARIZED
ZONES, LONGSTANDING SCENE STRUGGLE, AND SOME SENSE
RIGHTEOUSNESS IN FACT THEY SEEKING MINIMUM OF ENFORCE-
MENT GAA'S WHILE ISRAEL DEMANDING MORE. MOST UN
OBSERVERS ACCORD CERTAIN AMOUNT CREDIT TO SYRIANS
FOR RESTRAINT OVER LONG PERIOD IN FACE ISRAEL
SEIZURE CONTROL IN D/Z'S BY FORCE OR CONSTANT THREAT
USING IT. THEY BELIEVE FREQUENTLY EXPRESSED SYRIAN
DISAPPOINTMENT AT FAILURE UNTSO EFFECTIVELY RESTRAIN
ISRAELI INROADS IN D/Z'S BEING TRANSLATED INTO
ACTION AGAINST ISRAEL BY LOW LEVEL SYRIAN
MILITARY IN MOST CONVENIENT ARENA UNDER

PAGE 5 RUQMJR 535 ~~S E C R E T~~
INFLUENCE FACTORS MENTIONED ABOVE. [THEY FEAR
ESCALATION AND SPREAD BECAUSE NO CHANGE ISRAEL
PRESSURES DISCERNIBLE.]

IN RESPONSE QUESTION WHAT IMMEDIATE STEPS
POSSIBLE TO EASE TENSIONS, ACOS MARSH SAID UNTSO
CONVINCED ISRAEL HAS THIS WITHIN ABILITIES BY:

1) CEASE USE IN DEFENSIVE AREAS OF
VEHICLES VISUALLY IDENTIFIABLE AS ARMORED TYPES.
UNMOS AND PRESUMABLY SYRIANS USE US DEPT ARMY
PAMPHLET 30-115 "WEAPONS AND EQUIPMENT HANDBOOK
MIDDLE EAST" DATED 1958, TO IDENTIFY FROM VISUAL
SIGHTINGS.

2) STOP PATROLLING IN DEMILITARIZED ZONES.

3) REDUCE PATROLLING IN DEFENSIVE AREAS,
EVEN OF TYPE USING MEN AND EQUIPMENT APPARENTLY
WITHIN MEANING GAA'S. MARSH NOTES MOVEMENT ANY
MILITARY TYPE VEHICLE INVITES ATTENTION, UN
PERSONNEL HAVE SUGGESTED TO ISRAELIS ON MANY
OCCASIONS THAT FIXED POSITIONS IN DEFENSIVE AREA
BE SUBSTITUTED FOR VEHICLE PATROLLING.
CFN 1) 30-115 19#28 2) 3)
BT

MESSAGE UNSIGNED

~~SECRET~~

SECTION ONE OF TWO
ACTION DEPT 29 INFO AMMAN 20 BEIRUT 18 DAMASCUS 20
TELAVIV 22 USUN 21 FROM JERUSALEM JULY 21, 3PM

LIMDIS NOFORN

ISRAEL-SYRIA

FOLLOWING THOUGHTS ON CAUSES AND CURES CURRENT
SURGE BORDER UNREST SUMMARIZES NUMBER RECENT CON-
VERSATIONS SENIOR UNTSOP OFFICIALS. THEY SEE LOW LEVEL
SYRIAN MILITARY AS MOST LIKELY SOURCE TROUBLE. ANALY-
SIS SITUATION PRESAGES CFN 29 20 18 20 22 21 21 3PM

PAGE 2 RUQMJR 535
GREATER DIFFICULTIES, HOWEVER.

CUSHIONED BY THOUGHT WHOLE THING IMPOSED BY OUTSIDE
FORCES RATHER THAN MILITARY DEFEAT, ARABS WERE
REACHING POINT WHERE LAST UN PARTITION PLAN COULD BE
CITED PUBLICLY AS ACCEPTABLE, WHILE TERMS GAA'S SUB-
STANTIALLY OPERATIVE AS DE FACTO MODUS VIVENDI WITH
ISRAEL. PRINCIPAL CONTINUING "LUKEWARM WAR" CON-
CERNED STATUS DEMILITARIZED ZONES AND AREAS BETWEEN
LINES WHERE ARABS CONCERNED SELVES BASICALLY WITH
PRESERVATION SITUATION ENVISIONED IN GAA'S WHILE IS-
RAEL CONSISTENTLY SOUGHT GAIN FULL CONTROL. EVEN THIS
ASPECT STRUGGLE VISIBLY COOLING DURING PAST EIGHT
YEARS.

WITH ISRAEL EMERGING VICTORIOUS LARGELY BECAUSE UN
NEVER ABLE OPPOSE AGGRESSIVE AND ARMED ISRAELI OC-
CUPATION AND ASSERTION ACTUAL CONTROL OVER SUCH
AREAS, AND ARAB NEIGHBORS NOT REALLY PREPARED FOR

REQUIRED FIGHTING. IF END JUSTIFIES MEANS, ISRAEL'S RE-LIANCE ON FORCE AND THREAT USING IT SEEMED PROVING SUCCESSFUL.

PAGE 3 RUQMJR 535
CHANGE IN TREND IS RESULT ISRAEL INITIATIVES, A VARAB REACTION BASICALLY ONE OF FEAR DERIVED FROM IMPRESSIONS THAT:

1) LARGE SCALE ISRAELI PUMPING JORDAN WATERS IS INCURSION ON ARAB RIGHTS SECOND IN SCALE TO PALESTINE WAR.

2) FOREGOING MAKES POSSIBLE MAJOR INCREASE ISRAEL POPULATION WHICH IS PRELUDE FURTHER ISRAEL EXPANSION.

3) ISRAEL PROGRESS IN ATOMIC ENERGY FIELD IS MORTAL THREAT TO ARAB SECURITY.

4) ISRAEL HAS SUCCEEDED IN GAINING AMERICAN AND WESTERN SUPPORT FOR FOREGOING, WHICH GREATLY ENHANCES ISRAELI CHANCES OF SUCCESS.

5) IDENTIFICATION THESE DANGERS BY ARAB LEADERS SERIOUS ENOUGH TO BRING MAJOR EFFORTS RECONCILE DIFFERENCES BETWEEN THEM AND COORDINATE NEW ANTI-ISRAEL INITIATIVES, WHICH CONCEIVED AS DEFENSIVE DESPITE SPEECHMAKING.

SIMPLE ARAB BEHIND GUN CARRIES ON FROM THERE CFN 1) 2) 3) 4) 5)

PAGE 4 RUQMJR 535 SECRET
WITH TRADITIONAL EASE. IF ARABS ABOUT TO DO SOMETHING BIG, WHY NOT CONTRIBUTE MY BIT NOW? IF INDIVIDUAL FORE-

SEES "IMPERIALIST FRUSTRATION ARAB INITIATIVES" BLIND RAGE AT IMPOTENCE CAN EASILY COMMUNICATE TWITCH TO TRIGGER FINGER.

SYRIANS MOST SUSCEPTIBLE THIS LINE REASONING. THEY NEVER SUFFERED MAJOR MILITARY DEFEATS AND HAVE FEELING SECURITY FROM TACTICALLY SUPERIOR POSITIONS. THEY HAVE BEFORE THEM THE DEMILITARIZED ZONES, LONGSTANDING SCENE STRUGGLE, AND SOME SENSE RIGHTEOUSNESS IN FACT THEY SEEKING MINIMUM OF ENFORCEMENT GAA'S WHILE ISRAEL DEMANDING MORE. MOST UN OBSERVERS ACCORD CERTAIN AMOUNT CREDIT TO SYRIANS FOR RESTRAINT OVER LONG PERIOD IN FACE ISRAEL SEIZURE CONTROL IN D/Z'S BY FORCE OR CONSTANT THREAT USING IT. THEY BELIEVE FREQUENTLY EXPRESSED SYRIAN DISAPPOINTMENT AT FAILURE UNTSO EFFECTIVELY RESTRAIN ISRAELI INROADS IN D/Z'S BEING TRANSLATED INTO ACTION AGAINST ISRAEL BY LOW LEVEL SYRIAN MILITARY IN MOST CONVENIENT ARENA UNDER

PAGE 5 RUQMJR 535
INFLUENCE FACTORS MENTIONED ABOVE. THEY FEAR ESCALATION AND SPREAD BECAUSE NO CHANGE ISRAEL PRESSURES DISCERNIBLE.

IN RESPONSE QUESTION WHAT IMMEDIATE STEPS POSSIBLE TO EASE TENSIONS, ACOS MARSH SAID UNTSO CONVINCED ISRAEL HAS THIS WITHIN ABILITIES BY:

1) CEASE USE IN DEFENSIVE AREAS OF VEHICLES VISUALLY IDENTIFIABLE AS ARMORED TYPES. UNMOS AND PRESUMABLY SYRIANS USE US DEPT ARMY PAMPHLET 30-115 "WEAPONS AND EQUIPMENT HANDBOOK MIDDLE EAST" DATED 1958, TO IDENTIFY FROM VISUAL SIGHTINGS.

2) STOP PATROLLING IN DEMILITARIZED ZONES.

3) REDUCE PATROLLING IN DEFENSIVE AREAS, EVEN OF TYPE USING MEN AND EQUIPMENT APPARENTLY WITHIN MEANING GAA'S. MARSH NOTES MOVEMENT ANY MILITARY TYPE VEHICLE INVITES ATTENTION, UN PERSONNEL HAVE SUGGESTED TO ISRAELIS ON MANY OCCASIONS THAT FIXED POSITIONS IN DEFENSIVE AREA BE SUBSTITUTED FOR VEHICLE PATROLLING.
CFN 1) 30-115 19#08 2) 3)
BT

MESSAGE UNSIGNED

Document #13—as cited in Chapter 8, Note 40.

"Confidential" note to the President from Walt Rostow, dated June 6, 1967, National Security File, NSC History Middle East Crisis, May 12–June 19, 1967, Volume 4, Tabs. 111–127, Lyndon Baines Johnson Library.

THE WHITE HOUSE
WASHINGTON

SECRET

Monday, June 5, 1967
9:05 p. m.

Mr. President:

Herewith the account, with a map, of the first day's turkey shoot.

W. W. Rostow

SECRET

DETERMINED TO BE AN
ADMINISTRATIVE MARKING.
BY DLH ON 10-18-XX

The White House
WASHINGTON

Monday, June 5, 1967
9:05 P.M.

Mr. President:

Herewith the account, with a map, of the first day's turkey shoot.

W. W. Rostow

Document #14—as cited in Chapter 9, Note 18.

"Secret" State Department telegram 3928 from U.S. Embassy, Tel Aviv, to Secretary of State, dated June 5, 1967, declassified at the request of the author on December 13, 1982, under the federal Freedom of Information Act.

INCOMING TELEGRAM *Department of State*

ACTION COPY

SECRET

004353

3
Action

SS
Info

```
   VZCZCQMA786
····ZZ RUEHC
DE RUQMVL 3928 1560910
ZNY SSSSS
Z 050905Z JUN 67
FM AMEMBASSY TEL AVIV
TO SECSTATE WASHDC FLASH
STATE GRNC
BT
S E C R E T TEL AVIV 3928

EXDIS
```

1. HAVE JUST SEEN EBAN AT HIS REQUEST. AFTER REQUESTING GOI ASSESSMENT OF NASSER'S AGGRESSIVE INTENT, HIS BUILD-UP IN NEGEV, HIS CLOSING OF STRAITS, HIS RALLYING OF OTHER ARAB COUNTRIES, EBAN SAID THAT EARLY THIS MORNING ISRAELIS OBSERVED EGYPTIAN UNITS MOVING IN LARGE NUMBERS TOWARD ISRAEL AND IN FACT CONSIDERABLE FORCE PENETRATED ISRAELI TERRITORY AND CLASHED WITH ISRAELI GROUND FORCES. CONSEQUENTLY, GOI GAVE ORDER TO ATTACK. MILITARY SITUATION SOMEWHAT CLEAR. ONLY FIGHTING SO FAR IS WITH EGYPT. GOI BELIEVES ITS ATTACK ON EGYPTIAN AIRFIELDS HAS BEEN A SUCCESS. ALSO EBAN THINKS EGYPTIAN GROUND MOVEMENT FROM GAZA PROBABLY STOPPED.

PAGE 2 RUQMVL 3928 S E C R E T
EBAN INTERPRETS ERRONEOUS JORDANIAN CLAIM OF ISRAELI ATTACK ON MAFRAG AS POSSIBLE RUSE BY HUSSEIN TO JUSTIFY KEEPING HIS FORCES BACK TO PROTECT HIS AIR FIELDS. SYRIANS HAVE NOT MOVED.

2. EBAN, AFTER CONSULTING ESHKOL, DRAFTING MESSAGE TO PRESIDENT FOR DELIVERY LATER TODAY. HE SAYS LETTER WILL REHEARSE DEVELOPMENTS RE NASSER'S BUILD-UP, REASONS FOR ISRAELI ACTION WHICH BASED ON ART 51 OF CHARTER (ISRAELI REP UN INSTRUCTED BY PHONE TO INFORM SECURITY COUNCIL), AND CONVICTION THAT WORLD UNDERSTANDS ISRAEL IS VICTIM OF NASSER'S AGGRESSION. LETTER WILL ADD THAT OI HAS NO RPT NO INTENTION TAKING ADVANTAGE OF SITUATION TO ENLARGE ITS TERRITORY, THAT HOPES PEACE CAN BE RESTORED WITHIN PRESENT BOUNDARIES, THAT IT ALSO HOPES CONFLICT CAN BE LOCALIZED AND IN THIS REGARD ASKS OUR HELP IN RESTRAINING ANY SOVIET INITIATIVE.

SECRET

SECRET

-2- TEL AVIV 3928, JUNE 5

3. THERE IS TO BE A BRIEFING ON DETAILS OF MILITARY SITUATION AT
DEFENSE MINISTRY AT NOON WHICH I WILL ATTEND.

4. THERE HAVE BEEN TWO BRIEF AIR RAID ALERTS IN TEL AVIV SO
FAR BUT WITHOUT ANY APPARENT PENETRATION. BARBOUR
BT

ADVANCE COPY TO S/S-O 6-5-67, 5:58 A.M.
PASSED TO WHITE HOUSE 6-5-67, 5:58 A.M.

SECRET

1. HAVE JUST SEEN EBAN AT HIS REQUEST. AFTER REQUESTING GOI ASSESSMENT OF NASSER'S AGGRESSIVE INTENT, HIS BUILD-UP IN NEGEV, HIS CLOSING OF STRAITS, HIS RALLYING OF OTHER ARAB COUNTRIES, EBAN SAID THAT EARLY THIS MORNING ISRAELIS OBSERVED EGYPTIAN UNITS MOVING IN LARGE NUMBERS TOWARD ISRAEL AND IN FACT CONSIDERABLE FORCE PENETRATED ISRAELI TERRITORY AND CLASHED WITH ISRAELI GROUND FORCES. CONSEQUENTLY, GOI GAVE ORDER TO ATTACK. MILITARY SITUATION SOMEWHAT CLEAR. ONLY FIGHTING SO FAR IS WITH EGYPT. GOI BELIEVES ITS ATTACK ON EGYPTIAN AIRFIELDS HAS BEEN A SUCCESS. ALSO EBAN THINKS EGYPTIAN GROUND MOVEMENT FROM GAZA PROBABLY STOPPED.

PAGE 2 RUQMVL 3928 S E C R E T
EBAN INTERPRETS ERRONEOUS JORDANIAN CLAIM OF ISRAELI ATTACK ON MAFRAG AS POSSIBLE RUSE BY HUSSEIN TO JUSTIFY KEEPING HIS FORCES BACK TO PROTECT HIS AIR FIELDS. SYRIANS HAVE NOT MOVED.

2. EBAN, AFTER CONSULTING ESHKOL, DRAFTING MESSAGE TO PRESIDENT FOR DELIVERY LATER TODAY. HE SAYS LETTER WILL REHEARSE DEVELOPMENTS RE NASSER'S BUILD-UP, REASONS FOR ISRAELI ACTION WHICH BASED ON ART 51 OF CHARTER (ISRAELI REP UN INSTRUCTED BY PHONE TO INFORM SECURITY COUNCIL), AND CONVICTION THAT WORLD UNDERSTANDS ISRAEL IS VICTIM OF NASSER'S AGGRESSION. LETTER WILL ADD THAT OI HAS NO RPT NO INTENTION TAKING ADVANTAGE OF SITUATION TO ENLARGE ITS TERRITORY, THAT HOPES PEACE CAN BE RESTORED WITHIN PRESENT BOUNDARIES, THAT IT ALSO HOPES CONFLICT CAN BE LOCALIZED AND IN THIS REGARD ASKS OUR HELP IN RESTRAINING ANY SOVIET INITIATIVE.

3. THERE IS TO BE A BRIEFING ON DETAILS OF MILITARY SITUA-TION AT DEFENSE MINISTRY AT NOON WHICH I WILL ATTEND.

4. THERE HAVE BEEN TWO BRIEF AIR RAID ALERTS IN TEL AVIV SO FAR BUT WITHOUT ANY APPARENT PENETRATION.
BARBOUR
BT

ADVANCE COPY TO S/S-0 6-5-67, 5:58 A.M.
PASSED TO WHITE HOUSE 6-5-67, 5:58 A.M.

Document #15—as cited in Chapter 9, Note 28.

"Secret" State Department telegram 209182 from Secretary of State to American Embassy, Tel Aviv, dated June 8, 1967, in NSF Country File, Middle East Crisis, Vol. 4, Box 107, Lyndon Baines Johnson Library.

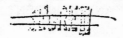

```
                                     · RECEIVED
                                       WHCA

                           :57 JUN 8  10 56

EHB614
••••·ZZ RUEHEX
DE RUEHC 209182 1590655
ZNY SSSSS ZFH-2
Z P 081031Z JUN 67 ZFF-4
FM SECSTATE WASHDC                                    · ·
TO RUQMVL/AMEMBASSY TEL AVIV FLASH 1750           ***
INFO RUQMKG/AMEMBASSY AMMAN PRIORITY 2027
RUQMAT/AMEMBASSY ATHENS 2238
RUQMBE/AMEMBASSY BEIRUT 2226
RUQMDM/AMEMBASSY DAMASCUS 760            THE RUSK TELEX
RUQMJR/AMCONSUL JERUSALEM 454
RUDTCR/AMEMBASSY LONDON 8973                                        S
RUEHDT/USUN NEW YORK 3435
RUEDPSA/CINCSTRIKE
STATE GRNC
BT
S-E-C-R-E-T STATE 209182

REFERENCE:  JERUSALEM 1053
```

UNTSO REPORT REFTEL DEEPLY DISTURBING. YOU SHOULD URGENTLY APPROACH FONOFF AT HIGHEST LEVEL TO EXPRESS DEEP CONCERN THIS NEW INDICATION MILITARY ACTION BY GOI. IF REPORTED BOMBARDMENT CORRECT, WE WOULD ASSUME IT PRELUDE TO MILITARY ACTION AGAINST SYRIAN POSITIONS ON SYRIAN SOIL. SUCH A

PAGE 2 RUEHC 209182 S-E-C-R-E-T
DEVELOPMENT, FOLLOWING ON HEELS ISRAELI ACCEPTANCE SC CEASE-FIRE RESOLUTION WOULD CAST DOUBTS ON ISRAELI INTENTIONS AND CREATE GRAVEST PROBLEMS FOR USG REPRESENTATIVES IN ARAB COUNTRIES. YOU SHOULD STRESS WE MUST AT ALL COSTS HAVE COMPLETE CESSATION ISRAELI MILITARY ACTION EXCEPT IN CASES WHERE CLEARLY SOME REPLYING FIRE IS NECESSARY IN SELF-DEFENSE.

GP-2, RUSK
BT

```
IBNN                                                    ·  COPY
                     : COPY                             Lyndon B. Johnson
```

REFERENCE: JERUSALEM 1053

UNTSO REPORT REFTEL DEEPLY DISTURBING. YOU SHOULD URGENTLY APPROACH FONOFF AT HIGHEST LEVEL TO EXPRESS DEEP CONCERN THIS NEW INDICATION MILITARY ACTION BY GOI. IF REPORTED BOMBARDMENT CORRECT, WE WOULD ASSUME IT PRELUDE TO MILITARY ACTION AGAINST SYRIAN POSITIONS ON SYRIAN SOIL. SUCH A

PAGE 2 RUEHC 209182
DEVELOPMENT, FOLLOWING ON HEELS ISRAELI ACCEPTANCE SC CEASE-FIRE RESOLUTION WOULD CAST DOUBTS ON ISRAELI INTENTIONS AND CREATE GRAVEST PROBLEMS FOR USG REPRESENTATIVES IN ARAB COUNTRIES. YOU SHOULD STRESS WE MUST AT ALL COSTS HAVE COMPLETE CESSATION ISRAELI MILITARY ACTION EXCEPT IN CASES WHERE CLEARLY SOME REPLYING FIRE IS NECESSARY IN SELF-DEFENSE.

GP-2, RUSK
BT

Document #16—as cited in Chapter 9, Note 43.

"Secret" State Department telegram 20317 from American Embassy, Paris, to Secretary of State, dated June 17, 1967, National Security File, Middle East Crisis, "Liberty File," Lyndon Baines Johnson Library, declassified February 16, 1983, in response to a request from the author.

INCOMING TELEGRAM *Department of State*   W 10

SECRET

CONTROL: 14897
RECD: JUNE 17, 1957, 1:29 P.M.

PR RUEHC
DE RUFWCR 20317 1681702
ZNY SSOSS
R 171902Z JUN 67
FM AMEMBASSY PARIS
TO SECSTATE WASHDC
STATE GRNC
BT
S E C R E T PARIS 20317

NATUS

NODIS

FOR UNDERSECRETARY BOSTON FROM CLEVELAND

SUBJECT: ISRAELI ATTACK ON LIBERTY

REF: STATE 01073 AND PARIS 1873 (NOTAL 5 STATE ...)

1. QUITE APART FROM NEWSPAPER PUBLICATION, MY TALKS WITH ...
IN CAIRO AND SEVERAL FOREIGN MINISTERS AT ... G ...
ISRAELI FOREIGN OFFICE HAS INDICATED AS A RESULT ... A GREAT
DEAL OF CURIOSITY AMONG HIGH GOVERNMENTS. WOULD ... GUIDANCE AS TO HOW MUCH OF THIS CURIOSITY I CAN SATISFY, AND WHEN.

2. IN PARTICULAR, PERHAPS I SHOULD INFORM SAG OF RESULTS OF BOARD OF INQUIRY IF SCHEDULE PERMITS THIS TO BE DONE BEFORE IT GETS INTO NEWSPAPERS.

GP-3. CLEVELAND
BT

SECRET

FOR UNDERSECRETARY ROSTOW FROM CLEVELAND

SUBJECT: ISRAELI ATTACK ON LIBERTY

REF: STATE 211672 AND PARTICULARLY PARA 5 STATE 212139.

1. QUITE APART FROM NEWSWEEK PERISCOPE ITEM, SECRE-TARY'S COMMENTS TO BROSIO AND SEVERAL FOREIGN MINIS-TERS AT LUXEMBOURG ABOUT ISRAELI FOREKNOWLEDGE THAT LIBERTY WAS A US SHIP PIQUED A GREAT DEAL OF CURI-OSITY AMONG NATO DELEGATIONS. WOULD APPRECIATE GUIDANCE AS TO HOW MUCH OF THIS CURIOSITY I CAN SAT-ISFY, AND WHEN.

2. IN PARTICULAR, PERHAPS I SHOULD INFORM NAC OF RE-SULTS US BOARD OF INQUIRY IF SCHEDULE PERMITS THIS TO BE DONE BEFORE IT GETS INTO NEWSPAPERS.

GP-3. CLEVELAND
BT

Document #17—as cited in Chapter 10, Note 2.

"Secret" memorandum of conversation dated October 24, 1967, National Security File—Israel, Volume 12 (1965–1968), Box 142, Lyndon Baines Johnson Library.

TELECOMMUNICATIONS OPERATIONS DIVISION   WORK COPY

96a

SECRET   10 3

INFO: Amembassy TEL AVIV   IMMEDIATE

USUN   1980/2014

STATE
EOIS
XXXXXX

FOR THE AMBASSADOR

1.   Prior to departure Foreign Minister Eban for UNGA Sept 15 you should seek opportunity to make following points clear. If time not available, Charge should deliver message through appropriate Foreign Ministry channel soon as possible, with request it be conveyed to Eshkol and Eban. XXXXXXXXXXXXXX
XXXXXXXXXXXXXXXXXXXX

2.   There is growing concern among governments friendly to Israel at XXXXXXXXXXXXXXXXXXXXXXXXXXX(indications Israeli objectives may be shifting from original position seeking peace with no xxx no territorial gains toward one of territorial expansionism. Israel's refusal to authorize the return of all refugees desiring to resume residence on West Bank, reported breaking off of West Bank banking negotiations and statements by senior Israeli officials quoted in American press give rise

NEA:YAM:CW a Drakis:
/Latherton, Jr:IO/UNP:AWDay: 2942   The Secretary
       Jun:9/14/67   White House -
     NEA - Ambassador Battle   S/S -
     IO - Mr. Sisco (draft)
     NEA - Mr. Davies   _____ The Under Secretary

COPY
Form
0-65   US 522

TEL AVIV

~~SECRET~~

to impression that Israeli Government may be moving toward policy of

seeking security simply by retaining occupied areas rather than by

achieving peaceful settlement with Arabs. In this connection, the concern
of Israel's friends

/is reenforced by increasing GOI emphasis on form of settlement (direct

negotiations and formal peace treaties) rather than substance (peaceful

borders and Arab renunciation of belligerent rights and actions). The

tactical usefulness of this posture can be appreciated There is

~~xppoedebececcocicebcesefulnessxofecbbeposecccs~~ up to a point.

concern,

~~Eveeeineiy~~ however, that taken in context of Israeli administrative and

other actions in occupied areas including Old Jerusalem, public statement

of GOI officials and developing Israeli attitudes toward occupied areas,

it could in fact become rationale for territorial acquisitions.

3. With the approach of the 22nd General Assembly, we are entering

period which could well be vital for future of Middle East. US

Government hopes to use this period to continue and intensify its efforts

to help Israel and Arabs reach settlement satisfactory to both. For

such efforts to have any chance of success, parties directly concerned

must keep open possibilities of compromise and avoid creating impression

that solution acceptable to both sides is not a serious goal. Ability

of US to work for more realistic position on part of Arabs depends to

great degree on assumption among Arabs and in world community generally

~~SECRET~~

Corrections made on original green MUST be made on this and other
flimsy work copies before delivery to Telecommunications Operations. LYNDON B. JOHNSON LIBRAR

COPY

3   TEL AVIV

~~SECRET~~

that Israel sincerely wishes peaceful settlement above all.

CP-3

End

FORM DS-322A
8-63

Corrections made on original green MUST be made on this and other
flimsy work copies before delivery to Telecommunications Operations Division

FOR THE AMBASSADOR

1. Prior to departure Foreign Minister Eban for UNGA Sept 15 you should seek opportunity to make following points clear. If time not available, Charge should deliver message through appropriate Foreign Ministry channel as soon as possible, with request it be conveyed to Eshkol and Eban.

2. There is growing concern among governments friendly to Israel at indications Israeli objectives may be shifting from original position seeking peace with no rpt no territorial gains toward one of territorial expansionism. Israel's refusal to authorize the return of all refugees desiring to resume residence on West Bank, reported breaking off of West Bank banking negotiations and statements by senior Israeli officials quoted in American press give rise to impression that Israeli Government may be moving toward policy of seeking security simply by retaining occupied areas rather than by achieving peaceful settlement with Arabs. In this connection, the concern of Israel's friends is reenforced by increasing GOI emphasis on form of settlement (direct negotiations and formal peace treaties) rather than substance (peaceful borders and Arab renunciation of belligerent rights and actions). The tactical usefulness of this posture can be appreciated up to a point. There is concern, however, that taken in context of Israeli administrative and other actions in occupied areas including Old Jerusalem, public statements of GOI officials and developing Israeli attitudes toward occupied areas, it could in fact become rationale for territorial acquisitions.

3. With the approach of the 22nd General Assembly, we are entering period which could well be vital for future of Middle East. US Government hopes to use this period to continue and intensify its efforts to help Israel and Arabs reach settlement satisfactory to both. For such efforts to have any chance of success, parties directly concerned must keep open possibilities of compromise and avoid creating impression that solution acceptable to both sides is not a serious goal. Ability of US to work for more realistic position on part of Arabs depends to great degree on assumption among Arabs and in world community generally that Israel sincerely wishes peaceful settlement above all.

CP-3

End

Index